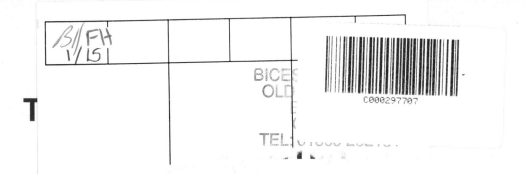

SIXTH EDITION

Janet Few

THE FAMILY HISTORY PARTNERSHIP

Published by
The Family History Partnership
57 Bury New Road
Ramsbottom, Bury
Lancashire BL0 0BZ

www.thefamilyhistorypartnership.com

Previous editions all published by
The Federation of Family History Societies (Publications) Ltd

First published 1985
Second edition 1986
Third edtion 1988
Fourth edition 1991
Fifth edition 1995

Sixth edition published 2014

ISBN: 978 1 906280 11 6

Printed and bound by
Berforts Information Press
Southfield Road, Eynsham
Oxford OX29 4JB

INTRODUCTION

The last edition of this book was published in 1995. Since then, family history research has changed beyond all recognition, not least because of the internet. It is a tribute to the volume's usefulness that, despite the many innovations since it was produced, the last edition was still the one book I would turn to when asked to man a family history 'help desk'. An update was long overdue and I am honoured to have been involved in such a family history classic.

This book is not designed to tell you everything you need to know. Instead, its purpose is to point you in the right direction, so you can find out more. The number of people who have been involved in this and earlier, editions means that the entries are wide ranging and have a variety of regional slants. We have aimed to be as comprehensive as possible but inevitably, there will be topics that some feel are missing. We hope however that we have covered everything that most family historians will require. Equally, in the fast moving world that is family history of the C21st, new books and websites will be appearing all the time. We have endeavoured to be up to date and indeed additions were still being made to the 'A' entries as we worked our way through later letters of the alphabet.

I would like to pay tribute to the late Fred Markwell and to Pauline Pedersen, formerly Pauline Saul, who conceived the original concept and to Paul Gaskell, Stuart Raymond and Richard Ratcliffe, who made significant contributions to this edition.

Janet Few

Please note that many of the books referred to are available in research libraries, such as that of the SOG, or via inter-library loan. Older volumes may be accessible as online downloads.

All TNA research guides can be downloaded from the website free of charge. Go to www.nationalarchives.gov.uk – 'Records', then 'Browse our Guidance A-Z'.

The following abbreviations have been used:

C   Century e.g. C17th - seventeenth century
CRO   County Record Office
DRO   Diocesan Record Office
FFHS   Federation of Family History Societies
FHP   Family History Partnership
FHS   Family History Societies

GRO   General Register Office
HMSO Her Majesty's Stationery Office
IHGS Institute of Heraldic and Genealogical Studies
LMA   London Metropolitan Archives
q.v.   quod vide – this indicates that the topic has an entry of its own in
          this volume.
SOG   Society of Genealogists
TNA   The National Archives

A

ABBREVIATIONS Abbreviations are useful when setting out your family tree. There is no absolute agreement on this but one golden rule is to be careful if you use 'b' as it might be interpreted as born, baptised or buried. Similarly, the use of 'c' for christened can be confused with 'circa', meaning about, which is usually used before a year. Here are some suggestions:

b	born
Bapt or bpt	baptised/christened
C	century or christened
c	christened or 'about' when referring to a date
= or m	married
d	died
bur	buried
unm	unmarried
d unm	died unmarried
d.s.p.	decessit sine prole - died without children
dau	daughter
s	son
div	divorced
re-m	re-married
ob	obit - died
o.t.p.	of this parish
b.o.t.p.	both of this parish

Abbreviations of Christian names are often found in parish registers. To avoid confusion and the possibility of misinterpretation you are advised not to use abbreviations for names in your own records. Months are best abbreviated by using the first three letters.

ABRAHAM MEN A class of pretended lunatics who wandered about England seeking alms after the dissolution of the religious houses in the C16th, hence beggars.

ABSENT VOTERS' LISTS See also World War I and World War II. Absent voters' lists contain the names and addresses of personnel who were not at home during the 1918 general election. For each individual listed, there is also information on their military service, ship, regiment, number and rank as appropriate. Most will now be in CROs. For details of online access to some lists see www.longlongtrail.co.uk then 'Find Your Soldier' and 'Articles and Insights'.

ACCESS TO ARCHIVES (A2A) This database www.nationalarchives.gov.uk/a2a/ is part of the UK archives network. It can be used to locate documents that are held in participating archives in England and Wales. The catalogues of most CROs and many other repositories can be accessed in this way. Note that this is not complete and no further additions are being made. It should be used in conjunction with the repository's own catalogue.

ACHIEVEMENT An heraldic term referring to a full display of armorial bearings, including shield, crest, helm, torse and mantling, together with motto, supporters and compartment where permitted. A badge or badges may be included.

ACT BOOKS Records of Ecclesiastical Courts (q.v.). Prior to 1733, they are usually written in Latin. They are useful for references to wills when the originals do not survive.

ADMINISTRATION or **LETTERS OF ADMON** See Intestacy.

ADMIRALTY See Royal Navy.

ADOPTION See also British Home Children and Children's Societies. Adoption as a legal process was begun in England and Wales on 1 January 1927. Anyone "adopted" before that date was fostered and the following does not apply. Tracing the natural parents of a fostered child, especially if there was a change of surname, is a very difficult and specialist exercise.

Registers of adopted children commenced on 1 January 1927 and give the adopted name of the child and date of adoption but not the real parentage. The indexes can be seen at numerous locations, see www.gov.uk then 'Births, Deaths and Marriages', 'Certificates and Register Offices' and 'Adoption Records' for an up to date list of holders, including online holders, of the GRO indexes.

There are formal procedures laid down by the Children's Acts (1975 and 1989) whereby an adopted person over the age of eighteen can obtain a copy of their original birth entry, assuming it was in this country. Counselling is required, for all those adopted before 12 November 1975, before a certificate can be issued. From 30 December 2005, changes to the law have enabled birth relatives to also apply for access to an adopted person's adoption registration; see www.gov.uk/adoption-records for further information. For adoption in Scotland, see www.gro-scotland.gov.uk. Records are confidential; there may be very few available before 1945. Adoption records date from July 1953 for the Republic of Ireland; see www.groireland.ie. For records in Northern Ireland see www.groni.gov.uk.

Adoption records have not survived evenly across the country. Their whereabouts are described in Stafford, Georgina *Where to find Adoption Records: a guide for counsellors, adopted people and birth relatives* (British

Agencies for Adoption and Fostering (BAAF) 2001). BAAF produces a range of leaflets and books on adoption; see www.baaf.org.uk.

Adoption Search Reunion www.adoptionsearchreunion.org.uk assists those researching adoptions.

ADVERTISING The History of Advertising Trust www.hatads.org.uk has amassed the largest archive of British advertising in the world. It is a unique collection dating from the early 1800s to the present. It provides examples of advertising and of the stories behind the names and brands on our High Streets. The Trust's website gives details of the Trust's study room, library and research facilities in Norfolk and also contains some very interesting online collections that are free to browse.

ADVOWSON The right of presenting a clergyman to a benefice.

AERIAL PHOTOGRAPHS See Britain from Above.

AFFIDAVIT See also Parish Registers. A written statement, confirmed by oath, to be used as judicial evidence.

AG. LAB. Commonly used abbreviation for agricultural labourer. Several books will help with background to the lives of the many ag. labs that appear on almost everyone's family tree. Waller, Ian *My Ancestor Was an Agricultural Labourer* (SOG 2008). Handford, Kay *The Agricultural Labourer in 19th Century England* (Grosvenor House Publishing 2011). Brown, Jonathan *Tracing Your Rural Ancestors: a guide for family historians* (Pen & Sword 2011). Hammond, John & Barbara *The Village Labourer* (The History Press 2005). Porter, Valerie *Yesterday's Farm: a taste of rural life from the past* (David and Charles 2008).

AGRA See Association of Genealogists and Researchers, The and Professional Researchers.

AGRICULTURE See Ag. Lab., Farm Survey, Rural Life, Museum of Englsh and Swing Riots.

AIM25 The website www.aim25.ac.uk provides access to collection level descriptions of the archives of more than a hundred institutions within the London area. These include the records of London livery companies, higher education institutions and learned societies.

AIR FORCE See Royal Air Force.

ALE ASSIZE An assessment to ensure that ale was of good quality. An ale-taster, usually chosen by the local inhabitants, had to report malpractices to the manorial court.

ALE DRAPER An Innkeeper.

ALEHOUSES Victuallers and alehouse keepers have had to be licensed by the Justices since the Alehouse Act of 1552. Lists of licences (recognisances and certificates) granted are often found in Quarter Sessions (q.v.) records, most of which have been deposited in the relevant CROs. See Gibson, Jeremy *Victuallers' Licences: records for local and family historians* (3rd ed. FHP 2009).

ALFRED GILLETT TRUST The Alfred Gillett Trust exists as a Clark's family trust alongside the well-known shoe business C & J Clark Ltd. and is responsible for the care and custody of the firm and family's heritage collections. The trust operates as an archive and museum of the company. Further details of the archive and of the company's history and heritage can be found on its website at www.clarks.co.uk.

ALIAS The Master of the Rolls said in 1730 that he was "satisfied that anyone may take upon him what surname and as many surnames as he pleases". In 1822, Lord Chief Justice Abbot added "A name assumed by the voluntary act of a man adopted by all who know him and by which he is constantly called, becomes as much and as effectively his name as if he had obtained an Act of Parliament to confer it upon him". Those statements are still pertinent if one considers entertainers (Frances Gumm was better known as Judy Garland) or a child who takes the surname of its step-father but there is still a widely held view that there were other reasons for using an alias. One of them related to copyhold land and occurred when the mother of a family remarried, having had children by her first marriage. Quite often, if the children were very young, they could take the surname of their step-father but in order not to lose their claim to their natural father's copyhold land, they would use both names as their surname. In the absence of birth certificates, it was easier to continue the surname in order to prove descent from a particular person. Hence, the alias would continue for generations and would be used very much as a hyphenated surname of today.

Other occasions on which aliases were also used include: To indicate the father's name in cases of illegitimacy. To distinguish between two possible spellings of a surname, for example Shaw and Shore. When a foreign surname was Anglicised. Where couples had married in Roman Catholic or Nonconformist chapels rather than in an Anglican church and therefore the marriage was not valid in law.

Alias is often abbreviated to "als".

ALIENS See also Immigration, Naturalization and Passenger Lists. From 1792, aliens were required to register with the Justices of the Peace, giving name, address, rank and occupation. Householders who provided lodgings for aliens had to give notice to the parish authorities and returns were sent to the Clerk of the Peace. Such records are likely to be in the CROs. Other sources of information are to be found in TNA. There are several relevant research guides that can be downloaded from their website www.nationalarchives.gov.uk. See also Bevan, Amanda *Tracing Your Ancestors in The National Archives: the website and beyond* (7th ed. TNA 2006). Kershaw, Roger *Migration Records: a guide for family historians* (TNA 2009).

ALNAGER A sworn officer appointed to examine and attest the measurement and quality of woollen goods.

ALUMNI See also Universities. Latin for 'students'. Alphabetical list of former school or university students, often with genealogical details. For a list see *Registers of Universities, Colleges and Schools of Great Britain and Ireland* by P M Jacobs (Athlone Press 1964). Many such records are available on CD or online.

AMERICAN IMMIGRANTS The United States Government kept Passenger Lists starting in 1820 and they still do so. The earlier records were kept by the Customs' Bureau (1820-1883) and are called Customs' Passenger Lists. In 1883, what is now the Immigration and Naturalisation Service was given the responsibility of keeping the records which are called Immigration Passenger Lists. The Customs' Passenger Lists provide only the immigrant's name, age, sex, occupation, nationality (place of origin) and their destination. The Immigration Passenger Lists were much more informative giving the immigrant's name, age, sex, marital status, occupation, last residence, final destination in the US, date of previous arrival and place of previous residence in the US, name, address and relationship to relatives or friends they are joining. In 1903 they added race to the form. In 1906 they added a personal description and in 1907 they added the name and address of the immigrant's nearest relative in the country they had come from.

In TNA, under Treasury Papers there are details of bound servants (indentured servants) between the ages of 15 and 21 who entered into an indenture for a term not exceeding 8 years in return for a passage to the Plantations in North America. The records follow an Act of 1717. They are important in that in addition to names, ages and occupations they give the former place of residence. Kaminkow, M & J (ed.) *Original Lists of Emigrants in Bondage from London to the American Colonies 1719 to 1744* (Magna Carta Book Co. 1981) is based on a series of documents in the Guildhall Library (q.v.) entitled "Memoranda of Agreements to serve in America and the West Indies". They date from 1718 to 1759 and are records of 3,000 Englishmen who emigrated to the colonies as indentured servants. *The Complete Book of Emigrants* (4 volumes: (1) 1607-1660, (2) 1661-1669, (3) 1700-1750, (4) 1751-1776), *Emigrants from England to the American Colonies 1773-1776* and *American Wills and Administrations in the Prerogative Court of Canterbury 1610-1857* all compiled

9

by Peter Wilson Coldham are just a few of the books on the impressive list of The Genealogical Publishing Co. Inc. www.genealogical.com. Gale Research Co. http://gale.cengage.co.uk also publish similar books, an example is Filby, P W & Meyer M K *Passenger and Immigration Lists Index* (13 volumes with supplements to 1993). This mammoth work, an index to published lists, not manuscript materials, covers nearly half a million passengers who reached North America c.1583 to 1900. See also a series of volumes by Carl Boyer and others *Ships' Passenger Lists* (Carl Boyer). There is also the earlier *A Bibliography of Ships' Passenger Lists 1538 to 1825* by Harold Lancour (New York 1963). Currer-Briggs, Noel *English Adventurers and Virginian Settlers* (3 vols. Phillimore 1970), is based on a very detailed study of relevant C17th British and American records. The index contains more than 12,000 names and places mentioned in the abstracted documents.

ANCESTRY www.ancestry.com and its UK subsidiary www.ancestry.co.uk, offer a variety of subscription packages, enabling researchers to search indexes of many classes of documents and access images of original records. The basic package allows access to Birth, Marriage and Death indexes and census information and higher rates of subscriptions open up access to millions of records that are being added to all the time. These include military records, immigration records, probate records and much more. Ancestry also enables users to create their own family trees. These are stored in the OneTreeWorld section and can be searched by other users. In addition, there are learning videos, tailored to UK research. Other features include, blogs, message boards, the ability to contact those with similar interests and free monthly e-newsletters.

ANCIENT ORDER OF FORESTERS FRIENDLY SOCIETY (AOF) Founded in 1833, membership not only gave security in time of sickness and death but participation in the running of the Brothers' court (branch) affairs long before most had a parliamentary vote.

Their website www.foresters.ws includes a history of the society and a list of the society's historical publications. See Fisk, Audrey & Logan, Roger *Grandfather was a Member of the Foresters* (AOF 1994).

The website of The Foresters' Heritage Trust www.aoforestersheritage.com details the holdings of their museum and archives in Southampton and includes a virtual tour. Displays in the museum include early minute books and printed material.

ANGLICAN CHURCH The Church of England is commonly known as the Anglican Church. All English and Welsh parish records (q.v.) relate to this denomination.

ANGLO-GERMAN FAMILY HISTORY SOCIETY See Germany.

ANGLO-IRISH FAMILY HISTORY SOCIETY See Ireland.

ANGLO-ITALIAN FAMILY HISTORY SOCIETY See Italy.

ANGLO-SCOTTISH FAMILY HISTORY SOCIETY See Scotland.

ANGULINE RESEARCH ARCHIVES http://anguline.co.uk/ provides access to old books, such as parish register transcripts, directories and school registers on CD or as a download.

ANNUAL REGISTER This has been published since 1758. The earlier volumes contain a great deal of miscellaneous information to interest the family historian. For example, 24 May 1802 "Lately, the wife of Alexander Ratcliffe, of Blackleach, in Saddleworth, three sons, baptised Abraham, Isaac and Jacob; all, with the mother, likely to do well. The mother is herself a twin, and has been before delivered of twins".

Volumes for the C20th are perhaps more in keeping with its sub-title "A view of the history, politics and literature for the year". Published by the Longman Group Limited, they should be available in larger libraries. Some early copies are available, free of charge, to browse online as part of the Internet Library of Early Journals (q.v.) www.bodley.ox.ac.uk/ilej.

ANNUITY An annuity is defined as "an investment of money entitling the investor to a series of equal annual sums" and tontine as an "annuity shared by subscribers to loan, the shares increasing as subscribers die till last survivor gets all, or till specified date when remaining survivors share the proceeds".

The British State Tontine and Annuity records of the C17th and C18th are in TNA and the British Library. They are said to be vast, disordered and dirty.

The records contain unique information about whole families, though these were largely of middle class origin. Masters frequently took out annuities for their own benefit, running on the lives of young and healthy servants or employees however, so more humble people figure in the records. As with modern annuities, it was essential to have accurate details of age, status and parentage and to update the records with changes of status, for example marriage, changes of address and death. There are sometimes supporting documents such as baptismal, marriage and death certificates, wills and certificates of existence.

For further information, consult Leeson, F L *Guide to the Records of the British State Tontines and Life Annuities in the 17th and 18th centuries* (Pinhorns 1968). In 1987, a list was found of survivors of the British State Tontines and Annuities earlier than those of 1730 and 1749 which were listed in the above Guide. A list printed in 1764 is in the Library of the Institute of Historical Research www.history.ac.uk/library/. This covers nominees not only of the first State Tontine of 1693 but also of the Life Annuitants of 1745, 1746 and 1757 who died before 4 January 1764, giving their ages and dates of death. A photocopy of the list has been deposited in the SOG library.

ANTIQUARIAN AND ARCHAEOLOGICAL SOCIETIES See also Chetham Society and Dugdale Society. Don't be put off by the word 'archaeological'. It frequently had a much wider connotation in the C19th, when the societies were named, than it does today. Many county societies have useful libraries and have published *Transactions*. These may be indexed and often contain research material on families relating to quite recent times for the area they cover. A list of such societies can be found at www.britarch.ac.uk.

The London Society of Antiquaries was formed in the C16th to discuss historical matters. Although it was banned for most of the C17th, it was subsequently revived. Details of its library, museum, events and publications are given on its website www.sal.org.uk. There is a Society of Antiquaries of Scotland www.socantscot.org.

APOTHECARIES The Worshipful Society of Apothecaries of London was founded in 1617. The majority of the society's historical records have been deposited at the Guildhall Library (q.v.). The guide *Sources For Tracing Apothecaries, Surgeons, Physicians and other Medical Practitioners at Guildhall Library* is available free of charge at www.history.ac.uk/gh/apoths.htm.

Two informative books are Copeman, W S C *Apothecaries of London* (Wellcome Institute 1967) and Burnby, Junaita L *A Study of the English Apothecary from 1660 to 1760* (Wellcome Institute 1983). See also Hunting, Penelope *A History of the Society of Apothecaries* (Wellcombe Institute 1998). This narrative is illustrated by pictures, plans and photographs taken from the society's archives. The Wellcome Institute (q.v.) have copies of *A List of Persons who have obtained Certificates of their Fitness and qualification to Practice as Apothecaries* (Society of Apothecaries 1840-1877) Two consolidated lists cover 1815-40 and 1840-52, followed by individual annual lists for 1852-53, 1853-54, 1855-56, 1867-68, 1871-73, 1875-77.

The Pharmaceutical Society was founded in 1841. Details of its archives and London museum, including its current exhibitions, are at www.rpharms.com/about-pharmacy/our-museum.asp.

APPRENTICESHIP See also Poor Law. A private apprenticeship indenture was an agreement between a master and usually the parents or guardians of an apprentice, whereby the master agreed to train the apprentice in return for a monetary payment, or premium. A stamp duty was imposed on apprenticeship indentures by an Act of 1710. The records of the tax, up to 1811, are in a series of Apprenticeship Books in TNA. Details are given in the TNA research guide entitled *Apprenticeship Records as Sources for Genealogy* at www.nationalarchives.gov.uk. The books give the name of the apprentice, address, name of father (until 1750), name and trade of master. These apprenticeship books from 1710 to 1811 (TNA class IR1) can be searched on the subscription website Ancestry (q.v.) www.ancestry.co.uk by the name of the master or apprentice. The SOG also has an index 1710-1774, which can be searched online at FindmyPast (q.v.). The apprenticeship registers of many London Livery Companies are abstracted in London Apprenticeship Abstracts from 1442-1850, and can be accessed via the Origins (q.v.) subscription website www.origins.net.

The Overseers of the Poor in each parish were responsible for apprenticing the orphans of the parish or the children of paupers. It suited the overseers to apprentice them to a master in another parish, for then they would be liable to receive parish relief, if needed, in that parish. In the towns where Guilds were established, their records often include lists of apprentices and masters. For example, the apprenticeship books of Bristol run to twenty-three volumes for the period 1532 to 1849. Between 1802 and 1844 overseers were required to keep registers of pauper apprentices. The apprenticeship records were usually kept with other parish documents and have generally found their way to the CRO if they were not previously lost or destroyed. Many records of apprenticeship have been published. For example *Oxford City Apprentices 1697-1800* (Oxford Historical Society 1986). Coldham, Peter Wilson *Child Apprentices in America from Christ's Hospital, London 1617-1778* (Genealogical Publishing Company 1990), lists approximately 1,000 names from the registers of Christ's Hospital scholars. Details of the child are given plus father's name and occupation, name of the master and destination in America. See also Raymond, Stuart *My Ancestor was an Apprentice* (SOG 2010).

ARCHAEOLOGICAL SOCIETIES See Antiquarian Societies, Historical Societies and Record Societies.

ARCHDEACON He was the Bishop's deputy with jurisdiction over incumbents in his Archdeaconry. The Archdeacon's Court dealt with probate, granting of licences etc..

ARCHES, COURT OF See Court of Arches.

ARCHER SOFTWARE www.archersoftware.co.uk. Publishes the mapping software Genmap (q.v.) and Surname Atlas, which generates maps of surname distributions based on the 1881 census.

ARCHITECTS Those who have an ancestor who was an architect of some note will wish to read Colvin, H M *Biographical Dictionary of English Architects 1660-1840* (John Murray 1978); Chancellor, Beresford *Lives of British Architects* (Duckworth 1909) and Ware, Dora *Short Dictionary of British Architects* (George Allen & Unwin 1967).

ARCHIVE CD BOOKS A large collection of facsimile UK Directories, maps and county histories produced on CD by this firm are available at www.familyhistoryresearch.org/cdindex.htm.

ARCHIVES See also Access to Archives, Aim25, Archives Hub, County Record Offices, Muniments, National Archives, National Trust, Record Offices and Royal Archives. Archives is the term used for a repository of documents and records of all kinds relating to the past. These may be official or unofficial. TNA holds the National Register of Archives, which lists the whereabouts of archive material that may be of historical value. These include private collections of deeds of large or small estates, records of charitable institutions, public bodies, journals, diaries, family photographs, marriage settlements, manorial records and many others. The National Register of Archives can be searched free of charge at www.nationalarchives.gov.uk/nra.

Scotland has its own National Register of Archives www.nas.gov.uk/nras, which can be searched free of charge.

Some excellent books of relevance are Iredale, David *Enjoying Archives* (David and Charles 1973, re-issued Phillimore 1980). Emmison, F G *Archives and Local History* (Phillimore 1978). Macfarlane, Alan *A Guide To English Historical Records* (Cambridge University Press 1983). Foster, Janet & Sheppard, Julia *British Archives* (2nd ed. Macmillan 1989) lists over 1300 institutions from national and local libraries to specialist and lesser known institutions.

The Database of Non-governmental Organisations (DANGO) has a website www.dango.bham.ac.uk that provides information on the availability of records relating to non-governmental organisations and pressure groups active in the UK since 1945.

ARCHIVES AND RECORDS ASSOCIATION This association www.archives.org.uk aims to "represent the interests of the record-keeping profession nationally in discussions with central and local government, with allied information professionals and with the archive user community."

ARCHIVES HUB This gateway website http://archiveshub.ac.uk/ allows searches in archives held by 220 institutions, primarily universities and colleges.

ARMIGER Person entitled to bear heraldic arms.

ARMORIAL BEARINGS See also Heraldry. This is a synonym for an Achievement of Arms, or what is commonly called today a Coat of Arms, though originally this term meant just the arms borne on the coat worn over the armour itself. Armorial bearings include the arms, crest, supporters, motto and the like. Between 1793 and 1882, a tax of two guineas had to be paid for displaying arms on a carriage and one guinea if displayed in some other way. The tax was not formally abolished until 1945. Few records survive. Those that do are in CROs.

ARMOURERS AND BRAZIERS A brazier was a worker in brass. A history of the Worshipful Company of Armourers and Braziers, a London Livery Company, is on the Company's website at www.armourersandbrasiers.co.uk.

ARMY See also Chelsea Royal Hospital, Civil Registration, Commonwealth War Graves Commission, Household Cavalry, Imperial War Museum, Light Brigade, Medals, Medical Profession, Militia, Prisoners of War, Royal Marines, Servicemen's Wills and Soldiers Died in the Great War 1914-1919.

It is a popular fallacy that it is only possible to trace a soldier ancestor if he was an Officer; this is not so. It is possible to trace an ordinary soldier but it is much easier if you know his regiment or a campaign in which he fought. As with everything, there are exceptions to this.

Many military records are in TNA. Numerous TNA research guides deal with Army research. These are listed at www.nationalarchives.gov.uk. In particular, *Armed Forces in Records Held in the UK* contains a list of many other repositories that hold records that could be useful. TNA published two books by William Spencer in 2008, *Army Records: a guide for family historians* and *First World War Army Service Records: a guide for family historians*. These and a wide range of military books from several other publishers, are available via its online bookshop. Kitzmiller, John F *In Search of the Forlorn Hope: a comprehensive guide to locating British regiments and their records 1640 to WW1* (Manuscript Publications Foundation 1988), does what the title suggests. See also White, A S *A Bibliography of Regimental Histories of the British Army* (Naval and Military Press 2009) and Chant, Christopher *Handbook of British Regiments* (Routledge 1988).

The titles of the Regiments of the British Army have changed many times since the first regular units were raised in the late 1600s. It was not until 1881, when Childers completed the Cardwell reforms by amalgamating units into Regiments of two Battalions and giving them territorial and other titles, that the familiar proud names of the Victorian Wars became standard. By and large, these remained in use until after the 1914-1918 war. See also *Regiments of The Empire: a bibliography of their published histories* compiled and published by Roger Perkins (1994). In addition to the 1,000 regiments and 900 book titles listed, the Appendices cover Rolls of Honour, battle honours etc..

Some other more recently published books that may help are Fowler, Simon *Tracing Your Army Ancestors: a guide for family historians (*2nd ed. Pen & Sword 2013). Ingham, Mary *Tracing your Servicewoman Ancestors* (Pen & Sword 2012). Watts, Michael J & Christopher T *My Ancestor was in the British Army: a guide to British army sources for family historians* (2nd ed. SOG 2009). Holding, Norman *World War I Army Ancestry* (revised and updated by Iain Swinnerton 4th ed. SOG 2004). In addition, books on specific conflicts by Philip Tomaselli, *The Crimean War 1854-56: military history sources for family historians* (FFHS 2006). *The Second World War 1939-1945: military history sources for family historians* (FFHS 2006). *The Zulu War 1879: military history sources for family historians* all (FFHS 2006).

Another useful book, concentrating on the work of the Labour Corps and where relevant records might be found, is Starling, John, & Lee, Ivor *No Labour, No Battle: military labour during the first world war* (The History Press 2009).

The book includes a list of members of the Corps who received honours and awards. It is well worth looking at the publications by Pen & Sword (q.v.) www.pen-and-sword.co.uk, many of which relate to individual campaigns or wars.

Post First World War service records are held by the Ministry of Defence. Next-of-kin or descendants should write to The Ministry of Defence, CS(R)2b, Bourne Avenue, Hayes, Middlesex UB3 1RF. There is a fee for this service.

See Civil Registration for notes on relevant indexes for servicemen and their families. At TNA, there are French and Belgian certificates of deaths for British soldiers who died in hospitals or elsewhere outside the immediate war zone, 1914-20, arranged by first letter of surname. For the Second World War, there are retrospective registers of deaths from enemy action in the Far East 1941-1945.

Muster Rolls and Pay Lists refer to soldiers on the strength, on detachment, on leave and the like. They often give details of a man's pay and enable you to ascertain when a man was taken on the strength or was discharged or if he served in a particular regiment at all. TNA research guide *British Army Muster Rolls and Pay Lists, c1730-1898* gives more information.

Description Books give names of recruits, age, trade, physical features, place of birth and where enlisted. They are exceedingly patchy especially for earlier years.

Casualty Lists are in existence for 1809 to 1857 and give name, rank, trade, birthplace, next of kin and a copy of a will if one was made.

More can be learned about the Records of Courts Martial from TNA research guide *Courts Martial and Desertion in the British Army 17th-20th centuries.*

War Office District Pension Returns 1842-83 are in class WO22 at TNA. The majority end in 1862. 1862-1882 are nearly all colonial ones; some Irish and New Zealand returns and a volume relating to pensioners who were prisoners on convict ships during the period 1862-67. These returns are arranged by the district where the pension was paid. Therefore, if you have a soldier ancestor whose regiment is unknown but whose place of residence after discharge to pension is known, it is possible to locate him in these returns. They give details of regiment, which will lead to other War Office sources. The returns occasionally include pensions paid to the widows and children of men of the Mercantile Marine.

Army Lists have been printed since 1740 (with a gap between 1741-53) and list all officers with their dates of commission, promotion and regiments. In addition there is Peterkin, Johnston and Drew's *Commissioned Officers in the Medical Services of the British Army: 1660-1960* (Wellcome Historical Medical Library 1968).

The British Army has always permitted fathers and sons, brothers and other relatives to serve together in the same regiment. Although regimental muster returns do not disclose relationships between men, the existence of namesakes should alert the astute family historian to the possibility of a relationship. A young lad who enlisted for Boy Service under age 18 may often be found to have had a father serving in the same regiment. In general if nominated as his next-of-kin, the names of a soldier's parents may be found in his discharge document, where discharge took place after 1882. Earlier references to parents as next-of kin normally only appear in regimental casualty returns. Although army wives have followed their husbands on service from the earliest times, mention of them in regimental records before the mid-1860s is wholly exceptional, save when named as next-of-kin in casualty returns reflecting deaths. These normally show the names of next-of-kin and his or her last known place of abode. From 1865, muster returns may include a married roll listing those wives who had permission to accompany the regiment. Such rolls normally provide the wife's Christian names, the date on which she was placed on the married establishment and the ages and sexes (but not names) of any children accompanying her. The places at which the regiment was stationed, as shown by the returns, are often good indications of children's birth places.

Military wills of small estates did not have to be proved in court, so there is no record of these unless they have survived among pension applications and casualty returns in the War Office records. If a soldier died abroad before 1858 and left assets over a certain amount, grants of probate or administration were issued in the Prerogative Court of Canterbury.

After the 1914-1918 war, a Next-of-Kin Memorial Plaque, known colloquially as the Dead Man's Penny, with scroll was commissioned as a memento, the cost to be borne by the State. The medal bears the inscription "He died for Freedom and Honour" and the name of the deceased. Some 1,150,000 plaques and scrolls were issued from 1919 onwards to the next-of-kin of those of HM Forces (Army, Navy and RFC) who fell between 4 August 1914 and 10 January 1920 for Home Establishments, Western Europe and the Dominions (but not to Indian troops) whilst the final date for other theatres of war or for those who died subsequently as a direct result of the war was 30 April 1920. Canada, Australia and New Zealand had a similar commemoration in the form of a silver Memorial Cross but these were issued to wives and mothers only.

The Roll of Honour (class WO304) for the War of 1939-45 has been transferred to TNA by the Ministry of Defence. It comprises a list of army servicemen and women who died during the War of 1939-1945 and gives details of rank, regiment, place of birth and domicile (by town, county and country) and the theatre or country where the fatal wound was sustained. The Roll of Honour, which is dated 1947, is in two parts, one part arranged by regimental code, the other by surname in alphabetical order.

Ireland's Memorial Books 1914-18 (Naval and Military Press 2004) contains names, not only Irish, of soldiers, sailors, officers and other ranks. Regimental numbers, rank and regiment are given, also where born and died.

In Scotland, Rolls of Honour are maintained on public display in the Memorial of the names of Scottish casualties of the 1914-1918 and 1939-1945 wars and in campaigns since 1945; separate rolls are kept for each branch of the services,

Scottish regiments, and Scots in other than Scottish regiments. Scottish casualties include all those killed while serving in Scottish regiments and all those of Scottish birth in other regiments, corps or units. See www.snwm.org or write to the Secretary, The Scottish National War Memorial, The Castle, Edinburgh EH1 2YT. The staff are unable to undertake genealogical research.

Study of photographs and postcards of a soldier in uniform will often reveal clues about him, his regiment and whereabouts he served. See Pols, Robert *Dating Old Army Photographs* (FHP 2011).

Various societies may be able to provide useful information:

The Arms and Armour Society, PO Box 10232, London SW19 2ZD
    www.armsandarmour.net.

The Military History Society, 38 Hawthorn Way, Shipston on Stour,
    Warwickshire CV36 4FD www.themilitaryhistoricalsociety.co.uk.

The Society for Army Historical Research, Wychwood, Scotland Lane,
    Haslemere, Surrey, GU27 3AB www.sahr.co.uk.

The Victoria Cross Society, 7 Oakham Road, Exton, Rutland LE15 9AX
    www.victoriacrosssociety.com.

There is a database of George Cross recipients at www.marionhebblethwaite.
    co.uk/gcindex.htm.

The Police Gazette, known as *The Hue and Cry*, lists army deserters.
    Information is very detailed as to origins and personal descriptions. Copies
    can be found at TNA (Class HO75/11 and elsewhere).

Fitzmaurice, Yvonne *Australia: army deserters from H.M. Service Vol.1 1853-
    1858* and *Vol 2: 1859-1870* (Melbourne 1988) has hundreds of entries
    compiled from material held at the archives in Melbourne and police
    records. All the men at this period came from the British Isles.
    Comprehensive details are recorded. This is the first volume in a series
    intended to continue to 1900.

Hughes, Hugh & Lyn *Discharged in New Zealand: soldiers of the Imperial
    Foot Regiments who took their discharge in New Zealand 1840-1870*
    (New Zealand SOG 1988). If you have a soldier ancestor who did not
    return to the UK you may find him in this book as having taken his
    discharge from one of the fourteen regiments and miscellaneous units
    covered. There is an index in alphabetical order for each regiment.

An increasing number of military records are appearing on pay per view and subscription websites. It is worth revisiting these from time to time as new classes of record may be added. For example, those available on www.findmypast.co.uk include, 1861 Worldwide Army Index; Armed forces births 1761-2005; Armed forces marriages 1796-2005; Armed forces deaths 1796-2005; Army Deserters 1828-1840, British Army Pensioners – Kilmainham, Ireland 1783-1822; British Army Service Records 1760-1915; Military Nurses 1856-1994; Napoleonic War Records 1775-1817; Army Roll of Honour 1939-

1945; Distinguished Conduct Medal Citations 1914-1920 and more. The Forces War Records website www.forces-war-records.co.uk, describes itself as follows, "The definitive location for military genealogy records from WW2, WW1, Boer War, Crimean War and beyond. Our Military Records site is the ONLY location where you can find military records of over 4 million British Armed Forces personnel exclusively cross matched with over 4,000 Regiments, Bases and Ships of the British Armed Forces going back to before 1350." Sources covered include numerous medal rolls and army lists and such things as TNA's UK Army Roll of Honour 1939-1945 Class WO304, World War 1 Mutineers and members of the armed forces from the 1861 census.

ARMY MUSEUMS See also Imperial War Museum and National Army Museum. The Army Museums website www.armymuseums.org.uk lists the museums of the British Army, its regiments and corps. At the time of writing, 136 museums are listed, with contact details, an indication of each museum's facilities, resources and links to the museums' own websites.

ARTISTS Books of reference that may help are Samuel Redgrave's *Dictionary of Artists of the English School* (Kingsmead Reprints 1970); M H Grant's *Dictionary of British Etchers* and *Dictionary of British Sculptors*, both (Rockliff 1952) and Algernon Graves' *A Dictionary of Artists who have exhibited works in the principal London exhibitions from 1760 to 1863* (reprinted RareBooksClub.com 2012).

ASHKENAZIC JEWS See also Jewish Ancestors. These Jews are those whose origins are in north eastern Europe and the Russian Empire. Many emigrated in order to escape persecution in the late C19th.

ASIA, PACIFIC AND AFRICA COLLECTIONS See Cemeteries in South Asia. Formerly known as the Oriental and India Offices collections. Records of those who served in India either as servants of the East India Company, or in the services, are kept in the British Library, 96 Euston Road, London NW1 2DB www.bl.uk/onlinegallery/onlineex/apac/.

The Library contains a remarkable collection of documents and is a rich source of biographical information. They have published Baxter, Ian A *A Brief Guide to Biographical Sources* (2nd ed. 1990). Moir, Martin *A General Guide to the India Office Records* (British Library 1988). See also Taylor, Neville C *Sources for Anglo-Indian Genealogy in the Library of the Society of Genealogists* (SOG 1990). Some records deal with areas other than India, for example Aden, Afghanistan, Central Asia, China and the Persian Gulf States. There are over 1,000 volumes of returns, births, marriages and deaths, c.1698 to 1947.

The best introduction is Jolly, Emma *Tracing your British Indian Ancestors* (Pen & Sword 2012). See also Keay, John *The Honourable Company: a history of the English East India Company* (Harper Collins 1993) and Wild, Antony *The*

East India Company Trade and Conquest from 1600 (Harper Collins 1999). The Families in British India Society www.new.fibis.org is dedicated to helping those with ancestors in British India.

For most of the time the British were in India there were two armies there, the Indian Army and the British Army in India. The latter was made up of British Regiments serving in India but controlled from the War Office in London. The first Indian troops to serve under the British were recruited by the Honourable East India Company to guard their trading posts; under the command of their own Indian officers they wore native dress and used their own weapons. As the company expanded and its military commitments increased, these grew into fully fledged battalions. India was divided by the Company into three great administrative areas, called Presidencies, Bombay, Madras and Bengal. The huge size of India and the difficult terrain, coupled with the almost total lack of communications meant that there was very little contact between them at first so each developed its own entirely separate army and these continued until after the Mutiny in 1857.

In 1748, all three armies of the Presidencies were put under one Commander-in-Chief, Major Stringer Lawrence. Nine years later, in the Bengal Presidency, Robert Clive organised the first battalions of Indian troops to be equipped and trained on the same lines as the British Army; to be commanded by a small core of British officers with subordinate Indian officers. Madras followed in 1759 and Bombay in 1767. This set the pattern for nearly 200 years although many attempts were made to improve the organisation. One of the changes to take place was the introduction of the 2-battalion regimental system in 1796 but with its attendant problems it was not wholly a success.

Units were formed to police particular areas such as the Punjab Frontier Force and the Hyderabad Contingent but these were under the control of the Civil Power not the military. Some cavalry regiments were raised as irregular regiments for use in an emergency and commanded by the local ruler or landowner with a minimum of British officers to provide training and organisation. In 1784 some regular cavalry regiments were raised. All except three were disbanded after the Mutiny, when all the troops of the East India Company that were not disbanded were transferred to the Crown. In 1861 the whole Army in India was reorganised. The Presidency Armies remained until 1895 when they were replaced by area commands which still however operated quite separately.

In 1866, a further re-organisation took place; the Punjab Frontier Force was transferred to the Commander-in-Chief and all battalions were grouped, usually in pairs. A voluntary reserve was created at the same time. This still proved unwieldy and it was left to Lord Kitchener as Commander-in-Chief in 1902 to properly unify the army. He renumbered all the regiments in order of seniority so that all traces of the three Presidency Armies disappeared completely except in the historic names of the regiments. The Frontier Force was abolished on the premiss that all regiments were to serve there in turn. Most of Kitchener's ideas had been put into practice by the outbreak of World War I in 1914.

In 1921 further changes took place, included the disbanding of all part-time cavalry units. Indianisation, the replacement of all British officers with native Indians, commenced in 1923 and the Indian Military Academy for training Indian officers was established in 1931. An Indian Territorial Force was founded in 1920 and there were also the Auxiliary Forces consisting of Europeans or persons of mixed race who volunteered to serve for home defence. British Officers and NCOs were known by the same ranks in the Indian Army as in the British Army but Indians had their own rank names.

When India was granted independence in 1947 the old Indian Army was disbanded and split between India and Pakistan (with the exception of the four 2-battalion Gurkha Regiments who were transferred to the British Army) and many of those famous old names with which we were so familiar, Hodson's Horse, Sam Browne's Cavalry, disappeared for ever.

As an example of the research done on these records see Hodson, Major V C P *Lists of Officers in the Bengal Army 1758 to 1834* (Naval and Military Press 2001). It is packed with biographical and genealogical information about thousands of people, from all levels of society. Another valuable source of information is Wilkinson, Wynyard R T *The Makers of Indian Colonial Silver: a register of European goldsmiths, silversmiths, jewellers, watch-makers and clockmakers in India and their marks 1760-1860* (W Wilkinson Publishing 1987). Many names are cross-referenced to other non-trade names.

ASSESSION ROLLS In some manors, the assessment of rents was supposed to be carried out every seven years. They were recorded in Assession Rolls, which also recorded land transactions.

ASSISTED EMIGRATIONS See Emigration.

ASSIZE COURTS Judges from the central courts went on circuit throughout the country twice a year to hear cases at the Assizes. Records were kept by the Clerks of the Assize and have been deposited in TNA. Four TNA research guides are relevant, see www.nationalarchives.gov.uk, *Civil Trials in the English Assize Courts 1656-1971: key to records*; *Criminal and Civil Trials in the Welsh Assize Courts 1831-1971: key to records*; *Criminal Trials in the Assize Courts 1559-1971* and *Criminal Trials in the English Assize Courts 1559-1971: key to records*. Crimes that were too serious for the Petty Sessions (q.v.) or Quarter Sessions (q.v.) would be referred to the Assizes. Serious cases of crime were dealt with at these courts, although the records have not survived in their entirety. It is interesting to note that what are now viewed as comparatively trivial offences were not so regarded formerly and hence many apparently minor offences will be found here. There is little of genealogical value about the accused in the records, except the parish of residence. More information is given about those who made depositions: names, ages and places of residence. Few details of the circumstances of the crime are given.

Copies of Assize Calendars are often found in CROs. These are lists of prisoners to be tried with a statement of the charge against them. It is possible that some more colourful details appear in newspaper reports on the Assizes.

ASSOCIATION OATH ROLLS In 1695-96, all persons in England and Wales holding public office had to sign a pledge of loyalty to the Crown. These rolls are in TNA.

ASSOCIATION OF GENEALOGISTS AND RECORD AGENTS, THE (AGRA) See also Professional Researchers. These letters in advertisements by professional researchers signify that the researcher is a member of The Association of Genealogists and Researchers in Archives. The Association aims to maintain a high standard of integrity and efficiency amongst its members, who agree to abide by a Code of Practice. A complaints procedure is also in operation. A list of members who offer professional services, together with their addresses and areas of expertise, is available at www.agra.org.uk.

ASTON MARTIN The Aston Martin Heritage Trust www.amht.org.uk was formed in 1998 by the Aston Martin Owners' Club. The Trust is responsible for preserving the history of Aston Martin to both educate and inform people about the history and legacy of the organisation. A museum and archive is located in Drayton St Leonard, Oxfordshire. The archive contains a large collection of photographs, books, documents and other artefacts.

ASYLUMS See also Hospitals. An Act of 1808 gave Justices in Quarter Sessions (q.v.) the authority to build a county asylum for lunatics. In 1815, parish overseers had to send lists of pauper lunatics to the Clerk of the Peace to be forwarded to the Quarter Sessions. Asylum records are often found in CROs but only those relating to individual inmates over a hundred years old may be consulted by the public. The records of the Office of Commissioners in Lunacy, which should not be overlooked, are held at TNA. A TNA research guide *Looking for Records of Asylum Inmates*, downloadable at www.nationalarchives.gov.uk gives further information. See also Faithfull, Pamela *Basic Facts about Lunatics in England* (FFHS 2002).

ATLAS AND INDEX, THE PHILLIMORE See Parish Maps.

ATTAINDER Forfeiture of estate following sentence of death or outlawry.

ATTORNEYS See Legal Profession.

AUGMENTATIONS, COURT OF This was created by statute in 1535, after the dissolution of the monasteries, to administer the property of religious houses and foundations dissolved. It subsequently dealt with chantries and the like, paying any revenues to the Crown. It was abolished in 1554 and its functions transferred to the Exchequer. At that time an Augmentations Office was established to keep the records of the Court, the keeper being appointed by the Clerk of the Pipe. When the Clerkship was discontinued in 1833 no further keepers were appointed so the very rich collection of records was taken over by the King's Remembrancer. The collection now forms part of the Exchequer Records in TNA.

AUSTRALIA see also The Australian War Memorial, Convicts, Emigration, Lacemakers, Parkhurst Boys and Transportation. Researchers should bear in mind that, unlike England, Australia is divided into states and each is responsible for its own record-keeping. There is no national system of recording birth, death or marriage information, nor are arrivals and departures centralised. It is therefore essential to determine an accurate location before commencing research.

The standard introduction to Australian research is Vine-Hall, Nick *Tracing your Family History in Australia* (3rd ed. Vine-Hall 2002), although this does not take account of more recent developments. The following are just a few of the websites that may assist with Australian research. Births, Deaths and Marriages, Victoria, Australia at www.bdm.vic.gov.au. A Select List of Resources held at the Australian Institute of Genealogical Studies, The Genealogical Society of Victoria and the State Library of Victoria http://members.optusnet.com.au/ guthrigg/ shipres.htm. New South Wales State records www.records.nsw.gov.au. New South Wales Registry of Births, Marriages and Deaths at www.bdm. nsw.gov.au. Queensland State Archives www.archives.qld.gov.au.

The Society of Australian Genealogists is situated at Richmond Villa, 120 Kent Street, Observatory Hill, Sydney, NSW 2000, Australia www.sag.org.au. There are also state and regional family history societies in Australia. A list of societies can be found at www.coraweb.com.au/society.htm.

The National Library of Australia is at Parkes Place, Canberra ACT 2600 Australia www.nla.gov.au.

The Australian Biographical and Genealogical Record (ABGR), an independent research body, formed to compile biographical and genealogical details about early Australians, claim that their first published series "contains over 1,500 submitted biographies of Australia pioneers who were settled or born in the colonies prior to 1841. The Series 2 Supplement contains more biographies for the period 1842-1899. An estimated nearly 80,000 persons are named in the biographies: parents, spouses, spouse's parents and children. In addition (where known) years of birth and death of sons and daughter and daughter's married names are also included. As an added bonus there are over 1,700 photographs included in this book." ABGR has also published a series of surviving Musters, which were taken on a regular basis to provide the government with information on both free settlers and convicts including: *Musters & Lists for NSW and Norfolk Island 1800-1802*; *Muster of NSW and Norfolk*

Island 1805-1806; The General Muster of 1811; The General Muster and Land and Stock Muster of NSW 1822 and the General Return of Convicts in NSW 1837.

Smee, C J & Selkirk, J The Bicentenary Pioneer Register: containing the genealogical details of 500 pioneers, their children and grandchildren Vol 3 (2nd ed. Smee 1987) contains details of families who arrived in New South Wales and Van Diemen's Land 1788-1820.

Perhaps not so well known is that many emigrants had assistance with their passage from the parish under the provisions of the 1834 Poor Law (TNA class MH12). Effective for rather a short time 1834-c.1860 it can account for that missing link. Based on this, Pat Button has compiled A Free Passage to Paradise?: passenger lists of UK emigrants who applied for free passage to South Australia 1836-1840 (South Australian Society 1993).

About 4,000 Irish girls, teenagers and orphans, emigrated to Australia 1848-50 under a scheme instigated by Earl Grey, British Secretary of State for the Colonies. This topic is covered in McLaughlin, Terence Barefoot and Pregnant? Irish Famine Orphans in Australia (Genealogical Society of Victoria 1991). The second part is a register of the orphans, listed alphabetically, according to the ship in which they travelled, with age, home town, names of parents (where known) and religion. Further information discovered since (e.g. marriage) is also given.

Ozships is a searchable list of passengers and convicts on selected ships to Australia www.ozships.net.

The Founders and Survivors project www.foundersandsurvivors.org is tracking the lives of 73,000 transportees to Tasmania.

Many English records relating to Australia were filmed by the Australian Joint Copying Project www.nla.gov.au/microform-australian-joint-copying-project. The microfilm are now held in a number of Australian research libraries.

AUSTRALIAN IMMIGRANTS It must be remembered that not all the early settlers in Australia were convicts. For instance, many of the crew of the First Fleet remained in Australia, as did those of the Second and Third Fleets (q.v.). The census of New South Wales and Tasmania for 1828 is the most complete record for the early years and contains names of more than 35,000 persons with their ages, religions, families, land held etc.. In addition there is an indication of whether they came to the colony free or in bond or were born in the colony and the ship and year of arrival. A copy of this census is on microfilm at TNA Class HO10 21-27; this copy can be searched at www.ancestry.co.uk. It is also available on CD from www.gould.com.au/New-South-Wales-1828-Census-p/lah130.htm.

For emigration to Australia see also www.records.nsw.gov.au/state-archives/indexes-online/indexes-online#immigration-and-shipping. A select list of sources relevant to emigration to Australia can be found at http://members.optusnet.com.au/guthrigg/shipres.htm.

Charlwood, Don *The Long Farewell* (Penguin 1981) provides a good backcloth to the lives of the early settlers in Australia. It has an extensive bibliography. There is also publication No.2 in the Great Expectations Series, Kitson, Jill *The British to the Antipodes* (Gentry Books Ltd. 1972).

AUSTRALIAN WAR MEMORIAL, THE The Australian War Memorial, GPO Box 345, Canberra, ACT 2601, Australia www.awm.gov.au, is the repository for official Australian Commonwealth Government archival records relating to periods when Australia was involved in wars and warlike activities. Holdings are strongest relating to the period following the establishment of the Commonwealth, ie. since 1901. Colonial records are of a miscellaneous nature, as the various state archives hold the majority of records for this pre-Federation period. The records cover all branches of the armed services, though the Army has traditionally been the most prolific in generating records.

The printed books and maps, official records and photograph collections include material from the Sudan War to date, with many items in these collections readily available for public access via their database.

Many personnel records are included in the official records and there are good indexes to most of these. A strength is the official unit diaries, for both World Wars. They often mention individual soldiers. The Embarkation Rolls and the Nominal Rolls for members of the 1st AIF (Australian Imperial Force) who served in World War I are published in microform. The Embarkation Rolls list next of kin (who are sometimes living at overseas addresses), age and occupation. The Nominal Rolls include date of enlistment, date returned to Australia, or date killed. As published material, these are widely available in other libraries. The official histories of Australia in the two World Wars mention many individuals by name and frequently give date and place of birth and occupation, together with date of death (often many years after the war).

Collections preserved by private individuals or organisations such as the Red Cross are held by the Memorial. They include letters, diaries, and photographs. Recent acquisitions cover activities involving Australians in peacekeeping, for instance in Somalia and Cambodia.

There are many items in the collections relating to places where Australians served e.g. villages in France, air bases in England, stately homes in Scotland, which supplied hospitality to servicemen. Many Allied servicemen feature in collections beside their Australian colleagues; for instance photographs of Australian prisoners of war may include British or Canadian airmen in the group, in many instances with their names. The Memorial also has collections of medals, weapons, and a fine art collection. The Memorial will supply a list of researchers on request, as it is unable to reply to mail enquiries unless they are specific. See Anderson, Nola *Australian War Memorial: treasures from a century of collecting* (Murdoch Books 2013).

B

BACSA See Cemeteries in South Asia.

BADGER See also Higgler and Pedlar. An itinerant trader, usually of food. Also refers to a corn dealer or miller. The term derives from an Act of 1697, which obliged paupers to wear a capital "P" on their clothing, a badge. Also known in various dialects as Cadger, Hawker or Huckster. Badgers had to be licensed by the Quarter Sessions (q.v.). Their names, with those of sureties, were registered, sometimes with other details and these records are known as "Badgers' Recognizances".

BAILIFF He was employed by the lord of the manor to administer some of the farms and lands of the manor. The overall administration was however in the hands of a Steward. See the booklet Plunknett, T F T *The Mediaeval Bailiff* (University of London Athlone Press 1954).

BAIRMAN A Pauper.

BAKERS The Worshipful Company of Bakers www.bakers.co.uk is one of the oldest City of London Livery Companies with a history dating back over 800 years.

BANK OF ENGLAND The Bank has an extensive archive covering every aspect of its administration from the Bank's foundation in 1694 to the present day. It holds a wide range of material of interest not only to genealogists but to social, economic and business historians and biographers. The Bank also has a museum, which hosts various exhibitions and events. For further details of both the archive and museum see www.bankofengland.co.uk/archive.

A useful reference book is Pressnell, L & Orbell, John *A Guide to the Historical Records of British Banking* (Gower Publishing 1985).

An *Index to the Bank of England Will extracts 1807-45* can be purchased from the SOG's on-line bookshop or searched on-line at www.origins.net or www.findmypast.co.uk.

BANKRUPTCY See also London Gazette. In bankruptcy, proceedings are taken whereby the state gains possession of the property of a debtor through an officer appointed for the purpose. Such property is realised, subject to certain priorities and distributed amongst the persons to whom the debtor owes money or has incurred pecuniary liabilities. An Act of 1914, subsequently amended, now regulates the proceedings in bankruptcy. Before then, most debtors were subject to legal proceedings and to imprisonment if convicted of being unwilling or unable to pay their debts. From 1543-1841 those who were traders or who owed large sums were usually exempt from the laws relating to debtors, did not suffer imprisonment but were subject to proceedings for bankruptcy. After 1861 bankruptcy proceedings were extended to all those unable or unwilling to pay their debts although imprisonment for debt continued until 1970, in certain cases.

From 1684, notices appeared in *The London Gazette* (q.v.) of official proceedings of bankruptcy. These are indexed and in print from 1690. The indexes are variable, some names appear which are not found in the official records and some names are omitted which are. There are several competitive indexes which can be found in larger libraries such as the Guildhall Library. *The London Gazette* and its Scottish and Northern Ireland counterparts, *The Edinburgh Gazette* and *The Belfast Gazette*, can also be searched freely and downloaded from www.gazettes-online.co.uk.

Two TNA research guides www.nationalarchives.gov.uk are of relevance: *Bankruptcy Records After 1869* and *Bankrupts and Insolvent Debtors, 1710-1869.*

It should also be noted that amongst the court and gaol records in TNA are some which relate particularly to debtors.

BANKS See Bank of England, Barclays Bank, Lloyd's Banking Group and Royal Bank of Scotland.

BANNS The reading of banns as a declaration of intent to marry goes back to Medieval times. From 1653-1660 banns were read either in the church or market place. These might be recorded in a separate book or in the parish register, sometimes with the annotation 'M' to denote a declaration in the market place. After Hardwicke's Marriage Act of 1753, all marriages from March 1754 had to be by banns or licence and a banns register had to be kept. Unfortunately, these have not always been preserved by the parish. If you are unable to locate a marriage in the marriage register in the parish where you believe it should have taken place, it is worth checking if a banns register has survived. It might contain the entry you want and give the name of the parish where the marriage was to take place. It was more usual for this to be the bride's parish and this would be given in the banns entry.

BAPTISM A religious rite signifying (for Christians) admission to the Church; generally accompanied by name-giving, christening. The two words are very often used interchangeably. Children christened privately, not in church, perhaps because they were not expected to survive, are sometimes referred to as "half-baptised".

BAPTISM REGISTERS See Non-conformists and Parish Registers.

BAPTISTS The Baptists were founded by an English refugee, John Smyth, in Amsterdam in 1609. They believed in adult baptism but split into factions with differing beliefs, the General Baptists and Particular Baptists. The General Baptists then split into the "New Connection" and the "Old Connection" and the latter became Unitarians. A Baptist Union in 1813 attempted to bring about co-operation between the divisions. The Particular Baptists and the New Connection united in 1891. As with other nonconformist registers, those of the Baptists up to 1837 were deposited with the Registrar General and are now in TNA and available for a fee via www.bmdregisters.co.uk.
The most comprehensive library and archive of information relating to Baptist churches and their history is held at the Angus Library in Oxford http://anguslibraryandarchive.blogspot.co.uk/. The Baptist Historical Society www.baptisthistory.org.uk has an informative website, which includes a section particularly devoted to family history.
The Baptist Magazine, from 1809, is a useful source of information for the family historian. See Breed, G R *My Ancestors were Baptists* (SOG 1986).

BAR THE RECOVERY See Entail.

BARBERS Until 1745, barbers were also surgeons. From that year onwards surgeons had their own identity. They have a London Livery Company, the Worshipful Company of Barbers, the records of which have been deposited at the Guildhall Library (q.v.). The Company's website at www.barberscompany. org.uk gives a full history of the Company, details of relevant memorials and the like.

BARBER SURGEONS See Medical Profession.

BARCLAYS BANK Barclays Group Archives http://group.barclays.com/about-barclays/about-us/our-history/barclays-group-archives preserves and provides access to records with permanent business value or historic importance. Barclays can trace its history back to 1690. The archives contain records dating back to then, including documents and products from Barclays businesses around the world. Amongst the oldest pieces in the collection is Barclay's first formal balance book, dated 1733.

More than 55,000 entries are listed on a searchable database, available to access onsite at the archives premises in Manchester. A reference library, containing books and magazines, is also open for daily use. For further information and to make an appointment to use the archives and library contact Barclays Group Archives, Dallimore Road, Wythenshawe, Manchester M23 9JA.

BAREMAN See Bairman.

BARGAIN AND SALE A method of transferring property by private agreement. This was usually superseded by lease and release (q.v.) by the C17th.

BARGES See also Boatmen, Canals and Watermen. From 1795-1871, all boats and barges exceeding thirteen tons burden used on inland navigations had to be registered with the Clerk of the Peace. Such records are with the Quarter Sessions (q.v.) records in CROs.

Information on the history of the sailing barge can be obtained from the National Maritime Museum www.nmm.ac.uk. The Society for Sailing Barge Research website is at www.sailingbargeresearch.org.uk. A website entitled Thames Sailing Barges www.thamesbarge.org.uk is also very informative and details a number of museums and other sources of information.

BARING ARCHIVE www.baringarchive.org.uk provides an introduction to the organisation and content of the archive and enables potential users to understand the wealth of material held. Its holdings illustrate the range of Baring's business activities. For much of the C19th, the firm specialised in issuing bearer bonds for overseas governments and businesses, especially railway companies. Towards the end of the C19th, work for domestic companies commenced, beginning with the flotation of Arthur Guinness Sons & Co. Ltd. in 1886.

The website also includes details of its art collection and the digitised collections that can be downloaded from the website. It also contains a brief history of Baring's, information about the Baring family, with biographical and genealogical material and an interactive timeline that lists key events and transactions in Baring's history.

BARKER A tanner of leather.

BARNARDO'S HOMES See Children's Societies

BARRISTERS See Legal Profession.

BASKETMAKERS This was a thriving trade in earlier times since baskets were used for transporting most goods. There are a number of books describing this craft, one of which is Heseltine, Alistair *Baskets and Basket Making* (Shire Publications 1982). The website of The Basketmakers' Association www. basketassoc.org gives details of various museums with relevant displays and exhibitions.

There is also a London Livery Company, the Worshipful Company of Basketmakers, which was established in 1569 to control the manufacture of baskets within the City of London. A full history of the Company features on its website at www.basketmakersco.org.

BASTARDY See Illegitimacy.

BBC See British Broadcasting Association.

BEADHOUSE An almshouse or workhouse.

BEADLE A parish or ward officer who had various duties. He summoned parishioners to attend vestry meetings, kept children in order with a cane, whipped vagrants and is generally associated with administration of the poor law.

BEALEY FAMILY ARCHIVE Bury Archives Service received funding from the National Cataloguing Grants Scheme in 2009 to catalogue the papers of the Bealey Family and Bleachworks of Radcliffe, near Bury. A blog has been set up to track the project's development and gives different perspectives on the project. Anyone wanting to know more about how a record office or archive catalogues a major set of papers should look at http://bealey.wordpress.com.

BEDEHOUSE See Beadhouse.

BEDLAM A contraction for the Hospital of St. Mary of Bethlem (or Bethlehem). It was founded in 1247 and first referred to as a hospital in 1330. It was the first hospital for the mentally ill in England. The website for its archives and museum service is at www.bethlemheritage.org.uk.

BELLFOUNDERS Jennings, Trevor *Bellfounding* (Shire Publications 1988) is a good introduction to the process. Two of England's oldest bellfounders have websites, The Whitechapel Bellfoundry www.whitechapelbellfoundry.co.uk and John Taylor & Co. www.taylorbells.co.uk.

BERMUDA Hollis Hallet, C F E *The Bermuda Index 1784-1914* (2 vols. Juniperhill Press 1992), contains details of births, marriages and deaths recorded in Bermuda newspapers. See also Hollis Hallet, C F E *Early Bermuda Records 1619-1826* (Juniperhill Press 1992) and Mercer, Julia E *Bermuda Settlers of the 17th Century: genealogical notes from Bermuda* (Genealogical Publishing Co. 2012), which contains genealogical notes culled from abstracts of wills, deeds, letters, colonial and parish records

BERNAU INDEX See also Chancery Proceedings and Depositions. This index was compiled by the late Charles Bernau, one of the founders of the SOG. It forms part of the Bernau Collection, along with Bernau's Notebooks and Bernau's Correspondence.

Although it does not give comprehensive coverage this is a most important index, the contents of which relate to unindexed material in TNA, mainly

Chancery and Exchequer Court Depositions and Proceedings from the C18th. It includes every litigant in Chancery between 1714 and 1758.

Bernau employed a team of workers to examine every document in 2,793 huge bundles and to extract all names of those involved in each case. Evidence of witnesses, often people of humble origin, was taken by Commissioners sent to the provinces. There is often genealogical information about these witnesses. The statements are known as depositions. Depositions in the Court of the Exchequer also figure in the index, which amounts to some four and a half million slips.

The index has been microfilmed and can be viewed at the Library of the SOG. See Sharp, Hilary *How to Use the Bernau Index* (SOG 2000). Further background information features in TNA research guide *Equity Proceedings in the Court of Exchequer* www.nationalarchives.gov.uk.

BEVIN BOYS Hickman, Tom *Called Up, Sent Down: the Bevin Boys' war* (The History Press 2008) describes how labour shortages in the Second World War led to Ernest Bevin, Minister of Labour in Churchill's government, deciding that one in ten conscripts would not join the armed forces to fight for their country but would instead dig for their country in the coal mines. These conscript miners, who quickly became known as "Bevin Boys", came from the length and breadth of the country and from all walks of life. Hickman describes the lives of these Bevin Boys, who were often sent many miles from home to settle in hostels or lodgings in tightly-knit and occasionally hostile mining communities. The book is also a fascinating insight into an industry that whilst vital to the economy, was riddled with vested interests, poor industrial relations and antiquated equipment. See also the Bevin Boys' Association www.bevinboysassociation.co.uk, who produce a newsletter.

BIBLE CHRISTIANS The Bible Christians were an offshoot of the Methodist Church, formed in 1815 by William O'Bryan. They were particularly strong in the south-west of England. Large numbers of Bible Christians emigrated in the 1830s-1860s, many moving to Canada but congregations were also established in the U.S.A., Australia, New Zealand and China. The English Bible Christians amalgamated with the United Methodist Free Churches and the Methodist New Connexion in 1907, to form the United Methodist Church. In Canada, the Bible Christian Church was amalgamated into the Methodist Church of Canada in 1884, later becoming part of the United Church of Canada.

Several books provide background information: Bourne FW *The Bible Christians: their origins and history* (reprinted Tentmaker Publications 2004). Shaw, Thomas *The Bible Christians 1815-1907* (Epworth Press 1965) and Wickes, Michael *The West Country Preachers: a history of the Bible Christians* (Wickes 1990). For the Canadian connection see three books by Sher Leetooze, all published by Michael-John Associates in 2005. *Bible Christian Chapels of the Canadian Conference*, *The Damascus Road: the Bible Christian Preachers of the Canadian Conference* and *A Corner for the Preacher*. The Bible Christian Project co-ordinates research, more information can be found here http://freepages.history.rootsweb.ancestry.com/~biblechristian/.

BIBLIOGRAPHIES See also Books, Digitised, Houses, The History of, Local History Bibliography, Social History Bibliography and Surnames. References to many books and pamphlets are made under appropriate sections of *Enquire Within*. Bibliographies for tracing ancestors in Scotland and Ireland will be found under the relevant headings.

Bibliographies are an important aid to Family History Research and give essential pointers for further information about research methods, sources and context for your family history. Stuart Raymond has compiled a county by county series of bibliographies that should be consulted for specific information about a particular area. They list all published works that are likely to be of relevance and generally enable a systematic search to be made in published sources. See www.stuartraymond.co.uk.

The Bibliography of British and Irish History (BBIH) www.royalhistorical society.org/respubs.php is an online subscription service listing over 518,000 records, relating to British and Irish history. Reduced rate subscriptions are available through the British Association for Local History (q.v.). There are many guides to tracing ancestors. The following can be recommended:

Adolph, Anthony *Collins' Tracing Your Family History* (Collins 2008).

Annal, David *Easy Family History: the stress free guide to starting your research* (Bloomsbury and TNA 2012).

Barrett, Nick *Beginners' Guide to Family History* (Pen & Sword 2010).

Barrett, Nick *Who Do You Think You Are? Encyclopedia of Genealogy: the definitive reference guide to tracing your family history* (Harper 2008).

Bevan, Amanda *Tracing Your Ancestors in TNA: the website and beyond* (TNA 2006).

Cole, Jean & Titford, John *Tracing your Family Tree* (Countryside Books 2000).

Davis, Graeme *Solving Genealogy Problems: how to break down 'brick walls' and build your family tree* (How to Books 2011).

Davis, Graeme *Your Family Tree Online: how to trace your ancestry from your own computer* (How to Books 2009).

Fowler, Simon *Family History: digging deeper* (The History Press 2012).

Heber, Mark D *Ancestral Trails: the complete guide to British genealogy and family history* (The History Press 2005).

Hey, David *Family History and Local History in England* (Longmans 1987).

Hey, David *The Oxford Guide To Family History* (Oxford University Press 1993).

Oates, Jonathan *Tracing Your Ancestors from 1066 to 1837* (Pen & Sword Books 2012).

Raymond, Stuart *Introducing Family History* (FFHS 2006).
Rogers, Colin *The Family Tree Detective: a manual for tracing your ancestors in England and Wales* (4th ed. Manchester University Press 2008).

The Family History Partnership (q.v.) www.thefamilyhistorypartnership.com publish family history books on a wide variety of topics. See in particular their "Basic Facts" series. Jeremy Gibson has edited a series of books, known as "Gibson Guides", which list the whereabouts of various classes of record on a county by county basis; these are available from FHP and other outlets. The SOG (q.v.) www.sog.org.uk/publications/publications.shtml publish a "My Ancestor was a ………." series, in which most titles relate to a particular occupation or religious denomination. Pen & Sword Books (q.v.) www.pen-and-sword.co.uk are publishing an increasing number of family history titles, including guides to researching in particular regions of Britain. TNA (q.v.) also have an online bookshop www.nationalarchives.gov.uk/BOOKSHOP. Genfair www.genfair.co.uk (q.v.) and Parish Chest www.parishchest.com (q.v.) are two online sellers who specialise in family history books. Most family history societies have publishing programmes, producing booklets, CDs or pdfs relating to their particular areas of interest.

BIGAMY The crime of going through a form of marriage whilst a previous marriage is still in existence. Until 1858, when it became easier to obtain a divorce (q.v.), bigamy appears to have been much more common than most people imagine. Unless the offence was discovered and brought to court, it is very difficult to detect or prove. It should be noted that after 1837, even following a conviction, no correction was made to the Registrar General's records.

In ecclesiastical law, bigamy (literally meaning "twice married") can be used to mean a second marriage or of a marriage to a widow or widower.

BIOGRAPHICAL DICTIONARIES See also Dictionary of Naval Biographies, Family Histories and Peerage. Over 16,000 biographical dictionaries are listed in Slocum, R B *Biographical Dictionaries and Relate works: an international bibliography* (2nd ed. Gale Research 1991), which is also available on CD. Some of these dictionaries are indexed in *Biography and Genealogy Master Index: a consolidated index to more tan 3,200,000 biographical sketches in over 350 current and retrospective biographical dictionaries* (8 vols. Gale 1980), with many subsequent supplements.

The *Oxford Dictionary of National Biography* (DNB 2001-8) is an illustrated collection of more than 50,000 biographies of the men and women from around the world who shaped all aspects of Britain's past. The printed version comprises sixty volumes of around one thousand pages each. The cost of these means that institutions are increasingly using the online version www.oxforddnb.com. The link entitled "Read the Oxford DNB at Home using your Library's Subscription" is a good starting point. Free online access is frequently provided by public library websites.

Boase, Frederick *Modern English Biography* (Reprinted Frank Cass 1965). The six volumes contain 30,000 biographies.

Between 1898 and 1912, W T Pike produced *A Dictionary of Edwardian Biography*. Each of its thirty-three volumes combines a guide book with an illustrated dictionary of biography covering county areas and the cities of Belfast, Birmingham, Bristol, Cork, Dublin, Durham, Edinburgh, Leicester, Liverpool, London, Manchester and Sheffield. Except for Bristol and Manchester the titles are in the format *Hertfordshire in the Twentieth Century: contemporary biographies*. The volumes generally contain several hundred detailed and illustrated sketches of major local figures. The number printed was very limited so these volumes are quite rare and their value to the family historian is often overlooked. See also Bell, Peter *A Dictionary of Edwardian Biography: master index* (Edinburgh: Peter Bell 1986).

Another useful publication is *Who was Who*, which covers all those in *Who's Who*, first issued in 1897, who had subsequently died. There are numerous books on the lines of *Who's Who* but specialising in a particular field such as art, sport and the theatre, or in a particular geographical location. The website of S & N Genealogy Supplies www.genealogysupplies.com shows that they sell facsimile copies of the following titles on CD: *Who's Who in Staffordshire 1844-1930*; *Who's Who 1897*; *Who's Who in Sport 1935*; *Who's Who in the Theatre 1922*; *Who's Who in Yorkshire 1912*.

BIRTH CERTIFICATES See Civil Registration.

BISHOPS' TRANSCRIPTS (BTs) In theory, these were copies of the parish registers sent at intervals to the Bishop. No doubt most were but in some cases, the BTs are believed to have been the notes written at the time of the events, to be written up later in the parish registers; thus the BTs are the original records. There are cases where there are such considerable differences both of spelling and dates, omissions and inclusions, that the registers and transcripts would appear to have been maintained by different persons. Because of this, it is worth checking entries extracted from original registers with those of the transcripts and vice versa.

BTs began in 1598, even earlier in a few dioceses but few have survived from the C16th and they rarely go beyond the mid C19th. There are usually gaps in the sequence either because of failure to make the returns or because they have been destroyed. There are none for the Commonwealth Period of 1649 to 1660.

Bishops' Transcripts will be found in Diocesan Record Offices (DROs) or in CROs; the latter frequently incorporates the former. For example, Devon Heritage Centre is also the DRO for Diocese of Exeter.

Gibson, Jeremy *Bishops' Transcripts and Marriage Licences, Bonds and Allegations: a guide to their location and indexes* (5th ed. FFHS 2001) is a survey on a county by county basis of where these may be examined.

BLACKSMITHS An index of Blacksmiths, together with contact details of these researching the individuals, can be found at http://blacksmiths.mygenwebs.com/. See McDougall, David *The Country Blacksmith* (Shire Publications 2013) and Bailey, Jocelyn *The Village Blacksmith* (Shire Publications 1980).

BLAZON See also Heraldry. A narrative description of arms in armorial terminology, so that they can be accurately rendered from the verbal description.

BLETCHLEY PARK See also World War I and World War II. Located at Milton Keynes, this was the historic site of secret British code-breaking activities during World War II www.bletchleypark.org.uk. It is now a museum and archives incorporating a wartime mini-cinema and an outstanding Churchill collection. Special events and talks are held in the building that was headquarters to intelligence staff during the War. The Bletchley Park Archives safeguards the documentary heritage of Bletchley Park and has over 14,000 items of text, image, sound, software and physical objects in its collections. Of particular interest to researchers are likely to be: ISOS and ISK Series Reports, intelligence intercepts; Government Code and Cypher School Card Indexes. The latter contains vast quantities of information which was obtained as a result of decoding enigma and other enciphered signals. As each message was decoded and translated it was passed to the indexing team who identified the words and phrases to be indexed, including many named individuals.

BLUECOAT SCHOOLS Charity schools, often boarding, whose uniform was a blue coat of varying design. Christ's Hospital School www.christs-hospital.org.uk was the first, and perhaps the best known. Formerly in London, it survives today at Horsham. This is the only school where the boys wear the bluecoat as part of their normal dress, as do the girls in the winter. Its archives are at the Guildhall Library (q.v.).

There were at least eighty other bluecoat and various other colour coat, schools. Local libraries should know if there was one in their area. Birmingham and Reading have Bluecoat Schools which are now run independently. An extensive collection of records relating to the Bluecoat School in Liverpool is held by Liverpool Record Office, see http://archive.liverpool.gov.uk.

BOARDS OF GUARDIANS See Guardians, Boards of.

BOATMEN See also Barges, Canals, Salters and Watermen. The term "Boatmen" usually refers to those who worked solely on the boats of the inland waterways. Canalmen could be working in any capacity on the canal or its bank. Flatmen worked on "flats", flat-bottomed boats, which were usually canal boats or those used for river or coastal traffic. These were very common in the Cheshire salt trade.

There is an Inland Waterways Index of Canal and River Boatmen and Allied

Trades working on inland waterways. These references come from a wide variety of sources and cover many occupations. Enquiries may be made, with a stamped addressed envelope, to John Roberts, 52 St Andrews Rd, Sutton Coldfield, West Midlands B75 6UH. General details can be obtained from:

The Canal and River Trust http://canalrivertrust.org.uk.

The Canal Museum Stoke Bruerne www.stokebruernecanalmuseum.org.uk.

The London Canal Museum www.canalmuseum.org.uk.

The Linlithgow Canal Centre www.lucs.org.uk.

Ellesmere Port Boat Museum www.boatmuseum.org.uk.

The Boat Museum Society www.boatmuseumsociety.org.uk.

The Railway and Canal Historical Society www.rchs.org.uk.

There have been many books published on canals and the lives of those who lived on them. A good example is Hanson, Harry *Canal Boatmen 1760-1914* (reprinted Alan Sutton 1984), also Wilkes, Sue *Tracing your Canal Ancestors* (Pen & Sword 2011).The Eureka Partnership www.eurekapartnership.com have published several booklets about boat people of various canals.

BODLEIAN LIBRARY See University Libraries.

BOER WAR See Army and South Africa.

BOND OF INDEMNIFICATION This term has two meanings, in the context of family history. It relates to the sum of money obtained from a putative father to pay for the up-keep of his child. It was also the indemnity given by people in respect of potential paupers who might be allowed to settle in a parish, or servants who gained settlement because of twelve months' employment.

BOOKPLATES Many bookplates are either armorial, dated or give the name of an estate, which may give clues as to the whereabouts of particular individuals, their alliances (impaled coats of arms) or their station in life. Bookplates can also be dated from their style in the same way as silver or furniture. The best known collection is the Franks' Collection of British and American Bookplates, which is in the Prints and Drawings Department of The British Library. Franks, Sir A W *Catalogue of British and American book-plates (ex libris) collected by the late Sir Augustus Wollaston Franks* (Ellis 1906) is available online http://archive.org. Another collection is the Marshall Collection at the Heraldry Society, London www.theheraldrysociety.com. The Bookplate Society has a most informative website www.bookplatesociety.org, publishes *The Bookplate Journal*, and a newsletter.

BOOKS, DIGITISED Many of the older titles recommended in this books have been digitised and are available on sites such as:

Google Books http://books.google.co.uk/

The Internet Archive http://archive.org

Family Search Books www.familysearch.org/learn/wiki/en/BYU-
    FHL_Digital_Book_Collection
Project Gutenburg www.gutenberg.org

BOOTH'S SURVEY OF LONDON See London.

BOOTMAKER See Shoemaker.

BOOTS UK The company archive for Boots stores contains a diverse collection of documentation, audio-visual/electronic records and museum objects illustrating the company's years of trading, firstly as a herbalist and latterly as chemists, healthcare and beauty retailers. The history of the company can be found at www.boots-uk.com.

BORTHWICK INSTITUTE, THE The Borthwick Institute for Archives, is at the University of York, Heslington, York, YO10 5DD www.york.ac.uk/library/borthwick. Amongst other things, they hold records relating to the diocese of York, including wills proved at the Prerogative Court of York. Full details can be found on their website.

BOWYER A maker and dealer in archery bows or an archer. There is a London Livery Company, the Worshipful Company of Bowyers, whose website www.bowyers.com gives a full history of the Company, details of relevant memorials and the like.

BOYD'S LONDON BURIALS See Burial Indexes.

BOYD'S MARRIAGE INDEX See also Marriages. This remarkable index, containing about seven million names, was the work of Percival Boyd, a Fellow of the SOG. The index covers the period 1538-1837, with the information having been extracted from Parish Registers, Bishops' Transcripts and Marriage Licences. Many CROs or libraries have microfilms of the volumes covering their own counties. The index is divided by counties but does not cover all counties by any means. It must be stressed that this is an index only and the parish register must be consulted for full particulars of the entry. It does however enable one to find the entry without too much searching since one is given the parish and the year of marriage. The index includes a number of "strays". When the slips for the index were made, if it was found that one of the partners of a marriage came from a county that was not adjacent to the county in which the marriage took place, a second slip was made for that county's index. It was felt that any competent searcher would naturally search adjacent counties, so only the references to more distant counties were thus dealt with. Hence, if at any time you are looking at Boyd's volumes for a particular county and see another county given alongside the entry, one of the partners to the marriage was from that given county.

The data is now available for searching on the FindmyPast (q.v.) website www.findmypast.co.uk. The free to view help pages on that website give a more detailed description of the index, as well as listing the counties and parishes included in the index and the period that the records cover in each case.

BREWERS or BREWSTERS The Worshipful Company of Brewers is an ancient London Livery Company, ranking fourteenth in the order of precedence, established by an Act of the Court of Aldermen in 1515. The Company's history is detailed on its website at www.brewershall.co.uk. Richardson, John *The Local Historian's Encyclopaedia* (3rd ed. Historical Publications Ltd. 2003), contains details of ancient legislation relating to brewing and public houses.

Many breweries have websites containing historical pages and some have museums or have published histories. An example is the National Brewery Centre, incorporating the Bass Museum, at which a history of brewing is on display. Further details are at www.nationalbrewerycentre.co.uk. The records of Courage Limited cover those of nearly eighty constituent companies and included records of licensees, deeds of public houses, tenants' registers, directors' minutes, photographs and magazines. Following the take-over of Courage by Scottish and Newcastle in 1995, these records are now part of the Scottish Brewing Archive www.archives.gla.ac.uk/sba. The Scottish Brewing Archive holds an annual Open Day and also publishes a newsletter and an annual journal. The Brewery History Society www.breweryhistory.com has a bookstall containing many interesting publications. Further guidance can be found in Fowler, Simon *Researching Brewery and Publican Ancestors* (FHP 2009).

BREWSTER SESSIONS These were instituted in 1729 when local justices granted licences to sell alcoholic liquor. Why the word "Brewster" was used is uncertain. Its origin is feminine, a woman that brews. Certain women were fined for charging too much for their ale but usually referred to as the wives of their husbands, with no mention of their own surname and often without their christian name. In *Middle English Surnames of Occupation*, Fransson concludes that the difference between "Brewer" and "Brewster" is topographical, the former being common in the South and the latter more common in the Midlands and North.

BRICKMAKERS The British Brick Society www.britishbricksoc.free-online.co.uk promotes the study and recording of all aspects of the archaeology and history of bricks, brickmaking and brickwork. There are several useful links on their website. Hammond, Martin *Bricks and Brick making* (Shire Publications 1990) gives a good general introduction. Some work on regional brick making has been done, for example that for the Isle of Wight at http://freespace.virgin.net/roger.hewitt/iwias/bricks.htm.

BRIDEWELL A common term for a county gaol. Later the term referred specifically to a London prison at Blackfriars.

BRITAIN FROM ABOVE A project by English Heritage and its Scottish and Welsh partners to digitise 95,000 Aerofilms aerial photographs taken between 1919 and 1953. See www.britainfromabove.org.uk.

BRITISH AGRICULTURAL HISTORY SOCIETY The society promotes the study of agricultural history and the history of the rural economy and society. They publish the journal *Agricultural History Review* and *Rural History Today* newsletter. They hold conferences twice a year. See www.bahs.org.uk.

BRITISH AND FOREIGN SCHOOLS SOCIETY (BFSS) See Education.

BRITISH ASSOCIATION FOR CEMETERIES IN SOUTH ASIA (BACSA) See Cemeteries in South Asia

BRITISH ASSOCIATION FOR LOCAL HISTORY (BALH) See Local History Societies.

BRITISH BROADCASTING CORPORATION (BBC) ARCHIVE COLLECTIONS These are a collection of films covering a wide range of topics that can be accessed without charge via the website of the BBC www.bbc.co.uk/archive. A substantial number of the films in the "Events", "Family and Lifestyle", "Politics and Government", "Transport and Travel" and "War and Conflict" categories might well be of interest to those researching their ancestors. The BBC has digitised the programme listings from 4,500 copies of *Radio Times* dating from 1923-2009. These will be used to create an online database, allowing access to as many of the 5 million programmes as possible, as well as photos, scripts and other material from shows from which recordings have no longer survived.

BRITISH HISTORY ONLINE www.british-history.ac.uk describes itself as a digital library containing some of the core printed primary and secondary sources for the medieval and modern history of the British Isles. Sources include: C19th Ordnance Survey maps, journals of the House of Lords and House of Commons, the Victoria County History of the counties of England, the Survey of London, calendars of state papers, letters, diaries and a number of Gazetteers. A large number of regional documents are included and the site can be searched by surname or place name.

BRITISH HOME CHILDREN Children's societies and organisations in Britain sent over 100,000 children, to the colonies between 1869 and 1967. These are referred to as British Home Children. Home Children, who were not necessarily orphans, were sent abroad, mainly to Canada, Australia and South Africa. Often no records were kept of their origins and many suffered incredible hardships. See Harrison, Phyllis *The Home Children* (3rd ed. Watson Dwyer 1979); Bagnell, Kenneth *The Little Immigrants* (Macmillan of Canada 1980); Snow, Perry *Neither Waif Nor Stray: the search for a stolen identity* (Universal Publishers US 2000) and Corbett, Gail H *Barnardo Children in Canada* (Woodland Publishing, Ontario 1981). Wagner, Gillian *Children of the Empire* (Weidenfield and Nicolson 1982), tells of the children shipped not only to Canada but to Australia, New Zealand and South Africa; also Ben, Philip & Melville, Joy *Lost Children of The Empire* (Hymans 1989).

The National Archives of Canada have records of juvenile immigration ships' passenger lists showing names of children, see the database at www.collectionscanada.gc.ca also http://jubilation.uwaterloo.ca/~marj/genealogy /homeadd.html.

Records for the Kingsley Fairbridge Child Emigration Scheme, also known as the Society for the Furtherance of Child Emigration to the Colonies and The Child Emigration Society, are at the University of Liverpool Archives, Sydney Jones Library, University of Liverpool PO Box 123 Liverpool L69 3DA http://liv.ac.uk/library/sca/.

The Child Migrant Trust www.childmigrantstrust.com, 124 Musters Road, West Bridgford, Nottingham NG2 7PW, is an organisation formed to help these children find their records and in some cases relatives.

Between 1939 and 1965, over nine hundred children in the care of Catholic Diocesan child care agencies were sent to Australia. See the timeline at www.cathchild.org.uk/pages/history.html. The emigration of children to Australia during this time was undertaken by a number of British child care agencies in England, Scotland, Wales and Northern Ireland, following government policy. Catholic child care agencies arranged the migration of children through the Catholic Child Welfare Council, a federation of Roman Catholic Diocesan Children's Societies, Religious Congregations and other Catholic organisations providing social care services for children and families in need, not necessarily Roman Catholics. The principal Catholic agencies involved with the migration were:

The Crusade of Rescue (Westminster Diocese) established 1859, linking
several existing groups, with aim of protecting the faith of Catholic children
and families.

Father Hudson's Homes (Birmingham Diocese) who hold their own records
and those of other similar societies, going back to 1884. A form to request
information can be downloaded from their website www.fatherhudsons.
org.uk.

Liverpool Catholic Children's Protection Society (Liverpool Diocese) founded
in 1881.

The Catholic Children's Rescue Society (Salford Diocese) now known as
Caritas Diocese of Salford www.caritassalford.org.uk.

Southwark Catholic Children's Rescue Society (Southwark Diocese) now part of The Cabrini Children's Society www.cabrini.org.uk.

Children were also sent from independent Catholic children's homes such as those run by the Sisters of Nazareth. The Catholic Child Welfare Council St James Presbytery, Pendleton Way, Salford, Lancashire M6 5JA employs a researcher to help former child migrants to the colonies and their families seeking information about their relatives and family background.

BRITISH LEGION See Royal British Legion.

BRITISH LIBRARY See also Asia, Pacific and Africa Collections. The British Library www.bl.uk 96 Euston Road, London NW1 2DB is a repository that no serious researcher should ignore. Amongst the 150 million items that the library holds are 14 million books, 920,000 journal and newspaper titles, 58 million patents and 3 million sound recordings. Note that researchers are normally only admitted to the British Library to view material if it is not easily available elsewhere. Their website is crammed with information for those not proposing to make a personal visit. It comprises in excess of 10,000 pages of information and is the access route to a gallery of 30,000 treasures from the Library's collections, to a catalogue of more than 14 million items and to extracts of some 9 million articles taken from more than 20,000 journals. The website also contains a vast amount of information about the Library's holdings and how to use them. This includes:
Details of events, exhibitions and lectures for visitors to the library.
Online exhibitions, which are often linked to ongoing exhibitions at the Library itself.
Virtual books, which enables digital images of some books in the Library's collection to be viewed online.
Reader Guides, which can be downloaded free of charge. Of particular interest to family historians are Reader Guide no 6 *English Places: sources of information*, Reader Guide no 8 *Researching Your Family History* and Reader Guide no.10 *British Family History, Printed Sources in the Department of Printed Books*.

BRITISH NEWSPAPERS ONLINE See Newspapers.

BRITISH OVERSEAS See also Civil Registration, Deaths Overseas, Emigration and Parish Registers. The Guildhall Library (q.v.) holds many records called "International Memoranda" from the Bishop of London's Registry, for the C19th and early C20th. See Yeo, Geoffrey ed. *The British Overseas: a guide to records of their births, baptisms, marriages, deaths and burials, available in the United Kingdom* (3rd ed. Guildhall Library Publications 1995).

BRITISH PATHE This is one of the oldest media companies in the world, with its roots lying in Paris in the 1890s where its founder, Charles Pathe, pioneered the development of the moving image. The company was established in London in 1902 and by 1910 was producing its famous bi-weekly newsreel the Pathe Gazette.

The company has now released archive footage dating back to the 1920s on its website at www.britishpathe.com. This is free to view and shows subjects ranging from the opening of Minehead's Regal Cinema to a maharajah playing polo and a gypsy burial. Although Pathe covered the big stories of the day, from the Hindenberg to Queen Victoria's funeral and the Second World War, they also covered the fun and interesting side of life, with plenty of the newsreels having been filmed in Somerset.

BRITISH POSTAL MUSEUM & ARCHIVE See Post Office.

BRITISH RECORDS ASSOCIATION (BRA) This was founded in 1932 to co-ordinate and encourage the work of individuals, authorities, societies and institutions interested in the preservation and use of records www. britishrecordsassociation.org.uk. It should not be confused with the British Record Society (q.v.), which is a separate body. BRA members include historians, genealogists and other researchers, owners of records, archivists, librarians and others responsible for keeping archives. This breadth of support ensures that the BRA has a strong voice in promoting the interests of archives and archive users at a national level. Its journal, *Archives*, contains many articles on useful sources.

BRITISH RECORD SOCIETY (BRS) BRS www.britishrecordsociety.org was founded in 1889. In the following year it took over the "Index Library" which had commenced in 1888. Many indexes have been published, especially of wills. A more recent project involves the transcription and indexing of the Hearth Tax Returns. BRS volumes can be seen in most major reference libraries and record offices. Membership of the BRS is available to both individuals and institutions. Copies of old volumes can often be seen in good second-hand bookshops, or purchased direct from the society. Further details of the BRS including a history of the society, a list of volumes published to date and how to join can be seen on its website.

BRITISH RED CROSS ARCHIVES AND MUSEUM The British Red Cross is part of the largest voluntary humanitarian organisation in the world. It promotes humanitarian values, and provides emergency help to people in short-term crisis in the UK and overseas. Its museum and archives are based in the Moorgate area of Central London, and maintain the corporate memory of the British Red Cross. The website at www.redcross.org.uk/museumandarchives includes numerous fact sheets, which contain details of their historic collections and has some online collections which are free to view. There is also an archives' blog at http://blogs.redcross.org.uk/tag/history/ which is well worth reading.

BRITISH TELECOM (BT) See also Telephone Directories. British Telecom Archives preserves the historical information of British Telecommunications plc and its predecessors. The Archives are open to the public. Contact BT Archives, Third Floor, Holborn Telephone Exchange, 268-270 High Holborn, London WC1V 7EE. Their collections include a vast number of historic telephone directories. Their catalogue is online at www.btplc.com/thegroup/btshistory/btgrouparchives/.

BRODERERS They were embroiderers. The Worshipful Company of Broderers is an ancient London Livery Company, which received a Grant of Arms in 1558 and was granted its first Charter on 25 October 1561. The Company's history is detailed on its website at http://www.broderers.co.uk/.

BRUSHMAKERS The Brushmakers were believed to be the first trade to form a Union. There is a Society of Brushmakers' Descendants. Their website gives some useful background to the occupation http://homepage.ntlworld.com/kdoughty/tramp.html.

BURGAGE AND BURGAGE PLOTS Tenure of land in town on yearly rent. Burgage plots were long narrow strips of land, tenanted by town dwellers. Most could only afford a narrow frontage on to the market place, hence the shape of the plots.

BURIAL REGISTERS See Parish Registers.

BUILDER, THE A journal that relates to the building trade. It contains information about domestic and public buildings erected in England and is particularly valuable for the C19th. The first ten volumes, 1843-1852, are available online via the Bodleian Library (q.v.) website www.bodley.ox.ac.uk. The Building News website www.builderindex.org/?q=scope allows searches, by architect, building, client and town of both *The Builder* and *The Building News*.

BURGESS ROLLS See also Electoral Registers. A burgess is defined in the Oxford Dictionary as an "Inhabitant of a borough with full municipal rights, citizen". Burgess lists of those entitled to vote, mostly for Borough representatives, continued in parallel into the C20th but sometimes survive from much earlier (even mediaeval) times. These and C18th lists of county free-holders, are included in Jeremy Gibson's county by county guide to the whereabouts of such documents, *Electoral Registers 1832-1948 and Burgess Rolls* (FHP 2008).

BURIAL GROUNDS See Cemeteries and Monumental Inscriptions.

BURIAL INDEXES A substantial number of burial indexes have been compiled by family history societies and other parties. They comprise details taken from any or all of parish registers and Bishops' Transcripts, church and cemetery records, monumental inscriptions and war memorials. When using an index, it is important to ascertain the period of time that it covers and the extent to which it is complete.

The format of such burial indexes varies. Some are sold on microfiche or CD, whilst others are accessed online. The National Burial Index (NBI) is a collection of burials transcribed from parish registers by member societies of the FFHS (q.v.). The 3rd edition contains over 18.4 million burial records taken from Anglican parish, non-conformist, Quaker, Roman Catholic and cemetery burial registers throughout England & Wales. The database on CD is fully searchable and results can be printed out or exported. More information is available under "projects" on the FFHS website at www.ffhsservices.com/National-Burial-Index-Ed.-3-23. Those considering acquiring the set should note that coverage is very patchy, with particularly few London burials featuring therein. The records are also available on FindmyPast (q.v.) www.findmypast.co.uk.

Another index available on FindmyPast is Boyd's London Burials. This can also be consulted at the SOG (q.v.). It is an index of about a quarter of a million entries from burial registers of London churches and cemeteries 1538-1872, including a large part of the registers of the Nonconformist burial ground of Bunhill Fields. The index contains names of males only and no children. Whilst far from complete it remains an extremely useful "lucky dip".

BURIAL REGISTERS See Parish Registers.

BURIALS IN WOOLLEN See Parish Registers.

BUSINESS RECORDS See Companies.

BUTCHERS See also Slaughter Houses. The Worshipful Company of Butchers is one of the seven oldest London Livery Companies, and is still active today. It has a website at www.butchershall.com, which gives a full history of the Company.

BY-NAMES See also Surnames. By-names were an additional name that developed when centres of population got bigger and a single forename was no long sufficient to identify an individual. These were imposed, rather than chosen by the individual, rather as nicknames are today. A person might have several by-names during their lifetime and might have more than one concurrently. Initially these were not hereditary although many did develop into hereditary surnames. A second name recorded for an individual pre C16th might be a by-name or a surname.

C

CADET An heraldic term referring to the younger son or junior branch of a family.

CADGER A carrier or pedlar of small wares by means of horse and cart. The word also refers to a street seller or a beggar, from which we get the verb "to cadge".

CAIRD LIBRARY See National Maritime Museum.

CALAIS See Lacemakers.

CALENDAR (1) See also Dates and Regnal Years. England continued to use the Julian "Old Style" calendar up to 1751 whereas the Gregorian or "New Style" calendar had been adopted on the Continent in 1582 and in Scotland in 1600. By 1751, the Julian calendar was eleven days out of step. In that year, Chesterfield's Act stated that 1 January should be the first day of the year, the year having previously commenced on 25 March. Thus the year 1750 had commenced on 25 March 1750 and ended March 24 1750/51. The year 1751 commenced on 25 March 1751 and ended on 31 December 1751. The year 1752 commenced on 1 January 1752 and ended on 31 December 1752. Eleven days of September were omitted to bring it into line with the Gregorian calendar. When citing a date between 1 January and 24 March before 1752 it is customary to put e.g. 2 March 1734/5.

When people in the UK shorten a date, we use the format date, month and year. For example, by 3.4.12, we mean 3 April 2012. An American would write it as 4.3.12, thereby putting the number of the month first. To avoid confusion, it is advisable not to use all numerical dates.

CALENDAR (2) A word used by archivists to describe a summary of the contents of a group of documents such as wills or estate papers.

CALLIGRAPHY A word describing handwriting, especially ornate handwriting. An excellent introduction to the subject is Lynskey, Marie *Creative Calligraphy* (Thorsons 1988).

CAMBRIDGE UNIVERSITY Venn J & Venn J *Alumni Cantabrigienses* (10 vols. Cambridge University Press 1922-1953) is a biographical register of students, graduates and officers at the University of Cambridge, from the earliest times to

1900. It was compiled from university records including matriculation registers, degree lists, written sources, college admission registers, episcopal registers, college accounts, genealogical collections and documents in record offices. More than 130,000 individuals are covered, with more extended biographical detail provided for post-1751 matriculants. Beyond details of an individual's progression at Cambridge University, the information may include dates and place of birth and death, the names of parents, siblings and spouses, schooling, occupation, notable accomplishments and references to sources. Cambridge University are in the process of providing a searchable database for *Alumni Cantabrigienses* http://venn.lib.cam.ac.uk/. It can also be searched on the Ancestry (q.v.) subscription website at www.ancestry.co.uk, where it goes under the name of "Cambridge University Alumni, 1261-1900".

CANADA See also British Home Children and Emigration. Births, marriages and deaths are registered on a provincial level and access varies from province to province. In general, privacy restrictions mean that birth records are closed for 100 years, marriages for 75 years and deaths for 20 years. Canadian censuses were taken on years ending in 1 and survival is rare before 1851. There are also censuses for 1906 and 1916 which are available, although these do not cover the whole country.

The website of the Archives of Canada is at www.collectionscanada.gc.ca. The address of their National Archives is 395 Wellington Street, Ottawa, Ontario, Canada K1A ON3; they will answer general enquiries. The researcher needs to be aware that some records will be in French.

Baxter, Angus *In Search of Your Canadian Roots* (3rd ed. Genealogical Publishing Co. 2000) is a province-by-province guide. A gateway site to other useful books is www.genealogysearch.org/free/bcanada.html. Indexes to many Canadian Records are freely available on Family Search (q.v.) https://familysearch.org, including baptisms, marriages and burials, censuses and some probate material. There is access to these and further records is at the subscription website Ancestry www.ancestry.com (q.v.). For access to census indexes go to http://www.bac-lac.gc.ca/eng/census/Pages/census.aspx; this includes some original images. See also the information on the Library and Archives of Canada website www.collectionscanada.gc.ca/census.

There are a number of Canadian Family History Societies, mostly specialising in a particular province. Links to the more prominent of these can be found on the Library and Archives Canada website www.collectionscanada.gc.ca. Some are members of the FFHS (q.v.) who provide contact details on their website www.ffhs.org.uk.

The Dictionary of Canadian Biography Online can be viewed at www.biographi.ca/index-e.html. A Canadian virtual war memorial, giving information on over 118,000 servicemen and women can be accessed www.veterans.gc.ca/eng/collections/virtualmem. The United Empire Loyalists' Association of Canada has a website that will be helpful for research in this field www.uelac.org.

See also The Canadian county Atlas Digital Project http://digital.library.mcgill.ca/countyatlas giving online access to copies of maps dating from the 1870s and 1880s. It is possible to search by the place name or by the name of the landholder.

CANADIAN IMMIGRANTS See www.cangenealogy.com/immigration.html and http://jubilation.uwaterloo.ca/~marj/genealogy/thevoyage.html. Library and Archives Canada www.collectionscanada.gc.ca have records of arrivals from 1865 to 1935. The names of those arriving from overseas are recorded in passenger lists. Border entry lists record those arriving from or via the United States. Their website gives access to a searchable database of "Home Children" arriving between 1869 and 1930. Those arriving at Grosse-Île Quarantine Station 1832-1937 can be searched via www.collectionscanada.gc.ca.

CANALS See also Barges, Boatmen and Watermen. A canal is an artificial watercourse for inland navigation or irrigation. Before the railways, the extension of water transport by cutting canals was the only means of significantly improving the transportation of many goods. Initiative by local companies who responded to the needs of the industrial revolution led to the creation of a national network of canals during the period 1750 to 1815. They were nationalised in 1947. Richardson, John *The Local Historian's Encyclopaedia* (3rd ed. Historical Publications Ltd. 2003) gives dates for completion of the more important canals. There are a number of sources of information about canals. David & Charles have published a series of books on the *Canals of the British Isles*, most of which have been written by Charles Hadfield. There is also a Shire Publication (q.v.) entitled *Discovering Canals* by Leon Metcalfe and John Vince 1975. Some more localised publications exist, for example two booklets entitled *The Boat People of the Oxford Canal*, which have been published by The Eureka Partnership and comprise records transcribed in the Oxfordshire Record Office.

The Railway and Canal Historical Society also publishes books and a journal. Further details can be obtained from their website at www.rchs.org.uk.

CARPENTER The Worshipful Company of Carpenters is a London Livery Company that can trace its origins back to the C13th. Its website at www.thecarpenterscompany.co.uk gives a full history of the Company and its activities. The records of The Worshipful Company of Carpenters have been published in a number of volumes by Phillimore, along with a name index.

CARIBBEAN ANCESTORS The Caribbean roots Website www.caribbean roots.co.uk is an excellent starting point. The key book on this subject is Guy Grannum's *Tracing Your Caribbean Ancestors: a national archives guide* (3rd ed. A & C Black 2012). TNA has several relevant research guides available for free download www.nationalarchives.gov.uk. The Encyclopaedia of British Slave-ownership at www.ucl.ac.uk/lbs/ lists all slave-owners in the British Caribbean at the time slavery ended, in 1833. The Caribbean Family History Group www.caribbeanfamilyhistorygroup.com is based in Birmingham. See also Mitchell, Madeleine *Jamaican Ancestry: how to find out more* (Heritage Books 2008).

CARS See Motor Cars.

CARTER A waggoner or a stable headman.

CASHMARIE A fish pedlar, one who took fish from the coast to the markets inland.

CATAGMAN See also Cottar. One who lived in a cottage.

CATHOLIC RECORD SOCIETY See Roman Catholics.

CATHOLICS See Recusants Rolls and Roman Catholics.

CAVALRY See also Household Cavalry. Shire Publications (q.v.) has published a title in its "Discovering" series on *British Cavalry Regiments* by Arthur Taylor 1973.

CAVEAT A warning notice lodged at the appropriate court that a will is to be disputed.

CEMETERIES See also Commonwealth War Graves Commission, Deceased Online, Royal British Legion and War Memorials. Burial Grounds, as distinct from parish churchyards, were started by nonconformists in the C17th, with many more being established in the C18th. The first public cemetery was started in 1827 in Kensal Green, London and other towns and cities followed suit. By 1850, some churchyards were full, so the General Board of Health was required to establish cemeteries to deal with the problem. By 1853, provincial cemeteries were being set up. Cemetery records are maintained by Cemetery Registrars. Often they are indexed and some contain details of memorial inscriptions. Registers of the old nonconformist burial grounds have been deposited with the Registrar General and are at TNA. One important example is that of Bunhill Fields, London, which covers the period 1713 to 1854. Abney Park, a large London Cemetery dating from 1840, has a website www.abney-park.org.uk with links to a searchable database of graves. The Find a Grave website www.findagrave.com enables details of cemeteries to be found and has partial listings for an increasing number of graves. Initially primarily US based this has now a much wider geographical coverage. See Rutherford, Sarah *Victorian Cemetery* (Shire Publications 2008).

CEMETERIES IN SOUTH ASIA The BACSA Association www.bacsa.org.uk records the locations of European cemeteries, isolated graves and monuments. It publishes cemetery and church records containing names, inscriptions and biographical notes on individual tombs and gravestones. It also supports local people active in the restoration and conservation of European graveyards. The BACSA website includes lists of Cemetery Record Books, other BACSA books and details of the BACSA archive, which contains records of over 1,300 cemeteries based on official sources with inscriptions and photographs.

CENSUS See also Ecclesiastical Census, Ireland and Scotland. The first official British census was taken in 1801 and thereafter every 10 years. Censuses normally become available to the public 100 years after they are taken, although statistical information is not subject to closure. Up until 1841, the returns were purely numerical, individual names were not required. Some enumerators took it upon themselves to make up their own lists of households and these sometimes turn up in the parish records held by CROs. Details of the survival and whereabouts of these pre 1841 censuses and other census like lists, often local in scope, can be found in the county by county guide Gibson, Jeremy & Medlycott, Mervyn *Local Census Listings 1522-1930: holdings in the British Isles* (FFHS 1997). See also Colin Chapman's *Pre-1841 Censuses & Population Listings in the British Isles* (Clearfield 2012) for a background to such listings.
Useful books on census returns in general include Edward Higgs' *Making Sense of the Census: the manuscript returns for England and Wales, 1801-1901* (H.M.S.O. 1991) and *Making Sense of the Census revisited: the manuscript returns for England and Wales, 1801-1901* (University of London 2005), which are guides to the historical and administrative background of these documents and the interpretation of the information therein. See also Raymond, Stuart A *The Census 1801-1911: a guide for the internet era* (FHP 2009) and Christian, Peter & Annal, David *Census: The Expert Guide* (TNA 2008). Two useful guides *Census* and *Census: further research* can be downloaded from TNA website www.nationalarchives.gov.uk. The Office for National Statistics website also has some interesting information www.ons.gov.uk.

The dates on which the censuses were taken are as follows: 1841 June 6th; 1851 March 30th; 1861 April 7th, 1871 April 2nd; 1881 April 3rd; 1891 April 5th; 1901 31st March; 1911 2nd April.

The 1841 census was the first to give the names of all people in a household but except in the case of children under 15, the age is only approximate, to the nearest 5 years below. Thus those aged 15 to 19 are recorded as 15 years of age, 20 to 24 as 20 and so on. Other information given is the sex, occupation and whether born in the same county as now residing in or not (indicated by a Y for yes or a N for no). Relationships are not given. For those born in Scotland we get an S and in Ireland an I, and F is used if born in foreign parts. The subsequent census returns are much more useful since they give the relationship to the head of the household, exact ages (as reported by the informant, so there

49

are possibilities of inaccuracy here), occupation and most important of all, where they were born. If born outside England or Wales however only the country is generally given. From 1891 censuses include additional information, such as the number of rooms in the house if less than 5. The 1911 returns are in a slightly different format, with one household per page. These give useful information concerning how long a couple has been married and for married women, how many children they have had and how many are surviving.

When using the census it is important to remember that members of the family who were not sleeping at home on the night of the census are not recorded with their family. A missing person in a family group in any of the census returns could be explained by the fact that the person was in hospital, in prison or in service. Soldiers and sailors serving abroad would not be included in their home census; those serving in Ireland however may be shown in the Irish census.

Access to census material is now normally through subscription/pay per view websites, where images of the original enumerators returns can be viewed. These include Ancestry (q.v.) www.ancestry.co.uk, FindmyPast (q.v.) www.findmypast.co.uk, The Genealogist (q.v.) www.thegenealogist.co.uk and UK Census Online www.ukcensusonline.com. For Scottish censuses see also Scotland's People (q.v.) www.scotlandspeople.gov.uk. There is free access to the indexes of the 1881 census at Family Search (q.v.) www.familysearch.org. See also FreeCen www.freecen.org.uk, which gives free but incomplete, access to census transcripts.

CENTRAL CRIMINAL COURT (THE OLD BAILEY) See Crime and Criminals.

CENTURY A period of one-hundred years. Often abbreviated as C18th, for eighteenth century. Bear in mind that any given century covers the preceding one hundred years. Thus the C19th covers the 1800s, the C18th the 1700s and so on.

CHANCERY, COURT OF See Court of Chancery.

CHANGE OF NAME See Deed Poll.

CHANNEL ISLANDS Civil Registration began in Jersey in 1842 and in Guernsey in 1840. Official censuses were taken every ten years from 1841 onwards. Guernsey also has records for the other smaller Channel Islands. Both Jersey and Guernsey have good research facilities in the form of the "Societe Jersiaise" and "Societe Guerniaise". See www.channelislandshistory.com for further details. The Channel Islands Family History society website is at www.jerseyfamily history.org. See Backhurst, Marie-Louise *Tracing Your Channel Islands Ancestors: a guide for family historians* (Pen & Sword 2011). Balleine G R *A Biographical Dictionary of Jersey* (Staples Press 1948), contains details of around 300 inhabitants of Jersey who have achieved some distinction.

CHAPMAN A pedlar and dealer in small wares.

CHAPMAN COUNTY CODES When the English Place Name Society was established in 1923 a series of abbreviations was produced for the English counties in existence at that time. Many of these consisted of only one letter, some of two and a few of three letters. In 1973 the SOG (q.v.) extended this system to cover the other counties in the British Isles.

The Post Office and other authorities over the years have been using other standards for abbreviating county names. With the creation of new counties and the amalgamation of others in 1974 the accepted, if not acceptable, contractions multiplied. The FFHS (q.v.) not only brought together many individuals and groups all frequently having cause to mention county names within the British Isles but also created interest among many thousands of other people all requiring to abbreviate a county name and each appearing to choose a different system. The advent of computers and the desirability of standardisation, to enable coding of computer programs to be effected with the least confusion, led those working on such projects to devise a Three Letter Coded System for each of the counties within the British Isles. Wherever possible the systems proposed and used by the English Place Name Society and the SOG were retained within the present system; where necessary, these systems have had the abbreviations extended to three letters. This has not always produced the most logical abbreviation if the three letters chosen were already allocated by a previous system to another county and in two cases the Utopian idea was impossible. For example, Co, the 1923 abbreviation for Cornwall, would logically be extended to COR, but as this had been allocated in 1973 to Cork, the code of CON was chosen; Sx, now being SSX for Sussex and IOW in place of Wt for the Isle of Wight (to bring it into line with the Isle of Man) are exceptions to the general rule used to derive the present coded system for the counties within the British Isles. As the post-1974 counties have also been included for completeness, and to obviate divergent applications in decades to come, other anticipated abbreviations could not be introduced; for example Cumberland, originally Cu, had to become CUL to prevent confusion with Cumbria which (post-1974) is abbreviated to CMA.

Colin Chapman, a Vice-President of the FFHS, was responsible for introducing the present County Codes when computerising some work on records. Over a period of time they have become generally known as the Chapman County Codes. With minor modifications (i.e. codes in current use ending in I or O have been altered to meet post office requests) this system has now been incorporated into the British Standard Specification Codes for the representation of names of counties and similar areas (BS 6879:1987).

England (ENG) before 1974

BDF	Bedfordshire
BRK	Berkshire
BKM	Buckinghamshire
CAM	Cambridgeshire
CHS	Cheshire
CON	Cornwall
CUL	Cumberland
DBY	Derbyshire
DEV	Devonshire
DOR	Dorset
DUR	Durham
ESS	Essex
GLS	Gloucestershire
HAM	Hampshire
HEF	Herefordshire
HRT	Hertfordshire
HUN	Huntingdonshire
KEN	Kent
LAN	Lancashire
LEI	Leicestershire
LIN	Lincolnshire
LND	London
MDX	Middlesex
NFK	Norfolk
NTH	Northamptonshire
NBL	Northumberland
NTT	Nottinghamshire
OXF	Oxfordshire
RUT	Rutland
SAL	Shropshire
SOM	Somerset
STS	Staffordshire
SFK	Suffolk
SRY	Surrey
SSX	Sussex
WAR	Warwickshire
WES	Westmorland
WIL	Wiltshire
WOR	Worcestershire
YKS	Yorkshire
ERY	Yks East Riding
NRY	Yks North Riding
WRY	Yks West Riding
IOW	Isle of Wight
IOM	Isle of Man

Wales (WLS) before 1974

AGY	Anglesey
BRE	Brecknockshire
CAE	Caernarvonshire
CGN	Cardiganshire
CMN	Carmarthenshire
DEN	Denbighshire
FLN	Flintshire
GLA	Glamorgan
MER	Merionethshire
MON	Monmouthshire
MGY	Montgomeryshire
PEM	Pembrokeshire
RAD	Radnorshire

Scotland (SCT) before 1975

ABD	Aberdeenshire
ANS	Angus
ARL	Argyllshire
AYR	Ayrshire
BAN	Banffshire
BEW	Berwickshire
BUT	Bute
CAI	Caithness
CLK	Clackmannanshire
DFS	Dumfriesshire
DNB	Dunbartonshire
ELN	East Lothian
FIF	Fife
Forfarshire (see Angus)	
INV	Inverness-shire
KCD	Kincardineshire
KRS	Kinross-shire
KKD	Kirkcudbrightshire
LKS	Lanarkshire
MLN	Midlothian
MOR	Moray
NAI	Nairnshire
OKI	Orkney Isles
PEE	Peebleshire
PER	Perthshire
RFW	Renfrewshire
ROC	Ross & Cromarty
ROX	Roxburghshire
SEL	Selkirkshire
SHI	Shetland Isles
STI	Stirlingshire
SUT	Sutherland
WLN	West Lothian
WIG	Wigtownshire

Channel Islands (CHI)

ALD	Alderney
GSY	Guernsey
JSY	Jersey
SRK	Sark

Ireland (IRL)

CAR	Carlow
CAV	Cavan
CLA	Clare
COR	Cork
DON	Donegal

52

DUB	Dublin	HUM	Humberside
GAL	Galway	KEN	Kent
KER	Kerry	LAN	Lancashire
KID	Kildare	LEI	Leicestershire
KIK	Kilkenny	LIN	Lincolnshire
Kings (see Offaly)		LND	London
LET	Leitrim	MSY	Merseyside
LEX	Leix (Queens)	NFK	Norfolk
LIM	Limerick	NTH	Northamptonshire
LOG	Longford	NBL	Northumberland
LOU	Louth	NTT	Nottinghamshire
MAY	Mayo	OXF	Oxfordshire
MEA	Meath	SAL	Shropshire
MOG	Monaghan	SOM	Somerset
OFF	Offaly (Kings)	STS	Staffordshire
	Queens (see Leix)	SFK	Suffolk
ROS	Roscommon	SRY	Surrey
SLI	Sligo	SXE	East Sussex
TIP	Tipperary	SXW	West Sussex
WAT	Waterford	TWR	Tyne & Wear
WEM	Westmeath	WAR	Warwickshire
WEX	Wexford	WMD	West Midlands
WIC	Wicklow	WIL	Wiltshire
		NYK	North Yorkshire

Northern Ireland (NIR)

		SYK	South Yorkshire
ANT	Antrim	WYK	West Yorkshire
ARM	Armagh	IOM	Isle of Man
DOW	Down	IOW	Isle of Wight
FER	Fermanagh		
LDY	Londonderry		
TYR	Tyrone		

Wales (WLS) after 1974

CWD	Clwyd
DFD	Dyfed

England (ENG) after 1974

		GNT	Gwent
AVN	Avon	GWN	Gwynedd
BDF	Bedfordshire	MGM	Mid Glamorgan
BRK	Berkshire	POW	Powys
BKM	Buckinghamshire	SGM	South Glamorgan
CAM	Cambridgeshire	WGM	West Glamorgan
CHS	Cheshire		
CLV	Cleveland		

Scotland (SCT): after 1975

CMA	Cumbria	BOR	Borders
CON	Cornwall	CEN	Central Region
DBY	Derbyshire	DGY	Dumfries & Galloway
DEV	Devonshire	FIF	Fife
DOR	Dorset	GMP	Grampian
DUR	Durham	HLD	Highland
ESS	Essex	LTN	Lothian
GLS	Gloucestershire	OKI	Orkney Isles
GTM	Greater Manchester	SHI	Shetland Isles
HAM	Hampshire	STD	Strathclyde
HWR	Hereford & Worcester	TAY	Tayside
HRT	Hertfordshire	WIS	Western Isles

CHARITIES Details of a charity's accounts had to be sent to Parliament by the Clerk of the Peace from 1786. Account books and other records of local charities often record in detail the donations, with the names of the recipients; these are usually to be found in CROs. An example of the records that might be found is contained in *An abstract of the Report of the Commissioners for inquiring concerning the Charities of the City of Oxford and the parishes of St Giles, St Clement and Binsey*, which is published by and available from Oxfordshire Family History Society www.ofhs.org.uk. Charity Commissioners were appointed to examine and supervise the way charities were run. Their reports can be examined in the larger reference libraries. Documents in the keeping of the Charity Commission are open to inspection. Further details are on the website of the Charity Commission at www.charity-commission.gov.uk. TNA guide *Conveyances of Land for Charitable uses in Trust Deeds 1736-1925* can be downloaded from their website www.nationalarchives.gov.uk.

CHARTISTS Chartists created a People's Charter in 1838, demanding an extension of the franchise to all males. Although the movement itself was unsuccessful and dwindled after 1848, it paved the way for later campaigns and working class associations. The lists of shareholders of the National Land Company, held at TNA (Class BT31), contain names of many Chartist sympathisers. See the website Chartists Ancestors www.chartists.net for further information.

CHATHAM CHEST A fund established about 1590 to relieve sailors hurt or wounded in service. It was maintained by regular deductions from the wages of all seamen in the Navy and administered by a corporation of Officers stationed at Chatham but within the jurisdiction of the Navy Board. In 1803 it came within the ambit of Greenwich Hospital, being known as "the Chest at Greenwich". The records include indexes of pensioners, records of payments made to them and other personal details relating in the main to the C17th and C18th. They are held at TNA.

CHELSEA ROYAL HOSPITAL This is a home for army pensioners. Old soldiers who could not be accommodated were known as "Out Pensioners". Registers are with the Registrar General: Baptisms 1691-1812. Marriages 1691-1765. Burials 1692-1856. Those records of the Royal Hospital Chelsea that are over thirty years old have been transferred to TNA. By 1792, there were over 20,000 pensioners. As the Commissioners of the Royal Hospital were responsible for the payment of army pensions up to 1955, the term "Chelsea Pensioner" tended to be used for all who received pensions from the Commissioners. For those who would like to know more about the "pensioners" and their home see Dean, C G T *The Royal Hospital, Chelsea* (Hutchinson & Co. 1950).

CHEMISTRY, ROYAL SOCIETY OF (RSC) The Society has a library and information centre in London. There are two main areas of historical chemistry at the RSC, the first being the historical collection which is composed of items of historical value. The second is the History of Chemistry, which is comprised of modern journals and books dealing with the lives of chemists and their discoveries. These are augmented by other resources such as the image collection, the genealogy enquiries database and a collection of biographies and obituaries of chemists, including past presidents of the RSC. Further details of the historical collection can be found on the website of the RSC at www.rsc.org.

CHEMISTS AND DRUGGISTS In 1893, Kelly's Directories published a Directory of Chemists and Druggists of England, Scotland and Wales and most principal towns in Ireland. The Royal Pharmaceutical Society of Great Britain has a library; its *Pharmaceutical Journal* contains obituaries www.rpharms.com/support/our-library.asp.

CHETHAM SOCIETY The Chetham Society is the oldest historical society, founded in Manchester in 1843, with the objective of publishing books of local and regional history within the counties of Lancashire and Cheshire. Over 260 volumes have now been published, covering a wide range of subjects. Further details of the society, its list of publications and how to join can be found on its website at www.chethams.org.uk.

CHILDREN'S SOCIETIES See also British Home Children and Foundlings. Dr. Barnardo's run a family history service, in return for a fee. Details can be found on their website www.barnardos.org. The records, dating from the 1870s, contain information about family circumstances, relatives and subsequent information about the child whilst in Barnardo's care. A photograph of the child can often be supplied as part of the family background information. According to their website, Barnardo's Photographic Archive, dating back to 1874, contains 500,000 images and 300 films of the visual history of the organisation, including their work overseas in Canada and Australia. The family history service can be contacted at Cottage 4, Barnardo's, Tanners Lane, Barkingside, Essex IG6 1QG. Records of some agencies who have ceased operating are also held by Barnardo's. In the event of them being unable to trace the subject of an enquiry in Barnardo's records they will also search the following: Children's Aid Society; MacPhersons Homes; Marchmont Home; Liverpool Sheltering Home; Sharmans Home.

Those requiring background information on this organisation and its founder should consult Wagner, Gillian *Barnardo* (Eyre & Spottiswoode 1980).
There were many other children's societies including:

The Children's Aid Society (founded in 1856 as The Reformatory and Refuge Union, name changed in 1933, amalgamated with Dr Barnardo's in 1966).

Children's Home and Mission (1899).

The Children's Society www.childrenssociety.org.uk (formerly The Church of England Children's Society, founded 1881 as The Waifs and Strays Society).

The Children's Society Records and Archives Centre is at Block A Floor 2 , Tower Bridge Business Complex, 100 Clement's Road, London SE16 4DG.

Thomas Coram Foundation for Children www.coram.org.uk (founded in 1739 as The Foundling Hospital), Coram Community Campus, 49 Mecklenburgh Square, London WC1N 2QA. Many Coram Foundation records are at The London Metropolitan Archives; many are subject to a 110 year closure rule. Some records have been retained by the Foundation and some C20th records are at Hertfordshire Record Office.

Incorporated Society of the Crusade of Rescue and Homes for Destitute Catholic Children (1905, now the Catholic Children's Society www.cathchild. org.uk), 73 St Charles Square, London W10 6EJ.

Mr Fegan's Homes Inc. (1870), 160 St. James Road, Tunbridge Wells, Kent TN1 2HE http://clutch.open.ac.uk/schools/watlingway99/Hist-Bldg.html.

John Grooms (1866, merged with the Shaftesbury Society in 2007 to form Livability).

Invalid Children's Aid Society (1888) Records from 1842(sic)-2000 are at London Metropolitan Archives.

The Muller Homes for Children Their website includes a heritage section www.mullers.org includes a "heritage" section and an historical archive of images (1836), Muller House, 7 Cotham Park, Bristol BS6 6DA.

National Children's Home (1869). Now known as Action for Children. Highbury Park, London N5 1UD.

Shaftesbury Homes and the Arethusa training ships run by the society www.ts_arethusa.talktalk.net/index.htm (1843), 3 Rectory Square, London SW4 OEG. Developed out of the Ragged School movement now known as Livability www.livability.org.uk.

Spurgeon's Child Care, a history can be found on their website www. spurgeons.org. (founded as Stockwell Orphanage, 1867), 74 Wellingborough Rd., Rushden, Northants NN10 9TY. Records up to 1979 are held by the society.

This list is by no means exhaustive.

Other organisations are listed in *Family Welfare Association Charities Digest*, which has been published annually since the C19th, or *Social Services Year Book*. It must be remembered that these books only give information about organisations that existed in the year of publication.

If you are inquiring about a child in care in a charity which either closed its work or amalgamated with another organisation, or in one of the Public Assistance Authorities' Children's Homes which operated under the old Poor Law, it is suggested you make enquiries at the record office/reference library in the area of the place where you think care may have taken place. For instance, records of the Middlemore Charity (Birmingham) including files, minutes etc. of the emigration of children to Canada and Australia are now deposited in the Local Studies Department, Birmingham Reference Library.

CHOLERA There were epidemics in Britain from 1831. A serious outbreak in 1848-9 caused 53,000 deaths and led to the creation of Medical Officers of Health.

CHRISTADELPHIANS This is a religious denomination founded in the U.S.A. about 1848 by John Thomas, an Englishman from London. They claim to represent the simple apostolic faith of the C1st. Branches of the sect were set up in this country. Their magazine *The Ambassador* was published between 1864 and 1871, when its name was changed to *The Christadelphian*. The magazine contains much useful genealogical information under "Intelligence", which contained notices sent in by meetings all over the country concerning the movements of individuals, adult baptisms, marriages, removals, deaths and the like. There are no central archives.

CHRISTENING See Baptism.

CHRISTIAN NAMES See Forenames.

CHURCH ALE Mediaeval equivalent of a church bazaar or vicarage garden party.

CHURCH COMMISSIONERS FOR ENGLAND See also Queen Anne's Bounty. A body formed in 1948 by the amalgamation of Queen Anne's Bounty (q.v.) and the Ecclesiastical Commissioners, which were constituted in 1836. In 1856, the latter became responsible also for the duties of the Church Building Commissioners. Records of these three bodies, together with the records created since 1948, are held by the Church Commissioners. Further details can be obtained from the Church Commissioners website at www.cofe.anglican.org. It should be noted that these records are primarily of an administrative nature, which are unlikely to be of interest to the family historian without a specialised interest in an individual parish.

CHURCH COURTS See Ecclesiastical Courts.

CHURCH MONUMENTS See Monumental Inscriptions.

CHURCH OF ENGLAND See Anglican Church.

CHURCH OF JESUS CHRIST OF LATTER-DAY SAINTS (LDS) See also Family Search. This is the correct title for what most people refer to as "the Mormons" or "the LDS". It was founded in 1830 by Joseph Smith in Fayette, New York, U.S.A.. Joseph Smith had a vision from God which instructed him to find some golden plates which were the basis of "The Book of Mormon". Latter-Day Saints use the Book of Mormon alongside the Holy Bible and other scriptures in their services of worship.

This Church has a special interest in family history studies. They believe in baptising ther dead and in order to do so, their ancestors need to be identified. All members are therefore encouraged to trace their family. The church has a thriving genealogical society based on Salt Lake City, where there is the largest genealogical library in the world. The address is 35 North West Temple Street Salt Lake City, Utah, 84150. There are nearly 2½ million rolls of microfilmed records, more than 700,000 microfiche and books and serial family history publications for every continent in the world.

The LDS have an active digitisation programme throughout the world. Many of the resulting films are available to be loaned to its branch libraries. Locations can be found on the Family Search website www.familysearch.org. There are such libraries in many UK cities and these are open to the public. An appointment should be made to use them. There is no charge but a donation towards administrative costs would be gratefully received.

The LDS's Family Search (q.v.) website www.familysearch.org is the gateway to their records, mostly in indexed form. The site also contains many helpful guides to sources.

A good introduction to researching Mormon ancestors is provided by Waller, Ian *My Ancestor was a Mormon* (SOG 2012).

CHURCH RATES Land or real property whether owned or leased was liable to a church rate. These were abolished in 1868. Rates lists in churchwardens' accounts (q.v.) can be a useful way to identify ancestors.

CHURCH REGISTERS See Nonconformists and Parish Registers

CHURCHES CONSERVATION TRUST This was set-up in 1969 as the Redundant Churches' Fund to preserve churches no longer needed for worship but which are of historic or architectural interest. Most of the churches are in sparsely populated areas and need substantial repair when they come to the Fund. The Fund's main income is provided by church and state equally and it relies heavily on volunteers for the maintenance of the churches. Further information can be obtained from www.visitchurches.org.uk.

CHURCHILL ARCHIVE Winston Churchill's papers were bought for the nation from his heirs in 1995 using £12 million of lottery money. They are now owned by the Churchill Archive Trust, and are currently stored at the Churchill Archives Centre (CAC) at Cambridge University. The archive includes about 2,500 archive boxes of letters, telegrams, documents and photographs, or about a million pages of material. The website of the Churchill Archives Centre www.chu.cam.ac.uk/archives gives further details about the collection and how to access it. Using the website's "Image Gallery", it is also possible to view a very small selection of the holdings online.

CHURCHWARDENS/CHURCHWARDENS' ACCOUNTS Churchwardens for each Anglican parish were elected by the vestry (q.v.), usually on Easter Tuesday. Two or four would serve at a time, according to the size of the parish. They had a great many duties which included managing the parish property and income, maintaining the church fabric, allocating pews, helping to keep the parish registers and the arranging of burials of strangers and baptisms of foundlings. Their accounts may survive among parish papers. The lists of payments for burials, found in some accounts, may serve as a substitute for burial registers. See Tate W E, *The Parish Chest* (3rd ed. Phillimore 2010).

CHURCHWARDENS' PRESENTMENTS These were reports to the Bishop relating to misdemeanours of parishioners. Here is an example: "A presentment made by the Churchwardens of Badsey and Aldington in the Diocese of Worcester delivered at the Visitation of the Right Rev'd Father in God John, Lord Bishop of Worcester, holden in the parish church of All Saints in Evesham, May 27th 1718. We present Mary Miland for being guilty of ye heinous sin of Adultery by having a child in the absence of her husband Anthony Miland".

Between 1660 and 1760, there are many presentments for non-attendance at Church; those so named were usually Roman Catholics or Quakers, although other non-conformists are also mentioned.

CINEMA MUSEUM, THE The Cinema Museum is housed at premises at 2 Dugard Way, Kennington, London SE11 4TH and has its website at www. cinemamuseum.org.uk. Those pages detail its history, whilst the museum itself houses a collection of artefacts, memorabilia and equipment that preserves the history and grandeur of cinema from the 1890s to the present day.

The Cinema Museum's publications collection includes: A run of *The Kinematograph Weekly* and its predecessor from 1889-1971. *The Cinema News and Property Gazette* from 1912 until it finished in the 1980s and then its later incarnation *Screen International*. The illustrated casting directory *Spotlight* from its beginning in 1927 to the 1990s, including bound copies of the first 10 years. Many other periodicals. A library of books on film actors and directors. A comprehensive collection of cinema sheet music and silent film music. Industry publications such as projector brochures, cinema company documents and share certificates.

CIRCUS FAMILIES Travelling circuses and fairgrounds employed numerous people, not only as entertainers but as support staff. In addition to their nomadic lifestyle many of the entertainers often adopted performing names. It follows that these families could pose difficult research problems. The National Fairground Archive www.nfa.dept.shef.ac.uk is maintained by the University of Sheffield www.nfa.dept.shef.ac.uk.National Fairground Archive, Western Bank Library, University of Sheffield, Western Bank, Sheffield S10 2TN.

CITATION A summons to appear before a court.

CITATIONS It is important to cite books, URLs and documents that have been used in research. There are different approved methods of doing this, the most common of which is the Harvard system but the important thing is to be consistent. If you are writing for a journal they may have their own preferred referencing style. *How to Cite Documents in The National Archives* is a research guide from www.nationalarchives.gov.uk. This suggests how the records in the custody of TNA should be cited in books, articles or theses. Although American in style the following may be useful: Mills, Elizabeth Shown *Evidence Explained: citing history sources from artefacts to cyberspace* (Genealogical Publishing Co. 2009) and Mills, Elizabeth Shown *Evidence! Citation and Analysis for the Family Historian* (Genealogical Publishing Co. 1997).

CIVIC TRUST See Local History Societies.

CIVIL REGISTRATION See also Civil Registration in Ireland, Civil Registration in Scotland and Registration Districts. The requirement to register a birth, marriage or death came into effect on 1 July 1837 in England and Wales, this is also the first date upon which a marriage could take place in a Register Office. Readers of this book will almost certainly have seen a birth, marriage or death certificate and details appear in all basic "how to" genealogy books, so the contents need not be described. There is no online access to English and Welsh birth, marriage and death certificates themselves. The Registrar General's indexes to birth, marriage and death certificates are now normally accessed via one of the online subscription/pay per view websites. It should be noted that free access to transcriptions of the original index books, together with images of these index books, are available at http://freebmd.rootsweb.com/. Although this index, compiled by volunteers, is not yet 100% complete, the search facilities are more flexible than those on the paid websites. Details of the availability of the indexes on microfiche can be found on the GRO website www.gro.gov.uk/gro.

The indexes give only the Surname, Christian names, name of Registration District, Volume and page reference. It is these details, together with the Year and quarter in which the event was registered, which are required to obtain a certificate from the GRO. Additional information appears in later indexes, which can be useful in identifying the correct entry. From the September Quarter 1911 the birth indexes also give the maiden surname of the mother. From the March Quarter 1912 the marriage indexes also show the surname of the spouse. From the March Quarter 1866, the death indexes show age at death and from June 1969, they show date of birth. The indexes are based on the date that the event was registered, not the date it occurred. The quarter in which the event took place is not necessarily the quarter in which it is registered. Always check at least the following quarter. This is particularly important for births.

The indexes supply the necessary references to enable a certificate to be purchased; the current fees are on the GRO website. The official online method of purchasing a certificate is via the GRO www.gro.gov.uk/gro. Please note however that there are other similar sites that purport to be the official site but will charge significantly more. Postal applications for certificates should be made to the Certificate Services Section, GRO, PO Box 2, Southport PR8 2JD. An application form is required. These are obtainable from the same address or can be downloaded online via the Home Office website www.homeoffice.gov.uk.

If the registration district is known, applications for certificates can also be made to individual register offices. Your local register office can supply the address for those elsewhere or the addresses can be obtained via www.ukbmd.org.uk/genuki/reg/regoff.html. Note that many indexes to the registers held by district registrars are available online at UKBMD www.ukbmd.org.uk/local_bmd.

Errors and omissions do occur both in the Indexes and on certificates issued, for a variety of reasons. Handwriting and dates can be mis-read both by staff and by researchers. Bear in mind that the Registrar or Incumbent wrote down what he thought he heard and as many people could not read or write in the early years of Civil Registration, there was no way of checking his entry. Regional accents, speech impediments, even the common cold can affect what is written on a certificate. The national indexes are copies of the district registrar's books and copying errors may have occurred. Now access is normally via transcribed indexes there is additional room for error. Remember that the spelling of surnames varied. Beware of any surnames beginning with a vowel or with an H (the former may well collect an H, the latter lose it). Always check, for example, MacDougall and McDougall and look out for such names as (K)Nowles, W(Roe), and (Y)Eardley. Michael Foster has written and published two volumes highlighting errors in the civil registration records *A Comedy of Errors or the marriage records of England and Wales, 1837-1899* (Mike Foster 1998) and *A Comedy of Errors Act 2* (Mike Foster 2002). The GRO registers are currently being re-indexed in the light of Foster's work although the new database is unlikely to be available for some years.

During the early years of civil registration many births, particularly those of illegitimate children, were not registered. Until 1875 there was no penalty for failure to do so. Parents were given six weeks (42 days) to register; after six weeks and up to six months the birth could be registered on payment of a fine. After six months, with very few exceptions, a birth could not be registered. It was fairly common for parents, arriving to register a child a few days late, to adjust the birth date to come within 42 days. Since 1875, the father of an illegitimate child can only be named on the birth certificate if he is present at the registration and consents.

A child that had not been named at the time of registration will have been indexed under the surname in question, as "Male" or "Female". Reversing of christian names was common; a man married as "Henry John" may well have been registered at birth as "John Henry". If the time of birth is given on an English or Welsh certificate, it frequently implies a multiple birth.

Identical entries in the indexes in successive Quarters can also occur. This is basically due to a flaw in the administrative system.

Ages on marriage certificates are often unreliable. "21" and "of full age" both mean that the person was 21 and upwards, if they were telling the truth. In theory, a marriage certificate should state if father of bride or groom is deceased; in practice, this requirement was often ignored. It is not safe to presume he is still alive because the certificate does not state that he is deceased.

Do not assume that a marriage took place nine months or more before the birth of the first child. A high percentage of brides were pregnant when they married and a surprising number of couples did not marry until after the birth of their first child.

A widow will be listed in the index under her previous married name and not under her maiden name but her maiden surname will appear on the certificate. Marriages which took place in non-conformist chapels prior to 1898 had to be carried out in the presence of a (civil) Registrar. Such marriages will often be located in the Registrar's own register (also used to record marriages which took place in the Register Office) and not in the register of the chapel concerned. Marriage registers for Church of England marriages were compiled in duplicate. One copy was retained by the church. These are now likely to be in CROs.

Prior to 1900, 4 marriages were entered on one page of the register (since 1900 this has been reduced to 2). Births and deaths registers can have up to 8 entries on the same page. This can cause confusion when, for example, cousins bearing an unusual surname are born, in the same area, some days apart but are registered on the same day, thereby receiving an identical registration reference and making it seem like a registration of twins. It can also be misleading when searching for a marriage between a couple who both bear common (for the area in question) surnames as, with 8 names on the page, it is possible to find an apparent match which, on checking, turns out to be the groom from one marriage on the page and the bride from another.

In 1837 a death had to be registered within 8 days; in 1875 this was reduced to 5 days. Do not place too much reliance on the age given on a death certificate. The only person who should know the true facts was not there to give them! The accuracy of the age given depends on the person giving the information (relative/employer/neighbour/workhouse master). Particularly in the early days, when there were no birth certificates to verify the statement, ages at death may be years out. Many people deliberately "lost" several years from their age at some stage in their lives. You will sometimes find a discrepancy between the age given on a death certificate and that given in the burial register.

"Present at the death" means what it says; "In attendance" means that the person registering the death was not actually present at it but is attending at the Register Office to register it.

With very few exceptions, a death cannot be registered until a positive identification of the body has been made. Unless a body is legally identified, it cannot be registered under a specific name, hence entries in the indexes for, for example, "Old Joe aged about 65", for an itinerant worker with no known surname and the entries for "unknown" or "unidentified" bodies with estimated ages.

If an inquest was held, the death will be registered in the quarter when the inquest was completed. Particularly if there was an adjournment, this may be some time after the actual death and the entry may be in a later quarter than you anticipate. If there is no body, a death cannot be registered. If the body is recovered (e.g. from a mining accident or a shipwreck) several years later and is identified, the death will be registered as at the date of recovery but the age given will be that which applied when the person actually died. If a ship goes down at sea with no survivors then, generally speaking, none of the deaths of those on board can be registered because the bodies cannot be legally identified.

Sometimes you are faced with a choice between two or more entries and the place of registration could lead you to the entry most likely to be correct. However, the name of the registration district does not always give you a clear idea as to where it was located. Sometimes old Hundred names for the area are used, names which no longer appear on modern maps. It is a help to be able to locate the county by a knowledge of the "code" (the first part of the reference you have to quote on your application form). The reference numbers that follow are only a guide, however, for often the same reference is used for more than one county, though these are usually adjacent.

From 1837 to 1851 Roman numerals were used. From 1852 we have Arabic numerals followed by a letter.

Anglesey XXVII 11b
Bedfordshire VI 3b
Berkshire VI 2c
Brecknockshire XXVI 11b
Buckinghamshire VI 3a
Caernarvonshire XXVII 11b
Cambridgeshire XIV 3b
Cardiganshire XXVII 11b
Carmarthenshire XXVI 11b
Cheshire XIX 8a
Cornwall IX 5c
Cumberland XXV 10b
Denbighshire XXVII 11b
Derbyshire XIX 7b
Devonshire IX, X 5b
Dorset VIII 5a

Durham XXIV 10a
Essex XII 4a
Flintshire XIX, XXVII 11b
Glamorganshire XXVI 11a
Gloucestershire XI, XVIII 6a
Hampshire| VII, VIII 2b, 2c
Herefordshire XXVI 6a
Hertfordshire VI 3a
Huntingdonshire XIV 3b
Kent V 1d, 2a
Lancashire XX, XXI, XXV 8b, 8c, 8d, 8e
Leicestershire XV 7a
Lincolnshire XIV 7a
London (with suburbs) I, II, III, IV 1a, 1b, 1c, 1d
Merionethshire XXVII 11b
Middlesex I, II, III 1a, 1b,1c,3a
Monmouthshire XXVI 11a
Montgomeryshire XXVII 11b
Norfolk XIII 4b
Northamptonshire XV 3b
Northumberland XXV 10b
Nottinghamshire XV 7b
Oxfordshire XIV 3a
Pembrokeshire XXVI 11a
Radnorshire XXVI 11b
Rutland XV 7a
Shropshire XXVI, XVIII 6a
Somerset X, XI 5c
Staffordshire XVI, XVII, XVIII 6b
Suffolk XVI, XII, XIII 3b, 4a
Surrey IV 1d, 2a
Sussex VII 2b
Warwickshire XI, XVI, XVIII 6b, 6c, 6d
Westmorland XXV 10b
Wiltshire VIII 5a
Worcestershire XVIII 6b, 6c
Yorkshire XXI, XXII, XXIII, XXIV 9a, 9b, 9c, 9d

The Registrar General also holds other records relating to births marriages and deaths; these indexes are usually available from the same sources as the mainstream indexes. They include:

Births and Deaths at Sea since 1st July 1837: events occurring at sea on any ship registered in Great Britain and Northern Ireland (Marine Register Book).

Births and Deaths in Aircraft from 1949: events occurring in any part of the world in any aircraft registered in Great Britain and Northern Ireland. (Air Register Book)

Service Records: events among members of H. M. Forces and certain other persons working for or attached to H. M. Forces. Army Registers date mainly from 1881, Royal Air Force from 1920 and Royal Navy 1959.

Consular and High Commission: events of British subjects in most foreign countries registered by British Consuls; births and deaths of British subjects in most Commonwealth countries registered by British High Commissioners.

Miscellaneous Records including certain Regimental Registers dating from 1760.

There are separate registers containing the registration of deaths of Servicemen in World Wars I and II, certificates of marriage forwarded by the British High Commissioners in India, Bangladesh, Sri Lanka and Ghana from 1950 and foreign certificates of marriage forwarded by British Consuls: births and deaths aboard British registered hovercraft and deaths occurring on off-shore installations.

Copies of Records of Still-Births registered in England and Wales since 1st July 1927 can be obtained only with special permission of the Registrar General.

There are several useful books and booklets on this topic. Collins, Audrey and Annal, David *Birth, Marriage and Death Records: a guide for family historians* (Pen & Sword 2012). Langston, Brett *A Handbook to the Civil Registration Districts of England and Wales* (Brett Langston 2001). Raymond, Stuart A *Civil registration* (FHP forthcoming). Three other books by Stuart Raymond are also relevant: *Birth and Baptism Records for Family Historians* (FHP 2010); *Marriage Records for Family Historians* (FHP 2010) and *Death and Burial Records for Family Historians* (FHP 2011). Watts, Christopher T & Michael J *Tracing Births, Deaths and Marriages at Sea* (SOG 2004). See also Nissel, Muriel *People Count: a history of the General Record Office* (HMSO 1987), which was published to mark its 150 years in existence. It tells of the origins and developments of civil registration and of the statistical work, including the census, of the Office plus results of social and economic changes on the service.

CIVIL REGISTRATION IN IRELAND The general registration of births, marriages and deaths did not begin until 1864 and until 1921 it covered the whole of Ireland. Registration of Protestant marriages began in 1845.

These records are held, together with those for Eire since 1921, by the General Register Office (Republic of Ireland) for online ordering of these certificates go to www.birthsdeathsmarriages.ie.

Registrations for Northern Ireland after 1921 are in the General Register Office (Northern Ireland) and certificates can be ordered via the website www.nidirect.gov.uk.

Indexes to Irish birth, marriage and death records, up to 1958, are available via FindmyPast www.findmypast.com.

CIVIL REGISTRATION IN SCOTLAND Registration commenced on 1 January 1855. Certificates for that year gave an astonishing amount of information but the authorities found it too difficult to keep up such a standard and modifications were introduced. Birth certificates in 1855 and from 1861 give the date and place of the parents' marriage. Marriage certificates give the names of both parents of each party. Death certificates give parents' names.

In Scotland, the public is allowed to see not just the indexes but the full details on the certificates themselves, subject to certain limitations. Some local Registrars also allow limited access to the registers by arrangement. See the webpages of the GRO for Scotland for more details see www.gro-scotland.gov.uk. Scotland's People (q.v.) www.scotlandspeople.gov.uk gives online pay per view access to Scottish civil registration indexes.

CIVIL SERVANTS Records will usually be amongst those of the Department in which the individual served and will generally be found in TNA. A very detailed Research Guide dealing with *Civil or Crown Servants* is available for download from www.nationalarchives.gov.uk.

CLANDESTINE MARRIAGES See Marriages.

CLARK'S FOOTWEAR See Alfred Gillett Trust.

CLASSMAN A term used particularly in Suffolk in the 1840s to describe unemployed labourers.

CLERGY See also Non-conformists. For those looking to research clergy in the period from 1540 to 1835, "The Clergy of the Church of England Database" (CCEd) is a collaborative project gathering biographical data on clergymen from archives in England and Wales. There is also information on dioceses, including lists of bishops, and on locations where clergy served. It is available at www.theclergydatabase.org.uk.

For those looking to research clergy in the period from 1835 to 1967, Lambeth Palace Library is the historic library of the archbishops of Canterbury and the principal library and record office for the history of the Church of England. The Library focuses on ecclesiastical history, but its rich collections are important for an immense variety of topics from the history of art and architecture to colonial and Commonwealth history and for innumerable aspects of English social, political and economic history. More details about the library and its holdings can be found at www.lambethpalacelibrary.org. It also has a guide to biographical sources for Anglican clergy see 'About Collections', 'Research guides' and then 'Anglican Clergy'.

Crockford's Clerical Directory www.crockford.org.uk has been published at frequent intervals since 1858. It lists the names of all Church of England clergy. The website gives information from 1968, the first time that the database was put in an electronic form. There are no current plans to retrospectively digitise the earlier editions. The 1929 edition of Crockford's Clerical Directory has been scanned and is sold on CD by S & N Genealogical Supplies (q.v.) www.genealogysupplies.com. In addition, some editions of Crockford's are made available online by Ancestry (q.v.) to their paying subscribers www. ancestry.co.uk.

The *Clergy List*, a professional directory for the Church of England, appeared from 1841-1917. Early editions included Wales, with more limited information relating for Scotland, Ireland and other churches within the Anglican Communion. It merged with Crockford's in 1917.

The *Index Ecclesiasticus* compiled by Joseph Foster lists clerical appointments from 1800 to 1840. The Institution Books held at in Classes E331 to E347 at TNA list earlier appointments of clergy. Their website www.nationalarchives. gov.uk has a downloadable guide entitled *Looking for Records of a Member of the Clergy.*

John le Neve's *Fasti Ecclesiae Anglicanae* gives details of all the higher clergy of the Church of England from early times to the mid C19th. A modern edition can be viewed at www.british-history.ac.uk/catalogue.aspx?gid=157.

Noblemen were allowed to have their own chaplains, the number depending on their rank. Certain Officers of State were also allowed to have them. These chaplains were permitted to enjoy two benefices. There is a record of the appointment, death or dismissal of such people in the Faculty Office (q.v.) from 1660. The C18th volumes have been indexed under the names of the Peers who appointed. These records can be consulted at Lambeth Palace Library.

In the case of Clergy of the Church of Scotland, *Fasti Ecclesiae Scoticanae* is regularly reissued and details ministers in parish churches from 1560.

There was a school for the orphans of clergy, boys only. See Simmonds M J (ed.) *The Register of the Clergy Orphan School for Boys 1751 to 1896* (Simmonds 1897). The school was in Yorkshire from 1751 to 1804, in Acton from 1804 to 1812, in St Johns Wood from 1812 to 1855 and in Canterbury from 1855 to 1896. It then became St Edmund's School www.machadoink.com/ St%20Edmunds%20College.htm. The Register gives the year of birth, date of admission, name of father and the parish where he served. There are some footnotes stating to whom some children were apprenticed or a profession entered.

A detailed guide to tracing clergymen is provided by Towey, Peter *My Ancestor was an Anglican Clergyman* (SOG 2006).

CLERK In addition to its present meaning, this term was often applied to a clergyman who was officially a "Clerk in Holy Orders". Occasionally "clerk" will follow a parish register entry, often a burial. This usually indicates that the individual was the parish clerk (q.v.).

CLIMBING BOYS See Sweeps.

CLOCKMAKERS AND WATCHMAKERS See also Oriental and India Office Collections. The Worshipful Company of Clockmakers www.clockmakers.org of London is a London Livery Company that was granted a Charter in 1631. The Company owns an extensive library of books, documents and portraits. Further details of its history are on its website. The Clockmakers' Company Museum is housed at the Guildhall Library (q.v.).

British & Irish Clock and Watch Makers (c1600-c1940), the website for Historical Clock & Watch Research is at www.clockswatches.com. The "Gershom-Parkington Collection of Time-keeping Instruments" is displayed at Moyse's Hall Museum, Cornhill, Bury St. Edmunds www.moyseshall.org. See also the growing list of clock and watch makers at http://blacksmiths. mygenwebs.com/clockmakers-1.php.

Some relevant books are: Britten, F J *Old Clocks and Watches and their Makers* (Pub Marketing Enterprises 1973), which has a list of nearly 12,000 makers. Wallis R V & P J *Index of British Mathematicians: Pt 3 1701-1800* (revised ed. PHIBB 1993), contains many references to clock and watchmakers. *Westmorland Clocks and Clockmakers* (David & Charles 1974) and *Lancashire Clocks and Clockmakers* (David & Charles 1975) are two of a series by Brian Loomes. Each has an alphabetical list of clockmakers, with considerable genealogical information. In the Westmorland book there are two five-generation pedigrees of clockmaking families. Elliot D J *Shropshire Clock and Watchmakers* (Phillimore 1979). *Wiltshire Watch and Clockmakers*, a projected series of books by John Young (Sedgehill Publishing) of which the first three volumes have now been published www.wiltshireclocks.co.uk. Tribe, Tom & Whatmoor, Philip *Dorset Clocks and Clockmakers: with a supplement on the Channel Islands* (Tanat Books 1981).

CLOSE ROLLS These documents are in TNA Class C54. They are records of deeds, conveyances between individuals, sales of lease and release and many other similar transactions. They date from 1204-1903. There are printed calendars, in 47 volumes, for the period 1227-1509. In the C19th changes of name by deed poll and naturalisation certificates were enrolled in the close rolls.

CLOTHWORKER The Clothworkers' Company was an amalgamation of the Fullers and Shearmen. It is an ancient City of London Livery Company, 12th of the "Great Twelve". Originally founded to promote the craft of cloth-finishing, the Company now exists to promote charitable work and fellowship amongst its members. Details of the company's archives and other collections are at www.clothworkers.co.uk.

COACHMAKER AND COACH HARNESSMAKER The Worshipful Company of Coach Makers and Coach Harness Makers of London was an historic London Livery Company. It has a website at www.coachmakers.co.uk, which gives extensive details of its history.

COAL MINERS See Mining.

COASTGUARDS Most records are held at TNA. Two research guides entitled *Coastguard* and *Coastguard Officers*, are available for download from their website at www.nationalarchives.gov.uk. See Carson E *The Ancient and Rightful Customs* (Faber and Faber 1972) and Webb, W *Coastguard: an official history of HM Coastguard* (H.M.S.O. 1976). For coastguards who served in Irish coastguard stations see www.coastguardsofyesteryear.org. An index to British Coastguards, largely taken from the 1841-1891 censuses, is available via GENUKI (q.v.) www.genuki.org.uk/big/Coastguards.

COAT OF ARMS See Armorial Bearings and Heraldry.

CODICIL An addition to a will, either modifying or revoking it.

COINAGE See also Inflation and Money. The coins most likely to be referred to are the guinea (which was worth 21 shillings), the shilling, the groat (which was worth four old pennies), the farthing (a quarter of an old penny) and the penny. There were 240 pennies in a pound, twelve pennies in a shilling and twenty shillings in a pound, until the introduction of decimal coinage in 1971. For more information see www.coins-of-the-uk.co.uk/coins.html and http://gwydir. demon.co.uk/jo/units/money.htm.

COLLEGES See Education.

COLLEGE OF ARMS See also Heraldry. This is the name usually given to the Corporation of the Kings, Heralds and Pursuivants of Arms. The present College, built after the Great Fire of 1666, stands on the site of Derby House on London's Queen Victoria Street. There is no direct public access to their library.

The College of Arms is the official repository of the coats of arms and pedigrees of English, Welsh, Northern Irish and Commonwealth families and their descendants. Its records also include official copies of the records of Ulster King of Arms the originals of which remain in Dublin. The College houses a great variety of records and many thousands of pedigrees.

Further details can be found on the College's website at www.college-of-arms.gov.uk. This details the officers of the College, contains news and has back editions of the College's newsletter that can be downloaded free of charge. Future editions of the College's free electronic newsletter, which is delivered by e-mail, can be subscribed to via the website.

COLLIER Originally a charcoal seller but later the name came to mean a coal miner.

COMBMAKERS This London Livery Company received its charter in 1635 and appears to have ceased to exist sometime between 1862 and 1892. The Guildhall Library (q.v.) holds limited records of the Combmakers' Company in its Manuscripts Section, namely a court minute book 1744-50. An index to freedom admissions recorded in this book, together with names of combmakers outside London, is available in Bowers, Ron *Combs, Combmakers and the Combmakers' Company*, which is kept in the Printed Books Section of Guildhall Library (q.v.) www.cityoflondon.gov.uk. This contains over 2300 entries and is principally compiled from City of London Alphabets of Freedom 1681 to 1893 but also from York, Bristol, other leading cities and overseas records.

COMMON PLEAS See Court of Common Pleas.

COMMON RECOVERY See Entail.

COMMONWEALTH, THE This is the period, from 1649 to 1653, of the English republic, established after the execution of Charles I and ruled by the Rump Parliament and a Council of State. The Commonwealth proper ended with the establishment of Oliver Cromwell's Protectorate in 1653. Although 1649-1660 is usually referred to as the "Commonwealth Period", strictly this is "The Interregnum", the period between the execution of Charles I (1649) and the Restoration (1660), embracing various governments of the Commonwealth and Protectorate. This is a difficult period for the family history researcher, as there is a hiatus in many of the records such as parish registers, often referred to as "The Commonwealth Gap". Virtually all wills for this period should be in TNA. See the research guide *State Papers Domestic 1642-1660* downloadable from TNA website www.nationalarchives.gov.uk and Aylmer, G E & Morrill, J S *The Civil War and Interregnum, sources for Local Historians* (NCVO 1979).

COMMONWEALTH WAR GRAVES COMMISSION (CWGC) The Commission was established in 1917. Its duties are to mark and maintain the graves of the members of the forces of the Commonwealth who were killed in the two World Wars, to build memorials to those who have no known graves and to keep records and registers. Its records include sunken ships and the Runnymede Memorial to Royal Air Force personnel whose bodies have remained undiscovered. The CWGC hold a copy of the Roll of Honour Civilian War Deaths 1939-1945, the original of which is in Westminster Abbey.

The website of the CWGC www.cwgc.org enables researchers to learn more about the Commission's work, to search its records and to explore various interactive histories. It is possible to download certificates for individual service personnel and see photographs of various military cemeteries and memorials. A film entitled *A Debt of Honour*, which illustrates the work of the Commission, is also available. Their searchable Debt of Honour Register is available on their website.

COMMUNITY HISTORY See Local History.

COMPANIES Since 1864 a Register of Companies has been maintained on behalf of the Department of Trade and Industry. Records give details of people associated with companies, addresses, relationships etc.. See the website of Companies House www.companieshouse.gov.uk for a searchable database leading to basic information about companies. For more detail concerning current companies and some that have now been dissolved, contact or visit the main office of the Registrar of Companies is at Crown Way, Maindy, Cardiff, CF4 3UZ; a fee is required.

Three research guides are available from TNA website www.nationalarchives. gov.uk *Businesses, Business History Records held in the UK* and *Companies and Businesses: further research*.

An extensive collection of business information is held by British Library Business & IP Centre, The British Library, 96 Euston Road, London NW1 2DB www.bl.uk/bipc/.

The Business Archives Council, 4 Maguire Street, Butlers Wharfe, London SE1, www.businessarchivescouncil.org.uk is a registered charity founded in the 1930s. It is the leading agency in the UK concerned with the preservation of historical records of British industry and assists in the rescue and preservation of records, advises companies on archives policy, publishes an annual journal and a quarterly newsletter.

Records of Scottish Companies can be found in Companies House, 4th Floor, Edinburgh Quay 2, 139 Fountainbridge, Edinburgh EH3 9FF. The Business Archives Council of Scotland is responsible for preserving the records of Scottish businesses. They can be contacted c/o Archive Services, University of Glasgow, 77-87 Dumbarton Road, G11 6PW, Scotland www.gla.ac.uk/services/archives/bacs/.

For Irish Companies see the Companies Registration Office website www.cro.ie.

Books on this subject include: Probert, Eric *Company and Business Records for Family Historians* (FFHS 1984) Richmond, Lesley & Stockford, Bridget *Company Archives: the survey of the records of 1,000 of the first registered companies in England and Wales* (Gower Publishing 1986), is the result of a survey of 1,200 companies, the only survivors of the 30,334 registered between 1856 and 1889 and extant in 1980. Orbell, John *A Guide to Tracing the History of a Business* (History Press 2009). Goodall, Francis *Bibliography of British Business Histories* (1987). Zarach, Stephanie *British Business History: a bibliography* (Palgrave MacMillan 1993). Jeremy, D J (ed.) *Dictionary of Business Biography* (Butterworths 5 volumes 1984-86). Armstrong, John & Jones, Stephanie *Business Documents, their Origin, Sources and uses in Historical Research* (Continuum International Publishing 1987).

The whereabouts of various business archives can be found in the National Register of Archives, now part of TNA website www.nationalarchives.gov.uk. See also the Database of Archives of Non-governmental Organisations www.dango.bham.ac.uk.

The three oldest Trading Companies are the Levant Company, whose records are at TNA. Hudson's Bay Company, whose records are in the Archives of Manitoba, 200 Vaughan Street, Winnipeg, Manitoba, Canada R3C 1T5 www.gov.mb.ca/chc/archives/hbca with microfilm copies at TNA. The third is the East India Company whose records form part of the Asia, Pacific and Africa Collections (q.v.)

COMPTON'S CENSUS This was an ecclesiastical census taken in 1676 and named after Henry Compton, the Bishop of London. The incumbents of each parish were recorded as Conformists, Papists, or Nonconformists, although in many cases the number of Conformists may have been the total population of the parish over 16. These statistical returns relate to parishes in the Midlands, Wales and the South and also include estimates of population and the numbers of dissenters.

Being an ecclesiastical census, this census was collected by ecclesiastical parishes, which were then aggregated into arch-deaconries and diocese, rather than into the civil hundreds and ancient counties. For some nineteen parishes, more detailed returns survive. These record the names of individual residents.

Copies of the Compton Census can be found at The William Salt Library, Stafford www.staffordshire.gov.uk/leisure/archives/williamsalt/home.aspx and The Bodleian Library, Oxford www.bodleian.ox.ac.uk.

For further details of the Compton Census including the nineteen parishes for which more detailed returns survive, see Gibson, Jeremy & Medlycott, Mervyn *Local Census Listings 1522-1930 - Holdings in the British Isles* (3rd ed. FFHS 1998).

The census has been published in full: Whiteman Annie (ed.) *The Compton Census of 1676: a critical edition* (Oxford University Press 1986).

COMPUTERS IN GENEALOGY See also Society of Genealogists. This was the title of a quarterly journal issued by the SOG, which dealt with the use of computers in genealogy and family history. It was first published in 1982 and ceased publication in 2005. A full series is available for perusal in the SOG Library, whilst copies for the period from March 1994 to June 2001 have been published on the web site of the SOG www.sog.org.uk.

COMPUTER SOFTWARE There are numerous commercial software packages that can store data and create family trees and reports. Many commercial programmes have free trial versions and there are also independent free downloads available. It is difficult to make recommendations as each researcher's requirements are different. It is a good idea to ask other users and ideally, see demonstrations, before deciding on a package that will suit your needs. Some of the most widely used programmes include: Brother's Keeper (a free download) www.bkwin.org. Family Historian www.family-historian.co.uk. Family Tree Maker, which is produced by Ancestry (q.v.) www.familytreemaker. com. Legacy Family Tree www.legacyfamilytree.com. Reunion (for Mackintosh users) www.leisterpro.com. Roots Magic www.rootsmagic.com. Personal Ancestral File (PAF) Family Search's (q.v.) free software https://familysearch. org/products. The Master Genealogist (TMG). Comparisons of software can be found http://genealogy-software-review.toptenreviews.com/ and http://en. wikipedia.org/wiki/Comparison_of_genealogy_software.

CONGREGATIONALISTS See also Dr Williams' Library and United Reformed Church. This denomination believed in the control of their church by the congregation. They were originally known as Independents. In the C19th, many became Unitarians (q.v.). There are many relevant records in the Dr Williams' Library www.dwlib.co.uk/congregational. The Congregational Historical Society published a number of early records in its "Transactions". This society ceased to exist in 1972 when it merged with the Presbyterian Historical Society of England to form the United Reformed Church History Society www.urc.org.uk. Most Congregational registers were handed over to the Registrar General in compliance with the 1840 Act and are now held at TNA. Many registers are now available online on a payment basis at either The Genealogist website www.thegenealogist.co.uk or The Official Non-Conformist and Non-Parochial BMDs website www.bmdregisters.co.uk.

For further information, see Clifford, David *My Ancestors were Congre-gationalists* (SOG 1998).

CONSISTORY COURT See also Ecclesiastical Courts and Wills. This was a diocesan, or Bishop's, court. It was one of several courts through which wills were proved.

CONSTABLE See also Verderers. As the name suggests, in simple terms he was the parish policeman. He was appointed by the Justices of the Peace, from names suggested by the Vestry, or sometimes by the manorial Court Leet. He had to supervise "Watch and Ward" (q.v.), maintain the local prison and the stocks, remove itinerant strangers, apprentice pauper children, was involved in the training of the local militia, collected taxes and had many other duties. Any parishioner might be nominated to act as Constable. It was not a popular job and the parishioner chosen often opted to pay someone else to act in his place. See Kent, Joan *The English Village Constable 1580-1642* (Oxford University Press 1986).

CONVEYANCES See Title Deeds.

CONVICTS See Crime and Criminals, Prisons and Prisoners and Transportation.

COOKS The smallest of London's Livery Companies, the Worshipful Company of Cooks can trace its origins back to the C12th. Thirty-fifth in order of seniority in the City Livery Companies, it was founded from two guilds of cooks in medieval London, the Cooks of Eastcheap and the Cooks of Bread Street. Receiving its first charter in 1482, the Cooks' Company still exists. Its website www.cookslivery.org.uk includes a detailed historical section.

CO-OPERATIVES Robert Owen and The Equitable Pioneers of Rochdale formed the first successful co-op in 1844. This became The North of England Wholesale Society and later The Co-operative Wholesale Society (CWS). These bought goods in bulk and resold them to their members at competitive prices. Co-operative societies also undertook benevolent activities. The National Co-operative Archive www.archive.coop hold records relating to history of the co-operative movement, printed histories of many co-operative societies, records of the Women's Guild and convalescent homes. Their website also gives details of the National Co-operative Film Archive. Few personal records survive but individuals may appear in minute books. Records may also be found in CROs or other archives. The archive is held at Holyoake House, Hanover Street, Manchester, M60 0AS and can be consulted by appointment only.

COOPERS These were makers and repairers of barrels and other wooden vessels such as tubs and buckets that were much in demand in earlier times. The Worshipful Company of Coopers is a London Livery Company that was granted its royal charter in 1501 and is thirty-sixth in order of seniority. It still exists. Its website www.coopers-hall.co.uk includes an extensive history of the Company.

COPEMAN Originally he was a dealer but by the C18th the word had come to mean a receiver of stolen goods.

COPYHOLD See also Freehold. This term is often found in old wills. It refers to lands held by copy of the Manorial Court roll. On the death of the tenant, the land reverted to the Lord of the Manor who normally transferred it to the deceased's heir. This was abolished in 1922, when all copyhold land became freehold.

COPYRIGHT See also Stationers' Hall. This is covered by the Copyright Designs and Patents Act 1988, which replaced the repealed Copyright Act 1911. The Act can be found on the website of the Office of Public Sector information (OPSI), at www.opsi.gov.uk. OPSI itself is part of TNA.

The Copyright Designs and Patents Act 1988 requires that, within one month of publication, British and Irish publishers must deposit one copy of each of their publications at the Legal Deposit Office, The British Library, Boston Spa, Wetherby, West Yorkshire LS23 7BY. Certain other libraries are entitled to free copies of publications provided that they make written demand within twelve months after publication. These libraries are Cambridge University Library; the Bodleian Library, Oxford; the National Library of Scotland; Trinity College, Dublin and the National Library of Wales.

A brief overview of the subject is contained in an article *Copyright Issues for Archivists*, which was written by Tim Padfield, Copyright Officer at TNA. It can be found on the website of the Society of Archivists at www.archives.org.uk. A more detailed look at the topic can be found in Padfield's book *Copyright for Archivists and Records Managers* (Facet Publishing 2010).

CORDWAINER Originally a worker who used leather from Cordoba in Spain. The term became more generally used for a leather worker, making anything from leather bottles and shoes to horse harnesses. The term was most commonly used of shoemakers. The Worshipful Company of Cordwainers is a London Livery Company, founded in 1272 and incorporated by Royal Charter in 1439. The Company's website at www.cordwainers.org includes details of its history.

CORONERS AND CORONERS' INQUESTS A coroner is a doctor or lawyer responsible for investigating deaths in particular situations. He does have other duties but this is his primary role and the one most relevant to family history. The coroner can arrange for a post-mortem examination of the body if he deems it to be necessary. An inquest is a legal inquiry into the causes and circumstances of a death. If an inquest into a suspicious death is held and adjourned, then the death cannot be registered until the inquest has been closed. In certain circumstances, this may be several months later and might account for why the death registration does not take place when it might be expected, that is shortly after the time of actual death.

Unfortunately, many records of coroners' inquests have been destroyed, although there are many that are extant. Those for the City of London have survived and are in the London Metropolitan Archives. This repository's Information Leaflet No 34 is entitled *Coroners' Records for London and Middlesex* and is splendidly informative. It can be downloaded from www. cityoflondon.gov.uk. Gibson, Jeremy & Rogers, Colin *Coroners' Records in England and Wales* (3rd ed. FHP 2009) attempts to itemise all extant coroner's records in England and Wales which are now in public repositories.

More coroners' records survive from the mid C19th onwards and an enquiry at the CRO might be worthwhile. Newspapers often give very detailed reports of coroners' inquests and it is worth checking the relevant newspapers in the absence of any other record. Some abstracts of coroners' records have been published. For example, Oxfordshire Black Sheep Publications have published three volumes of *Oxfordshire Coroners' Inquests* covering the periods 1820-1826, 1827-1832 and 1833-1837 (2008). These are available from www.ofhs. org.uk/books.html.

COSTERMONGER Originally he was a seller of apples. It later became a general term for a seller of fruit and vegetables from a barrow.

COST OF LIVING See Inflation.

COTTAR He was a cottager with a small landholding, obliged to provide labour on the estate of the lord of the manor.

COUNCIL FOR BRITISH ARCHAEOLOGY See Local History Societies.

COUNTESS OF HUNTINGDON'S CONNEXION This was connected with the Methodist denomination. The Countess Selina (1707-1791) advocated the principles of Methodism and appointed George Whitfield, a notable preacher, as her chaplain. Her name was given to Whitfield's followers. The Countess founded a college in Wales and built many chapels.

The earliest register of this sect comes from Norfolk and dates back to 1752. The movement spread throughout the country. Registers were deposited with the Registrar General in accordance with the 1840 Act and are in TNA.

COUNTIES Please note that the names and boundaries of British Counties have not remained constant. Those commonly in use prior to 1974 are shown on the maps. There have been some minor changes over the centuries but those of 1974 were the most significant for England and Wales. Similar reorganisation took place in Scotland in 1975. These changes included the creation of new counties, such as Avon and the amalgamation of others. In Wales, for example, twelve historic counties were reduced to six. There were further changes in the 1990s, which reversed some of the 1974 changes. See http://jonathan.rawle. org/hyperpedia/counties/history.php.

COUNTY CODES See Chapman County Codes.

COUNTY HISTORY See Victoria County History.

COUNTY MAPS See Maps.

COUNTY RECORD OFFICES (CROs) CROs were initially established to house records of the Quarter Sessions courts (q.v.). Now they house a wealth of information relating to their area including parish registers, deeds and leases, maps, probate material and much more. The starting-point before visiting a CRO is to study its web pages, which will usually be found as part of the website of the relevant county council. Amongst other things, these will give the office's address and telephone number, opening hours and details of facilities for the disabled. The web pages will also give the procedure for document ordering and some include a copy of the office's catalogue.

A visit to a record office will be much more rewarding if you do your homework beforehand and arrive well prepared. The staff are usually most helpful. If you have a specific enquiry and know that it would take only a little time for a reference to be verified or a photocopy produced, you can write or e-mail. A modest charge may be made, if only to cover the cost of photocopying. Some record offices have a minimum charge for supplying photocopies by post. Most will allow the use of a lap top and digital camera, although there may be a charge for the latter.

Almost all Record Offices require some kind of identification. You are advised to check what is necessary before your visit. Many CROs are part of the County Archive Research Network (CARN) scheme, whereby one identity card suffices for all. See www.archives.org.uk.

If any long search is required, the record office might well have staff who undertake research on payment of a fee, Alternatively, you may be supplied with a list of local researchers who undertake such work for a fee (see AGRA and Professional Researchers).

COUPER One who buys and sells, especially in cattle and horses. Sometimes used in combination, for example horse-couper or a herring-couper. Confusion can arise from its being mis-spelt "cooper".

COUPLE BEGGAR An itinerant "hedge-priest" an often illiterate priest of low status who performed marriages in the period pre-1754.

COURSES IN FAMILY HISTORY See also Family History Societies, Institute of Heraldic and Genealogical Studies, National Institute for Genealogical Studies, Pharos Teaching and Tutoring and SOG. Some universities also offer extra mural family history courses. There is a list of some of the courses available at www.ffhs.org.uk/education/courses.php.

COURT BARON See also Manorial Records. This was part of the manorial system. The Court Baron concerned itself mainly with the changes of copyhold tenancies and the organisation of open fields, meadows and common land. Its records are found with other manorial documents (q.v.) usually in CROs.

COURT LEET See also Manorial Records. This manorial court dealt with matters relating to law and order on the manor. In some cases the jurisdiction extended over a wider area than the Manor, often that of a Hundred. It was also known as the Court Customary since it dealt with customary tenants, that is those who held land according to the custom of the manor as against those who were copyholders dealt with by the Court Baron. The functions of the two courts were apt to overlap.

COUNTIES OF ENGLAND AND WALES
before 1st April 1974

COUNTIES OF ENGLAND AND WALES
after 1st April 1974

COUNTIES OF SCOTLAND
before 16th May 1975

ORKNEY ISLES

CAITHNESS

SUTHERLAND

ROSS &
CROMARTY
INV.

ROSS & CROMARTY

INV.

INVERNESS

NAIRN-
SHIRE

MORAY

BANFFSHIRE

ABERDEENSHIRE

INVERNESS-SHIRE

KINCARDINE-
SHIRE

ANGUS

(FORFARSHIRE)

ARGYLL

PERTHSHIRE

FIFE

ARGYLLSHIRE

KRS

CLK

CLK = CLACKMANNANSHIRE
KRS = KINROSS-SHIRE

STIRLINGSHIRE

DUNBARTON-SHIRE

WEST
LOTHIAN

MIDLOTHIAN

EAST
LOTHIAN

ARGYLL

RENFREWSHIRE

BUTE

LANARKSHIRE

BERWICKSHIRE

PEEBLE-
SHIRE

SELKIRK-
SHIRE

ROXBURGHSHIRE

ARGYLL

BUTE

AYRSHIRE

DUMFRIESSHIRE

KIRKCUDBRIGHT-
SHIRE

WIGTOWN-
SHIRE

COUNTIES OF SCOTLAND
after 16th May 1975

ORKNEY ISLES

WESTERN ISLES

HIGHLAND

GRAMPIAN

TAYSIDE

FIFE

CENTRAL REGION

LOTHIAN

STRATHCLYDE

BORDERS

DUMFRIES & GALLOWAY

COURT OF ARCHES This was the Court of Appeal for the Province of Canterbury dealing with matters such as disputed wills, probate, defamation, matters relating to church property and other causes. The court dates from the C13th but very few records survive before 1660. The records are at Lambeth Palace Library www.lambethpalacelibrary.org. See *Records of the Court of Arches 1554-1911: Lambeth Palace Library* (Chadwyck-Healey 1983) partially indexed in Houston J (ed.) *Index of Cases in the Records of the Court of Arches at Lambeth Palace Library 1660-1913* (British Record Society 1972).

COURT OF CHANCERY See Bernau Index and Six Clerks, The. The Court of Chancery dealt with disputes over inheritance, lands, debts and the like. Its records run from the C14th to the C19th. They are held by TNA. Relevant TNA research guides can be downloaded from www.nationalarchives.gov.uk: *Chancery Proceedings: equity suits before 1558*; *Chancery Proceedings: equity suits from 1558* and *Chancery Cases in the Supreme Court after 1875*.

COURT OF COMMON PLEAS This Court was in operation from 1194 to 1875 and was concerned with disputes between subjects of the Crown. There is much family history hidden away in the proceedings of this court. The records are in TNA and in the British Museum; they include the Feet of Fines (q.v.).

COURT OF DELEGATES This was a Court of Appeal for the provincial courts of Canterbury and York.

COURT OF KING'S BENCH See also Curia Regis Rolls. This was the highest court of common law in the realm, with jurisdiction over both civil and criminal actions. Its records in TNA are extensive. The depositions of witnesses are of great use to family historians. See TNA research guides *Court of King's Bench 1200-1600* and *Court of King's Bench: criminal cases 1675-1875*.

COURT OF REQUESTS Between 1485 and about 1642, this court dealt with land and monetary matters. Its records are in TNA. A research guide entitled *Court of Requests 1485-1642* can be downloaded from www.nationalarchives. gov.uk and gives details of the records, how to use them and the various indexes and finding aids that make them accessible.

COURT OF STAR CHAMBER This court was the judicial arm of the King's Council. It became a separate court of law in 1485 and was abolished in 1641. Many of the cases relate to private property disputes or corrupt judicial officials. Records are in TNA (Class STAC). See TNA research guide *Court of Star Chamber 1485-1642*, which can be downloaded at www.nationalarchives.gov.uk.

COURT OF WARDS AND LIVERIES The court was responsible for collecting money due in connection with the inheritance of land held by tenants in chief, for the period 1540-1645. The Records are in TNA (Class WARD) but many are in very poor condition. See TNA research guide *Land inheritance in the Court of Wards and Liveries 1540-1645*, which can be downloaded at www.nationalarchives.gov.uk.

COURT ROLLS See also Court Baron, Court Leet and Manorial Records. These recorded the decisions of the manorial courts. Where they survive, they contain useful genealogical information as they record the descent of land from father to son. A notable series is the Wakefield Court Rolls, which are being published by the Yorkshire Archaeological Society; further details can be obtained from the society's website at www.yas.org.uk.

COURTS MARTIAL A court martial tries offences against military discipline, or offences committed by members of the armed forces. Civilians would be tried by courts martial if martial law was in force. The research guide *Courts Martials and Desertion in the British Army 17th-20th centuries* can be downloaded from TNA Website www.nationalarchives.gov.uk.

COUSIN GERMAN A first cousin.

COVENTRY See Herbert Art Gallery and Museum, Coventry.

CREST The crest is an heraldic device, modelled onto the top of the helm and part of an achievement of arms. The term is frequently used incorrectly for the whole achievement.

CREW LISTS See Royal Navy and Merchant Seamen.

CRICKET Marylebone Cricket Club (MCC) is the owner of the Laws of Cricket and keeper of the game of cricket's history. Its collections comprise fine and decorative art, a library and archive held at Lord's Cricket Ground in Central London. Archival material includes minute books, manuscripts, scorecards and photographs. A fully searchable database and on-line catalogue is being developed. Further details can be obtained from www.lords.org/history/mcc-museum.

The Association of Cricket Statisticians and Historians has a website at http://acscricket.com. That website invites those searching for information on a team or a particular player to make contact. The "Cricinfo" website at www.espncricinfo.com includes a searchable database of all those who have played or umpired in first class cricket at any time and anywhere in the world. It also includes details of many who played a just below the first class level.

Many obituaries of cricketers are printed in Green, Barry *The Wisden Book of Obituaries: obituaries from Wisden's cricketers' almanac 1892-1985* (Queen Anne Press 1986). Numerous collective and individual bibliographies are listed in Padwick, E W *A Bibliography of Cricket* (2nd ed. Library Associarion 1984).

CRIME AND CRIMINALS See also Assize, Parkhurst Boys, Prisons and Prisoners and Transportation. The key work on this topic is Hawkings, David T *Criminal Ancestors: a guide to historical criminal records in England and Wales* (The History Press 2009). The eight appendices list hundreds of classes of criminal records and their whereabouts. See also Wade, Stephen *Tracing Your Criminal Ancestors: a guide for family historians* (Pen & Sword 2009). TNA have several useful guides that can be downloaded from their website www.national archives.gov.uk. These include *Prisons, Prisoners* and *Criminals and Convicts*.

A brief study of the Quarter Sessions records will bring home the realisation that until the late C19th, the words "crime and criminals" implied something very different than they do now. People were transported or hanged for acts which today would be considered more a misdemeanour, such as the theft of clothing. Between 1688 and the early C19th, the number of offences for which the nominal penalty was death had risen from about fifty to over two-hundred. Criminals, like paupers, were often well-documented, though the location of records is not so easy, since criminal justice was administered locally but prisons might be organised locally or nationally. The website Old Bailey Online www. oldbaileyonline.org Includes a free searchable database of nearly 200,000 criminal trials that took place at the Central Criminal Court 1674-1913.

The Galleries of Justice Museum in Nottingham www.galleriesofjustice.org.uk has free exhibitions, audio and performance led tours and a themed café that enable visitors to learn more about crime and punishment.

CRIMEAN WAR See also Florence Nightingale Museum. A good starting point in researching the Crimean War is Tomaselli, Philip *The Crimean War 1854-56: military history sources for family historians* (FFHS 2006). A TNA guide entitled *Crimean War* is of relevance. This can be downloaded from www.national archives.gov.uk. The website of the Crimean War Research Society http://crimeantexts.russianwar.co.uk/index.html also contains much useful information.

CROCKFORD'S CLERICAL DIRECTORY See Clergy.

CROFTER This is the usual term for a Scottish smallholder although there are regional variations. It is also used for a bleacher or dyer in the textile trades.

CURATE Usually the vicar's or rector's assistant. A Perpetual Curate was in fact a vicar.

CURATION See also Tuition. Guardianship over orphaned minors aged under twenty-one but over fourteen in the case of boys or twelve in the case of girls.

CURIA REGIS ROLLS See also Court of King's Bench. These relate to the records of the Court of King's Bench covering the period 1193 to 1272. The Rolls, later known as Common Pleas, record the proceedings of the Bench and the court "Coram Rege". They are held in class KB26 at the TNA and include all the surviving rolls of itinerant justices for the reign of Richard I and some for those for King John.

Those interested in using these records should refer to TNA research guides *Court of King's Bench 1200-1600* and *Court of King's Bench: criminal cases 1675-1875*, which can be downloaded from www.nationalarchives.gov.uk. Some of the Rolls have been transcribed and published. They are useful not only to those studying Mediaeval law but also as a source reflecting the social and economic life of the times. Increasing numbers of the plea rolls from 1272 onwards are freely available in the form of digital images on The Anglo-American Legal Tradition http://aalt.law.uh.edu/, which is a website maintained by the O'Quinn Law Library of University of Houston, Texas.

CURRENCY See Coinage and Money.

CURRER-BRIGGS See Indexes.

CURRIER Curriers were dressers of leather for further treatment and were originally linked to the cordwainers. The Worshipful Company of Curriers is a London Livery Company that is number 29 in the order of seniority of the 108 Livery Companies of the City of London. The Company's website is at www.curriers.co.uk and includes details of its history. Many of the documents owned by the Curriers' Company are available for study in the Guildhall Library (q.v.). That website also contains information about the history of the curriers' craft.

CURSITOR A clerk in a Chancery Court who drew up writs.

CURTILAGE This is a term sometimes found in wills and means a plot of land near the house, usually a vegetable garden.

CUSTUMAL/CUSTUMNAL This was a written document setting out the "customs" of the manor and the services owed by tenants, the duties of town burgesses and the rights and duties of the lord of the manor.

CUSTOMS AND EXCISE Customs duties are imposed on goods imported into or exported from the country, excise duties are imposed on goods within the country. Customs duties date back to the reign of Edward I and until 1671 were administered by the Exchequer. In that year six commissioners were appointed and formed a Board of Customs which set up Customs Houses with salaried officers throughout the country. The administration of Excise duties on the manufacture, sale or consumption of goods began in 1642 and was transferred to Customs in 1909. In 2005 HM Customs and Excise merged with the Inland Revenue to form HM Revenue & Customs (HMRC).

There are 300 volumes at TNA, dating from the late C17th relating to provincial ports (headquarters' records were destroyed by fire in 1814). The correspondence in these volumes contains much information about government staff, such as recommendations, adverse reports, baptismal certificates and notes about sickness and death. Excise Board records in the form of indexed minute books from 1695 to 1867 fill 749 volumes and contain similar information. Relevant guides that can be downloaded from TNA website www.national archives.gov.uk are: *Customs Officers*, *Medieval Customs' Accounts* and *Excise and Inland Revenue Officers*.

There is a Museum of Customs and Excise at Merseyside Martime Museum, Albert Dock, Liverpool L3 4AQ and their website has information about tracing ancestors who worked in this field www.liverpoolmuseums.org.uk/maritime.

CUTLER The word "cutler" is derived from the Latin "cultellarius" through the Old French "coutelier" and signifies a maker or seller of knives and weapons with a cutting edge. Hence, a cutler made swords, knives and instruments. The term cutler was later applied to those who made domestic cutlery, with Sheffield being the centre of the modern industry. The Worshipful Company of Cutlers is a London Livery Company that received its Charter in the early C15th. The Company's website at www.cutlerslondon.co.uk records its history and its collections of both cutlery and medals.

CYNDI'S LIST This is a gateway website containing a vast number of genealogy links, covering all aspects of worldwide family history www.cyndislist.com.

D

DADE REGISTERS See Parish Registers.

DANCE See Rambert Dance Company.

DATABASE OF ARCHIVES OF NON-GOVERNMENTAL ORGANISATIONS (DANGO) See Archives.

DATA PROTECTION ACT In 1984, legislation was passed about the way personal information is handled by computers. This was updated by the 1998 Act and from 2001, also applied to paper records. It affects everyone who owns a computer or who has any data processed on someone else's equipment. The Act is highly complex but is summarised in SOG' Information Leaflet No 18, which is entitled *The Data Protection Act 1998 and Genealogists*. This can be downloaded from www.sog.org.uk/leaflets/dpa2.pdf The Data Protection Act is administered by the Information Commissioner's Office. It has a website at www.ico.gov.uk.

DATES See also Calendars and Regnal Years. A wide variety of means of dating have been used in historical documents. These are described in Webb, Cliff *Dates and Calendars for the Genealogist* (SOG 1984). This booklet has short sections dealing with the Roman, French Revolutionary, Jewish and Moslem Calendars in addition to the more familiar Julian and Gregorian Calendars. Cheney C R *Handbook of Dates for Students of English History* (revised ed. Cambridge University Press 2000), is a more comprehensive guide and includes a six-page bibliography. Haydn's *Dictionary of Dates* has been published in various editions since 1841.

DEAN He presided over the Chapter (q.v.). A rural dean, like the Archdeacon, was a bishop's deputy but inferior in status.

DEATH, CAUSES OF There are several online lists of epidemics, the best of which can be found on the website of Keighley and District Family History Society www.kdfhs.org.uk. See also Wills, Simon *How our Ancestors Died: a guide for family historians* (Pen & Sword 2013).

DEATH DUTIES Death duty was a tax payable on legacies and residues of personal estates of deceased persons commencing in 1796. Initially, it was a tax on particular legacies but it was gradually extended until, by 1811, all estates going through probate courts were included, except those that were very small. The registers of abstracts for the whole country from 1796 through to 1903 are now in TNA class IR26. They record the date of probate, the names of beneficiaries, details and value of property and the duty paid.

There are three main uses of the Death Duty Registers: As a finding aid to ascertain in which court a will was proved or an administration was granted. In order to discover what actually happened to an estate as opposed to what was intended because the registers give a list of people who shared the estate and its value. In the case of an administration, to ascertain the value of the estate, as the administration will simply record the name and address of the administrator or next of kin.

A research guide entitled *Death Duty Records 1796-1903: further research* can be downloaded from TNA website www.nationalarchives.gov.uk. The Discovery catalogue facility on TNA website also enables an online search of the Death Duty Registers 1796-1811 and the relevant documents can be downloaded for a fee. Indexes to Death Duty registers are available at FindmyPast (q.v.) www.findmypast.co.uk.

DEATHS See also Burial Indexes, Cemeteries, Civil Registration, Deceased Online, Funerals, Inquisitions Post Mortem, Monumental Inscriptions, Parish Registers and War Memorials. In England and Wales, death certificates are available from 1837. Prior to this, parish registers can be used, although these are records of burials rather than deaths. Some do give dates of death. Many family history societies have compiled burial indexes. Most of these were combined by the FFHS in The National Burial Index (NBI).

Publications such as *The Gentleman's Magazine* (q.v.) and *Miscellanea Genealogica et Heraldica* (published from about 1880-1920) contain a vast amount of assorted genealogical information and can be consulted at the SOG and larger reference libraries. Some editions are also available online. Whilst not exclusively genealogical, *Notes and Queries* etc. also include Obituaries and Memorial Inscriptions. Besides the national edition some counties had their own editions. For overviews of death records see Raymond, Stuart *Death and Burial records for Family Historians* (FHP 2011) and Heritage, Celia *Tracing your Ancestors through Death Records* (Pen & Sword 2013).

DEATHS OVERSEAS See also Cemeteries in South Asia, Civil Registration, Commonwealth War Graves Commission and Sea Deaths. There are various registers of deaths of British subjects overseas and of servicemen in the indexes of the Registrar General. Yeo, Geoffrey (ed.) *The British Overseas: a guide to the records of their births, baptisms, marriages, deaths and burials, available in the UK* (3rd ed. Guildhall Library 1995), deals primarily with sources pre-1945 and Part: I "Introduction to the Sources", is particularly helpful. Part II: "Lists of known Registers for Individual Places Overseas" deals with everywhere from

Aden (South Yemen) to West Indies. It is also worthwhile checking at the SOG (q.v.) as they hold a considerable amount of material relating to events overseas. A good introduction to Britons abroad can be found on The Family Relatives website www.familyrelatives.com, which also provides access to some relevant material.

DECEASED ONLINE The "Deceased Online" website at www.deceased online.com is a database of statutory burial and cremation registers for the UK and Republic of Ireland. It has facilitated burial and cremation authorities in the digitisation of their register records, maps and photographs and has brought them together into a central searchable collection. The database holds records mainly from the 1850s onwards and can reveal previously unknown family links from different interments recorded in the same grave. The vast collection of records is being expanded all the time and users of the site can leave an e-mail address in order to receive a notification whenever any new data is added. The site's "Database Coverage" page details all of the authorities who have contributed data to the site, when it was added and how many records were involved.

Searching the "Deceased Online" database is free, although a payment is required to access any further information associated with any record that is found. Depending on what has been provided by the originating authority, the further information might include: Burial and cremation register entries in computerised form. Digital scans of register pages. Scans of book of remembrance pages. Grave details and other interments in a grave, which can be the key to making new family links. Pictures of graves and memorials. Maps showing the exact locations of graves and memorials. The site has also launched a blog to detail developments http://deceasedonlineblog.blogspot.co.uk. Another way to keep up with developments is via Facebook www.facebook.com/ DeceasedOnline.

DECEASED WIFE'S SISTER, MARRIAGE TO See Marriage.

DEED POLL There is no law to prevent anyone from changing their name, it is done by merely using the new name of choice. There comes a time however when legal proof of identity is required. Hence, it is advisable to make a simple statutory declaration, drawn up by a solicitor, of any change of name. Those wanting complete formality in a change of name use a process called Deed Poll, which is done through Royal Courts of Justice. A document entitled *Enrolling a Name Change in the Royal Courts of Justice* can be downloaded from www.justice.gov.uk.

Family historians are often more interested in those who changed their names in the past. It was sometimes done in order to inherit an estate or title. TNA have produced a research guide entitled *Changes of Name* which can be downloaded from www.nationalarchives.gov.uk. Indexes to enrolled deeds poll 1850-2003 are at TNA.

From 1914, changes of name by deed poll had to appear in the *London Gazette*, www.london-gazette.co.uk, *Edinburgh Gazette* www.edinburgh-gazette.co.uk or *Belfast Gazette* www.belfastgazette.co.uk. Online searches can be made. Change of name declarations 1939-1945 are of interest. During the Second World War, people wanting to change their name had to make a declaration to that effect and publish details three weeks beforehand. This was to allow the National Registration records to be altered and an identity card and ration book to be issued in the new name. The original declarations were destroyed when National Registration was abolished in 1952 but the researcher can search the relevant Gazette.

See Phillimore, W P W & Fry, E A *An Index to Changes of Name 1760 to 1901* (London 1905). It is available on CD from S & N Genealogical Supplies (q.v.) www.genealogysupplies or online at http://archive.org.

DEEDS REGISTRY See Title Deeds.

DELEGATES, COURT OF See Court of Delegates.

DELINQUENT A word used mainly during the Commonwealth (q.v.) to describe those who took the Royalist side in the Civil War or those who were described as Papists or Recusants.

DEMESNE This term refers to the lord's land, farmed on his own behalf, as distinct from the land farmed by tenants on their own behalf. An "ancient demesne" refers to Crown land. In effect, tenants of land belonging to the Crown had special privileges, even though the land may later have been given to another lord.

DEMISE Another word for a conveyance of land. It can also mean to lease land or to bequeath or transmit to a successor.

DENIZATION See Naturalization.

DENTIST The British Dental Association (BDA) www.bda.org 64 Wimpole Street, London W1M 8AL houses the BDA library, which has an index to articles from periodicals containing the names of dentists; this index commences in 1839. The BDA Museum, at the same address, preserves and interprets collections relating to the social history, practice and professional development of dentistry in the UK. It has some 30,000 objects and images that tell the story of how dentistry has developed from a marketplace spectacle to the complex procedures and treatments of today. See the page *Was your Ancestor a Dentist* on the BDA website via 'BDA Museum' and 'Enquiries'.

Dentists' Registers dating back to the 1880s are held in the library of the SOG (q.v.) www.sog.org.uk.

DEPOSITIONS See also Bernau Index. These are statements of evidence, usually relating to a court case. Disputes between individuals were heard in various courts including the Court of Chancery (q.v), Quarter Sessions (q.v.) and Ecclesiastical Courts (q.v.).

DESERTERS During the C18th and early C19th, notices of deserters from the armed forces were printed in local newspapers and the *Police Gazette* or *Hue and Cry*. These give detailed physical characteristics and often place of birth and trade, so there was a good chance that a deserter who returned home might be caught.

This is an example from *Aris's Birmingham Gazette* for 15th March 1756: "Owen who enlisted the 26th February and deserted the 10th of March. He was born in the parish of St Chad in Shrewsbury, is 16 years of age, 5ft 6 inches and a quarter high, dark brown hair, very much marked with the Small-Pox, a dimple on his chin, by trade a leather dresser; had on a dark brown wig, a dark brown frize coat, greasy leather breeches and a black velvet stock with ribbons to it, round his neck".

Army Deserters from HM Service Vol 1 1853-1858 by Yvonne Fitzmaurice was privately published in 1988 but is now out of print. It contains over 800 entries compiled from material held at TNA and from police records. It gives comprehensive details of the men, all of whom at this period came from the British Isles. See also TNA research guide *Courts Martial and Desertion in the British Army 17th-20th centuries*, downloaded from www.nationalarchives.gov.uk.

DEXTER He was a dyer. It is also a heraldic term referring to everything placed on the right hand side of the shield, as opposed to Sinister, the left hand side. The terms right and left in heraldry are as seen from the back by the person holding the shield and are therefore the reverse of the normal positions.

DIAGEO ARCHIVE The Diageo Archive www.diageo.com is based in Clackmannanshire and holds records relating to more than 1,500 brands past and present, including household names such as Johnnie Walker Scotch Whisky and Smirnoff Vodka. The collections span 402 years of history with brands such as Bushmills Irish Whiskey having heritage and history dating back to 1608.
The archive's holdings tell the histories of these brands, as well as the group's distillery sites, companies and people. Holdings include C18th ledgers, sales records, letter books, minute books, old company magazines and early advertising material.

DICKENS, CHARLES The Charles Dickens Museum is based at 48 Doughty Street, Camden, which is the only one of the author's former homes that still exists. The house is where Dickens wrote Oliver Twist, Nicholas Nickleby and other works. The museum has a collection of 100,000 items relating to the author, including manuscripts and rare editions. More information including details of the museum's exhibitions and holdings can be found on its website at www.dickensmuseum.com.

DICTIONARY OF NATIONAL BIOGRAPHY (DNB) See Biographical Dictionaries.

DIOCESAN RECORD OFFICES (DROs) The diocese is the district over which a bishop has authority. Records were deposited in what was called the Diocesan Registry. These have formed the basis of the DROs, which are open to the public. Many CROs are also DROs.

DIRECTORIES See also Kelly's Directories and Poll Books. Directories of large towns date from the middle of the C18th and County Directories from the early C19th. They serve both as gazetteers and as a guide to people living in the area, although the early ones contain only the names of persons of substance or people in business. Some of the more prolific producers of such directories were Kelly's (q.v.), Pigot's and White's.

The most comprehensive sets of directories are held at the British Library (q.v.) and the Guildhall Library (q.v.); the SOG (q.v.) has a good collection as do many local libraries.

A useful reference book is Shaw, Gareth & Tipper, Alison *British Directories: a bibliography and guide to directories published in England and Wales (1850-1950) and Scotland (1773-1950)* (Leicester University Press 1988). This volume is divided into three parts: Introduction and Evolutionary Trends in Directory Publication; Bibliography and its Organisation; Library Holdings by Location and Index by place and subject. For the earlier period see Norton, Jane *Guide to National & Provincial Directories of England and Wales (excluding London) before 1856* (reprinted The Royal Historical Society 1984). For London see Atkins, P J *The Directories of London 1677-1977* (Marcell 1980). The SOG has published a *Catalogue of Directories and Poll Books in the Possession of the SOG* (1994).

When using directories make allowances for the lapse of time between the collection of information and the publication year. Thus, a Directory of 1845 may well be recording addresses of residents a year or more earlier. Also valuable as a source of information are trade and professional directories and telephone directories.

Historical Directories www.historicaldirectories.org gives access to a wides range of digitised UK directories.

DIRECTORIES OF MEMBERS' INTERESTS See Surname Interests' Lists.

DISCOVER MY PAST ENGLAND AND DISCOVER MY PAST SCOTLAND MAGAZINES *Discover My Past England* and *Discover My Past Scotland* are two monthly magazines that are made available online and for which the subscriptions payable are modest. *Discover My Past Scotland* is said by its publishers to be "the only available genealogical and historical reference resource dedicated to Scottish ancestry". Further details of both magazines can be obtained from www.discovermypast.co.uk.

DISSENTER See Nonconformist.

DISTRESSED PROTESTANTS IN IRELAND 1642, COLLECTION FOR On the eve of Civil War in England, rebellion broke out in Ireland. Thousands of Protestant "planters" were massacred, whilst thousands more fled to the fortified garrison towns or to England. There was an urgent need to provide emergency relief to the refugees and to pay for a small force to suppress the rebellion. Parliament and King passed an emergency act to receive loans and gifts for these purposes.

Those charged with collecting the gifts were also responsible for recording and submitting the names and contributions of the donors. Many of the returns survive and are in TNA. The returns are split between two separate classes: Lay Subsidies (E179), and State Papers Domestic (SP28).

Details of the places covered by the returns are given in Gibson, Jeremy & Dell, Alan *The Protestation Returns 1641-42 and other contemporary listings* (FFHS 2004).

DISTRICT PROBATE REGISTRY See also Wills. Where probate was taken out at a district registry, that registry retained the original will and made a copy before forwarding a further copy to the Principal Registry in London. District Probate Registries generally covered the counties in which they lay and there were none in the Home Counties. See Stuart Raymond's *The Wills of our Ancestors* (Pen & Sword 2013).

DISTRICT REGISTRAR See Civil Registration.

DIVORCE See TNA research guides *Looking for Records of a Divorce* and *Divorces: further research*, which can be downloaded from www.national archives.gov.uk.

Under early Catholic church law there was no such thing as divorce; although Henry VIII had annulled two of his marriages there was no general "divorce" in the sense that these marriages were dissolved by a formalised legal process. By the end of the C16th and despite the introduction of a reformed Protestant religion, England was the only European Protestant country to have no divorce law as such. There was no legal change in the law of divorce before 1857. In practice, however, various ways were found to separate partners in unsatisfactory marriages. The remedies were available through the church courts, common law courts and through Parliament but only to those who could afford them. Within the poorer classes of society separations were straight forward desertions. The sale of wives was one means used by poor people to obtain a separation. The practice is described in Thomas Hardy's *The Mayor of Casterbridge*. *Wives for Sale* by Samuel Pyeatt Menefee (Blackwell 1981) makes fascinating reading. Between 1670 and 1857 divorce was obtainable only by an Act of Parliament and private divorce acts are mainly to be found at the House of Lords Record Office (q.v.).

The 1857 Divorce Act finally became law as the Matrimonial Causes Act on 1 January 1858 and made divorce possible by use of the civil courts. The 1857 Act did not apply to Ireland (Scotland had a fairly liberal divorce law by the C17th). Before searching for divorce records in TNA it is necessary to have an idea of when the separation took place, or whether an appeal was made from a local court in questions of separation before 1858.

After 1858, all divorce cases in England and Wales were heard before the new court for divorce and after 1873 by the Probate, Divorce and Admiralty Division of the Supreme Court of Judicature. Files from these courts can be found in TNA Principal Probate Registry Divorce Files, 1858 to 1938. Some files are restricted under a 75 year closure but the indexes are subject to the normal 30 year rule. Permission to see closed files may be sought from the Principal Registry of the Family Division, at the address given below. Records from 1938 to the present (England and Wales only) and copies of records from 1858, are at the Principal Registry of the Family Division, First Avenue House, 42-49 High Holborn, London WC1V 6NP. Indexes to divorce records from 1858-1903 are available via FindmyPast (q.v.) www.findmypast.co.uk.

See Stone, L *Road to Divorce: England 1530-1987* (Oxford University Press 1990) and Stone, L *Broken Lives, separation and divorce in England 1660-1857* (Oxford University Press 1993).

Divorces were extremely newsworthy items. It is therefore worth consulting The Times Archive www.thetimes.co.uk/tto/archive; which covers 1785-1985. Other newspapers (q.v.) also carried reports.

DNA Many family historians are now making use of DNA testing. There are various commercial companies who administer the tests and allow for comparison of results with other testees. The most prominent company in this field is Family Tree DNA www.familytreedna.com.

There are an increasing number of books on the subject. Pomery, Chris *DNA and Family History: how genetic testing can advance your genealogical research* (TNA 2004). Pomery, Chris *Family History in the Genes: trace your DNA and grow your family tree* (TNA 2007). Savin, Alan *DNA for Family Historians* (FFHS 2000). Fitzpatrick, Colleen & Yeiser, Andrew *DNA & Genealogy* (Rice Book Press 2005). Redmonds, George, King Turi & Hey, David *Surnames, DNA and Family History* (Oxford University Publications 2011). Kennett, Debbie *DNA and Social Networking: a guide to genealogy in the twenty-first century* (The History Press 2011).

Information about the Scottish DNA project can be found at www.scottishdna.net. For the Ulster Heritage DNA Project go to http://ulsterheritagedna.ulsterheritage.com/.

Further background information can be found on the website of the International Society of Genetic Genealogy www.isogg.org.

DOCKYARD EMPLOYEES Until 1832, dockyards and naval establishments were the responsibility of the Navy Board but victualling yards and depots were controlled by the Victualling Board, itself answerable to the Navy Board. Jetties used specifically for loading gunpowder and ordnance stores onto warships, known as gun wharves, were the responsibility of the Ordnance Board. After 1832, all yards and establishments in each port, excepting gunwharves, were amalgamated under a single authority.

The records at TNA relate to employees prior to 1832, both tradesmen and salaried staff. After that date, there are pension records of salaried staff, but yard musters survive only to the mid C19th. A TNA research guide entitled *Royal Naval Dockyard Staff* gives further information and can be downloaded from www.nationalarchives.gov.uk. The website of Dockland Ancestors Ltd. www.parishregister.com contains useful information and includes indexes and access to original documents.

DOCTORS See Medical Profession.

DOCTORS' COMMONS The College of Doctors of Civil Law in London. Five courts were held in the buildings, Prerogative Court of Canterbury (q.v), Court of Arches (q.v), Court of Faculties, Consistory Court and High Court of Admiralty. Business included divorce suits, marriage licences, probate matters, ecclesiastical law, Prize claims, etc.. It ceased to function after 1858.

Cox, Jane *Hatred Pursued Beyond The Grave* (HMSO 1993), draws on material from the records of Doctors' Commons and comprises stories taken from the unique and invaluable records of these courts. TNA research guides entitled *Wills and Probate: further research* and *Wills 1384-1858* give further information and can be downloaded from www.nationalarchives.gov.uk.

DR BARNARDO'S See Children's Societies.

DR WILLIAMS' LIBRARY See also Congregationalists and Non-conformists. The births of many London nonconformists were registered at this theological library. The register was intended for nonconformists living within twelve miles of central London but there are entries for those living further afield. The registers are now in TNA (Class RG5) and cover the period 1742 to 1837. They are available via www.bmdregisters.co.uk.

Amongst the special collections at the library are many histories of individual congregations, both printed and duplicated. These relate to both the different nonconformist denominations, and to nonconformity generally on a geographical basis. There is also a card index comprising brief biographies of all Congregationalist ministers and yearbooks of a variety of denominations, some of which contain obituary notices of ministers.

The website of the Dr Williams' Trust and Library at www.dwlib.co.uk includes sections on: Dr Williams' Library; Dr Williams' Trust; Congregational Library. The website also contains information on Dr Williams' Centre for Dissenting Studies, which was set up in 2004 in collaboration with the School of English and Drama at Queen Mary, University of London.

DOCUMENTS The preservation of any document of value, either historical or sentimental, is of paramount importance. See Baynes-Cope, A D *Caring for Books and Documents* (British Museum Publications 1989). Suppliers of preservation materials are numerous but include: www.conservation-resources.co.uk and www.my-history.co.uk.

DOMESDAY BOOK This was a Survey of England drawn up by order of William the Conqueror in 1086. The Survey's function is disputed by historians. It records manors but not necessarily all of them. Before its rebinding in the 1980s into a more-manageable five volumes, the Survey consisted of two volumes. The first covered Essex, Norfolk and Suffolk, whilst the other comprised the remainder of England, with the exception of Cumberland, Durham, Northumberland and northern Westmorland. London and Winchester are also omitted. The two volumes of the Survey acquired the name *Exchequer Domesday* (Great and Little) as there was no appeal against the judgements based on the evidence in their pages. Northumberland and Durham were subsequently covered by what is known as the Boldon Book. There are many related documents such as The Exeter Domesday, held at Exeter Cathedral Library.

The original Survey is in TNA. See TNA Research Guide *Domesday Book*, which can be downloaded from www.nationalarchives.gov.uk. Colour facsimiles of Domesday entries can be downloaded from Discovery, TNA catalogue.

See Williams, Ann & Martin, G H (ed.) *Domesday Book: a complete translation* (Viking/Allen Lane 2003).

There is an online searchable list of landowners from Domesday at www.domesdaybook.co.uk, which also contains a wealth of background information. The website Open Domesday www.domesdaymap.co.uk is searchable by modern place name and describes itself as "the first free online copy of Domesday Book".

DOMESTIC SERVANTS Many women, particularly young, unmarried women and a not inconsiderable number of men, worked as domestic servants. In the C19th about 25% of working women were in service. Pamela Horn has written several books on this subject including: *The Rise and Fall of the Victorian*

Servant (Sutton 1995); *Life Below Stairs in the Twentieth Century* (Sutton 2003); *Flunkeys and Scullions: life below stairs in Georgian England* (History Press Ltd. 2004) *My Ancestor was in Service* (SOG 2009) and *Life Below Stairs: the real lives of servants, the Edwardian era to 1939* (Amberley Publishing 2004). See also May, Trevor *The Victorian Domestic Servant* (Shire Publications 2007).

DORMANT FUNDS See Funds in Chancery.

DOWER A widow's share for life of one-third of her deceased husband's land, not just his "estate" which would include cash, investments and the like. The word is also used for dowry, property brought by woman to husband at marriage, a practice quite common amongst the middle and upper classes until the C20th.

DRAPER The Drapers' Company of the City of London is an ancient City of London Livery Company, which was ranked third in precedence of the Great Twelve. Originally founded to promote the craft of cloth-finishing, the Company now exists to promote charitable work and fellowship amongst its members. A detailed history of the company and its collections is at www.thedrapers.co.uk.

DUBLIN UNIVERSITY Sadleir, Thomas U & Burtchaell, George D *Alumni Dublinenses* (3 vols. Thom 1935) now available on CD (Archive CD Books Ireland 2005) is a register of the students, graduates, professors and provosts of Trinity College in the University of Dublin 1593-1860. It mentions individuals who were at Trinity between 1593 and 1846 and is especially valuable for its list of over 32,000 names from 1593 through to 1637, a period for which no registers survive. Students at Trinity College Dublin came not just from Ireland but also Britain and the British Empire. Included in the register is the individual's full name, date of entering the college, age of entering, father's name and address, the degree they received and their graduation date.

Alumni Dublinenses can be searched online using the subscription websites FindmyPast Ireland www.findmypast.ie and Family Relatives www.family relatives.com. The blog of FindmyPast Ireland http://blog.findmypast.ie/2011/06/interesting-finds-in-the-alumni-dublinenses also carries an interesting article about these records.

DUGDALE SOCIETY The Dugdale Society www.shakespeare.org.uk, named after Warwickshire's distinguished antiquary Sir William Dugdale, was founded in association with the Shakespeare Birthplace Trust in 1920. Its objectives were to publish original documents relating to the history of the County of Warwick, to foster interest in historical records and their preservation and to generally encouraging the study of local history. The Society publishes volumes of original documents relating to the County of Warwick.

DYERS The Worshipful Company of Dyers is a City of London Livery Company which received its first Charter in 1471 and stands thirteenth in the order of precedence. It has a website www.dyerscompany.co.uk, which includes a detailed history of the company and its collections

E

E179 DATABASE www.nationalarchives.gov.uk/E179 This database enables the records in Class E179 at TNA to be searched. These are records of taxation of both the clergy and laity. Unfortunately there are no name indexes but the documents are searchable by place.

EAST ANGLIAN FILM ARCHIVE This is part of the University of East Anglia and comprises about 12,000 hours of film and a further 30,000 hours of video, relating to the eastern counties of England. See www.eafa.org.uk/browse.aspx.

EAST EUROPEAN FAMILY HISTORY SOCIETIES The Federation of East European Family History Societies (FEEFHS) http://feefhs.org/index.html is an umbrella organization that promotes family research in eastern and central Europe. It is primarily for North Americans attempting to link back to Eastern Europe but will also assist others with Eastern European ancestry.

EAST INDIA COMPANY See Asia, Pacific and Africa Collections.

EASTER DUES See Church Rates.

EASTMAN'S ONLINE GENEALOGY NEWSLETTER This is a long-standing family history newsletter which is made available free of charge via a website. Whilst the articles are primarily of a technological nature and often have a strong US bias, it is nevertheless worth a look. To read the newsletter, go to http://blog.eogn.com.

ECCLESIASTICAL CENSUS In 1851, the Home Office took a census of all places of worship in the country. It contains a record of every church or meeting house of all denominations and gives its location, its date of erection or foundation, the name of the minister and the size of its congregation on 30th March 1851. The Ecclesiastical Census of 1851 is held in TNA and is arranged by county or by Poor Law Unions. Sometimes, the information is incomplete because of the ignorance or reluctance of the informant. These records have been published for some counties. As an example of these records, see Tiller, Kate (ed.) *Church and Chapel in Oxfordshire incorporating the Religious Census of Oxfordshire 1851* (Oxfordshire Record Society 1987).

ECCLESIASTICAL COURTS See also Prerogative Courts of Canterbury and York and Wills. Ecclesiastical, or church, Courts were held by Archdeacons, Bishops (Consistory Courts and Commissary Courts) and Archbishops (PCC & PCY), as well as by priests and others who held title to a "peculiar" (q.v.). They dealt not only with ecclesiastical matters but also with many aspects of C15th-C19th life. Thus attendance at and especially behaviour in, church or churchyard, the conduct of parish officers, matters connected with the church fabric, furniture and its maintenance, parish dues and tithes were considered as well as all aspects of betrothal, marriage and wills. Offences against ethical codes such as libel, slander, defamation of character, bastardy, bigamy, incest, quarrels and much else were dealt with.

Penalties were awarded, usually private penance after lesser or public penance after more serious offences, though these could be accompanied by fines or castigation. Act Books record the proceedings, often verbatim. The accused was presented to the Court for his fault, usually by church-wardens or constables, witnesses made depositions (q.v.) on oath and a judgement was pronounced by the ecclesiastic presiding. An accused could purge his fault by producing witnesses who would make depositions on oath as to his innocence, but failure to appear before the court generally involved excommunication. Cases could last for many sessions, the account being correspondingly scattered throughout the text.

Their records, especially from Elizabethan times, are of immense value to the local, and family, historian but suffer from two disadvantages. Where they have survived, they can be very extensive, when diligent and time-consuming searches may be necessary and for the amateur, there is the problem of ancient handwriting. When an item of interest is found, the detail is usually far-reaching. The availability of this class of record varies but the whereabouts of surviving Act Books is generally known by the Diocesan Archivist. A few of these records have been transcribed, either in full or in extract form. For example Christie, Peter *Of Churche-Reves and of Testaments* (1994) Devon Family History Society, is a transcription of the Archdeaconry Court of Barnstaple records for 1570-1579.

The most comprehensive introduction is Tarver, Anne *Church Court records: an introduction for family and local historians* (Phillimore 1995). See also Chapman, Colin *Sin, Sex and probate: ecclesiastical courts, officials and records* (Lochin 1997).

ECCLESIASTICAL LAWYER See Proctor.

ECCLESIASTICLAL VISITATIONS See Visitations.

EDE AND RAVENSCROFT This firm of tailors and robe makers was founded in 1689, and are upheld as tailors of distinction. They have received commissions from the royalty to the judiciary. In particular, they enjoy the privilege of being the tailors and robe makers of choice for twelve coronations. A company history detailing some three hundred years of ceremonial dress and forensic wig-making and their royal warrants can be found at www.edeandravenscroft.co.uk/company-history.

EDUCATION See also Alumni, Cambridge University, Dublin University and Oxford University. Many famous schools are of very old foundation; many were set up originally to educate poor boys but developed into Public Schools (which, for the benefit of overseas readers unfamiliar with the quirks of our educational system, are now private schools). The old school registers of most of the Public Schools have been published, together with other records; they can contain valuable genealogical information such as names of parents and even details of what subsequently happened to the pupils, e.g. marriage, careers and distinctions obtained. Details will be found in Jacob, P M *Registers of the Universities, Colleges and Schools of Great Britain and Ireland* (University of London 1964) available online at http://onlinelibrary.wiley. Some relevant records have been published on CD by Anguline Research Archives http://anguline. co.uk.

Other useful reference books are Walesby, P J *Histories of Old Schools; a revised list for England and Wales* (Department of Education, University of Newcastle upon Tyne 1966) and Thomas, D H *Reformatory and Industrial Schools (certified by the Home Office 1854-1933)* (Newcastle upon Tyne Polytechnic Products Ltd. 1986).

The SOG Library has a fine collection of printed records and copies are likely to be found in libraries in the locality of the individual school. See *School, University and College Registers and Histories in the Library of the SOG* (SOG 1988). TNA has several relevant guides see www.nationalarchives.gov,uk.

The National Society (formerly The National Society for Promoting the Education of the Poor in the Principles of the Established Church) www. churchofengland.org/education/national-society.aspx was formed in 1811 to provide education for poor children. The Church of England Record Centre, 15 Galleywall Road, London SE16 3PB holds indexed registers of teachers trained at their Central School 1812-51, plus admission registers for training colleges at St. Marks, Chelsea 1841-48 and Battersea 1844-48. Unindexed copies of *National Society Monthly Paper* 1849-74 and *School Guardian* 1875-1930s can be consulted by appointment. They contain many references to teachers. A guide to records can be downloaded from www.lambethpalacelibrary.org/content/education. Burgess, Henry *Enterprise in Education: the story of the work of the established church in the education of the people prior to 1870* (National Society and S.P.C.K 1958) is a history of the National Society.

The British and Foreign Schools Society was formed in 1808 www.bfss. org.uk. The archives of the British and Foreign School Society are at Old School House, 1 Hillingdon Hill, Uxbridge, Middlesex UB10 0AA, close to Brunel University's Uxbridge Campus. Access to the archives is by appointment only.

Records include: Material concerning founder Joseph Lancaster's work . Minute books from 1808. Financial papers and papers on the Lancastrian Institution and the BFSS prior to 1833. C19th foreign correspondence. Correspondence regarding individual British schools, reports and school inspection returns from the C19th. Printed sources, including The Annual Reports of the BFSS 1814 to date. *The Educational Record* 1848-1929.

Industrial schools were set up from 1857 for children in need of care and protection and magistrates sent children there to learn a trade. There were numerous private schools, which charged a small weekly fee, some run by women teachers being known as Dame Schools. Ragged Schools were begun in 1818 by John Pounds who provided a school which was free for the poorest children. In 1844 Lord Shaftesbury helped to organise an official union of these schools. By 1869 there were about 200 establishments. The Ragged School Museum website is at www.raggedschoolmuseum.org.uk. The Sunday School movement was popularised by Robert Raikes who founded a school in Gloucester in 1780, although it is thought the first Sunday School was in Yorkshire in 1763. He charged pupils a penny each week. The Sunday School Union was founded in 1803 to improve such schools in the London area.

Forster's Education Act of 1870 divided England into areas and arranged that schools should be set up where provision was insufficient. Legislation in 1876 laid down the principle that all children should receive elementary education but it was not until 1880 that school attendance became compulsory up to the age of 10.

Numerous aspects of schooling are dealt with in Chapman, Colin R *The Growth of British Education and its Records* (Lochin 1991). See also Berry, George *Discovering Schools* (Shire Publications 1970), which gives much background information. Stephens, W B & Unwin, R W *Materials for the Local and Regional Study of Schooling 1700-1900* (British Records Association 1987) is also useful. For an account of the life of school children, see Horn, Pamela *The Victorian and Edwardian Schoolchild* (Alan Sutton 1969).

Records of the old School Boards and of the schools themselves, are often to be found in CROs. School Log Books may record punishments, school outings and local epidemics. They were first required to be kept in all schools supported by the state in 1862. The Family and Community Historical Research Society have a School Log Books project, see www.fachrs.com/slb/slb.htm. Admissions' Registers may include family information: parents' names and occupation, date of birth, as well as details of future and previous schools of entrants and leavers. The registers for 843 London schools 1840-1911 are available on www.ancestry.com, the original records are at London Metropolitan Archives (q.v.). See www.scan.org.uk/knowledgebase/topics/schooladmissions.htm for information about Scottish Admissions' Registers.

The Museum of the History of Education is located at The University of Leeds, Parkinson Court, Leeds LS2 9JT http://library.leeds.ac.uk/special-collections. The Institute of Education Library, University of London, 11-13 Ridgmount Street, London WC1E 7AH www.ioe.ac.uk, specialises in the history of education.

The government's Edubase2 lists all current educational establishments in England and Wales www.education.gov.uk/edubase/home.xhtml.

ELECTORAL REGISTERS See also Poll Books. The 1832 Reform Act greatly widened the franchise and enacted that the names of all those qualified to vote be published annually. The resultant electoral registers continue to this day but the printed lists for the C19th and earlier C20th survive much more rarely than might be expected. A useful county by county guide to the whereabouts of these records is Gibson, Jeremy *Electoral Registers 1832-1948 and Burgess Rolls* (FHP 2008).

EMIGRATION See also Aliens, American Immigrants, Australian Immigrants, Canadian Immigrants, Children's Societies, New Zealand Immigrants, Passenger Lists, Passports, Population and Scottish Emigrants. The chief sources of information are in the numerous classes of Colonial Office records and in a few classes of Home Office, Board of Trade and Treasury records at TNA. You are strongly advised to obtain a copy of the relevant research guides from their website www.nationalarchives.gov.uk, *Emigration* and *Looking for Records of an Emigrant* and to consult Kershaw, Roger *Migration Records: a guide for family historians* (TNA 2009). An increasing number of records relating to emigrants are becoming available on subscription websites such as Ancestry (q.v.) and FindmyPast (q.v.).

The amount of material is vast, so much so that chances of tracing particular persons is related to the amount of information one has to start from. If one knows only a name, the chances of success are remote. Note that it is far easier to locate a person from within the country to which they emigrated as shipping lists usually survive at the port of arrival and not that of departure. The numerous family history societies in the respective countries may also be able to advise on what records are available. What follows is far from being comprehensive but seeks to point researchers in the right direction.

Parish Assisted Emigrants, where emigrants were given financial help by their parish, took place between 1834 and 1890. Destinations included U.S.A. (mid1830s only), Canada, Australia, Tasmania, New Zealand and South Africa. Records may be found in CROs and in the destination country. New South Wales, Australia, Assisted Immigrant Passenger Lists, 1828-1896 are available on www.ancestry.co.uk.

Prior to 1834, British subjects could not go to India without the consent of the East India Company. Application records and permission to trade are with the Asia, Pacific and Africa Collections (q.v.). Lists of East India Company employees up to 1794 are also there.

Not strictly within the category of either emigration or immigration there is a class of records covering a thirty year period which could be overlooked. They are the Records of Cross-Channel Passengers at Boulogne, 1822-58. These include: 26 Oct 1833-26 Aug 1834 & 29 July-11 Oct 1836. Passenger

Disembarkation Lists: Arrivals from England 21 Sep 1825-14 Apl 1858 with a short gap; 4 July 1836-12 Oct 1836. Alphabetical Indexes to Passenger Lists 1826-1844. Registers of Visas 26 Dec 1822-31 Dec 1855 with 2 gaps 6 Jan 1836-19 Oct 1843 and 28 Nov 1845-31 Jan 1846. Ferry Movements: January 1853-September 1855. Records are at the Municipal Archives in Boulogne www.ville-boulogne-sur-mer.fr/les-archives-municipales. The records give a cross-section of persons travelling to and from Britain; whilst British passengers are in the majority there is an astonishing range of nationalities from all over the world.

Books that will give you background information are Guillet, Eric *The Great Migration: the Atlantic crossing by sailing ships since 1777* (University of Toronto Press 1937). Carrothers, W A *Emigration from the British Isles* (P S King 1929). Coleman, T *Passage to America* (Hutchinson 1972).

The Maritime Record Centre, Merseyside Maritime Museum, Albert Dock, Pierhead, Liverpool L3 1DN www.liverpoolmuseums.org.uk/maritime/archive has a section devoted to emigration through Liverpool, which is very useful for social, local and family history.

Increasing numbers of journals of emigrant voyages are appearing online; see for example http://freepages.history.rootsweb.ancestry.com/~biblechristian/other/robins_paul_voyage.html.

There are a number of regional studies of emigration. See, for example, the North Devon Exodus Database http://genuki.cs.ncl.ac.uk/DEV/DevonMisc/NDevonExodusListing.html. The Cornish Global Migration Project has a website www.murdochhouse.org/CGMP/how.html For Cornish emigrants to New Zealand see http://www.cornwall-opc.org/Resc/emigration_nz.php or to Australia http://www.cornwall-opc.org/Resc/emigration_australia.php.

ENCLOSURE AWARDS Between 1760 and 1860, a process of enclosing and re-allotting open fields, common meadows, commons, heaths, greens and forests took place as part of what has come to be called the Agrarian Revolution. Following the enactment of a Parliamentary Enclosure Act, Commissioners were appointed to work out the details. Their decisions are generally accompanied by maps showing the land involved with details of owners and tenants. These are invaluable to family historians as they pinpoint where particular lands were. They are usually found in CROs. In some areas, Enclosure Maps and Awards are found where Tithe Maps (q.v.) are not. The term "Inclosure" is often found to describe these awards. A TNA research guide *Enclosure Awards* is relevant and can be downloaded from www.nationalarchives.gov.uk. A comprehensive list of enclosure awards is provided by Tate, W E *A Domesday of English Enclosure Acts and Awards* (University of Reading Library 1978).

ENFEOFFMENT See Feoffment.

ENGLISH HERITAGE See also Britain from Above. English Heritage www.english-heritage.org.uk is responsible for the preservation of many monuments and historic sites. Their Archives (see the "Professionals" tab on their website) have over 12 million items. Its collections include the National Buildings Record and it has taken on the remit of the Royal Commission on the Historical Monuments of England (RCHME). This Commission was established to publish an inventory of ancient and historical monuments on a parish by parish basis. This resulted in a large collection of research notes, plans and photographs. They are also responsible for the national record of archaeological sites that was previously the responsibility of the Ordnance Survey. This inventory has been added to and is available on the PastScape website www.pastscape.org.uk. They also maintain the Images of England website www.imagesofengland.org.uk, which contains photographs and descriptions of England's listed buildings recorded at the turn of the C21st. "Portico" is the part of their website (accessed via the "Professional" and "Archives and Collections" tabs) that gives historical details on the properties that they own. This is being built up into a valuable online library and catalogue. It includes links to sources about particular properties, held both by English Heritage and elsewhere.

ENTAIL See also Fee Simple. An entail or fee tail was a way in which an estate could be kept within a family. The heir would usually not be able to sell the land or bequeath it to anyone but a relative. There were also normally prohibited from bequeathing it to an illegitimate child. Tail Male or Tail Female restricted the descent of the property to the specified gender. The person entitled to the entail was a Tenant in Tail. He or she could "Bar the Entail". This would convert the Fee Tail or entail into a Fee Simple. This was done by a Common Recovery. A fictional court action was brought against the Tenant in Tail who failed to defend the action and then 'lost' the case, giving the life tenant the ability to make a new settlement. The Fines and Recoveries Act 1833 abolished the Common Recovery and a Disentailing Assurance was substituted to effect the barring of the entail.

EPIDEMICS See Causes of Death.

EPIPHANY The name for 6 January (twelfth night). The term was applied to that Court of Quarter Sessions held sometime between 25 December and 25 March.

ESTATE See also Manorial Records. Many of our ancestors were tenants on the estates of the landed gentry or nobility. Farm Bailiffs kept careful records of payments made to workers and details of the work assigned to them. Usually these vast collections of records, which include a great many property deeds as well as rentals, surveys and maps, have been deposited at a CRO but not necessarily in the record office of the county you would expect, for many landowners held estates in various parts of the country and preferred to have their muniments kept intact as a collection. They may be tracked down via the Manorial Documents Register (see Manorial Documents) or the National Register of Archives (see Archives). Some of the larger estates have their own archives offices; the principal ones are listed in Richardson, John *The Local Historian's Encyclopaedia* (3rd ed. Historical Publications Ltd. 2003).

It is a good idea to find out the names of the landowners in the parish in which your ancestor lived. An easy way to do this is to study the monuments in the church. You can then enquire, at the CRO as to the estate records of those families. Many estate records are voluminous; some collections are calendared, others unsorted. Estate maps may have the names of occupiers of farms marked on them. With the maps there may be schedules describing the nature of the farming done and the acreage.

The National Register of Archives and the Manorial Documents Register are maintained by TNA. Relevant guides that can be downloaded from their website are *Looking for Records of Landed Estates* and *Using the Manorial Documents Register and how to find Manorial Lordships*.

Much land was held by the Crown, most Crown Estate papers are either at TNA www.nationalarchives.gov.uk (particularly land in the Duchy of Lancaster), or at the Crown Estate Commissioners, 13-15 Carlton House Terrace, London SW1Y 5ES. Papers relating to the Duchy of Cornwall are at the Estate Office, 10 Buckingham Gate, London SW1E 6LA. www.duchyofcornwall.org.

ESTATE DUTY OFFICE REGISTERS See Death Duties.

EXAMINATION See Illegitimacy and Settlement.

EXCISE See also Customs and Excise. A tax on goods for the home market, or tax paid for a licence to carry out a trade or sport.

EXCOMMUNICATION Exclusion from communion and from privileges and public prayers of the church. Lists of those excommunicated for serious misdemeanours are to be found amongst ecclesiastical records in DROs. They can sometimes also be identified in records from the parish chest (q.v.).

EXTRA-PAROCHIAL DISTRICT See also Liberty. This was an area outside the jurisdiction of any parish. Neither poor rates nor church rates were paid, though tithes, in theory, went to the Crown. A resident could choose to worship in the adjoining parish of his choice. In 1894, extra-parochial areas were abolished and either added to an existing parish or given parish status.

E-ZINE The journal of the FFHS (q.v.) for more than twenty years was *Family History News & Digest*. This was published twice a year in April and September, until it was discontinued on the grounds of cost. Its last edition was published in

September 2006. The replacement publication is the Federation's "e-zine", which is published electronically six times per year. This is a free of charge publication, which is delivered to each subscriber's computer by e-mail. Further details can be obtained from www.ffhs.org.uk.

F

FACTORY ACTS See also Legislation. From 1802 onwards, numerous Acts of Parliament were passed relating to conditions in factories and mines, many of them concerned with the exploitation of children. Measures included: workhouse apprentice children were not to work more than twelve hours a day and were to receive elementary education. In the cotton mills, no children under nine were to be employed and others were not to work more than twelve hours a day. Workers were not to be paid in kind nor by tokens exchangeable only in employers' shops, this was known as the Truck Act. No women or boys under the age of ten were to be employed underground in the mines. In the textile mills, women were not to work more than twelve hours a day and children were to spend half their day at school. Children were to be employed from 6am to 6pm with one and a half hours for meals.

Such Acts gradually improved the situation with regard to children but it must be realised that there was little enforcement of some of the earlier Acts.

FACULTY OFFICE See also Marriage Licences. In simple terms, this is the Archbishop of Canterbury's Legal Department. Historical records issued by this office survive from 1660 and are now housed in Lambeth Palace Library www.lambethpalacelibrary.org. Lambeth Palace Library has separate online catalogues, which are freely accessible via the URL above, for its collections of printed books, archives and manuscripts. The Holdings of the Church of England Record Centre can also be checked via that website.

FAIRGROUNDS See Circus Families.

FAMILY AND COMMUNITY HISTORY RESEARCH SOCIETY, THE (FACHRS) www.fachrs.com/index.html. This developed out of the, now defunct, Open University course DA301, Family and Community History. The society under-takes research projects, produces a journal and arranges meetings and conferences.

FAMILY BIBLES It was a custom to record family events, such as births, marriages and deaths, in a family Bible, which would then be handed down from generation to generation. Some Bibles have pages especially designed for this purpose. Be sure to check the front and back of a Bible, as well as between the Old and New Testaments, for family information.

FAMILY HISTORIES See also Writing up. Make sure that your family history has not already been written or at least the history of some branch of your family. Apart from the obvious internet search engine trawls, which may reveal the results of more recent work, there are lists of earlier printed pedigrees in the following books: George Marshall's *Genealogists' Guide* (Lightning Source UK Ltd 2012). It records all known family histories up to 1903, when it was first published. Major J. B. Whitmore's *A Genealogical Guide* (The Harleian Society 1953), brought the listings up to that date. The task was continued by Geoffrey Barrow in *The Genealogists' Guide: an index to printed British pedigrees and family histories 1953 to 1975* (Research Publishing Company 1977). In the back of T R Thomson's *A Catalogue of British Family Histories* (3rd ed. Research Publishing Company 1980) is an Appendix of family histories printed between 1975 and 1980, the only compilation of its kind for this period. More up to date and comprehensive listings are provided in the county volumes of Stuart Raymond's genealogical bibliographies series (see Bibliographies).

Those interested in Scottish families should consult Stuart, Margaret *Scottish Family History* (reprinted Genealogical Publishing 2009) and Ferguson, Joan P S *Scottish Family Histories Held in Scottish Libraries* (The Scottish Central Library revised ed. 1986). The latter details some 3,200 entries held in libraries, including separately printed histories and articles in periodicals.

For Irish families consult de Breffny, Baron Brian *A Bibliography of Irish Family History and Genealogy* (1973). Also Edward MacLysaght's *Irish Families* (1957); *More Irish Families* (revised ed. 1982); *A Guide To Irish Surnames* (Helicon 1964) and *Bibliography of Irish Family History* (Irish Academic Press 1982). This bibliography was previously published in MacLysaght's *The Surnames of Ireland* (revised and corrected Irish Academic Press 1978) but was omitted from the 4th edition (1980) and subsequently published separately.

FAMILY HISTORY CENTRE See Church of Jesus Christ of Latter Day Saints (LDS).

FAMILY HISTORY PARTNERSHIP LLP A firm set up in 2007 with the objective of publishing and selling a range of books of relevance to the genealogist and family historian. Their website is at www.thefamilyhistorypartnership.co.uk.

FAMILY HISTORY SOCIETIES There has been a phenomenal growth of these societies since 1970, not only in the size of their membership but in their number. Virtually every county has its society; in some areas there are several for example, in Yorkshire and the London area. A list of societies is available on the FFHS website at www.ffhs.org.uk, although it should be borne in mind that not all societies are members of the Federation. Links to the websites of family history societies are also available from www.ffhs.org.uk. A society's website will give an indication of its activities. These are likely to include some or all of the following: the holding of regular meetings, often in more than one centre. The production of a journal, which is issued free of charge to members. The organisation of courses at all levels on "Tracing Your Ancestors" and allied topics. The giving of help and advice on matters relating to the tracing of ancestry. The running of projects that are designed to help to preserve records and cut down the time it takes to consult them. Typical of such projects are the production of baptism, marriage and burial transcriptions and indexes, the recording of memorial (or monumental) inscriptions and indexing other valuable source materials. The end products of such projects are likely to be published on paper, microfilm, CD or DVD or to become part of a society database. The running of a research centre where visitors can carry out their own research with assistance from experienced volunteers.

FAMILY RELATIVES www.familyrelatives.com. A subscription website, providing access to UK records including births, marriages and deaths, parish registers, military records and trade directories.

FAMILY SEARCH See also Church of Jesus Christ of Latter-day Saints (LDS). This remarkable free index, with world-wide coverage, has been produced by the LDS. The coverage is particularly strong for the U.S.A., Canada and England. The index contains many millions of baptisms and marriages but fewer burials, as well as links to census and other records. It incorporates the International Genealogical Index (IGI), although this may also be searched separately. The IGI indexes transcripts of registers that have been microfilmed. These microfilms can be viewed at LDS branch libraries. Where the index contains some entries from a particular register this does not necessarily indicate coverage of the whole period of the register. Access is via the website www.familysearch.org. It is much more than just an index as it also contains many digitised images, which are un-indexed.

The site also contains research hints and educational videos. The Family Search Wiki has a huge amount of background information. There are an increasing number of links to the images of documents themselves. It should be remembered that indexed items vary in accuracy and should be checked with original records where possible. Items taken from LDS transcriptions of registers are more reliable than "patron submitted entries", which have been added to the database from individual research and vary greatly in accuracy. A frequent error in this is the use of "born" for what is actually a baptism. The extensive catalogue of the LDS library is also available via this site.

FAMILY TREE MAKER (FTM) See Computer Software.

FANMAKER The Worshipful Company of Fan Makers is a London Livery Company that received its Charter in 1709. A history of the Company and a great deal of other information about it can be found on its website at www.fanmakers.com.

FARM SURVEY The National Farm Survey was conducted in 1941 to ensure optimum productivity during the Second World War. A series of documents was produced for each farm with details of owner, occupier, acreage, crops, livestock, equipment and the condition of the farm. It is available at TNA class MAF32, with related maps in MAF73. See its research guide, *National Farm Surveys of England and Wales 1940-1943* www.nationalarchives.gov.uk. A more detailed guide is included in Beech, G and Mitchell, R *Maps for Family and Local History* (National Archives 2004).

FARMING See Rural Life.

FARRIER A farrier was a shoeing smith of horses. The Worshipful Company of Farriers is a London Livery Company that can trace its history back to 1356. Its modern role is to promote the welfare of horses. A history of the Company and other information about it can be found on its website www.wcf.org.uk.

FEDERATION OF FAMILY HISTORY SOCIETIES (FFHS) This umbrella organisation was formed in 1974, as a result of the growing interest in the study of family history. Since its inception, its membership has grown to include family history societies throughout the world. These include national, regional, special interest and one-name groups. The FFHS's principal aims are to co-ordinate and assist the work of societies or other bodies interested in family history, genealogy and heraldry and to foster mutual co-operation and regional projects in these subjects. It was granted charitable status in 1982.

Membership of the FFHS is open to any Society or body specialising in family history or an associated discipline. It is run by an Executive Council, which includes representatives of member societies. Their website www.ffhs.org.uk includes a list of member societies and their contact details, as well as detailed information about the FFHS's activities in the fields of guidance for member societies, education and national projects. Details of the FFHS's "e-zine" (q.v.), published electronically six times per year, can also be found on the website.

The FFHS makes representations to official bodies on matters affecting the study of family history and related topics, and provides an authentic, audible and respected voice for the many thousands of individual family historians belonging to local and national societies.

The FFHS also maintain a list of recommended speakers on family history and related topics.

FEE ENTAIL OR FEE TAIL See Entail.

FEE SIMPLE See also Entail. This was an estate of freehold land that was not the subject of feudal service of a servile nature to the lord. After 1540, freehold land could be given away by will. Fee Simple was therefore described as an estate by inheritance which was free of conditions. This was unlike copyhold land, where the land could not pass to an heir unless it was surrendered back to the Lord of the Manor first, with a fine paid before the heir was admitted as the new tenant and his name added to the Manor Court Roll. It was also unlike entailed land, which limited descent to defined classes of descendant. Fee Simple land was inheritable by heirs regardless of whether they were male or female, descendants or collaterals.

FEET OF FINES The term "fine", or "final concord", refers to an agreement relating to land transactions kept by the King's Justices. The fine was written three times on a skin, then divided by wavy cuts or "indentures", there being an upper, a lower and a transverse section, the latter being termed the foot. The Foot was filed among the rolls of the Court of Common Pleas and the collection of these in TNA is familiarly known as "Feet of Fines", or in Latin pedes finium. The word "cyrographum", with variant spellings, was written where the cuts were to be made. Thus identification could be assured by matching not only the jagged cuts but the cut letters of the word, making forgery almost impossible. The procedure was only abolished in 1834.

With the exception of the Commonwealth period, the earlier records were written in Latin, but those for several counties have been translated and printed. They cover several centuries from the early C12th. Only an approximate date of the actual agreement can be surmised, as the date shown on the writ summoning the parties to appear is that on which it was due to be returned to court. In many cases, there is also an additional record known as a deed to lead the uses of a fine, which explains the purpose.

These are useful early references to those of our ancestors who owned land. The Fine was regarded as putting an end to any controversy as to ownership. A research guide that can be downloaded from the website of TNA www.nationalarchives.gov.uk is *Land Conveyances: feet of fines, 1182-1833.* For a full list of published fines, see Kissock, Jonathan 'Medieval Feet of Fines: a study of their uses with a catalogue of published sources' in *Local Historian* 24 1994 pp.66-82. Some of the older texts listed here can be read at www.archive.org.

FELL MONGER A dealer in hides, especially sheepskins. Sometimes written as one word.

FELTMAKERS See also Hatting Industry. The Worshipful Company of Feltmakers is a London Livery Company that received its Charter in 1604. A history of the Company and lots of other information about it can be found on its website at www.feltmakers.co.uk.

FEOFFEE A person to whom freehold estate in land is conveyed by a feoffment, a particular mode of conveying freehold estate, or a trustee invested with such estate.

FEOFFMENT A transfer of land or property, giving the new holder the right to sell it or bequeath it to heirs.

FERONER See Ironmonger.

FIFTEENTHS AND TENTHS See Subsidies.

FILM ARCHIVE See also East Anglian Film Archive. *Family Tree Magazine*'s website www.family-tree.co.uk hosts an "Archive Weekly Calendar" section, which gives access to archive film clips.

FINDMYPAST (FMP) FindmyPast www.findmypast.co.uk is one of the main sources of online records for UK research. A certain amount of information is available free of charge but detailed transcriptions and images of the documents are accessed via a subscription package or as pay-per-view items. Apart from the usual birth, marriage and death indexes and census returns there are an increasing number of counties who have submitted parish register entries. In addition, there is access to the British Newspaper library collection 1710-1950, criminal records, passenger lists, military records and much more.

FINE See Feet of Fines.

FIRE BRIGADES See also Insurance and Maps. Fire fighting became the responsibility of the parish as long ago as 1575, when orders were given that buckets, hooks and ladders were to be kept in churches. The equipment was however not always kept up to standard.

Fire insurance companies came into being in the late 1600s and many formed their own fire brigades to protect the properties of their clients, mainly in towns and cities. During the C18th and first half of the C19th fire fighting was principally organised and run by the various fire insurance companies. It was common practice for them to place a metal plate called a fire-mark on the wall of the insured property. This not only proved to the fire brigade that the premium was paid, it also acted as an advertising plaque. These plaques quite often had the insurance policy number beneath the company emblem. Folklore has it that if the first fire fighters to reach the scene were rivals of the company who insured the property at risk they were most likely to leave the fire burning.

The second half of the C19th saw the formation of the municipal brigades who took over responsibility from the parish and insurance companies.

The Auxiliary Fire Service manned by volunteers was formed in 1937 in readiness for war; they worked with the full-time brigades. In 1941 the National Fire Service (incorporating the Auxiliary Fire Service) replaced the independent fire authorities. This service continued until 1948 when the brigades were restored to local authorities and no further changes took place until the local government reorganisation in 1974 when many of the smaller brigades were merged with the larger ones.

The website www.fireservice.co.uk has a history section. The London Fire Brigade Museum www.london-fire.gov.uk/research.asp may be able to help you trace London members of the National Fire Service.

There are very few references to early fires and extant records vary greatly, as do those of the insurance brigades and companies. You are advised to check with your local CRO. Occasionally parish records contain details of fire equipment purchased and may even name the person in charge. Fires may be reported in newspapers but small fires were a regular occurrence so not always newsworthy.

Industrial fire brigades were run by many large firms and railway companies; any surviving records should be with their archive material at the CRO or local Reference Library. By law there must be a fire brigade present anywhere that planes or helicopters are flown. A minimum standard of operation is laid down. Large airports have their own fire stations and fire services which are independent of the local authority fire brigade.

See Ewen, Shane *Fighting Fires: creating the British fire service, 1800-1978* (Palgrave MacMillan 2009). Kirk, John L *History of Fire Fighting* (revised ed. Castle Museum, York 1960). Blackstone, G V *A History of the British Fire Service* (Routledge and Kegan Paul 1957) and Wallington, Neil *Images of Fire: 100 years of fire-fighting* (David & Charles, 1989).

FIRST AVENUE HOUSE See Wills.

FIRST FLEET See Australia, Crime and Criminals, Emigration and Transportation.

FIRST FRUITS The profits of an ecclesiastical benefice, for the first year after a vacancy, which, since the Reformation, had to be paid to the crown. Records from the mid C16th to the early C19th are held at TNA. They include details of payments made or defaulted, arrears, usually the names of the incumbents, vacant livings and valuation data.

FISHERMEN See also Merchant Seamen, as many fishermen also spent time in the merchant service. A useful book is Wilcox, Martin *Fishing and Fishermen: a guide for family historians* (Pen & Sword 2012).

FLATMAN See Boatman.

FLEET See Marriage.

FLETCHER See also Bowyer. A maker of, or a dealer in, bows and arrows. The Worshipful Company of Fletchers is a London Livery Company that can trace its history back to 1371. A history of the Company and lots of other information, including a history of the craft of fletching or arrow-making and of archery in general, can be found on its website at www.fletchers.org.uk.

FLORENCE NIGHTINGALE MUSEUM See also Nursing. The Florence Nightingale Museum www.florence-nightingale.co.uk is based at St Thomas' Hospital, London. This gives details of the life and achievements of Florence Nightingale, the opportunity to search the museum's collections and archives and the chance to view selected holdings. A downloadable file enables the researcher to explore some highlights from the museum's collection of oral history, whilst the Crimean War is looked at in some detail.

FOGGER This term has variously been used to mean a pedlar, a headman at a farm, a groom, a manservant, a middleman in the nail and chain trade, low-class lawyer (usually referred to as a pettifogger) or a farm labourer.

FOLIO A folio is two pages so folio numbers occur on every other page. The two sides are distinguished by recto (right side) and verso (reverse side) or obverse and reverse. Folio numbers are often referred to in connection with census returns/transcriptions and manuscripts.

FORENAMES There is a considerable amount of information about Christian names in Vol. I of Steel, Don *The National Index of Parish Registers* (SOG 1992). It also contains speculations on the influences on the choice of names and the practice of using a surname as a Christian name. There is a list of the Latin forms of Christian names found in early parish registers; a similar list is given in Richardson, John *The Local Historian's Encyclopaedia* (3rd ed. Historical Publications Ltd. 2003). See Withycombe, E G *The Oxford Dictionary of English Christian Names*, reissued Godfrey Cave Associates 1988 as *The Concise Dictionary of English Christian Names*. A study of Christian names appears in Weekly, Ernest *Jack and Jill* (John Murray 1939). See also Jarvis, S M *Discovering Christian Names* (Shire Publications 1989). More detailed are Hanks, Patrick & Hodges, Flavia *A Dictionary of First Names* (Guild Publishing by arrangement with OUP 1990) and Pickering, David *The Penguin Dictionary of First Names* (Penguin 2004).

Many Christian names were Latinised by adding "us" (masculine) or "a" (feminine) to the English form. A list of Latin Christian Names is given in Richardson, John *The Local Historian's Encyclopedia* (3rd ed. Historical Publications Ltd. 2003). Some of the more common ones that you are likely to encounter are Jacobus - James, Carolus - Charles, Gulielmus - William and Gualterus - Walter.

In some records, the census for example, diminutives, also called "pet names", are sometimes used. Vol. I of the *National Index of Parish Registers* has a very long list of these. Most are very obvious, since they suggest the formal name; exceptions are "Polly" which stands for Mary, often Mary Ann; "Peggy" for Margaret; "Molly" for Mary; "Jack" for John; "Harry" for "Henry"; "Sally" for Sarah and "Kitty" for Catherine.

See also http://onomastics.co.uk/.

FOUNDER See also Gunfounding. A worker in brass and brass alloy or tin plate. The Worshipful Company of Founders is a London Livery Company whose history is recorded in the following books: Williams, William Meade *Annals of the Worshipful Company of Founders, of the City of London* (privately published 1867). Hadley, Guy *Citizens and founders: a history of the Worshipful Company of Founders, London, 1365 - 1975* (Phillimore 1976). Hibbert, William N *History of the Worshipful Company of Founders, of the City of London* (privately published 1925).

FOUNDLING See also Children's Societies and Lying-in Hospitals. An abandoned baby. Baptisms and burials of foundlings are commonly found in parish registers, especially in London and particularly in the C16th and C17th. Foundlings were often named after the church where they were baptised, the vicar who baptised them, the person on whose property they were found or the geographical location where they were found; examples are Church, Field and Meadow.

The Thomas Coram Foundation for Children www.coram.org.uk was established by Royal Charter in 1739 and created a hospital for foundlings. The LMA holds records of the Thomas Coram Foundation's Foundling Hospital. A research guide *The Foundling Hospital* can be downloaded from their website www.cityoflondon.gov.uk. The Foundling Museum tells the story of the Foundling Hospital see www.foundlingmuseum.org.uk.

FRANCE See also Huguenots and Prisoners of War. There are many local family history societies in France, most are grouped in regional associations covering several departements. Many of these societies also belong to the French Federation of Genealogical Societies www.genefede.org, from whom the addresses of specific local societies may be obtained.
There are a large number of French entries in the Geneanet database http://en.geneanet.org.

FRANCIS FRITH See Photographs.

FRASER, HOUSE OF See House of Fraser.

FREE AND VOLUNTARY PRESENT TO KING CHARLES II See also E179 database. This was a voluntary levy collected in 1661. The lengthy lists of subscribers, by county or borough, are in series E179 at TNA and make a useful comparison with the Hearth Tax (q.v.) which was first levied the following year. The returns for some counties have been transcribed and printed.

FREEHOLD Freehold land is owned outright and will include the property and the land upon which it stands. Unlike leasehold land (q.v.) there is no time limit to the ownership. Freehold tenure was not subject to the custom of the manor and after death could pass to anyone named to inherit in the will of the deceased.

FREEMASONS Freemasons were originally what their name implied, freemen masons; members enjoying all the privileges of the guild of masons. These craftsmen travelled about to take part in building and were recognised and accorded hospitality after exchanging certain signs known only to members of the guild. A master was at the head of the central organisation and wardens presided over branches of it.

Modern freemasonry has no connection with a specific trade. The movement became worldwide and at times was regarded as a subversive movement but not in England. In 1799, an Act for the suppression of secret and unlawful societies was passed but freemasons' lodges were specifically exempted from its provisions.

From 1799, annual returns of members of freemasons' lodges had to be made to the Quarter Sessions (q.v.). Names and descriptions of the members are given and these records are housed in CROs. For further information, see Newton, Joseph Fort *The Builders: a story and study of freemasonry* (Forgotten Books 2008).

Freemasonry in England and Wales dates back to 1713. Thousands of documents have been created by Masonic lodges during this time. Local historians may have come across some of them in CROs or in specialist repositories. Now the Library and Museum of Freemasonry www.freemasonry.london.museum, Freemasons' Hall, 60 Great Queen Street, London WC2B 5AZ, has completed a survey of freemasonry records and their whereabouts. This covers the records of individual lodges and chapters that have been deposited by their creating body and the surviving lists of members of Masonic lodges submitted to the county magistrates and held among Quarter Sessions (q.v.) records under the 1799 Unlawful Societies Act. Whilst this is unlikely to be a complete record, as it has relied on catalogued material available on the internet, it should provide a useful starting point. The survey is available on their website. The Library and Museum has also completed a larger survey of the records held by all Masonic lodges and chapters in England and Wales. There are nearly 12,000 lodges and chapters, each holding records of their activities and membership. Some go back to the C18th; most hold records going back to the foundation of the lodge in question. Returns were received from two-thirds of the lodges and chapters surveyed. The survey details what records are held, their covering dates, their location and physical condition. Information was given on nearly 120,000 individual record items relating to freemasonry. Contact The Library and Museum of Freemasonry for further details of the whereabouts of records.

Lewis, Pat *My Ancestor was a Freemason* (SOG 1999) deals with the history of freemasonry and how to find the records of freemason ancestors. It also includes chapters on freemasonry publications, women freemasons, lodges, prisoners of war and record repositories.

FREEMEN See also Apprentices. In Corporations, a freeman is a person who has inherited or acquired by adoption, purchase or apprenticeship the rights of a citizen. By the Municipal Corporations Reform Act (1835) persons who had hitherto enjoyed the right of voting were placed on the Freemen's Roll, whilst those who obtained privileges by virtue of the act were placed on a separate list called the Burgess Roll. The title is now an honorary one.

Records of Freemen of the City of London are in the Guildhall Library (q.v.). Those of other towns will generally be found in the local CRO. A useful leaflet entitled *City Freedom Archives* can be downloaded from the website of the Corporation of London Records Office www.cityoflondon.gov.uk. See also *My Ancestors Were Freemen of the City of London* by Vivienne E Aldous (SOG 1999).

Some records of Freemen have been published, such as, Bennett, J H E *The Rolls of the Freemen of the City of Chester 1392-1805* (Lancashire and Cheshire Record Society vols 51 & 55 1906 and 1908). L'Estrange, John, Rye, Walter (ed.) *The Freemen of Norwich 1317-1603* (British Library, Historical Print Editions 2011) and *The Freemen of York 1272-1759* (Ulan Press 2012). Some are available on CD from S & N Genealogical Supplies (q.v.) www.genealogy supplies.com/. Oxfordshire Family History Society sell an *Index to the Freemen of the City of Oxford 1663-1997*, which details not only the Freemen but also their sponsors. This is available from www.ofhs.org.uk/mfiche.html.

FRIENDLY SOCIETIES See https://mutuals.fsa.gov.uk. The Friendly Societies Research Group www.open.ac.uk/socialsciences/friendly-societies-research-group, which operates under the auspices of The Open University, publishes a newsletter that can be downloaded from their webpages.

Other recommended websites are: Friendly Societies' online reference www.friendlysocieties.co.uk, which has an interesting history section. History of Nottingham Friendly Society www.nottinghamfriendly.co.uk, which details the history of what might be considered a typical Friendly Society and Sons of Temperance Friendly Society www.sonsoftemperance.abelgratis.co.uk, which has a page specifically devoted to family history research.

Some records of Friendly Societies have been published. An example is Morley, Shaun *Oxfordshire Friendly Societies 1750-1918* (Oxfordshire Record Society 2001).

FROBISHER An armour polisher. Sometimes spelled "Furbisher".

FRUITERER The Worshipful Company of Fruiterers is a London Livery Company that can trace its history back to 1463. A history of the Company and lots of other information, including details of the Company's current activities, can be found on its website at www.fruiterers.org.uk.

FUNDS IN CHANCERY These are also known as "Dormant Funds" or "Funds in Court", and are monies from the estates of deceased persons that have remained unclaimed for a minimum of fifteen years.

A research guide entitled *Funds in Court* can be downloaded from the website of TNA and gives much additional detail www.nationalarchives.gov.uk. Current dormant funds can be viewed at www.bonavacantia.gov.uk.

FUNERAL A ceremony at which a dead person is buried or cremated. Funeral Directors' Records can be a very useful source of information if you know when and where an ancestor died but cannot locate the burial place. Though not bound by law to preserve them, funeral directors may keep records for some considerable time (upwards of thirty years). Usually filed by date, not alphabetically, they include a number of personal details in addition to the funeral arrangements and will note if a burial is to be in a family grave. Some records may have found their way into CROs.

FURBISHER See Frobisher.

FURNITURE HISTORY SOCIETY This Society was founded in 1964 to study furniture of all periods, places and kinds, to increase knowledge and appreciation of it and to assist in the preservation of furniture and its records. It publishes an annual journal and a quarterly newsletter in addition to holding meetings and lectures. See www.furniturehistorysociety.org.

Baird, Geoffrey & Gilbert, Christopher (ed.) *A Dictionary of English Furniture Makers 1660-1840* (The Furniture History Society & W. S. Maney & Son Ltd 1986). The Dictionary covers the same period as Sir Ambrose Heal's *London Furniture Makers from the Restoration to the Victorian Era 1660-1840* (2nd ed. Batsford 1988) and includes both London and Provincial makers and their apprentices along with other details. Shire Publications have published *Discovering Furniture 1500 to 1720* and *Discovering Furniture 1720 to 1830*, both by John Bly 1971.

There are Furniture Museums located at the Victoria and Albert Museum and the Geffrye Museum, Kingsland Road, Shoreditch, London E2 8EA.

FWK See also Stockinger. A common abbreviation for a Framework Knitter in the textile industry.

G

GAFFMAN A bailiff. It is considered by some that this is the origin of the slang word "Gaffer" much used in the building trade. There is, however, a possibility that "Gaffer" was derived from "grandfather" or "godfather".

GAME DUTY Between 1784 and 1807, manorial gamekeepers and all who killed or sold game had to register with the Clerk of the Peace and pay a fee. These registers are useful since they also record the name of the lord of the manor and at what date he "deputed" the power of killing game to his keeper. The registers are likely to be found with the Quarter Sessions records (q.v.) in CROs. Lists of applications for licences might also be found in contemporary local newspapers.

GANGER A beggar or hawker.

GANNER See Ganger.

GAOL DELIVERY These are registers of prisoners delivered from gaol to stand trial at the Quarter Sessions (q.v). Older Gaol Delivery Rolls can be seen at TNA. See also Jewell, Helen M *English Local Administration in the Middle Ages* (David & Charles 1972) pp.144-145. More recent records, because of their close association with Quarter Sessions, are more likely to be found in CROs. A good example is provided by the Caledars of Prisoners at devon Quarter Sessions http://genuki.cs.ncl.ac.uk/DEV/CourtRecords/Prisoners.html.

GARTH An enclosed court, yard or garden.

GARTHMAN A yardman or herdsman. Also used for one who owned or worked in a fish-garth, which was a dam or a river for catching fish.

GAVELKIND A form of land tenure by which land was divided equally between the male heirs on the death of the father. Daughters would inherit equally if there were no male heirs. This was particularly associated with the county of Kent, where the system was not abolished until 1925 but is also found in Wales and Ireland.

GAYMERS The archives of Gaymers, cider and related beverage manufacturers, containing documents dating from1877-1992 are held at Norfolk Record Office. The content includes: photographs of staff, products and premises, price lists, promotional and marketing material, file cards, partnership deeds and lots of correspondence. Advertisements and promotional sketches, mainly from the 1920s and 1930s. Further details of the collection can be obtained by searching the online catalogue of the Norfolk Record Office www.archives.norfolk.gov.uk.

GAZETTEERS See also Vision of Britain through Time. These are directories of place names and often include very small hamlets e.g. *Bartholomew's Gazetteer of Britain* (Harper Collins 1977). These can be vital for locating obscure places.

GENEALOGICAL PUBLISHING CO INC An American company www. genealogical.com specialising in genealogy and family history books and CDs, some of which relate to the UK.

GENEALOGICAL SOCIETY OF UTAH (GSU) See Church of Jesus Christ of Latter-Day Saints.

GENEALOGIST, THE A subscription website for British genealogical records www.thegenealogist.co.uk. It's contents include census records, birth, marriage and death records and parish register entries, with a good selection of non-conformist records. There are also miscellaneous records such as trade directories and a good range of army records.

GENEALOGISTS' MAGAZINE See SOG.

GRO/GENERAL REGISTRATION See Civil Registration.

GENERATION Generally reckoned to last about thirty years.

GENEVA An online calendar of GENealogical EVents and Activities http://geneva.weald.org.uk, which is run on behalf of GENUKI (q.v.) and the Federation of Federation History Societies (q.v.). It comprises a listing of forthcoming family history events in the UK and Ireland.

GENFAIR An online retailer www.genfair.co.uk, bringing together numerous family history suppliers, whose books, CDs and other products can be purchased. It is also possible to purchase memberships to many family history societies through Genfair.

GENMAP Software produced by Archer Software (q.v.) www.archersoftware. co.uk. The program is designed for UK distribution mapping and makes it easy to compile maps of historical or genealogical data relating to the British Isles, such as surname distributions. It includes a large gazetteer of British places, with many synonyms based on historical usage, and features several styles of mapping.

GENTLEMAN'S MAGAZINE This monthly publication was begun in 1731 and continued until 1908. It is of particular value to genealogists because, until 1861, it published notices of births, marriages and deaths. These were not, as one would have supposed, only of the upper classes; middle class people and those in trade or commerce were often included. There are also obituary notices. Bound volumes are to be found in many libraries. There is a complete run in the Library of the SOG (q.v.). Online images are available, see http://onlinebooks. library.upenn.edu/webbin/serial?id=gentlemans. See also Internet Library of Early Journals (q.v.).

Specialist indexes of particular interest to family historians have been produced. Farrar, R H *An Index to the Obituary and Biographical Notes in the Gentleman's Magazine 1731 to 1780* (Index Society 1891).

There are also Farrar, R H *Index to Births and Marriages in the Gentleman's Magazine 1731 to 1862* (2 vols.1886) and Fry, E A *An Index to Marriages in the Gentleman's Magazine 1731 to 1768* (Pollard 1922).

If you do find an entry of interest it is worth checking further in newspapers of the time, since the Magazine used them as its source and often considerably pruned the original entry.

The Gentleman's Magazine also contains endless reports of unusual events involving people.

GENTRY Records of landed families other than those with titles, what one might call the "lesser nobility", can be found in Walford's *County Families* and also in *Burke's Commoners*, which later became *Burke's Landed Gentry*. These are available in most reference libraries. Some editions are available online. For a wide range of sources for tracing gentlemen see Raymond, Stuart *My Ancestor was a Gentleman* (SOG 2012).

GENUKI An online reference library of genealogical information of particular relevance to the UK and Ireland www.genuki.org.uk. It is a non-commercial service, maintained by a charitable trust and a group of volunteers. The pages include information of national interest as well as sections for each county and parish. The amount of detail is much greater for some counties than others. GENUKI includes a list of genealogy-related discussion groups for those with research interests in areas of the British Isles www.genuki.org.uk/indexes/ MailingLists.html. These may be mailing lists, web forums or newsgroups. There is also an index to surname interest lists at www.genuki.org.uk/indexes/ SurnamesLists.html.

GERMANY The Anglo-German Family History Society www.agfhs.org.uk was formed in 1987. They maintain large databases and physical files, which are only available to members. A quarterly magazine, *Mitteilungsblatt*, is issued to members. The society has published several books of interest to those with German ancestors. These include Roy Bernard's *Tracing German-speaking Ancestors* (2004). See also Towey, Peter *An Introduction to Tracing your German Ancestors* (3rd revised ed. Anglo German Family History Society 2013). Friedericks, Dr Heinz F *How To Find My German Ancestors and Relatives* (Degener & Co. 1969) is a booklet written in English, primarily for those living in the U.S.A. with German ancestry. It contains much useful information and lists of addresses for source material in Germany. Thode, Ernest *German-English Genealogical Dictionary* (Genealogical Publishing Co. 1992). For the researcher who has little or no knowledge of German; it covers thousands of German genealogical terms. With a standard German-English dictionary the user should be able to make a translation of any document. See also Powell, Kimberly *Researching German Ancestors* http://genealogy.about. com/od/germany/a/ basics.htm.

GIBRALTAR Civil registration, similar to that of the British Isles, commenced thus: Births 1848 (compulsory 1887); Marriages 1862 (compulsory 1902); Deaths 1859 (compulsory 1869), although some civil authorities registered Anglican Marriages from 1845. Jews and Roman Catholics tended to register their events with their own religious authorities though there are many instances of Catholics marrying in Protestant churches or the register office. Full censuses of the population were carried out by British Authorities in 1834, 1868/71, 1878/81, 1891, 1901, 1911, 1921 and 1931 though some, notably 1901, are incomplete. The records are in the care of the government archivist, 6 Convent Place, where they can be viewed by appointment. Gibraltar Archives can be contacted at archives@gibraltar.gov.gi. Gibraltar Genealogy www.gibraltar genealogy.com is a non-profit making site dedicated to and serving the online Gibraltar family researcher. Some records relating to Gibraltar have been filmed and are available at LDS libraries.

GILBERT'S ACT An Act of 1782 that reformed the Poor Law. The able-bodied poor were excluded from workhouses and given out relief. The Act encouraged parishes to join together in Unions and provide a single workhouse for a group of parishes.

GIPSIES See Gypsies.

GIRDLER A belt maker. The Worshipful Company of Girdlers is one of the 108 Livery Companies of the City of London. The Company, which was involved with the making of girdles and belts, received its Letters Patent from Edward III in 1327. The Company's website at www.girdlers.co.uk gives an introduction to the Company, its history, organisation and principal activities and relationships. See Baker Dr T C *The Girdlers' Company: a second history* (The Worshipful Company of Girdlers 1957). The Company's archives are held in the Manuscripts' Section of the Guildhall Library (q.v.) www.cityoflondon.gov.uk.

GIVEN NAMES See Forenames.

GLASGOW UNIVERSITY See also University Libraries. Addison, W I *The Matriculation Albums of the University of Glasgow from 1728 to 1858* (J Maclehose 1913). Is available on microfilm from the university, in the Library of the SOG (q.v.) www.sog.org.uk or can be downloaded free of charge from www.archive.org.

GLASS See also Glaziers. The Broadfield House Glass Museum www.glassmuseum.org.uk at Barnett Lane, Kingswinford, West Midlands, DY6 9QA, is situated in what was the heart of the glass making industry. See Dodsworth, Roger *Glass and Glassmaking* (Shire Publications 2003). Or for more specialised reading Guttery D R *From Broad-Glass to Cut Crystal: a history of the Stourbridge glass industry* (Leonard Hill 1956) or Haden, H J *Notes on the Stourbridge Glass Trade* (reprinted by Dudley Library 1969) and Grazebrook, H S *Collections for a Genealogy of the Noble Families of Henzey, Tyttery and Tyzack* J T Ford 1877). Consider the possibility that glass making families were Huguenots (q.v.).

GLASS-SELLERS The Worshipful Company of Glass-Sellers and Looking-Glass Makers of London received its Charter in 1664. It was initially founded to regulate the glass-selling and pot-making industries within the City of London. The company's website at www.glass-sellers.co.uk contains information about the company, its history and traditions and about glass as a product. A history of the Company is Ramsey, William *The Worshipful Company of Glass-Sellers of London* (reprinted Ulan Press 2012).

GLAZIERS, PAINTERS OF GLASS, STAINED GLASS See also Mediaeval Stained Glass. The Worshipful Company of Glaziers and Painters of Glass, which is often known as the Glaziers' Company, is one of the historic Livery Companies of the City of London. Although its origins can be traced back to the C14th, the Glaziers Company is currently active in promoting its craft through encouraging new artists and helping to restore and preserve the rich heritage of decorative glass in our churches and public buildings. Further information about the Company and its history can be found on its website at www.worship fulglaziers.com.

A history of the company is Ashdown C H *The Worshipful Company of Glaziers* (reprinted HardPress Ltd. 2013). Osborne, June *Stained Glass in England* (Frederick Muller 1981 contains many individual names of artists and firms throughout the UK, with contact addresses.

The British Society of Master Glass Painters (BSMGP) www.bsmgp.org.uk is devoted to the art and craft of stained glass. Its website gives further details of the society, its history and its extensive reference library on stained glass.

GLEBE TERRIERS See also Visitations. These are to be found in DROs. They are records of Church lands and property; "glebe" being the land held by the church on behalf of the incumbent. The terrier usually consists of a written survey or inventory of the church and its graveyard, the vicarage or rectory and associated land. The terrier would be drawn up during a visitation. Often the location of the glebe is given in relation to non church-owned property, with the tenants or owners named, which enables us to locate the sites of the latter. Sometimes the names of the occupiers of the church lands or property are given, which enables the researcher to pinpoint where an ancestor lived. Many glebe terriers have been published by County Record Societies. see, for example, Potts, Richard (ed.) *A Calendar of Cornish Glebe Terriers 1673-1735* (Devon and Cornwall Record Society 1974)

GLOSSARY OF TERMS FROM PROBATE INVENTORIES See Inventories.

GOAD MAPS See Maps.

GOLDSMITH See Heal, Sir Ambrose *The London Goldsmiths, 1200 to 1800* (Cambridge University Press 1936), which includes a list of nearly 8,000 goldsmiths, jewellers, bankers and pawnbrokers in London up to the year 1800. Similarly, Culme, John *The Directory of Gold and Silversmiths, Jewellers and Allied Traders, 1838-1914* (2 vols. Antique Collectors Club 1987).

The term "hallmark" means the mark originally applied at Goldsmiths' Hall, the headquarters of the London Livery Company. See Herbert, W *History of the Twelve Great Livery Companies Vol. 2* (David and Charles 1968).

GOONS See One Name Studies.

GOSSIP A sponsor in baptism, a god-father or a god-mother. The term can also mean a close friend, especially a female friend present at childbirth.

GOUGH MAP, THE See Maps.

GRAVESTONES See Monumental Inscriptions.

GRAVEYARDS See Cemeteries and Monumental Inscriptions.

GREAT WESTERN RAILWAY See also Railways. Also known as the GWR and nicknamed God's Wonderful Railway. One of the "big four" railway companies, whose name survived the amalgamation of smaller companies in 1922. It was formed in 1835 and primarily provided routes in and from the south west of England and Wales. See the Great Western Archive website at www.great western.org.uk. There are relevant records at TNA. See the research guide *Railways* at www.nationalarchives.gov.uk.

GREAVE A bailiff or foreman.

GREECE Lica Hariclea Catsakis has written the following to aid those conducting family history research in Greece. *Family History Research in Greece* (2nd ed. Bywater 2005) and *Greek Gazetteer, Volumes 1 and 2* (Bywater 2000) and *Your Family History* (2004). The latter is a manual with instructions for family history research written in Greek for those who live in Greece.

GREENWICH HOSPITAL This was a home for navy pensioners. The Greenwich Hospital archive comprises details of apprenticeships of pensioners' children, registers of the admission and discharge of pensioners 1704 to 1869, estate records, details of bequests to the Hospital and the minutes of meetings of the Greenwich Hospital commissioners, advisory panels, advisory board and the Royal Hospital School Board of Governors. These records are held at TNA (q.v.). See www.grenhosp.org.uk.

GREENWICH HOSPITAL SCHOOLS These were established to provide education for children of disabled or deceased officers of the Royal Navy. TNA (q.v.) has a collection of registers which include school admission papers 1728-1870. The latter are arranged under first letters of surnames and give details of the birth or baptism of the children, marriage of parents and father's naval service. The registers themselves include registers of claims and candidates, admissions and the apprenticing of children. Most are indexed. The Reference is ADM73. A second group which is similar in nature covers the period 1883-1922, reference ADM163. See Turner H D T *Royal Hospital School Greenwich* (Phillimore 1980).

GREGORIAN CALENDAR See Calendar.

GRETNA GREEN MARRIAGES A term widely used for Irregular Border Marriages which were performed at a number of places close to the English/Scottish border. Marriages recorded at Gretna since 1st January 1855 are in duplicate, one held by the local Registrar, the other by the Registrar General for Scotland at New Register House, Edinburgh EH1 3YT. The Old Parochial Registers of Gretna relating to the years 1730 to 1855, are also in the care of the Registrar General. These were kept by the ministers and/or session clerks of the parish church. The Lang Collection of Gretna Green Marriages Records 1794-1895, named after the father and son who acted as priests, is held at The Institute of Heraldic and Genealogical Studies, Canterbury (q.v.). The records are available at www.ancestry.co.uk. See *Irregular Border Marriages* by Meliora G. Smith (using the pseudonym Claverhouse) (Moray Press 1934).

GRIEVE See Greave.

GROAT This was small silver coin of the value of four old pence, in England. It was mediaeval in origin and about an inch in diameter. There were sixty groats to the pound. It was not minted in England after 1856.

GROCER The Worshipful Company of Grocers, commonly known as the Grocers' Company, is one of the twelve great Livery Companies of the City of London and ranks second in order of precedence. The Company still plays a significant role in the city's constitutional and ceremonial life, including the election of the Lord Mayor and Sheriffs. The Company's website at www.grocershall.co.uk contains a brief history, whilst a more detailed history can be downloaded via that website without charge. A history of the Company is Heath, Baron *Some Account of the Grocers' Company* (1869).

GUARDIAN AND OBSERVER ARCHIVES See also Newspapers. The Guardian News and Media Archive preserves and makes accessible records relating to the histories of the Guardian and Observer newspapers. As well as corporate records of the papers, records of staff and contributors and illustrative collections, the archive contains photographic material dating from the early 1920s to the present day. Further information about the archive collections can be found at www.guardian.co.uk/gnm-archive. It can also be followed on Twitter at @GuardianArchive.

GUARDIANS See Curation and Ward (2).

GUARDIANS, BOARDS OF See also Workhouses. Under the New Poor Law of 1834 individuals of some social standing in the area were elected to Boards in "Unions" of parishes. These Guardians of the Poor were to arrange and oversee the relief of the poor through the provision of "indoor" relief in workhouses and "outdoor" relief for those remaining in their own homes. The idea was to encourage people to work hard rather than to rely on official charity, with the result that most of the inmates were the sick, infirm and chronic unemployed who could not do so. These Unions rapidly became an important unit in local government and the Boards of Guardians were asked during the next seventy years to take on other functions. Their records therefore contain not only matters relating to the relief of the poor, including the settlement laws but also civil registration, rating, local health including vaccination, sanitation, school attendance, and infant life protection.

Their voluminous records are housed in CROs and TNA. They can provide an immense amount of detail on individuals. For example, they might contain a workhouse inmate's date and place of birth, entry to the institution, religion, addresses of relatives or friends, medical examination, diet, punishment, state of clothing and many other features.

A good example of these records are the annual reports of the Oxford City Guardians of the Poor, which have been scanned, indexed and published on

CD by Oxfordshire FHS www.ofhs.org.uk. The records are described and located in the Gibson Guide series by Jeremy Gibson and others *Poor Law Union Records* (4 vols. FFHS 1993-7).

GUERNSEY See Channel Islands.

GUIDE BOOKS A great many guide books were published for various areas from the mid C19th. These provide interesting background material about the areas in which our ancestors lived and worked and may provide clues to changes of occupation.

Many guide books have recently been reproduced on CD. An example is *A Book of North Wales* by Sabine Baring-Gould, which was originally published in 1903. This has been reproduced by Archive CD Books www.familyhistory research.org. Similar examples of reproduced guide books will be found by scouring the websites of other CD producers.

GUILDHALL LIBRARY A large collection of genealogical material, printed books, manuscripts and maps can be found in this public library. It concentrates on the City of London and the London area, and holds many Livery Company (q.v.) archives. It also holds extensive collections of printed books for the whole country, including large collections of poll books, directories, and family history society publications. Note that many archives formerly held, including registers and transcripts of the Anglican and diplomatic communities abroad, have now been transferred to the London Metropolitan Archives. Harvey, Richard *A Guide to Genealogical Sources in the Guildhall Library* (3rd ed. Guildhall Library 1988) contains much relevant information, as does the Guildhall Library's website at www.cityoflondon.gov.uk. The latter enables prospective visitors to download research guides and to search the online catalogue.

GUILDS See Apprenticeship Records and Livery Companies. The word "guild" derives from the Saxon word for payment, since membership of such societies was and still is, paid for. Guilds of craftsmen flourished in towns from the later Middle Ages. The first guild to be given a Royal Charter was the Worshipful Company of Weavers in 1155. The early companies were the medieval equivalent of trading standards departments, checking quality of goods and weights and measures. They also controlled imports, set wages and working conditions and supervised the training of apprentices.

The development of guilds in Britain was not confined to London. Examples of those still in existence around Britain today include: The Cutlers of Hallamshire in Sheffield www.cutlers-hallamshire.org.uk. The Merchant Venturers of Bristol http://merchantventurers.com. The Fellmongers of Richmond in Yorkshire www.fellmongers.org.uk. Guild Records for towns such as Shrewsbury, Norwich, Bristol and Coventry, for example, provide records of both masters and apprentices. These will often have been lodged at the relevant CRO.

GUILD OF ONE NAME STUDIES See One Name Studies.

GUNMAKERS The making of hand guns, as distinct from the casting of cannon, started in the C14th. From that time, records exist of the various makers, and of the specialist makers of gun components. Several books have been published which although primarily intended for those interested in the history and collecting of guns, do outline the business and biographical details of many of the people in the trades. Those researching gunmakers in London will find Blackmore, Howard L *A Dictionary of London Gunmakers 1350-1850* (Phaidon & Christies 1986) to be of relevance. For the remainder of England and Wales, there is Bailey, de Witt & Nie, Douglas A *The English Gunmakers: Birmingham and provincial gun trade in the eighteenth and nineteenth century* (Arms & Armour Press 1978). See also Whitelaw, Charles E *Scottish Arms Makers: biographical dictionary of makers of firearms, edged weapons and armour working in Scotland from the 15th century to 1870* (Arms and Armour Press 1977) and Kennard A N *A Directory of Cannon Founders from Earliest Times to 1850* (Arms & Armour Press 1986), which outlines the gunfounding process and includes an international list of Gunfounders with biographical information.

Much of the early trade was concentrated in the Tower Hamlets area of London, often contracting to the Board of Ordnance whose records are at TNA, or to trading companies such as the Hudson's Bay Company. TNA's research guide *Ordnance Board Records* is of relevance www.nationalarchives.gov.uk.

The Worshipful Company of Gunmakers was established by Royal Charter in 1637/8, and is one of the ancient London Livery Companies. They set up their Proof House in Whitechapel. Their website is at www.gunmakers.org.uk. The Highland Scots were noted for producing pistols. "Black Country" towns such as Darlaston and Wednesbury became major suppliers of gunlocks and barrels. The first evidence of the Birmingham trade was in the supply of guns to the Parliamentarians in 1643. The 1851 census recorded 7,731 gunsmiths and workers in England and Wales, of which 5,167 were in Birmingham and 1,223 in London. The trade was noted for work being done in family groups sub-contracting to others. After 1860 more industrialisation occurred, with the setting up of large companies.

GYPSIES A useful starting point for family enquiries is the Romany and Traveller Family History Society www.rtfhs.org.uk. In some cases, the broad term "Traveller" can serve to conceal the identity of a gypsy family. There were a number of associated occupational groups which were often of gypsy origin, including braziers, tinkers, chair-bottomers, sieve-makers, pot-hawkers, peg-makers and horse-dealers.

A list of publications of interest to those researching gypsy ancestry can be obtained from The Gypsy Studies Section of the Sydney Jones Library at the University of Liverpool see http://www.liv.ac.uk. The library's Special Collections Section holds the archives of the Gypsy Lore Society, which includes some pedigree notes on gypsy families. See also The Gypsy Lore Society at www. gypsyloresociety.org and Wedeck, H E *Dictionary of Gypsy Life and Lore* (Philosophical Library 1973). See Floate, Sharon Sillers *My Ancestor was a Gypsy* (SOG 1999).

H

HABERDASHERS The Worshipful Company of Haberdashers, established in 1516, is eighth in the order of precedence of London Livery Companies and thus is a member of the "Great Twelve Companies". Its website www. haberdashers.co.uk gives both a history of the Company and of its halls.

HALF-BAPTISED Privately baptised. Children baptised in this way, often because they were sickly, may have later been "received into the church".

HAMLET A grouping of houses with no church; although perhaps with a non-conformist chapel. A hamlet was thus part of a larger parish unit.

HANDWRITING See Palaeography.

HANWAY ACTS Jonas Hanway was an English philanthropist (1712-1786). Following the persistent lobbying of Jonas Hanway, Parliament passed two acts. That of 1761 required parish authorities to keep accurate records of infants in their care. The other, passed in 1767, directed parish authorities to send infants out of the city when placing them for care and nursing. Hanway also founded a hospital for fallen women.

HARLEIAN SOCIETY The Harleian Society was established in 1869. Its official objects are "the transcribing, printing and publishing of the heraldic visitations of counties, parish registers or any manuscripts relating to genealogy, family history and heraldry". It is particularly noted for its editions of the Heralds' Visitations (q.v.) in the possession of the College of Arms (q.v.).

   Their website at http://harleian.org.uk gives details of how to subscribe to the society and how to purchase back volumes. CD reproductions are available if a back volume is out of print. Some are online.

HATCHMENT Diamond-shaped funeral hatchments, on which the coat of arms of the deceased was painted. These are to be found in many of the older churches. A series of books entitled *Hatchments in Britain* by Peter Summers (Phillimore 1974-1988) records hatchments on a county basis.

HATTING INDUSTRY This was an important industry especially in London, Cheshire, Lancashire, Gloucestershire and South Wales. It was a very mobile industry with hatters frequently moving between these areas. For further information see Giles P M *The Felt-Hatting Industry c.1500 to 1850 with special reference to Lancashire and Cheshire* (Vol. 59 of the Transactions of the Lancashire and Cheshire Antiquarian Society 1959) www.landcas.org.uk. The expression "Mad as a Hatter" derives from the fact that many hatters suffered from mercury poisoning; mercury being extensively used in the felt hat making processes.

Straw hats have been made in the villages of South Bedfordshire and Buckinghamshire since before 1680. It became a cottage industry and the plait was often made by children in "Plait Schools". The product was then sold in the weekly plait markets in Luton and Dunstable. In 1869, a "Plait Hall" was built at Luton for these markets. Hat manufacturers worked from home or had small factories. The trade produced many allied occupations such as blockers, plait-dealers, dyers, leghorn merchants ribbon merchants and card board box makers. Hats were trimmed by out-workers who finished the rough "hoods" at home. Dony, Dr J G *The History of the Straw Hat Industry* (Gibbs Bamforth 1942), is the standard book on the subject. See also Grof, Laslo *Children of Straw: the story of straw plait, a vanished craft and industry* (Baron 2002) and Shire Publications' volume *Straw Plait* by Jean Davis (1981). The Guild of Straw Craftsmen have a website www.strawcraftsmen.co.uk.

HAWKER A travelling salesman who carries his wares. The Peddlers' Act of 1871 required travelling traders on foot to be licensed by the police. The Hawkers' Act of 1888 required travelling traders with a horse or other beast of burden to be licensed by the County or County Borough Council. License records can sometimes be found in CROs.

HEARTH TAX This tax was levied from 1662 to 1689, though incomplete lists of taxpayers only survive from 1662 to 1674. The records are useful to the family historian in that they enable us to identify our ancestors in place and time, indicate the size of the house and thus the degree of affluence or otherwise of our ancestors. Persons with houses worth less than 20/- per annum were exempt, as were those in receipt of poor relief. Otherwise, 2/- per hearth was payable. The parish constable made lists of householders with the number of hearths and the lists were submitted to the Justices at the Quarter Sessions. The tax was collected twice a year, at Michaelmas and Lady Day. A person with only one hearth was probably relatively poor. A yeoman or "gent" might have three or four and an esquire six or more.

The records of the Hearth Tax are held at TNA. A research guide *Taxation before 1689* can be downloaded from www.nationalarchives.gov.uk. Details of the records surviving in TNA and elsewhere, plus published and other copies, are given in Gibson, Jeremy *Hearth Tax Returns, other Later Stuart Tax Lists and the Association Oath Rolls* (2nd ed. FFHS 1996).

Occasionally, CROs have contemporary copies retained in Quarter Sessions (q.v.) records. The University of Roehampton has, with the assistance of a grant from the Heritage Lottery Fund, had master microfilm made of the Hearth Tax listings in TNA, which has made copies of the relevant portions available to every appropriate local record office in the country. A good many records of the Hearth Tax have been published, usually with indexes, or there may be locally held indexes to unpublished modern transcripts.

The British Record Society (q.v.) has joined with the University of Roehampton to produce a series of texts of the Hearth Taxes of the 1660s and 1670s. These are being published on a county by county basis. Eventually, there may well be some twenty volumes in the series. Copies of these volumes can be purchased from www.britishrecordsociety.org.

The Centre for Hearth Tax Research has transcribed the names of the householders and also produced statistical maps on its website, Hearth Tax Online www.hearthtax.org.uk. This is being added to and eventually all counties will be available. There is a bibliography listing all published hearth tax details on this site.

HELLIER A slater or tiler sometimes found as Hillier.

HERALDRY See also Armorial Bearings and College of Arms. It is important to be aware that a coat of arms does not 'belong' to everyone with that surname. Arms are granted to an individual and his direct descendants only. The social status of your ancestors will determine whether a knowledge of heraldry will assist your researches, although that is no reason why you should not enjoy the subject for its own sake. There are many introductory books on the subject. Brooke-Little J P *Boutell's Heraldry* (revised ed. Frederick Warne 1978). *A New Dictionary of Heraldry* (Alphabooks 1987) and *Heraldry for the Local Historian and Genealogist* (Grange Books 1997) both by Stephen Friar, are excellent hardback publications. More modestly priced and perhaps for the novice is Mackinnon, Charles *The Observer's Book of Heraldry* (Frederick Warne 1966) or Summers, Peter *How To Read A Coat of Arms* (A & C Black 1986).

New Register House, Princes Street, Edinburgh, EH1 3YT is the Head-quarters of the Court of Lord Lyon King of Arms www.lyon-court.com and can advise on matters of Scottish heraldry. The Chief Herald of Ireland www.nli.ie/en/heraldry-introduction.aspx Kildare Street, Dublin 2, deals with heraldic matters in that country.

The Heraldry Society, 44-5 Museum Street, London WC1A 1LH www.theheraldrysociety.com specialises in heraldic studies as does the Institute of Heraldic and Genealogical Studies (q.v.) www.ihgs.ac.uk.

If you come across a copy of a coat of arms in your family documents, do not assume it belonged to one of your ancestors. It could have been those of a family to whom he or she was a servant. J W Papworth's *Ordinary of British Armorials* (facsimile ed. Heraldry Today 1985) lists most known coats of arms according to "Ordinaries" or "charges" on the shields. Thus, if axes appear on the arms, you look up "axes" in the book and there you will find them listed and described. This will help identify a coat of arms.

See Evans, F E *Discovering Civic Heraldry* (Shire Publications 1968) and Storrry, J G *Church Heraldry* (Nettlebed Press 1983).

HERALDS' VISITATIONS In the C15th, the Senior Heralds, known as Kings of Arms, were given the right to grant arms. The Heralds began to compile registers both of the arms already in use and of those that they granted. Early in the C16th, conditions became more stringent, when certain property requirements had to be proven before a grant of arms would be approved. From 1530 onwards, at intervals of about thirty years, the Heralds made tours of the country to examine gentlemen's claims. They took account of records of previous visitations, monumental inscriptions, family muniments and traditions before allowing a claim. The Herald was empowered "to put down or otherwise deface at his discretion" all unlawful arms, crests, cognizances, and devices, "in plate, jewels, paper, parchment, windows, gravestones and monuments or elsewhere wheresoever they be set or placed". They could also summon before them any person who had unlawfully "usurped and taken upon him any name or title of honour or dignity as esquire, gentleman or other". Visitations continued until 1686. Many copies of visitation pedigrees have been published by The Harleian Society (q.v.) http://harleian.co.uk. Most of these are based on copies of visitations in the British Library, rather than on the originals in the Collge of Arms. Indeed, some volumes described as "visitations" actually have nothing whatsoever to do with the heralds. A significant number of Harleian Society volumes have now been reproduced on CD by S & N Genealogical Supplies (q.v.) www.genealogysupplies.com. The counties covered by these CD reproductions include Bedfordshire, Berkshire, Buckinghamshire, Cambridge-shire, Cheshire, Cornwall, Cumberland, Devon, Durham, Essex, Lancashire, Leicestershire, Lincolnshire, London, Norfolk, Northamptonshire, Northumber-land, Nottinghamshire, Oxfordshire, Somerset, Surrey, Wiltshire, Westmorland and Yorkshire. Some are available online.

HERBERT ART GALLERY AND MUSEUM, COVENTRY The "History Centre" at this repository is said to be a treasure trove of information on the history of Coventry and its citizens from medieval times to the present day. Its huge range of original documents available for consultation includes books, maps, newspapers, electoral registers and building plans. Photographs, oral history, microfilms and internet sources provide further evidence on the history of the city and its inhabitants. Further details about the "History Centre" and its holdings can be found at www.theherbert.org.

HERITAGE OPEN DAYS Heritage Open Days celebrate England's fantastic architecture and culture by offering free access to properties that are usually closed to the public or normally charge for admission. Every year on four days in September, buildings of every age, style and function throw open their doors, ranging from castles to factories, town halls to tithe barns, parish churches to Buddhist temples. It is a once-a-year chance to discover hidden architectural treasures and enjoy a wide range of tours, events and activities which bring to life local history and culture. For further information and to find out what is open in your area, visit www.heritageopendays.org.uk.

HIGGLER or HIGLER See also Badger. An itinerant dealer, usually with horse and cart. One who haggles or bargains.

HIGHWAYS These were public roads and usually main routes. Originally, the upkeep of the highways was the responsibility of the Manor but from 1555, the Parish became responsible for their maintenance. Each parishioner owning a ploughland in tillage, or keeping a plough, had to supply a cart for four days a year. If able-bodied, he also had to give four days' labour a year. In 1691, this was increased to six days. The custom arose to commute this obligation by paying a substitute.

The Accounts of the Surveyors of Highways, or Waywardens, which record expenses and payments received are a valuable source of information for the family historian. Where extant, they can be found in CROs. Further information can be found in Chapter IX of W E Tate's *The Parish Chest* 3rd ed. Phillimore 2010). The appointment of Surveyor was made by the justices. The person chosen, from a list supplied by the parish, sometimes paid to be excused from taking office.

A very useful early book containing details of the main routes of the time is *A New and Accurate Description of all the Direct and Principal Cross Roads in England and Wales and Part of the Roads of Scotland*. It includes references to some of the principal houses and their occupants. The book was compiled by Lt Col Daniel Paterson and by 1808 had reached its fourteenth edition (facsimile ed. Lightening Source UK 2012).

HILLIER See Hellier.

HIND A farm labourer or a household servant.

HIRING FAIR See Market Towns.

HISTORICAL ASSOCIATION, THE The Historical Association was founded in 1906 to promote the study of history. It is particularly concerned with history provision in schools. It publishes *The Historian* and the teaching related journals *Teaching History* and *Primary History* and arranges conferences and lectures. Its useful short guides to records, covering a variety of sources, have been published in two volumes and are available via their website www.history.org.uk.

HISTORY PRESS, THE A specialist history publisher, incorporating the Phillimore (q.v.) group, with genealogy, general history and many local history titles in its portfolio www.thehistorypress.co.uk.

HOCKEY The National Hockey Museum and archive is at Butts Road, Woking, Surrey. The collection, spanning the 125 years of hockey's existence, consists of books, magazines, photographs, videos, drawings, paintings, trophies, plaques, the changes of hockey clothing, balls, sticks and even hockey stamps. It contains some fascinating artefacts, as well as extensive statistical records both for the UK and international hockey. The focus is on hockey at all levels, including women's hockey. More details can be found on the repository's website at www.hockeyarchives.co.uk.

HOLOGRAPH WILL See Wills.

HOME CHILDREN See Canada, Children's Societies and Emigration.

HOME FRONT We tend to concentrate on our family's experiences on the battle fields of the world wars but it is equally important to realise what life was like at home. See for example, Beckett, Ian *The Home Front 1914-1918: how Britain survived the Great War* (TNA 2006). Raymond, Stuart *The Home Front 1939-1945: a guide for family historians* (FHP 2012). Hodge, Susie *The Home Front in World War Two: Keep Calm and Carry On* (Remember When 2013). Calder, Angus *The People's War: Britain 1939-1945* (Jonathan Cape 1969).

HONG KONG AND SHANGHAI BANKING CORPORATION, THE (HSBC) The website of HSBC Holdings plc www.hsbc.com/history includes details of HSBC's history, information about how the archives of HSBC reflect its long and colourful history, what is in the archive collections and how they can be accessed. There is an online gallery, exploring the organisation's heritage through its exhibitions of archives, artefacts, photographs and paintings. The site also contains an archive resource centre, enabling publications and resources about the organisation's history to be accessed and in some cases, downloaded.

HOSPITALS See also Census and Lying-In Hospitals. The majority of the early ones were charitable foundations; their records can often be found in TNA, LMA or CROs. The number of hospitals increased after c.1750 (a list of hospitals and asylums with foundation dates can be seen in Richardson, John *The Local Historian's Encyclopedia* (3rd ed. Historical Publications Ltd. 2003). In the C19th many hospitals/infirmaries were associated with workhouses; these often had their own burial grounds and burial registers; many have now been deposited in CROs or local libraries.

The Hospital Records database www.nationalarchives.gov.uk/hospitalrecords is a joint project between TNA and the Wellcome Library (q.v.). The database contains information about hospital and patient records held in public repositories and health authority archives. Here you can find: the location of records, details of catalogues and findings aids, historical information about the hospitals, details of the surviving administrative and clinical records. The database can be searched by town or hospital name. The appearance of a hospital on this list does not mean that all its records will be found, as the quantity of records held for any particular hospital varies. The records are also subject to the 30 year closure rule for administrative records and the 100 year rule for patient records. The Historical Hospital Admissions Records' Project www.hharp.org covers Victorian and Edwardian Admissions records for the Hospital for Sick Children at Great Ormond Street, the Evelina Hospital and the Alexandra Hospital for Children with Hip Disease in London and the Royal Hospital for Sick Children, Glasgow. The Royal Free Hospital is transferring its archive collections to LMA.

See Dainton, Courtney *The Story of England's Hospitals* (London Museum Press 1961); Abel-Smith, Brian *The Hospitals: 1800-1948: a study in social administration in England and Wales* (Heinemann 1964) and Clay, Rotha Mary *The Mediaeval Hospitals of England* (Frank Cass 1909), in which mediaeval hospitals are arranged under counties. For a listing of London Hospital Archives see Webb, Cliff *An Index of London Hospitals and their Records* (SOG 2002).

HOSTELLERS See Innkeepers.

HOSTLER See Ostler.

HOUSE OF COMMONS' RECORD OFFICE See Parliamentary Archives.

HOUSE OF CORRECTION A county gaol used to house vagrants, beggars and unmarried mothers where, by hard labour and other deprivations, an attempt was made to reform the prisoners, not merely punish them.

HOUSE OF FRASER The physical archive for the House of Fraser department stores is held and maintained by Glasgow University Archive Services. It dates back to the mid-C19th and is an extensive collection comprising 132 metres of records and some 10,000 items, including in-depth details of 200 former and current stores, product catalogues, wage ledgers, apprenticeship registers and staff newsletters. It is an outstanding source for the history of British design, fashion, tastes, lifestyles, consumerism and consumption from the early nineteenth to the end of the C20th. At www.housefraserarchive.ac.uk the researcher can search and browse a wide variety of House of Fraser archives, as well as viewing images related to the records.

HOUSE OF LORDS' RECORD OFFICE See Parliamentary Archives.

HOUSEHOLD CAVALRY The Household Cavalry Museum collection relates to The Life Guards, Horse Grenadier Guards, Royal Horse Guards (The Blues) and The Blues and Royals, covering over three hundred years of the history of the Sovereign's mounted bodyguard. The collection contains uniforms, weapons, standards, medals and horse furniture plus paintings, prints and many other curios of the Regiment. There is also a library containing the historical records of the Regiments. For details of access see www.householdcavalry museum.org.uk.

HOUSES, THE HISTORY OF The main sources of information about houses are located in CROs. If the house is old, it might be worth consulting the Victoria County History for the appropriate county. The relevant county in Pevsner's *Buildings of England* series should also be consulted.

These are some records which may help in tracing the history of a house:- Ordnance Survey maps, both 6" and 25". Early maps of the settlement in which it is located. Enclosure maps and awards from the late C18th and early C19th, as these usually have houses marked on them. The related Schedule will list names of owners or occupiers, and sometimes these are recorded on the maps. Tithe Maps and Awards. Estate Surveys. Wills. Manorial Records. Parish Records, in particular Terriers. Sale Catalogues. Land Tax Records. Rate Books. Census Returns. Registers of Electors. Title Deeds.

There are several books that cover tracing the history of houses. Some of the more recent ones include: Adolph, Anthony *Tracing your Home's History* (Harper Collins 2006). Barrett, Nick *Tracing the History of your House* (TNA 2006). Blanchard, Gill, *Tracing Your House History: a guide for family historians* (Pen and Sword 2013). Brooks, Pamela *How to Research your House: every home tells a story* (Howtobooks 2007), this contains a particularly good section on architectural styles. An interesting individual house history, together with an account of the research trail, is Myerson, Julie *Home: the story of everyone who ever lived in our house* (Harper Perennial 2005).

HUCKSTER A street seller of ale, often a woman, or a retailer of small wares in a shop or booth.

HUDSON'S BAY COMPANY See Companies.

HUGUENOTS French Protestants. The first Huguenot refugees arrived in England in the mid 1500s. In 1685 there was an influx of at least 40,000 after the Revocation of the Edict of Nantes. They tended to concentrate in London, the Cinque Ports, Norwich, Bristol and the West Country. They had their own churches and most of the registers have been published by the Huguenot Society www.huguenotsociety.org.uk, PO Box 444, Ruislip, HA4 4GU. The Huguenot Library is currently housed with UCL Special Collections at TNA. The Society has also published volumes listing naturalisations and aliens 1509 to

1800. Naturalisations are also in *Index to Local and Personal Acts, 1801 to 1947* (HMSO). *The Proceedings of the Huguenot Society* are worth study by anyone with a Huguenot ancestor in the family. A valuable General Index to its publications 1855-1991 compiled by C. F. A. Marmoy has now been published. The State Papers, Domestic, Edward VI, Mary and Elizabeth (the Calendars have been printed) contain references to strangers in London from 1560 onwards, many of whom were Huguenots. A useful book is Smiles, Samuel *Huguenots, their Settlements, Churches and Industries in England and Ireland* (reprinted Ulan Press 2012). Gwynn, Dr Robin *Huguenot Heritage* (Routledge & Kegan Paul 1985), is the first full-length study of the Huguenots in England to appear this century and marked the tercentenary of the Revocation of the Edict of Nantes. Published in the same year was Currer-Briggs, Noel & Gambier, Royston *In Search of Huguenot Ancestry* (Phillimore). A more recently published, and excellent, guide is Chater, Kathy *Tracing your Huguenot Ancestors* (Pen and Sword 2012).

HUNDRED A subdivision of a county or shire, having its own court. Hundred names and areas are detailed in the Victoria County History series and their derivations in the English Place Names Society's County volumes. A number of taxes, including Land Tax, are arranged under Hundreds or equivalent names in certain areas and many Registration Districts are named after the old Hundreds.

HUNDRED ROLLS These date from 1255-1280 and were enquiries into Crown rights over land and property. The originals are in TNA in class SC5. Those for the twelve counties that still survived in the early C19th were published in two volumes of *Rotuli Hundred rum* (Record Commission 1812 & 1818). Further details can be found at www.medievalgenealogy.org.uk. See Raban, Sandra *A Second Domesday?: the hundred rolls of 1279-80* (Oxford University Press 2004).

HUSBANDMAN A tenant farmer.

I

IGI See Family Search.

ILLEGITIMACY To be born of parents who were/are not married to each other at the time of birth. Illegitimacy is very common; there are few families without an example. In family history, often the father cannot be traced. Parish Poor Law Overseers usually tried to establish the name of the father of an illegitimate child, so that he could be made to pay weekly amounts to the mother and thus spare the Poor Rate funds. The matter was dealt with by the issue of a Bastardy Bond. Many cases are mentioned in Quarter Sessions (q.v.) records.

Under the Poor Law Amendment Act of 1834, mothers of illegitimate children could apply to the Petty Sessions for a Bastardy Order against the father. When an illegitimate child was registered, the father's name was normally omitted.

The term "illegitimate" was not employed in parish registers until the C18th, though the Latin form "illegitima" may be found, as also "filius naturalis et legitimus" (which in English might appear as "natural and lawful son").

However many other phrases, some quite extraordinary, have been found in registers. An article appeared in the Journal of the Birmingham and Midland Society for Genealogy and Heraldry February 1975 by Dr R. J. Hetherington, containing a collection of no fewer than 87 which he has noted including: Bantling, Base, Base-born, Bastardus, Begotten in adultery, Begotten in fornication, Born extra, By-blow, By-chip, By-scape, By-slip, Chance begot, Child of shame, Come by chance, In sin begotten, Love begot, Lovechild, Merrybegot, Misbegotten, Scape-begotten-child, Son of no certain man, Spuriosus, Supputed son, Whoreson.

An excellent introduction to sources for bastards is provided by Paley, Ruth *My Ancestor was a Bastard* (SOG 2011).

IMAGES OF ENGLAND See English Heritage.

IMMIGRATION See also Aliens, Emigration, Naturalisation and Population. There are several relevant research guides that can be downloaded from TNA website www.nationalarchives.gov.uk. Those entitled *Immigrants* and *Immigration* are good starting points. A more detailed guide is Kershaw, Roger *Migration Records* (TNA 2009).

IMPERIAL WAR MUSEUM (IWM) See also Army, Royal Air Force and Royal Navy. The IWM is situated in five locations: on London's Lambeth Road; at

Duxford in Cambridgeshire; at Manchester's Trafford Park; on HMS Belfast on London's Morgans Lane and in the "Churchill War Rooms" on London's King Charles Street.

The IWM illustrates and records all aspects of the two World Wars and other military operations involving Britain and the Commonwealth since 1914. The Museum was founded in 1917 and has been in its present Lambeth Road home, which was formerly the Bethlem Royal Hospital or Bedlam, since 1936.

The Department of Documents is a repository for documentary records of all types relating to warfare in the C20th. The collections fall into two main groups, one consisting of British private papers and the other largely of captured German material. There is a photographic library which has over five million photographs, as well as galleries in which relevant exhibitions take place.

The IWM has a selection of publications that can be purchased in person or online from its shop. These include *Tracing Your Family History - Merchant Navy* (2006), *Tracing Your Family History - Navy* (2006) and *Tracing Your Family History - RAF* (2006). The following guides can also be downloaded free of charge from the IWM website www.iwm.org.uk: *Tracing Royal Flying Corps and Royal Air Force Ancestry*; *Tracing Merchant Navy* Ancestry; *Tracing POWs*; *Tracing Royal Navy Ancestry* and *Tracing West Indian Service Personnel*, which deals with tracing West Indians who served with the British Armed Forces.

INCLOSURE AWARDS See Enclosure Awards.

INCOME TAX This was first levied in 1799 to pay for the war against France. The rate was 2/- in the £ (two shillings in the pound). It was abolished in 1802 but revived the following year. It has been a permanent feature of life ever since. Unfortunately, few records survive but see Colley, Robert (ed.) *Devizes Division Income Tax Assessments 1840-1860* (Wiltshire Record Society 2002).

INCUMBENT A general term which covered rector, vicar, parson, minister or perpetual curate (all q.v.). The incumbent was in charge of the parish.

INDENTURE This was originally a document cut into two pieces using an indented line; the authenticity of one piece being proved when matched with the other. The contents of the document were written twice and it was usual to add the word "Cyrographum" where a jagged cut between the two copies was to be made. Indentures were used for some types of apprenticeship and other contracts and title deeds.

INDENTURED SERVANT See Emigration.

INDIA See Asia, Pacific and Africa Collections, Cemeteries in South Asia and Emigration.

INDUSTRIAL ARCHAEOLOGY Useful references to such things as mines, railways and the like can be found in Cossons, Neil *The BP Book of Industrial Archaeology* (revised ed. David & Charles 1993). It lists sites, museums and organisations connected with these topics.

A comprehensive list of the various Industrial History Museums is also given in Richardson, John *The Local Historian's Encyclopedia* (3rd ed. Historical Publications Ltd. 2003). Shire Publications (q.v.) on individual trades often list relevant museums www.shirebooks.com.

INFLATION See also Wages. Although we think of inflation as largely a modern phenomenon, there was a period of considerable inflation in the C16th, one cause of which was the flow of gold and silver from the Americas. The value of money has altered dramatically over the past four hundred years.

For further reading see Burnett, John *History of the Cost of Living* (Pelican 1969). Priestley, Harold *The What it Cost the Day Before Yesterday Book* (Kenneth Mason 1979). Munby, Lionel *How Much is that Worth* (Phillimore 1989).

Historic inflation calculators that show how the value of money has changed (there are others) can be found at: www.measuringworth.com; www.bank of england.co.uk/education/Pages/inflation/calculator/flash/default.aspx and www. hisismoney.co.uk/money/bills/article-1633409/Historic-inflation-calculator-value-moneychanged-1900.html.

INHIBITION This was the period during the visitation of a bishop to an archdeaconry, when the archdeacon's court would be closed and probate business conducted in the consistory court. In theory, the visitation of an archbishop to a diocese would have the same effect on a consistory court but in post-mediaeval times this was likely to be "pro forma" only.

Some peculiars (q.v.) were entirely exempt from visitation and inhibition, others subject to visitation by a dean or a dean and chapter. Visitations would normally last several months at intervals of several years.

INLAND REVENUE See Valuation Office.

IN-LAW This phrase had a different meaning in the mid C19th and prior from that which it has today. For example, in the 1851 census, the terms daughter-in-law or son-in-law could mean "son or daughter in the eyes of the law" i.e. stepdaughter or stepson, the children of the wife of the head of the household by a previous marriage. In Dicken's novel *Pickwick Papers*, Sam Weller addresses his step-mother as "mother-in-law". It is important to remember this when studying early wills from which much important information about relationships can be gleaned.

INNKEEPERS See also Alehouses. They were also known as ostlers or innholders. The Worshipful Company of Innholders is number 32 of the 108

Livery Companies of London. The company began in the early C14th and became known as the Guild of Innholders in 1473. Its website www.innholders.org.uk gives further details. See also Warner, O *A History of The Innholders' Company* (The Innholders' Society 1962) and Coote, Stephen *The Innholders: a history of the worshipful company of innholders* (Dianthus 2002).

INNS OF COURT See Legal Profession.

INQUESTS See Coroners' Inquests.

INQUISITIONS POST MORTEM (IPM) If a person held land belonging to the Crown, on his death an inquiry was made into his possessions, services due and his rightful heirs. IPM (literally "enquiries after death"), detail the land holdings of the deceased. They cover the period from 1236 to the end of feudal tenures in 1646. Though they tended to relate to important people, quite humble folk might be called upon to give evidence, relating to the age of the heir. The person giving such evidence was named, his age given, and such information as: "He has lived in . . . for 45 years and remembers . . . was baptised the same week as his son John".

These records are in TNA. There are published Calendars of Inquisitions 1235-1392 and 1485-1509. Those for a number of counties have been printed by local record societies. TNA have produces a research guide *Landholders and Heirs in Inquisitions Post Mortem 1236-c.1640*, which can be downloaded from their website www.nationalarchives.gov.uk. See also www.medievalgenealogy. org.uk for further background information.

INSTITUTE OF HERALDIC AND GENEALOGICAL STUDIES (IHGS) See also Pallot Index and Parish Maps. Their headquarters, bookshop and library are at Northgate, Canterbury, Kent CT1 1BA and their website is at www.ihgs.ac.uk. The Institute is constituted as a registered charity and is an educational trust. It provides for training, study and research in genealogy and the history of the family. It acts as a qualifying body for genealogists, setting and maintaining professional standards. The Institute is supported by Achievements Ltd., which also provides practical experience for students of the Institute in genealogical and related research. It organises day, evening and residential courses at several levels. There is also a popular correspondence course. The Institute's training courses can lead to examinations in the method and practice of genealogy and heraldry. There are various levels of membership of the Institute. Fellows are elected by Council. The Licentiateship is awarded to those fulfilling qualification requirements. Graduate membership is also available to those qualified through examination. Associate membership is open to all wishing to support the Institute. Members may be granted free access to the library during normal opening hours. The journal *Family History* and newsletters are issued to members and subscribers.

A large number of publications on heraldry, genealogy and related subjects are available from the Institute's Family History Bookshop (on which members receive a discount). Also within the Institute here are accredited specialists who will advise on heraldry and associated artwork.

Along with other aids to research, the Institute publishes parish maps of the counties of England, Wales and Scotland and produces Cecil Humphrey-Smith's *Phillimore Atlas and Index of Parish Registers* (3rd ed. Phillimore 2002).

The library contains an extensive collection of works on heraldry, genealogy and local history, providing invaluable finding aids and useful background material. There are sources for the whole of the UK along with special collections for the counties of London, Kent, Sussex and Hampshire along with many specialist indexes. Non-members may use the library for a fee. All visitors should make an appointment with the librarian as space is at a premium. A research and advisory service is available for those who cannot visit the library.

INSURANCE See also Maps. The Guildhall Library holds records of over eighty London based insurance companies, approximately half of which were involved in insuring property against fire. These include the Hand-in-Hand Fire and Life Insurance Society (established 1696), Sun Insurance Office (established 1710 as Sun Fire) and the Royal Exchange Assurance (established 1720). The original registers of the Sun Fire Office are in the Guildhall Library, together with an index of policy holders between the years 1714 to 1730, arranged by counties but excluding London, Scotland and Wales. A leaflet about their holdings can be downloaded at www.history.ac.uk/gh/fire.htm. The surviving registers of both the Royal Exchange Assurance and the Sun Fire Office 1775-1787 are on microfiche, covering some 150,000 policies. The "A Place in the Sun" project www.history.ac.uk/gh/sun.htm has created an index to a part of the series of Sun Fire Office policy registers (Guildhall Library Ms 11936). The index to 125 volumes (nos. 419-560) of the policy registers, covering the period 1800-1839, is available via TNA www.nationalarchives.gov.uk.

A comprehensive list of some of the earlier Fire Insurance Companies, with their dates of foundation, is given in Richardson, John *The Local Historian's Encyclopaedia* (3rd ed. Historical Publications Ltd. 2003). The records of some companies have been deposited in CROs. The SOG (q.v.) has a collection of claims documents of the Sun Fire Office for 1770-88. Brief details of the records held in CROs and elsewhere are given in Cockerell, H A L & Green, Edwin *The British Insurance Business 1547 to 1970* (Heinemann Educational 1976).

Fire insurance offices were established in London from the late C17th and in the provinces from early C18th. Some London-based companies initially restricted their business to that area, gradually developing throughout Britain working through provincial agents. Insurance of property in Ireland and overseas was not undertaken by them in a significant way until the C19th.

Where fire policy registers exist they generally include the policy number; the name of agent and location of the agency; the name, status, occupation and address of policyholder; the names, occupations and addresses of tenants; the location, type, nature of construction and value of property insured; the premium and renewal date and some indication of endorsements. Entries are generally arranged in chronological order, that is in policy number order.

Indexes to the policy registers deposited at the Guildhall Library vary with each collection so searching can be a lengthy business. Other records available are committee minutes, agents' records, share records, endorsement books, claims records, investment records, surveyors' plans and reports, accounts and correspondence. Some records are on restricted access.

Two research guides can be downloaded from the website of the Guildhall Library www.cityoflondon.gov.uk/guildhalllibrary *Fire Insurance Records at Guildhall Library* and *A Place in the Sun Index Instructions*.

A key book on this topic is that by David Hawkings' *Fire Insurance Records for Family and Local Historians* (Francis Boutle Publishers 2003). There is useful background on the London Lives website www.londonlives.org/static/AHDSFIR.jsp.

INTERNATIONAL GENEALOGICAL INDEX (IGI) See Family Search.

INTERNET See also Cyndi's List. The internet is increasingly becoming essential for family historians. It must be remembered that the information it contains varies greatly in accuracy. Evidence gathered in this way needs to be evaluated. The ability to download digital images of documents is invaluable. Family trees uploaded by individuals, frequently unverified and lifted straight from other individuals, can be highly speculative. There are of course an ever increasing number of useful websites for family history research, the most notable of which are included in this volume. An umbrella site that enables a number of historical indexes to be search at once, either by place, personal name or keyword, is www.connectedhistories.org. Stuart Raymond has published a number of lists of websites to assist with various aspects of UK research, see www.stuart raymond.co.uk. These include *Family History on the Web* (6th ed. FHP forthcoming) and similar volumes for Ireland and Scotland. For a detailed discussion of the value of the internet see Christian, Peter *The Genealogists' Internet* (5th edition Bloomsbury 2012).

INTERNET LIBRARY OF EARLY JOURNALS (ILEJ) A searchable, digital library of C18th and C19th journals www.bodley.ox.ac.uk/ilej/. The journals included are *Gentleman's Magazine*; *The Annual Register*; *Philosophical Transactions of the Royal Society; Notes and Queries; The Builder* and *Blackwood's Edinburgh Magazine*.

INTERREGNUM (1649-1660) See Commonwealth, The.

INTESTACY A person who dies without leaving a will is said to have died "intestate". Many people die without leaving a will. Their goods are then divided between the children or taken over by a surviving partner by mutual agreement. If no property is owned, no legal process is involved. If property is involved or if there is money in a bank or savings scheme, an application for probate has to be made. "Letters of administration" (admon) are then granted to enable the heirs to sell the property or obtain the money. The records that are normally seen are the admistration bonds, rather than the actual letters of administartion and information is limited.

INVENTORIES These were lists of the belongings of a deceased person and were part of the process of obtaining probate. Common until the mid C18th, they are fascinating documents and give a vivid picture of the contents of the houses in which our ancestors lived. From the inventory we can often judge whether they lived in affluence or in poverty. Many of the items listed, however, may puzzle you. You are recommended to obtain a copy of a book such as Milward, Rosemary *A Glossary of Household, Farming and Trade Terms from Probate Inventories* (3rd ed, Derbyshire Record Society 1986) or Stuart Raymond's *Words from Wills and Other Probate Records 1500-1800: a glossary* (FFHS 2004); the latter lists many published collections of inventories. See also Moore, J S *The Goods and Chattels of our Forefathers* (Phillimore 1976). It has a useful glossary.

IRELAND See also Civil Registration in Ireland, Emigration, Family Histories, Parish Registers of Ireland and Townland. Since 1921, Ireland has been divided into two parts, the Republic of Ireland (sometimes referred to as Eire) with Dublin as the seat of Government and Northern Ireland (still part of the UK), governed from Belfast. Northern Ireland consists of the counties of Antrim, Armagh, Down, Fermanagh, Londonderry (referred to by Nationalists as Derry) and Tyrone. It is sometimes called the Six Counties. The other twenty-six counties form the Republic.

Most genealogical records are centralised in either Dublin or Belfast. The relevant repositories are: The National Library of Ireland, Kildare Street, Dublin 2 www.nli.ie.

The National Archives of Ireland, Bishop Street, Dublin 8 www.national archives.ie.

General Register Office, Joyce House, 8-11 Lombard Street East, Dublin 2 www.groireland.ie.

Representative Church Body Library, Braemor Park, Churchtown, Dublin 14 http://ireland.anglican.org/about/43.

Registry of Deeds, King's Inns, Henrietta Street, Dublin 1 www.landirect.ie/eng/ (land registration dates from 1708).

Public Record Office of Northern Ireland (PRONI), 2 Titanic Boulevard, Queens Island, Belfast, Antrim BT3 9HQ www.proni.gov.uk.

General Register Office, Oxford House, 49-55 Chichester Street, Belfast BT1 4HL www.nidirect.gov.uk/general-register-office-for-northern-ireland.

Other useful organisations are: The Association of Professional Genealogists in Ireland (APGI) www.apgi.ie. It represents most professionals in the Republic and Northern Ireland and has a complaints investigation procedure.

Ulster Historical Foundation, 49 Malone Road, Belfast BT9 6RY Northern Ireland www.ancestryireland.com.

The Irish Ancestral Research Association (TIARA) Dept. W, 2120 Commonwealth Avenue, Auburndale, Massachusetts 02466-1909 is an American based, non-profit making organisation aimed at promoting the growth, study and exchange of ideas amongst people and organisations interested in Irish genealogical and historical research and education. http://tiara.ie/index.php

Most of the valuable archival records deposited at the Public Record Office in the Four Courts, Dublin, were destroyed in 1922 as a result of the Civil War in Ireland. Therefore, it is no use pretending that tracing Irish ancestry is going to be easy. Records that were not housed at the Four Courts in 1922 were not affected by the Civil War.

Irish Origins www.irishorigins.com is a subscription website enabling those with Irish Ancestry to access records. The website www.irishgenealogy.ie allows searches in a variety of records including, church records, the 901 and 1911 censuses, the tithe applotments and Griffith's Valuations. For those whose families have left Ireland, www.irelandxo.com aims to reconnect the Irish diaspora with their roots.

Useful books about Irish research include: Maxwell, Ian *How to Trace Your Irish Ancestors* (2nd ed. How to Books 2009). By the same author *Tracing Your Northern Irish Ancestors: a guide for family historians* (Pen and Sword 2010). Grenham, John *Tracing Your Irish Ancestors* (4th ed. Gill and Macmillan 2012). Roulston, William J *Researching Scots-Irish Ancestors: the essential genealogical guide to early modern Ulster 1600-1800* (Ulster Historical Foundation 2005). Paton, Chris *Tracing your Irish Family History on the Internet* (Pen and Sword 2013). Raymond, Stuart *Irish Family History on the Web* (4th ed. FHP forthcoming).

The Irish Family History Foundation www.rootsireland.ie maintains county genealogy centres and is co-ordinating the creation of a database of Irish genealogical sources to assist those who wish to trace their Irish ancestry. These indexes but no images of original records, are available on their website. See also the Irish Genealogy website www.ireland-genealogy.com, which enables researchers to search a database of pension claims that relate back to the now destroyed 1841 and 1851 censuses. Copies of documents can be ordered for a fee.

There are a number of amateur organisations that have membership facilities. The oldest is the Irish Genealogical Research Society (IGRS), founded in 1936 and based in London Church of St. Magnus the Martyr, Lower Thames Street, London EC3 6DN, where its library is located. The IGRS publishes *The Irish*

Genealogist annually. It has a worldwide membership and there is an Ireland Branch for members within Ireland (Republic and N.I.). The Irish Family History Society, PO Box 36, Naas, Co. Kildare www.ifhs.ie also has a worldwide membership and publishes an annual journal. The North of Ireland Family History Society, Unit C4, Valley Business Park, 67 Church Road, Newtownabbey, Co Antrim, Northern Ireland, BT36 7LS www.nifhs.org has twelve branches in Northern Ireland and issues a journal.

The following research guides can be downloaded from the website of TNA www.nationalarchives.gov.uk *Births, Marriages and Deaths in Scotland and Ireland*; *Bloody Sunday Inquiry 1972*; *Ireland's Easter Rising 1916*; *Irish maps c.1558-c.1610*; *Royal Irish Constabulary* and *State papers Ireland 1509-1782.*

Wills for the period 1858-1899 probated at the Principal Registry (i.e. Dublin) were destroyed in 1922. Those probated in local offices (i.e. outside Dublin) for that period survive in Will Copy Books for places like Belfast, Armagh, Derry, Limerick etc. Wills 1900-1922 survive, those relating to people in what became Northern Ireland were transferred to PRONI in Belfast. TNA in Dublin have abstracts of many pre-1858 wills. Vicars, Sir Arthur *Index to the Prerogative Wills of Ireland, 1536-1810* (reprinted Genealogical Publishing Co. 1989). A time saver when searching for Irish wills and admons. for the years 1859-1876 inclusive in the indexes of the Principal Probate Registry (see Wills), is to look under the letter Z rather than the testator' name. Following the Z admons. appear: Irish Probates, sealed; Irish admons. sealed and Scottish confirmations, sealed. In each of these three sections testators' names are arranged in strict alphabetical order. These could be of great value since though calendared in TNA, Dublin, these wills and admons. are missing from some courts including the Principal Registry. Calendars of Wills and Administrations 1858 - 1920 at TNA of Ireland can be searched at www.willcalendars.nationalarchives.ie.

Cantwell, Brian J *Memorials of the Dead in Ireland* a series of volumes published by the Irish Memorials Association, contains many thousands of inscriptions from gravestones and other memorials. These are available via the FindmyPast Ireland website www.findmypast.ie and on CD (Eneclann Ltd. 2006.)

TNA website www.nationalarchives.gov.uk has a research guide *Irish Maps c.1558-c.1610.*

The Surnames of Ireland by Edward MacLysaght (Irish Academic Press 1989) lists over 4,000 family names with information on practically every surname found in Ireland. Recommended is Andrews, J H *History in the Ordnance Map: an introduction for Irish readers* (David Archer 1993). The introduction to the book is an evaluation of the historical and demographical use of ordnance survey maps; following on is a detailed analysis of each type of map; boundary sketches, fair plans etc.. Sources and references are quoted and there is a bibliography.

For Irish emigrants, Glazier, Ira A *The Famine Immigrants: lists of Irish Immigrants arriving at the port of New York, 1846-1851* (7 vols. Genealogical

Publishing Co. 1983-86). http://emigrationisle.com/ is an interesting website illustrating aspect of Irish emigration.

McClaughlin, Trevor *Barefoot and Pregnant? Irish famine orphans in Australia* (Genealogical Society of Victoria 1991) is about 4,000 Irish girls, teenagers and orphans, who emigrated to Australia in 1848-50 under a scheme instigated by Earl Grey, British Secretary of State for the Colonies. An interesting story, the second part particularly so, as this is a register of all the orphans, listed alphabetically, according to the ship in which they travelled, with age, home town, names of parents (where known) and religion. Any further information discovered since (e.g. marriage) is also given. On the same topic The Famine Orphan Girl Database is free to search www.irishfaminememorial.org/en/orphans.

For an Irish gravestone transcribing project see http://historicgraves.com/.

IRONMONGERS An ironmonger is also known as a "feroner" or a dealer in iron. Meadows, Cecil *Victorian Ironmonger* (Shire Publications 2000) gives more details of the work of an ironmonger. The Worshipful Company of Ironmongers, or the Ironmongers' Company as it is sometimes known, is ranked tenth in precedence among the Great Twelve Livery Companies of the City of London. Its website www.ironmongers.org, amongst other things, gives a brief outline of the company's history. See Nicholl, J *Some Account of the Worshipful Company of Ironmongers* (reprinted Ulan Press 2012). Noble, T C *A Brief History of the Worshipful Company of Ironmongers, London, AD 1351-1889* (Spottiswoode 1889). Glover, Elizabeth *A History of the Ironmongers' Company* (Ironmongers' Company 1991).

IRREGULAR MARRIAGES See Gretna Green Marriages and Marriages.

ISLE OF MAN Civil registration on the Isle of Man commenced in 1849 for marriages but not until 1878 for births and deaths. The records are held by the Island's General Registry, Deemsters Walk, Bucks Road, Douglas, Isle of Man, IM1 3AR www.gov.im/registries. Information about wills can also be obtained from the Registry. Other records are to be found in the Manx Museum Library, Kingswood Road, Douglas, Isle of Man www.gov.im/mnh/heritage/museums/manx museum.xml. The censuses for England and Wales also cover the Isle of Man. Family Search (q.v.) contains almost all Manx baptisms and marriages.

The Manx National Heritage website can be found at www.gov.im/mnh. They have also launched iMuseum online www.imuseum.im, giving online access to the Isle of Man national archives, library and museum collections. The records include baptisms, marriages and burials, newspapers, war memorials and a photographic archive. The Isle of Man Family History Society www.iomfhs.im holds regular meetings, produces a journal and maintains a library at at Derby Lodge, Derby Road, Peel IM5 1HH.

ITALY The Anglo-Italian Family History Society is a good starting point www.anglo-italianfhs.org.uk. L'Instituto Araldico Genealogico Italiano www.iagi. info, may also be useful.

J

JACOBITES Supporters of the Catholic James II and his descendants. The Jacobite Rebellion ended in 1745 with the Battle of Culloden.

JAGGER A jagger is an itinerant pedlar or hawker, carrier or carter, the term is often used for a seller of fish. The term also has a more specialised meaning in mining, the man who carried ore on a pack-horse from a mine to be smelted, or a boy in charge of the "jags" or train of trucks in a coal mine.

JAGUAR HERITAGE MUSEUM The Jaguar Heritage Museum www. jaguarheritage.org was based in Coventry but is currently closed following relocation. It was reported that the museum's archival holdings, when packed for storage, amounted to 43 tonnes-worth of boxes packed full of archive material, a total of 2,640 boxes, each holding 15kg worth of items. The museum's website gives updates on the future of the archive and museum. It also contains a company history, a library of photographs, and details of events connected to the history of this iconic company.

JAPANNING This was a thriving industry especially in Birmingham in the C18th and C19th and was often allied to Papier-Mache manufacturers, both trades usually being carried out in small factories. If an ancestor was engaged in this work any of the following books would be of interest. Devoe, Shirley Spaulding *English Papier Mache of the Georgian and Victorian Periods* (Barrie & Jenkins 1971). Dickinson, George *English Papier Mache: its origin, development and decline* (Courier Press 1925). Huth, Hans *Lacquer of the West: the history of a craft and industry, 1550-1950* (Chicago University Press 1971). Jones, Yvonne *Georgian and Victorian Japanned Ware of the West Midlands* (Wolverhampton Art Gallery & Museums 1982). Toller, Jane *Papier Mache in Great Britain and America* (Bell 1962).

JERSEY See Channel Islands.

JESUITS Members of the Society of Jesus, formed by Ignatius Loyola in 1534. Jesuit priests were sent to England in the 1580s to inspire Catholics at a time of an impending Spanish invasion. See Holt, Geoffrey *The English Jesuits 1650-1829: a biographical dictionary* (Catholic Record Society record series 70 1984).

JEWELLERS See Goldsmiths and Oriental and India Office Collections.

JEWELLERY QUARTER, BIRMINGHAM The Jewellery Quarter Research Group (JQRG) www.jqrg.org will be of interest to those studying local or family history with connections to Birmingham's Jewellery Quarter. In particular, they have put over 11,000 existing memorial inscriptions for Birmingham's Key Hill Cemetery online, with an intuitive search engine potted histories of some of the people mentioned. This cemetery was opened in 1837 by a group of non-conformist businessmen and contains over 20,000 graves and over 62,000 burials. The JQRG plan to add the memorial inscriptions for Warstone Lane cemetery to their website soon.

JEWISH ANCESTORS Joseph, Dr Anthony *My Ancestors were Jewish* (4th ed. SOG 2008) is a comprehensive guide to tracing Jewish ancestors in the UK and includes a chapter on researching Jewish ancestry abroad. Wenserul, Rosemary *Tracing Your Jewish Ancestors: a guide for family historians* (Pen and Sword 2008) is a detailed guide to research. A research guide *Jews and Jewish Communities in Britain 18th to 20th Centuries* is available on TNA website www.nationalarchives.gov.uk. LMA (q.v.) information leaflet no 16 *Records of the Anglo Jewish Community at the London Metropolitan Archives* can be downloaded from www.cityoflondon.gov.uk/Corporation. Avotaynu www.avotaynu.com is a publisher of works on Jewish genealogy, including *The International Review of Jewish Genealogy*. This has been published since 1985 and is said to be the world's largest circulation magazine devoted to Jewish genealogy, which each year publishes more than 300 pages of useful, interesting information that can help a researcher. An index to the first twenty-four volumes is available online, whilst its back editions can be obtained on CD.

The Bevis Marks Hall in London www.bevismarks.org.uk has a collection of Jewish registers 1687 to 1837. Its publications include birth registers 1780-1887 and circumcisions performed between 1715-1785, with many details of parentage, grandparentage and godparentage.

The Jewish Historical Society of England www.jhse.org has headquarters in London but has active branches in a number of centres. It holds lectures on a wide range of subjects relating to Anglo-Jewish history and publishes its biennial transactions *Jewish Historical Studies*. It and has also published Hyamson, Albert M *Anglo-Jewish Notabilities: their arms and testamentary depositions* (1949).

The Jewish Genealogical Society of Great Britain www.jgsgb.org.uk promotes and encourages the study of Jewish genealogy and assists those tracing the family history of their Jewish ancestors. It holds meetings, organises conferences, runs its own library and resource centre, publishes a journal *Shemot* and a newsletter and runs its own online discussion group. There is a JewishGen website www.jewishgen.org who operate the Jewish Genealogical Family Finder (JGFF) www.jewishgen.org/jgff, a database of ancestral areas and surnames currently being researched by Jewish genealogists worldwide. There are also active Jewish genealogical societies in many European counties including Holland, France and Switzerland, whilst further afield the Australian Jewish Genealogical Society www.ajgs.org.au can help to deal with Australian Jewish historical or genealogical enquiries. An internet search will reveal details of similar societies, many of which publish regular journals or newsletters.

Manchester's Jewish Museum www.manchesterjewishmuseum.com is located in a former Spanish and Portuguese Synagogue, which reopened in 1984 as a museum. It now chronicles the lives of Jewish people in Manchester and their contribution to making the city what it is today. The museum now hosts exhibitions and an events' programme. Its collection is made up of objects, documents, photographs and oral histories charting the many stories and experiences of Manchester Jewish life.

Family historians tracing the experiences of ancestors caught up in the Holocaust may be able to learn more following the relocation of The Wiener Library www.wienerlibrary.co.uk to Russell Square, London. It houses the world's oldest archive recording the impact of the Nazi regime during the Second World War.

The Special Collections Division of the Hartley Library at Southampton University www.southampton.ac.uk/library/resources/collections/specialcollections/hartley.html houses the Anglo Jewish Archives. The Division holds more than 850 collections of manuscripts, whilst its Parkes Library holds a printed collection of Jewish archival material.

JOHN RYLANDS LIBRARY See Manchester University and Methodists.

JOINER The records of the Joiners and Ceilers Company Livery Company www.joinersandceilers.co.uk are in the Guildhall Library (q.v.). See Lane, Sidney E *The Worshipful Company of Joiners and Ceilers or Carvers, a Chronological History* (Chesham Press 1868).

JOINTURE Money paid to a widow out of her late husband's freehold estate.

JOURNEYMAN Not someone who journeyed about for work, although they often did. The word comes from the French "journée", for day, so a worker who was paid by the day and not hired on a long term contract. Journeymen will have completed their apprenticeship but not yet set up on their own as a master.

JULIAN CALENDAR See Calendar.

JURORS There were various property qualifications necessary before a person could serve on a jury. In 1825, service was limited to men between the ages of twenty-one and sixty who owned property worth at least £10 a year, or leased property worth at least £20 a year, or rented property worth at least £30. Lists of jurors are to be found with Quarter Sessions (q.v.) records in CROs.

JUSTICES OF THE PEACE (JP) The office of Justice of the Peace was instituted in 1361 but the duties of the office had been performed by "Keepers of the Peace" since 1195, when Richard I commissioned certain knights to preserve the peace in unruly areas. An act of 1327 had provided that in every county "good and lawful men" should be appointed to guard the peace. For centuries, those appointed to the Commission of the Peace were either landowners or men of substance, whose social position was so strong that their authority went undisputed. An act of 1361 provided that JPs should meet four times a year, the origin of Quarter Sessions (q.v.), which continued until replaced by Crown Courts in January 1972. Between sessions, JPs could meet to settle very small matters in Petty Sessions (q.v.) and they oversaw the administration of the Poor Laws. They are named Commissioners of the Peace in various other Quarter Sessions records. For a listing of Welsh JPs see Phillips, J R S *The Justices of the Peace in Wales and Monmouthshire* (University of Wales Press 1975).

JUVENILE OFFENDERS From 1847, monthly returns of juvenile offenders were compiled with details of punishments. They are with Quarter Sessions (q.v.) records, usually in CROs.

K

KAY & CO LTD See University Libraries.

KELLY'S DIRECTORIES See also Directories. Generally regarded as the most important series of local directories. They began in 1799 with a volume for London and subsequently covered all counties and large cities of England. Whilst they largely ceased in 1939 some volumes appeared as late as the mid 1970s. Publication was about every eight years for county volumes, city volumes appeared more frequently. Earlier volumes contained names and addresses of commercial organisations, expanded to include those of wealthier private householders and eventually of all householders. Entry was free but the directory had to be purchased. Many are available online at www.historicaldirectories.org.

KIN In the phrase "Kith and Kin", strictly the former are friends and the latter are blood relatives although the phrase is often loosely interpreted. Next-of-kin is generally defined as a person's closest relative and nowadays is usually taken to mean a person's spouse. Technically, a person's next of kin is their child, parent or sibling, as a spouse is not a blood relative. This should be borne in mind particularly when interpreting wills.

KING'S BENCH See Court of King's Bench.

KITH AND KIN See Kin.

KNIGHT'S FEE Land held from a feudal lord in return for miliary service. This was later converted to a monetary payment before being abolished in 1662.

L

LACEMAKERS Lacemaking thrived as an industry from the early C17th to the late C19th, when lacemaking almost died out due to the advent of machines. Relevant publications are: Levey, S M & Maney, W S *A History of Lace* (Victoria and Albert Museum 1983). Earnshaw, Pat *A Dictionary of Lace* (Shire Publications 1982). Hopewell, Jeff *Pillow Lace and Bobbins* (Shire Publications 1999). Earnshaw, Pat *The Identification of Lace* (Shire Publications 2009).

The Australian Society of the Lacemakers of Calais www.angelfire.com/al/aslc/ represents descendants of machine lacemakers who worked in Calais in 1815-1848. The society has its own archives, publishes a journal entitled *Tulle* and has published a book by Gillian Kelly *Well Suited To The Colony* (1998).

LADY DAY One of four quarter days, 25 March. Until 1752, the year began on Lady Day. Traditionally, this was the day on which hiring-fairs for servants and the like took place.

LAMBETH PALACE LIBRARY See Clergy and Education.

LAND OWNERSHIP See Domesday Book, Ireland, Returns of Owners of Land, Scotland and Title Deeds.

LAND TAX This tax was first introduced about 1692 and was not finally abolished until the 1950s. The rate was usually 4/- (four shillings) in the pound.

The annual lists contain names of the owners and tenants of houses and land. These records survive mostly in CROs and are found in Quarter Sessions (q.v.) collections. This is particularly the case for the period 1780-1832, when the Clerks of the Peace used the tax lists to identify those entitled to vote in parliamentary elections. County taxpayers' lists for earlier years rarely survive but some boroughs, such as London and Bristol, have long runs.

For just one year, 1798, there is a duplicate set of taxpayers' lists for the whole of England and Wales (except Flintshire) in TNA, Class IR23. Post-1832 lists are of less use, as they omit the growing number of landowners who had commuted payment.

The book Gibson, Jeremy; Medlycott, Mervyn & Mills, Dennis *Land and Window Tax Assessments* (2nd ed. FFHS 1998) explains the purpose and collection of the tax. It contains a county-by-county list of surviving records and their location.

LATHE A term used in Kent for a grouping of several Hundreds.

LATIN See also Forenames and Relationships. Many ecclesiastical, manorial and legal records up to the early C18th (the cut off date is often 1732) were written in some form of Latin.

There are a number of published guides to reading Latin: Morris, Janet *A Latin Glossary for Family Historians* (FHP 2009). Stuart, Denis *Latin for Local and Family Historians* (Phillimore 2006). Gooder, Eileen A *Latin for Local History* (Longmans 1988). Kennedy, Benjamin *Kennedy's Revised Latin Primer* (Longmans 1965).

Martin, Charles Trice *The Record Interpreter* (facsimile of 2nd ed. Phillimore 1982), with an introduction by David Iredale, is a collection of abbreviations, Latin words and names used in historical manuscripts and records. It is accepted as one of the standard local history reference sources.

LATTENER Latten was a yellow metal compound very similar or identical to brass. It was used for the "brasses" found in churches. A lattener was a worker in this metal.

LAVENDER A washerwoman. This derives from the French "laver", to wash.

LAW TERMS A precise definition of law terms is impossible since not only are they dependable on moveable ecclesiastical feast days but there are variations over the centuries. Hence, a rough guideline is sufficient when searching legal records, bearing in mind that in Chancery records the legal year begins with the Michaelmas term.

Michaelmas - from late September to the end of November.
Hilary - from mid January to mid February.
Easter - from just after Easter to mid April or May, depending on the actual date of Easter.
Trinity - anywhere from mid May until 24 June.
Sittings customarily took place outside the terms as well.

LAWYER See Legal Profession.

LAY SUBSIDIES See Subsidies.

LDS See Church of Jesus Christ of Latter-Day Saints.

LEASE AND RELEASE A form of land transfer in use until the mid C19th. Two documents were created the lease and the release. The property was first leased to its purchasers. On the following day, the vendors' interest in the property was released to the purchaser. Technically this did not convey the freehold, so there was no need to enrol the deed.

LEASEHOLD LAND See also Entail, Fee Simple and Freehold. Leasehold land is held for a number of years (often 99) or a number of 'lives'. Leases for lives were in force whilst one of three persons named in the lease was alive, for this reason young children are often named. Names might be substituted when one of the original three 'lives' died or when a tenant sought greater security by changing a name, often for that of someone younger. Leasehold land could be bought and sold but a ground rent was normally payable to the freeholder.

LEATHERCRAFT Two museums with information about the history of leatherworking on their websites are: A Museum of Leathercraft www. museumofleathercraft.org and Walsall Leather Museum www.walsall. gov.uk/ leathermuseum. The latter website has access to sixteen booklets: *Leather: reference and general works. History of Tanning and Currying. The Craft of the Tanner and Currier. The History of the Saddlery and Harness Trades. Making Saddlery and Harness. The Evolution of Saddles. Leathercraft. Costume Accessories. Gloves and Glovemaking. History of the Leathergoods Industry. Bookbinding Techniques. The History of Bookbindings. The History of Shoes and Shoemaking. Making Boots and Shoes. Miscellaneous Leather Products and Crafts. Leather Conservation.*

LEATHERSELLERS The Leathersellers' Company or the Worshipful Company of Leathersellers www.leathersellers.co.uk is one of the ancient Livery Companies of the City of London and is ranked fifteenth in the order of precedence. It was founded by royal charter in 1444. Their website looks at both the ancient and modern functions of the company and contains details of the company's history and archives. See Black, W H *History and Antiquities of the Worshipful Company of Leathersellers* (1887, reprinted Lightening Source UK 2012).

LEET See also Court Leet. Equivalent of a Hundred in East Anglia.

LEGAL PROFESSION Barristers were admitted through the Inns of Court: Lincoln's Inn www.lincolnsinn.org.uk. Middle Temple www.middletemple.org.uk. Inner Temple www.innertemple.org.uk and Gray's Inn www.graysinn.info. Printed lists of entrants to the legal profession via the Inns of Court exist for all but the Inner Temple which has an admissions' database www.innertemple.org.uk/ index.php/history/admissions-database. See for example Foster, Joseph *Register of Admissions to Gray's Inn 1521-1889* (reprinted Ulan Press 2012) and *Register of Admissions to the Honourable Society of the Middle Temple from the Fifteenth Century to the year 1944* compiled by the Middle Temple (Butterworth 1949).

Barristers were usually University graduates, so records of them may be in the Alumni (see Universities). Judges had first to be barristers. The term Serjeant applied to a type of English barrister who practised in the Common Law courts.

He took precedence over "ordinary" barristers. This ceased in 1875. There was a Serjeants' Inn of Court in London.

A consolidated index of admissions to the Inns of Court from Indian and other non-British-born entrants 1859-1887 can be found at www.histecon.magd. cam.ac.uk/research/digitization/rfscott.html. This digitises a manuscript by Sir Robert Forsyth Scott's, the original of which is in Cambridge University Library MS Add.6707 vol. 9.

Solicitors were less frequently graduates, so are harder to trace. Their place of practice may be determined from the *Law List* first published in 1774 and thence annually. Once a name disappears from these lists one might conclude that one has the year of death or retirement. Solicitors usually left wills. Some individual law lists are available online, either via subscription websites or sites giving access to out of print books. TNA has copies for some years in its library

The Law Society, 110-113 Chancery Lane, London WC2A 1PL www.lawsociety.org.uk has a Register of Attorneys and Solicitors which include lists of admissions from 1845 (earlier to some courts) and Registers of Articles of Clerkship from 1860. Earlier Articles of Clerkship (plus indexes), Certificates of Admission and Chancery Oath Rolls are in TNA. Their research guides *Lawyers* and *Lawyers: further research* can be downloaded from their website www.nationalarchives.gov.uk. The Institute of Advanced Legal Studies hold some relevant records. See http://ials.sas.ac.uk/index.asp.

Enquiries regarding Scottish solicitors should be directed to The Law Society of Scotland, 26/28 Drumsheugh Gardens, Edinburgh EH3 7YR www.lawscot.org.uk.

See the detailed guide Brooks, Brian and Herber, Mark *My Ancestor was a Lawyer* (SOG 2009). Also Wade, Stephen, *Tracing your Legal Ancestors: a guide for family historians* (Pen & Sword 2012).

LEGENDS Family legends and stories of our ancestors handed down by word of mouth should be carefully recorded in every detail. They should then be treated with great circumspection and checked against the memories of other elderly members of the same family. There is usually a grain of truth in them but exaggeration, especially of things such as property ownership, is the most common snag. There was a tendency for people to assume, with no foundation of fact, that there was a relationship with some person of importance or renown who had the same surname. Another common fault is for the legend to refer to events which took place several generations earlier than the teller says.

LEGISLATION Access to both historic and current UK legislation can be obtained at www.legislation.gov.uk. This is free of charge, with the website being overseen by TNA. The site carries most but not all, types of UK legislation and their accompanying explanatory documents. See also British History Online (q.v.) www.british-history.ac.uk, which has some statutes of the realm for the C17th and will probably have more in due course.

LETTERS PATENT These are documents granting rights or privileges, in the form of open letters. A Grant of Arms is a typical example. The records run from 1201-1920 and are included within the Chancery Records held at TNA. See their research guide *Royal Grants in Letters Patent and Charters from 1199* at www.nationalarchives.gov.uk.

LEVANT COMPANY See Companies.

LIBERTY Area with freedom, generally by Royal Grant, from Royal Officials and jurisdictions. Marriages could be performed in some Liberties and being exempt from normal ecclesiastical jurisdiction, they became, until 1754, local Gretna Greens. An example is the Peak Forest, Derbyshire.

LIBRARIES See also British Library, Guildhall Library and University Libraries. No serious family historian can conduct research without the use of libraries. See Raymond, Stuart *Using Libraries: workshops for family historians* (FFHS 2001). We have made frequent references to standard works of reference which should be found in libraries. Remember there is an Inter-Library Loan Scheme, by which your library can obtain on loan a book you need which they do not stock.

A detailed list of Specialist Libraries, with addresses, is given in Blatchford, Robert *The Family and Local History Handbook* (14th ed. Blatchford 2013). See also www.genuki.org.uk/big/Archives.html. For a comprehensive listing of addresses and telephone numbers see *Libraries in the United Kingdom and the Republic of Ireland* published bi-annually by Facet. *Aslib Directory of Information Sources in the UK* (17th ed. Routledge 2013) has details of over 5,000 institutions.

The members of the Association of Independent Libraries www. independentlibraries.co.uk are all subscription libraries, founded between 1768 and 1841, before the creation of the public library service. They are not controlled or financed by outside bodies and many of them are still owned by their members. They combine care of their historic buildings with the supply of the latest books and periodicals. Some of the libraries house rare and important books.

The Friends of the National Libraries c/o Department of Manuscripts, The British Library, 96 Euston Road. London NW1 2DB was founded in 1931 to give the Nation's libraries and record offices the same kind of help that art galleries and museums receive from the National Art-Collections Fund. The purpose was to ensure that books and documents of national importance were retained in this country in suitable institutions, well cared for and accessible. The Friends have achieved this in many instances by making grants towards purchases of books and documents and by organising appeals and publicity. See www.friends ofnationallibraries.org.uk.

LIFE ASSURANCE See Insurance.

LIGHT BRIGADE See Crimean War.

LINNEAN SOCIETY OF LONDON, THE www.linnean.org. This society is a forum for natural history. Its Archive Collections, which include portraits, prints and drawings of naturalists, nomination certificates for Fellows of the society and accession registers, are likely to be of interest to family historians.
The society's online collections allow research material to be made available as images in digital formats. This includes the society's correspondence, which comprises over 4,000 letters from 600 different correspondents, with the earliest letters dating from the 1730s.

LIVERY COMPANIES See also Aim25, Apprenticeship Records and Guilds, as well as the entries for the individual livery companies. Livery Companies are the London equivalent of trade guilds. The word "livery" refers to uniform clothing. Livery companies probably existed in the UK prior to 1066 and flourish today as living institutions. Their survival has been achieved by doing what they have always done, namely fostering their trade in a wide context, serving the community and embracing modern skills and professions. Today there are 108 livery companies in the City of London, the most recent Royal Charter having been awarded to the Worshipful Company of Information Technologists (WCIT) in 2010.

The websites of the livery companies typically include details of the company's history, its treasures and its library and archives. The latter are of particular use to researchers, who might even find that an ancestor was a member of a company.

A list of the current London livery companies, with links to their websites, can be found on the website of the City of London at www.cityoflondon.gov.uk/about-the-city/working-with-and-for-others/Pages/city-livery-companies.aspx. The companies in question are: Actuaries. Air Pilots & Air Navigators. Apothecaries (medicine). Arbitrators. Armourers & Brasiers (armour-makers and workers in brass). Bakers. Barbers (also surgeons and dentists). Basketmakers. Blacksmiths. Bowyers (longbow makers). Brewers. Broderers (embroiderers). Builders Merchants. Butchers. Carmen. Carpenters. Chartered Accountants. Chartered Architects. Chartered Secretaries & Administrators. Chartered Surveyors. Clockmakers. Clothworkers. Coachmakers & Coach Harness Makers. Constructors. Cooks. Coopers (barrel makers). Cordwainers (workers in fine leather). Curriers (dressers of tanned leather). Cutlers. Distillers. Drapers. Dyers. Engineers. Environmental Cleaners. Fan Makers. Farmers. Farriers (shoers of horses and veterinary surgeons). Feltmakers (hats). Firefighters. Fishmongers. Fletchers (arrow makers). Founders. Framework Knitters. Fruiterers. Fuellers. Furniture Makers. Gardeners. Girdlers (girdles and belts as clothing). Glass Sellers. Glaziers. Glovers. Gold & Silver Wyre Drawers (gold and silver braid for uniforms). Goldsmiths. Grocers. Gunmakers. Haberdashers. Hackney Carriage Drivers. Horners. Information Technologists. Innholders. Insurers. International Bankers. Ironmongers. Joiners and Ceilers. Launderers. Leathersellers. Lightmongers. Loriners (stirrups and other harness for horses). Makers of Playing Cards. Management Consultants. Marketors. Masons. Master Mariners. Mercers (general merchants). Merchant Taylors (tailors). Musicians. Needlemakers. Painter Stainers. Pattenmakers (makers of wooden clog-style footwear). Paviors (paving, highways). Pewterers. Plaisterers (plasterers). Plumbers. Poulters. Saddlers. Salters. Security Professionals. Scientific Instrument Makers. Scriveners (writers of court letters and legal documents). Shipwrights. Skinners. Solicitors. Spectaclemakers. Stationers & Newspaper Makers. Tallowchandlers. Tax Advisers. Tinplate Workers. Tobacco Pipe Makers & Tobacco Blenders. Turners. Tylers & Bricklayers. Upholders (upholsterers). Vintners. Water Conservators. Wax Chandlers. Weavers. Wheelwrights. Woolmen (winders and packers of wool). World Traders.

There are also two recognised City companies but without the grant of livery, these being: Parish Clerks. Watermen & Lightermen. There are also several London Guilds, as follows: Educators. Public Relations Practitioners. Guild of Art Scholars. Dealers & Collectors.

After many years of fierce dispute, an order of precedence for livery companies was finally settled in 1515, starting with Mercers at number one. The City of London companies, now collectively known as the livery, are unique in their survival, number and diversity. Today, city street names, such as Milk Street, Bread Street, Ironmonger Lane, Poultry, Cloth Fair and Mason's Avenue, mark the sites where their trades began.

The website http://londonroll.org/ is a growing database enabling online searches for apprentices and freemen of various London Livery Companies 1400-1900.

Most of the records of the Livery Companies are in the Guildhall Library (q.v.), although one or two of the Livery Companies which still survive have their own archives.

There is an excellent book by John Kennedy Melling *Discovering London's Guilds and Liveries* (Shire Publications 1995). Also of relevance is the Guildhall Library research guide *Searching for Members or those Apprenticed to Members of City of London Livery Companies*, which can be downloaded from http://www.history.ac.uk/gh/livapp.htm. The websites of the individual Livery Companies will give further information. The Livery Companies Database is hosted by The Fishmongers' Company and can be accessed at http://www.fishhall.org.uk. This contains links to all of the Companies' websites. A similar list of Livery companies can be found at www.cityoflondon.gov.uk.

LLOYDS' BANKING GROUP When Lloyds' Banking Group was formed in 2009, it brought together many well-known companies, including Bank of Scotland, Halifax, Lloyds TSB and Scottish Widows. These businesses' combined histories stretch back to 1695, which means that Lloyds Banking Group holds one of the largest and richest business archives in the UK, with offices in London and Edinburgh.

The webpage at www.lloydsbankinggroup.com/about_us/company_heritage. asp details the group's history. It also contains links to other pages giving details of the group's archives and museums, as well as facilitating access to an interactive timeline that enables the researcher to explore more than three-hundred years of the group's history.

The Group's archives hold the records of all of their main companies. They include minute books, branch records, photographs, advertisements, staff registers and banknotes. The "Collections Index", accessed via the "Our Archives" page, gives an alphabetical list of the many businesses for which records are held in the archives. The "Our Historical Images" webpages include a collection of historical images, which are held in the archives and in many cases, are available online in digital format.

Two of the group's museums have their own websites. The Museum on the Mound in Edinburgh has a site at http://museumonthemound.com. The "Savings Banks Museum" has a splendid website at www.savingsbanksmuseum.co.uk.

LLOYDS' MARINE COLLECTION See Merchant Seamen.

LOCAL HISTORY BIBLIOGRAPHY See also Bibliography and Social history bibliography. Local history provides essential background for family histories, as well as being an interesting subject for research on its own right. Community History might be seen to combine both family and local history. What follows is a small selection of a wide range of books on this topic.

Bristow, Joy *The Local Historian's Glossary of Words and Terms* (Countryside Books 2001).

Brooks, Pamela *How to Research Local History* (How to Books 2006).

Dymond, David *Researching and Writing History: A Guide for Local Historians* (Carnegie Publishing Ltd. 2009).

Fowler, Simon *Starting out in Local History* (Countryside Books 2001).

Friar, Stephen *The Local History Companion* (The History Press 2001).

Hey, David *Family History and Local History in England* (Longman 1987).

Hey, David *The Oxford Companion to Local and Family History* (2nd ed. Oxford University Press 2010).

Hoskins, W G and Hey, David *Local History in England* (Longmans 1984).

Iredale, David *Discovering Local History* (Shire Publications 1973).

Morton, Ann and Donaldson, Gordon *British National Archives and the Local Historian* (The Historical Association 1981).

Porter, Stephen *Exploring Urban History: sources for local historians* (Batsford Ltd. 1991).

Richardson, John *The Local Historian's Encyclopedia* (3rd ed. Historical Publications Ltd. 2003).

Riden, Philip *Local History: a handbook for beginners* (2nd ed. Merton Priory Press 1998).

Riden, Philip *Record Sources for Local History* (Batsford 1987).

Stephens, W B *Sources for English Local History* (revised ed. Cambridge University Press 1981).

Tate, W E *The Parish Chest* (3rd ed. Phillimore 2010).

Tiller, Kate *English Local History: an introduction* (Alan Sutton 1992).

West, John *Town Records* (Phillimore 1983).

West, John *Village Records* (Phillimore 1997).

The are also some useful magazines and journals including:

Local History Magazine available via the Local History Online website www.local-history.co.uk.

The Local Historian www.balh.co.uk.

Local Population Studies www.localpopulationstudies.org.uk.

Family and Community History www.fachrs.com.

There are numerous individual local histories in publication, often privately published with small print runs. An increasing number have been published with the aid of lottery grants. It is worth taking some trouble to discover if an area of interest has been covered, especially as many of these publications are lavishly illustrated. Two major publishers of local histories are Phillimore, Coach Road, Chichester, West Sussex PO20 2BG www.phillimore.co.uk and Halsgrove www.halsgrove.com. Note that a number of local history societies are publishing online.

LOCAL HISTORY SOCIETIES See One Place Studies and Record Societies. If your aim is to write your family history you need as much interesting background material as you can get for the area in which your ancestors lived.

In many counties, towns and villages there are local history societies and in some cases they have published pamphlets about the way of life of people who lived there in the past. There is a British Association for Local History (BALH), PO BOX 6549, Somersal Herbert, Ashbourne DE6 5WH. Their website www.balh.co.uk includes links to many local history societies. A detailed *Directory of Local History and Allied* Societies is available at www.local-history.co.uk/ Groups.

Other organisations, all of whom have useful websites and information to offer, include:

Council for British Archaeology, 66 Bootham, York, Y030 7BZ http://new.archaeologyuk.org/contact-us/.

The Historical Association, 59A Kennington Park Road, London SE11 4JH www.history.org.uk.

Family and Community Historical Research Society www.fachrs.com.

Local Population Studies Society www.localpopulationstudies.org.uk.

Community Archives and Heritage Group www.communityarchives.org.uk

LONDON See also Burial Indexes, Guildhall Library, Livery Companies, Maps, Occupations and Pallot Index. Tracing ancestors who lived in London in the years between the late C18th and civil registration in 1837 can be very difficult as people mostly lived in rented accommodation and changed their addresses frequently. The Pallot Marriage Index (q.v.) can be very helpful.

Boyd's Inhabitants of London, formerly misnamed Boyd's Citizens of London, is a collection of 238 volumes covering the C15th to C19th and is in the Library of the SOG (q.v.). It can be searched via the subscription/pay per view website FindmyPast www.findmypast.co.uk (q.v.). Glass, D V ed. *London Inhabitants within these Walls 1695 Vol 2* (London Record Society 1966) is an index to a taxation "census".

The London Metropolitan Archives (LMA) is at 40 Northampton Road, Clerkenwell, London EC1R OAB. Their webpages are reached via www.cityoflondon.gov.uk, click on "Things to Do", "Visiting the City", "Archives and City History" and "LMA". They hold an enormous collection of archive material about the Greater London area. All records formerly held at the Corporation of London Records Office are now at the LMA. See also Cotton, Carolynne *London Local Archives, A Directory of Local Authority Record Offices and Libraries* (4th ed. Greater London Archives Network 1999).

Archives for London www.archivesforlondon.org, formed in 2005, incorporates several similar bodies. It is an umbrella organisation for professionals, associations and individual users of London archives. There are a wide range of other repositories that may also help with London research.

The website http://maps.thehunthouse.com/index.htm is useful for those interested in London's history and also provides access to old maps. The lists of street name changes are particularly useful.

There are numerous books available on London and its environs. many are listed in Creaton, Heather *Bibliography of Published Works on London History to* 1939 (Library Association 1994). See also Raymond, Stuart *London and Middlesex a genealogical bibliography* (2nd ed. 2 vols. FFHS 1998). General but useful, publications are Weinreb, Ben; Hibbert, Christopher; Keay Julia and Keay, John *The London Encyclopaedia* (3rd ed. MacMillan Reference 2010); Flanders, Judith *The Victorian City: everyday life in Dickens' London* (Atlantic Books 2012); Picard, Liza *Victorian London: the life of a city 1840-1870* (Phoenix 2006); George, M Dorothy *London Life in the Eighteenth Century* (Penguin 1966) and Dalzell, W R *The Shell Guide to The History of London* (Michael Joseph Ltd. 1981). See also Nick Barratt's *Greater London: the story of the suburbs* (Random House 2012).

The books written by Henry Mayhew supply detailed background to the living and working conditions of mid C19th Londoners; in particular a series of four volumes called *London Labour and the London Poor; a cyclopedia of the condition and earnings of those that will work, those that cannot work and those that will not work* (1861, reprinted Cosimo 2009).

The records and maps resulting from Charles Booth's survey of life and labour in late Victorian London are now available online at http://booth.lse.ac.uk/. Maps of bomb damage in London during World War 2 are available at the Bomb Sight website www.bombsight.org. See also the guide *Bomb Census Survey 1940-1945*, which can be downloaded from TNA website www.nationalarchives.gov.uk.

The Centre for Metropolitan History www.history.ac.uk/cmh/main has been set up at the Institute of Historical Research in collaboration with the Museum of London and other organisations. It supports and publishes the results of research projects and runs conferences and workshops. Further details can be obtained from the website or Institute of Historical Research, Senate House, Malet Street, London WC1E 7HU.

The London Topographical Society www.topsoc.org has published a number of books, plans, maps and views that could interest family historians with London connections.

The London Lives project, according to their website www.londonlives.org, "makes available, in a fully digitised and searchable form, a wide range of primary sources about C18th London, with a particular focus on plebeian Londoners. This resource includes over 240,000 manuscript and printed pages from eight London archives and is supplemented by fifteen datasets created by other projects. It provides access to historical records containing over 3.35 million name instances. Facilities are provided to allow users to link together records relating to the same individual, and to compile biographies of the best documented individuals".

A detailed guide to research in London is Webb, Clifford *My Ancestors were Londoners* (SOG 2010).

LONDON GAZETTE This is the official publication of the British government. It was first issued in February 1665/6 and originally appeared on a Tuesday and Friday though for many years it has been issued daily. There are quarterly indexes from the early 1800s.

It publishes official civil, naval, military, church and legal appointments and promotions. Also included are notices on the formation and dissolution of business companies and partnerships, settlements of claims and other financial and legal matters related to individuals and corporate bodies, including bankruptcies and insolvent debtors.

There is a complete set of the *London Gazette* in both the Guildhall Library (q.v.) and the British Library (q.v.). It can also be freely searched and downloaded online www.gazettes-online.co.uk. The similar *Edinburgh Gazette* and *Belfast Gazette*, which deal with matters in Scotland and Northern Ireland, are also available on that website. There is also a history of the *Gazette*.

LONDON METROPOLITAN ARCHIVES See London.

LONDON TRANSPORT MUSEUM The London Transport Museum www. ltmuseum.co.uk is located at Covent Garden. Its website details its collections, including its library and also gives access to a collection of online holdings.

LORD-LIEUTENANT He was appointed by the Crown. When first appointed, by Henry VIII, his main role was to control the crown's military forces. He had entire control of the militia between 1662 and the Forces' Act of 1871, which returned the role to the Crown. See http://www.royal.gov.uk/TheRoyalHousehold/ OfficialRoyalposts/LordLieutenants/LordLieutenants.aspx.

LORD WHARTON BIBLES These bibles were distributed by the trustees of Philip Lord Wharton in 1839, with instructions that family records be included and that they should only be passed on to someone who could read.

LORIMER A lorimer was a maker of bits, spurs and other small ironware for horses. He was sometimes known as a loriner.

LUNATICS See Asylums.

LYING IN HOSPITALS From the mid C18th, these hospitals were established in London and later in other cities. Their registers can be a useful source for missing baptisms.
The British Lying In Hospital at Holborn catered for the distressed poor, with special attention to the wives of soldiers and sailors, though many women appear to have been the wives of servants. Admission was supposedly by recommendation. The baptismal registers are supplemented by the hospital's own records of admissions which give vital and interesting details for the genealogist. The hospital records for the period from 1749 through to 1868 cover over 42,000 admissions and 30,000 baptisms. Many of the individuals mentioned therein do not originate from London. The records of the British Lying In Hospital at Holborn are included on the Family Search website (q.v.) www.familysearch.org. The originals are in TNA class RG8/52-RG8/66 and can be searched via www.bmdregisters.co.uk. Records for Chelsea and Greenwich Lying-in Hospitals are in TNA. A transcription of the Middlesex Hospital register is in the LMA. Their information leaflet *Records of Patients in London Hospitals*, available at www.cityoflondon.gov.uk/things-to-do/visiting-the-city/archives-and-city-history/london-metropolitan-archives/Documents/visitor-information/35-recor ds-of-patients-in-london-hospitals.pdf is relevant.

M

MACHINE BREAKERS See Swing Riots.

MAGAZINES A number of "glossy" magazines dealing with family history are available from larger newsagents or by subscription. Each has its own website, which usually gives an outline of the topics covered in the most recent edition, as well as detailing how back editions can be purchased. Most of these magazines are published every four weeks, making thirteen editions per annum. A selection are listed below:

Family Tree Magazine, the website also has an online bookshop stocking a range of family history titles www.family-tree.co.uk. *Family Tree Magazine* also offers combined digital and print subscriptions, more details of which can be found on their website.

Your Family History www.your-familyhistory.com.

Your Family Tree www.yourfamilytreemag.co.uk.

Who Do You Think You Are? magazine, a "spin-off" from the BBC TV series of the same name www.bbcwhodoyouthinkyouare.com.

The annual "bookazine" *Discover your Ancestors* www.ancestryshop.co.uk/products/books/dya-bookazine. See also the magazine website *Discover Your Ancestors* www.discoveryourancestors.co.uk, which offers a monthly magazine in both pdf and web ready formats.

Irish Roots www.irishrootsmedia.com.

Most Family History Societies (q.v.) also have their own magazines.

It is still worth checking the back runs of genealogical magazines published in the C19th and early C20th. They contain many pedigrees, family histories and original sources. For details see Raymond, Stuart *British Genealogical Periodicals: a bibliography of their contents* (3 vols. in 5 FFHS 1991-1993).

MAGISTRATE See Justices of the Peace.

MAJORITY, AGE OF Sometimes referred to as "of full age" in documents such as marriage certificates. This was lowered from 21 to 18 in 1969. Not to be confused with the age at which marriage was legal. With parental consent, this was 12 for girls and 14 for boys until 1929.

MAKER-UP A term used in the textile industry for a garment assembler. It can also refer to a chemist or druggist.

MANCHESTER A useful website for those with roots in Manchester is "Manchester Family History Research", which can be found at www.manchester-family-history-research.co.uk.

MANCHESTER UNIVERSITY See University Libraries.

MANORIAL RECORDS See also Court Baron, Court Leet, Court Rolls, Estates and Historical Manuscripts Commission. These can be extremely useful when tracing back to pre-parish register times and give background information about one's ancestors. Most are in the keeping of CROs but some are still in private hands. A great many have, unfortunately, been destroyed.

Manorial boundaries did not coincide with those of a parish; any one parish might include portions of several manors. The Manorial Documents Register, now in the care of TNA, assists with the identification of manors in a particular area and with the location of any surviving documents. Many counties can be searched via the Manorial Documents Register pages on TNA website www.nationalarchives.gov.uk/mdr. Additional counties will soon be available in the same way. In the meantime, the remaining English counties are available on microfilm in the Map and Large Document Reading Room at TNA.

Manors; *Manors: further research* and *Using the Manorial Documents Register and how to find Manorial Lordships* are three useful guides that can be downloaded from TNA website www.nationalarchives.gov.uk.

Court Rolls (q.v.) up to 1732 were often in Latin. They list cases for the consideration of the Lord of the Manor and are full of details relating to the tenants, their tenancies, activities and misdemeanours. They are particularly useful for tracing the inheritance of manorial properties.

See Stuart, Denis *Manorial Records: an introduction to their transcription and translation* (Phillimore 1992) and Park, Peter *My Ancestors Were Manorial Tenants: how can I find out more about them?* (SOG 1994).

The Manorial Society of Great Britain, 104 Kennington Road, London SE11 www.msgb.co.uk was founded in 1906. It publishes a journal for its members; information about recent sales of manorial rights may be available from the society though there is no obligation on their part to disclose this.

MANX See Isle of Man.

MAPS See also Enclosure Awards, Parish Maps, Tithes and Valuation Office (Field Books). It is well worth enquiring at CROs about the availability of maps for the areas in which you are interested. The oldest surviving map of Britain, known as the Gough Map, dates from the 1370s. Its website www.goughmap.org allows searches by modern and medieval place name.

Some early maps even give the names of property owners and tenants. Enclosure maps are particularly useful. Estate maps, produced for the benefit of individual landowners, have often also found their way in to CROs but some may remain in private archives.

Tithe maps were produced mainly between 1838 and 1854. The scale of the maps was generally between 13 and 26 inches to the mile, so all buildings are usually shown. They vary in quality, some being more accurately surveyed ("first class maps") than others ("second class"). Three copies were made, one for the parish authorities (this copy is now usually in the CRO), the second went to the Bishop (and may in the DRO) and the third to the Tithe Redemption Commission, whose copies are in TNA. About three-quarters of the country was covered.

Goad maps were drawn up for fire insurance companies in the C18th and C19th. They are named for the business that took over responsibility for their production in 1885. They cover urban and industrial districts of England and Wales. Each map was periodically updated so changes can be pinpointed. For information about more recent Goad maps see www.experian.co.uk/goad. Some are available on CD http://digitalarchives.co.uk/.

The Ordnance Survey www.ordnancesurvey.co.uk, founded in 1791 and originally called the "Trigonometrical Survey" had as its aim to map Great Britain to a scale of 1 inch to the mile. The "Old Series" was produced between 1805 and 1873 but the actual date of publication may have been anything up to 20 years after the survey was made. Before this was completed a "New Series", commencing in 1840, was undertaken, taking 20 years to complete. It covered 300 sheets. From the 1890s there were numerous other series. For some areas a scale as large as 60 inches to the mile was used and thus individual buildings and even outhouses are shown. There are even a few drawn at 10.56 feet to the mile.

The 110 maps of the original edition have been reduced to 97 by transferring small sections of coastline into spare space on adjoining maps and reproduced by David & Charles, of Newton Abbot, Devon TQ12 4YG www.david-archer-maps.co.uk.

See Hewitt, Rachel *Map of a Nation: a biography of the ordnance survey* (Granta Books 2011); Oliver, Richard *Ordnance Survey Maps: a concise guide for historians* (2nd ed. Charles Close Society 2005); Hindle, Paul *Maps for Historians* (Phillimore 1998); Smith, David *Maps and Plans for the Local Historian and Collector* (Batsford 1988), which is particularly intended as a guide to the maps of the British Isles produced before 1914 and Masters, Charles *Essential Maps for Family Historians* (Countryside Books 2009).

The TNA Map Room houses several hundred thousand items including the Tithe Apportionments and Maps (IR29 and IR30). There are 14 TNA research guides relating to different kinds of maps, downloadable from www.national archives.gov.uk.

A series of reproductions of 6" maps are published by Alan Godfrey, Prospect Business Park Leadgate, Consett, DH8 7PW www.alangodfreymaps.co.uk.

The London Topographical Society www.topsoc.org includes amongst its publications maps of C18th and C19th London. Bowles 1795 street map of London can be downloaded from http://commons.wikimedia.org/wiki/File:1795_Bowles_Pocket_Map_of_London_-_Geographicus_-_London-bowles-1795.jpg.

A number of historical maps are available for purchase as facsimiles or on CD or DVD see www.latitudemaps.co.uk/historicalmaps.html; http://digital archives.co.uk/ and http://www.old-maps.co.uk/index.html.

MARINE SOCIETY See National Maritime Museum.

MARINES See Royal Marines.

MARKET TOWNS Towns which had been granted charters permitting them to hold markets or fairs on particular days were known as "market towns". By the C18th, these towns were usually well-placed on the road network and market day served as the main social gathering point for the surrounding areas.

Couples often met at such markets but hailed from villages many miles apart and then married there. For elusive marriages, always check the registers of the nearest market town, which will sometimes be in a neighbouring county.

A comprehensive list of market towns is given in Richardson, John *The Local Historian's Encyclopedia* (3rd ed. Historical Publications Ltd. 2003). TNA website www.nationalarchives.gov.uk contains a research guide entitled *Markets and Fairs*.

Owen's New Book of Fairs (1824), gave a county by county, place-by-place listing of all fairs for the sale of cattle, pigs, sheep, cheese, pedlary and the like. It also contained a monthly list of fairs and an index of places. It is available at http://books.google.co.uk. Another source of contemporary information are directories (q.v.).

MARKS AND SPENCER See also Leeds University. The new company archive of Marks and Spencer has recently opened in the Michael Marks Building, located on the Western Campus at the University of Leeds. The archive and exhibition tracks the company's progress from a penny bazaar stall in Leeds market to its current position as one of the biggest names on the British high street, and houses. This includes: The Marks in Time Exhibition, celebrating the role that M&S has played in people's lives and featuring iconic items from the archive collection to show the development of M&S from Michael Marks' first market stall in Leeds in 1884 to the present day. More than 70,000 items including reports, letters, speeches, employee magazines, advertising material, photographs, films, oral history recordings and merchandise including clothing, food packaging, toys and household items are accessible to anyone wanting to do more in-depth research.

The website http://marksintime.marksandspencer.com/ includes interactive learning resources and an online catalogue. Particularly worth a visit is www.marksintime.marksandspencer.com/ms-history/timeline/.

MARRIAGE See also Civil Registration, Gretna Green Marriages, Parish Registers and Strays. In the case of marriages in Scotland see also Civil

Registration in Scotland, Parish Registers of Scotland and Scotland. For Ireland see also Civil Registration in Ireland, Ireland and Parish Registers of Ireland.

Until the Middle Ages the church had only a limited role in marrying couples, who performed a simple ceremony themselves, usually exchanging vows in a public place before witnesses. This gradually changed and by the C17th most weddings were carried out by the clergy, although many marriages did not comply with the laws of the church (canon law) in some way or other. Marriages that were not conducted within the dictates of canon law were known as common law marriages,

Church weddings are recorded in parish registers from their commencement in 1538. During the Commonwealth (q.v.), in 1653, officials known as "Parish Registers" were appointed. A marriage could only take place after a certificate had been obtained from the Register to state that banns had been called on three Sundays after the morning service, or on three successive market days in the market place. The marriages were solemnised by a Justice of the Peace. An Act of Parliament at the Restoration in 1660 legalised such marriages.

After the Restoration in 1660 the marriage scene became particularly chaotic. Clandestine weddings (without banns or licence, usually in a parish in which neither bride nor groom were resident) became common practice, with two London centres, St James Duke's Place and Holy Trinity Minories, leading the way. At Duke's Place some 40,000 weddings are recorded from the start of the registers in 1665 to 1694; these entries are included in Boyd's Marriage Index (q.v.) but parishes of origin of the parties are not regularly noted in the registers until 1696. At the Minories, although clandestine marriages appear to start in 1644, there is no continuous register sequence until 1676 and although weddings before 1663 are in Boyd, those after that date are not. Those for 1579-1692 are available via the subscription website FindmyPast www.findmy past.co.uk (q.v.) and have been published for 1676-1754 by the East of London Family History Society www.eolfhs.org.uk. Almost all register entries at the Minories contain details of the origins of those marrying. Between them, these two marriage centres accounted for around half of all marriages in London in the late C17th; those marrying came not only from surrounding east London and City parishes but also all over the South East and even further afield, including all social classes from the very rich to very poor, although mariners made up the largest group. After 1695 all weddings there were by licence, as various Acts of Parliament restricted the scope for carrying out clandestine weddings.

From the late 1690s marriages in the chapel of the Fleet Prison became more common, despite the effects of this legislation and by around 1710 the area around the prison, known as "The Rules", became the centre of the clandestine trade, with the weddings carried out in "marriage houses". Marriages in the Fleet reached a peak in the late 1720s and by the late 1740s some 6,500 weddings annually (over half the London total) were performed there, again attracting custom from far and wide. The Fleet became notorious for abuses of the marriage trade and some doubt has been cast over the accuracy of the registers.

Nevertheless, despite these concerns, dubious entries form a small minority and the registers are mostly well-kept, containing details of occupations, status and origins. There are 230,000 or so weddings, making these registers one of the greatest genealogical sources. The registers and notebooks covering the period 1675-1754 are held in class RG7 (with two volumes covering 1726-35 in PROB18/50) at TNA. Registers for other clandestine centres at the King's Bench Prison, the Mint and the Mayfair Chapel (also a major centre in the 1740s) are also found in RG7. These records can be accessed via www.bmdregisters.co.uk for a fee. See also Heber, Mark (ed.) *Clandestine Marriages in the Chapel and Rules of the Fleet Prison 1680-1754 (Fleet Marriage Registers)* (Francis Boutle 1998).

For further information see Benton, Tony *Irregular Marriage in London before 1754* (2nd ed. SOG 2000) and Outhwaite, R *Clandestine Marriage in England, 1500-1850* (Hambledon Continuum 2005).

Clandestine marriages were not confined to London and all over the country before 1754 local marriage "hot spots" are to be found. The introduction of Hardwicke's Marriage Act on 25 March 1754 curtailed the activities of the clandestine centres. With the coming of Civil Registration in 1837 (q.v.), Superintendent Registrars were allowed to issue licences for marriages either in the Registrar's Office or in a non-conformist church.

The Age of Marriage Act of 1929 forbade marriage under the age of 16. Until then, girls of 12 and boys of 14 could legally marry in England. It might, therefore, be worth checking back those few extra years for a missing marriage.

Marriage to a deceased wife's sister was not permissible under Canon law until 1907, as the relationship was within the prohibited degrees. Such marriages did however take place, usually well away from the couple's home area. Up to 1835 such marriages were not void but were voidable by legal action. Few such actions were instituted but the risk was always there.

A marriage is most likely to be found in the bride's parish which was often different from that of the bridegroom, hence marriages can be elusive. Remember that banns were valid for three calendar months after the third calling. There are a number of aids to the genealogist in the form of various indexes, see Boyd's Marriage Index (q.v.) and Family Search (q.v.). For background information see Chapman, Colin *Marriage, Laws, Rites Records and Customs* (Lochin publishing 2008). Gillis, John R *For Better, For Worse: British marriages 1600 to the present* (Oxford University Press 1986) deals with the whole subject of marriages and has an extensive bibliography. See also Stone, Laurence *Uncertain Unions: marriage in England, 1660-1857* (Oxford University Press 1995). Probert, Rebecca *Marriage Law for Genealogists: the definitive guide* (Takeaway publishing 2012). A wide variety of suggestions for tracing marriages can be found in Raymond, Stuart *Marriage Records for Family Historians* (FHP 2010.)

MARRIAGE LICENCES, BONDS AND ALLEGATIONS Licences were issued so that marriages could take place without the necessity for banns to be called.

This was useful if both parties were away from their normal place of residence, or if the parties did not wish to wait for the three week period during which the banns were called. It was also something of a status symbol to be married by licence; it avoided what was regarded as a private family affair being proclaimed to all and sundry.

The licence, which was valid for three calendar months from the date of issue, was generally granted by the Bishop or his surrogate of the diocese in which both parties lived. If they lived in different dioceses other rules applied. Surviving documents can usually be found in the records of the diocese where the marriage took place.

A licence gives names, places of residence, occupations, whether single, widow or widower, ages, parishes and in the case of minors, fathers/guardians and their consent and the place where the marriage was to take place. In 1822, an Act required applicants for licences to produce documentary evidence of their birth or baptism and these certificates were attached. Owing to administrative difficulties, the Act was repealed within a year.

The licence itself would be given to the parties who were being married but an "Allegation", i.e. a statement made by the parties affirming their intention to marry, was kept by the Diocesan registry. With it would be "Bonds", assurances by bondsmen, often friends or relatives (one was usually the groom himself), in which the sureties undertook to ensure that the couple would be married in a specified church or chapel. The license was presented to the celebrant, who very occasionally kept them; they can therefore sometimes be found amongst parish records.

Bonds and Allegations can be seen in Diocesan Record Offices or CROs. Those for York Province are at the Borthwick Institute of Historical Research, University of York, Heslington, York, YO10 5DD www.york.ac.uk/library/borthwick. Published indexes currently cover 1750-1839. Province of Canterbury records are at Lambeth Palace Library, London SE1 7JU www.lambethpalacelibrary.org.

Sometimes extensive searches for marriages fail, yet the evidence for a marriage survives in these documents. It is interesting to note that Shakespeare's marriage entry has not been found in a register. Yet at the Worcester Diocesan Registry two allegations have been found, one for the marriage of a William Shakespeare dated 27th November 1582 to Anne Whateley and another dated 28th November 1582 to Anne Hathaway. This strange duplication has been attributed to a clerical error!

MARRIAGE REGISTERS See Non-conformists and Parish Registers.

MARRIAGE TAX See Registration Tax.

MARSHALSEA Former prison in Southwark, London, principally a Debtors' Prison.

MASONS See also Freemasons. The Worshipful Company of Masons is a London Livery company that can trace its history back to 1356. It received its Royal Charter in 1677. The Company's website at www.masonslivery.co.uk contains details of its history, as does Conder, Edward *History of the Worshipful Company of Masons of the City of London* (Lightening Source UK 2012).

MASTER GENEALOGIST, THE (TMG) See Computer Software.

MECHANICAL ENGINEERS, INSTITUTION OF The Institution of Mechanical Engineers (IMechE) http://imeche.org/ has a library and archive, which retains the Institution's Council and Committee minutes from its founding in 1847. Other archival material held includes membership proposal forms, which give details of date and place of birth, schooling and early career of individual members. IMechE proceedings list dates of election to membership, any publications written and memoirs of the members. Also held are IMechE meeting attendance books.

The Institution also collects the papers of its members, for example personal manuscripts of George and Robert Stephenson and Frederick Lanchester are held. They also hold archives the Institutions of Automobile and Locomotive Engineers and the minutes of the Association of Railway Locomotive Engineers.

Company records held include: D. Napier and Son, engine builders. Livesey Henderson and Co., railway contractors. Joseph Whitworth and Co. and Nasmyth Gaskell and Co., both machine tool manufacturers. ICI Limited, chemical industrialists.

The IMechE has launched the Engineering Heritage website http://heritage.imeche.org/ which details: The history of mechanical engineering. The history of Institution of Mechanical Engineers. All of the past Presidents of the institution, with photographs and biographical details of each. The history of 1 Birdcage Walk, the headquarters of the Institution.

MEDALS Records of medal rolls are at TNA. There are several research guides available on their website, which might assist with this topic but see in particular *British Military Campaign and Service Medals; British Army medal index cards 1914-1920; British Military Gallantry Medals; Civilian Gallantry Medals; Merchant Seamen's Campaign Medal Records 1914-1918; Merchant Seamen's Campaign Medal Records 1939-1945* and *Merchant Seamen's Medals and Honours.* Army and Royal Flying Corps medal index cards give the soldier's name, corps (regiment), rank, regimental number and medals awarded, sometimes with additional information about where they served. These cover the 5.5 million records of those who served abroad in the First World War. The original cards are in class WO372 at TNA but they are indexed and available online via TNA's "Discovery" catalogue.

With a few exceptions, Gallantry and Meritorious Service Awards are "gazetted", published in *The London Gazette* (q.v.) and the Scottish and Irish equivalents.

Details of recipients of the Victoria Cross are held by The Victoria Cross Society www.victoriacross.org.uk. The George Cross database can be consulted at www.marionhebblethwaite.co.uk/gcindex.htm.

The website www.gov.uk/medals-campaigns-descriptions-and-eligibility contains no names but gives details of more recently awarded medals and who is entitled to them. In most cases, next of kin can apply for retrospective awards, if the recipient did not claim their medals. Soldiers of the First World War 1914-1918 were sent their medals automatically; officers had to apply for them. Circumstances made it impossible to adopt this procedure during the Second World War.

With the creation of the RAF in 1918, four gallantry awards were instituted for the new service. There are relevant records at TNA. Regulations governing the award of medals in the RAF are in Air Ministry Orders AIR 72. For the First World War surviving recommendations are in AIR1; from 1918 AIR2, "B", code 30 and AIR30. During the Second World War awards were of two types, immediate (for single acts of bravery) and non-immediate (given at conclusion of a tour of duty between 25 and 30 operations). Contact Ministry of Defence, RAF Personnel Management Centre, PMa.3 (d) (4), RAF Innsworth, Gloucestershire GL3 1EZ.

Campaign/War Medals awarded to Marines are recorded in Admiralty Medal Rolls TNA class ADM171. Gallantry Medals are in classes ADM1 and ADM116. During the First World War, many Royal Marines were given army gallantry medals. The Royal Marines Medal roll 1914-1920 is included on the FindmyPast (q.v.) subscription website www.findmypast.co.uk. Contact Ministry of Defence, Drafting and Record Office Royal Marines, HMS Centurion, Grange Road, Gosport, Hampshire PO13 9XA.

Campaign and War medal rolls are at TNA in class ADM171. Medal rolls for the First World War are in records class ADM171/89-134. Gallantry medal rolls are in ADM1, code 85 and ADM116, code 85. Registers of awards to naval officers during the First World War are in ADM171/78-88.

The Orders and Medals Research Society holds monthly meetings and issues a quarterly journal. Further details can be obtained from www.omrs.org.uk.

There are a number of books and articles to help you identify medals and in the case of war medals, to tell you more about the campaigns for which they were awarded: Duckers, Peter *British Gallantry Awards 1855*-2000 (Shire Publications 2005). Abbott, P E and Tamplin, J M A *British Gallantry Awards* (Guinness World Records Ltd 1971). Gordon, L L *British Battles and Medals* (6th ed. Spink & son 1988). Farrington, A *Guide to Medal Rolls* (India Office Library 1980). *The Register of the Victoria Cross* (This England 1981) and *The Register of the George Cross* (This England 1990). Joslin, Edward C *Observer's Book of Awards and Medals* (Frederick Warne 1972). Hall, Don *British Orders, Decorations and Medals* (Balfour Publications 1973). Dorling, H Taprell *Ribbons and Medals* (revised ed. Geo. Phillip & Son 1974). Carter, T and Long, W H *War Medals of the British Army: and how they were won* (reprinted Ulan Press 2012).

MEDIEVAL See also British History Online, Domesday Book and Wills. Denotes records kept before about 1485. If your research has progressed thus far, read TNA research guide *Medieval and Early Modern Family History* from www.nationalarchives.gov.uk. See also Franklin, Peter *Some Medieval Records for Family Historians* (FFHS 1994). The types of records available include: Inquisitions Post Mortem (q.v.), Close Rolls (q.v.), Pipe Rolls (q.v.), Manorial Records (q.v.), Feet of Fines (q.v.) etc.. Many of these were written in Latin. A very interesting and informative website is www.medievalgenealogy.org.uk. This gives background information and includes a search facility. See also Manuscripts Online www.manuscriptsonline.org, which enables many primary resources and catalogues for the period 1000-1500 to be searched.

For the C11th see the Battle Abbey Roll, which can be viewed online at www.robertsewell.ca/battleabbey.html.

To encourage the resurgence of interest in the country's medieval period The Ranulf Higden Society has been formed. Named after the monkish author of the *Polychronicon* it is principally a society for self-help to develop skills for those who read medieval manuscripts www.ranulfhigden.org.uk. Further information available from the Secretary, Southerton, Hazler Road, Church Stretton, Salop SY6 7AQ or the Departments of History at the Universities of Keele and Liverpool or the John Rylands University Library, Deansgate, Manchester.

The Foundation for Medieval Genealogy http://fmg.ac issues an annual journal *Foundations*, arranges conferences and the website contains online resources.

For Irish research during this period see Connolly, Philomena *Medieval Record Sources (Maynooth Research Guides for Irish Local History)* (Four Courts Press 2002).

MEDICAL PROFESSION See also Apothecaries, Florence Nightingale Museum and Nursing. The medical profession included physicians, doctors, barber surgeons and apothecaries and their comparative status was in that order. The vast majority of records relating to these are deposited at the Guildhall Library (q.v.). Physicians were usually university men or members of the College of Physicians. The internal records of the Royal College of Physicians of London are in the library of the College, 11 St Andrews Place, London, NW1 4LE www.rcplondon.ac.uk. Information concerning the medical profession in Scotland is available from the Royal College of Physicians of Edinburgh, 9 Queen Street, Edinburgh, EH2 1JQ www.rcpe.ac.uk who have lists of members since its foundation in 1681. William Munk's *Roll of the Royal College of Physicians* (3 vols. Harrison and Sons 1878) has been continued to the C21st by the Royal College of Physicians. These give details of well-known members of the profession. From the early C19th medical directories can be helpful, with an obituary notice in the volume covering the year of the physician's death. There are plans to make this available online. In the meantime indexes can be browsed here http://munksroll.rcplondon.ac.uk/. Important collections are also held at the Royal College of Physicians and Surgeons of Glasgow, 234-242 St Vincent Street, Glasgow, G2 5RJ www.rcpsg.ac.uk, which was established in 1599.

Wallis, P J & R V *Eighteenth Century Medics* (2nd ed. Project for Historical Bio-Bibliography, Newcastle upon Tyne 1988). It is advisable to read the Introduction before embarking upon the contents of this book, which contains brief summaries of the 80,000 entries for medical practitioners, physicians, surgeons, apothecaries, pharmacists, distillers, chemists, druggists, dentists, opticians, midwives and patent-medicine sellers. There is a bibliography and the index of places is printed as a separate booklet.

Many medical men qualified at Trinity College, Dublin, or at the universities at Glasgow or Aberdeen (see Alumni) so records of these establishments could be helpful. Leyden, in Holland, was also a popular place at which to qualify. See Smith, Robert William *English Operating Students of Medicine at the University of Leiden* (Oliver & Boyd 1932).

Medical Registers first appeared in 1858 and contain biographies of practitioners. The London and Provincial Medical Directory began in 1861.

From 1511 doctors should have been licensed. These were issued by bishops, archbishops and by the Royal College of Physicians. These may be found with the records of the ecclesiastical courts (q.v.). In 1858 regulation was transferred to the General Medical Council. Medical licences issued by the Archbishop of Canterbury 1535-1775 are held by Lambeth Palace Library www.lambethpalacelibrary.org.

Surgeons up to 1745 were associated with the Surgeons and Barbers Company of London. The Company of Surgeons was established in 1745. Detailed lists of Apprentices, Surgeons and Company Officials, those fined or disenfranchised and relevant bibliographies appear in the following: Wall, Cecil *The History of the Surgeons' Company 1745 to 1800* (Hutchinson 1937). Cope, Sir Zachary *The History of the Royal College of Surgeons of England* (Blond 1959). The Royal College of Surgeons www.rcseng.ac.uk was founded in 1800 and led to an improvement in status. Details of deceased fellows have been published by the College in several volumes of *Lives of the Fellows of the Royal College of Surgeons (England)*. This is now online at http://livesonline.rcseng.ac.uk.

Records held by the College include the following: Examination Books of the College from 1800 and the Examination Book of the Surgeons' Company 1745-1799. 1541-1745 are in the Guildhall Library (q.v.). These give names of candidates, examinations sat, whether passed or failed and occasionally place of residence. An Apprentice Book 1784-1846. The Medical Directory 1845 to date. Miscellaneous publications listing graduates of various universities and members of the Army and Indian Medical Services etc.. Specific enquiries should be addressed to The Librarian, Royal College of Surgeons, 35-43 Lincoln's Inn Fields, London WC2A 3PN www.rcseng.ac.uk.

Information about surgeons in the Army or Navy should be sought in military records (q.v.) but see also Peterkin, A and Johnston, W *Commissioned Officers in the Medical Services of the British Army 1660-1960, Volume I: 1660-1898* and Drew, Robert *Volume II: 1898-1960* both (Wellcome Historical Medical Library 1968).

The Royal Society of Medicine, 1 Wimpole Street, London W1M 8AE www.rsm.ac.uk, keeps the papers of the important societies that preceded its formation in 1907. The library is in the process of adding digital images of portraits to their online searchable catalogue.

The Wellcome Institute for the History of Medicine http://library.wellcome.ac.uk/ houses the medical history library at 183 Euston Road, London NW1 2BP. Records are available to the public by arrangement.

Glasgow University Library www.gla.ac.uk has a fine medical section with a particular emphasis on the William Hunter collection of manuscripts and books.

Death notices and obituaries often appeared in *The Lancet* (first published 1823) www.thelancet.com, *The British Medical Journal* (first published 1857) www.bmj.com and *The Medical Directory* (1845-1914 only). There are indexes to the first two publications.

MEDWAY ON SCREEN The "Medway on Screen" project comprises archive film of the River Medway and the towns and villages it passes through. It records the social, industrial and agricultural history of Medway and Kent in the last century. The film captures many of the industries and communities associated with the Medway as they were in the 1930s and 1940s. From the hop fields near Tonbridge to the breweries, factories and docklands at Maidstone and the Medway towns, the river connected contrasting ways of life and enabled the development of a thriving industrial base. The footage can be viewed free-of-charge at www.brighton.ac.uk/screenarchive/medway/index.html.

MEETING HOUSES See Toleration Act.

MEMBERS' INTERESTS See Surname Interests' Lists.

MEMORIAL INSCRIPTIONS See Monumental Inscriptions.

MERCER A mercer was a dealer in silk, cotton, woollen and linen goods. The Mercers' Company www.mercers.co.uk is the premier livery company of the City of London. It received its first charter in 1394 but its origins go much further back. Today the Company has around 360 members and 40 staff based at Mercers' Hall in the City of London. Its Archive holds records of the Company dating from the C14th to the present. They document the day-to-day operation of the Company, including management of its large property estate, schools, almshouses and associated charities and trusts as well as admission of members and apprentices. It is an important source for the history of the City of

London, British trade, the history of charity and philanthropy, education and genealogy. The archive is also responsible for the management and preservation of the Company's collections of art, plate, textiles and furniture.

MERCHANT The term tended to be used for those who carried on trade on a large scale, especially with foreign countries but an ordinary shopkeeper might describe himself as a merchant.

MERCHANT SEAMEN See also Fishermen and Sea Deaths. Useful books include: Wells, Simon *Tracing Your Merchant Navy Ancestors* (Pen and Sword Books 2012) and Watts, Christopher & Watts, Michael *My Ancestor Was A Merchant Seaman: how can I find out more about him?* (2nd ed. SOG 2002). The Crew List Index Project website www.crewlist.org.uk/index.html contains background information and lists of the whereabouts of various classes of record. The project's index can be accessed via the FindmyPast (q.v.) subscription or pay per view website www.findmypast.co.uk .

The records of the Registrar General of Shipping and Seamen 1835 to 1857 give place of birth for those in the merchant navy. These are at TNA and they produce a guide *Merchant Seamen Serving up to 1857: further research*. Several other useful research guides can be downloaded from their website www.nationalarchives.gov.uk including *Crew Lists, Agreements and Log Books of Merchant Ships 1747-1860*, *Officers in the Merchant Navy* and *Looking for Records of a Merchant Seaman Serving between 1858 and 1917*.

For earlier records, such as crew lists, you need to know the names of the ships and their ports of registration. Apart from the Register of Seamen, there are other registers such as: Certificates of competence and service of masters and mates. Certificates of competence and service of engineers. Certificates of competence of skippers and mates, fishing boats. Registers of the wages and effects of deceased seamen. Index of apprentices and apprentices' indentures. Registers of births, marriages and deaths of passengers at sea compiled from official ships' logs. Registers of births and deaths of British Nationals at sea.

Lloyd's' Marine Collection, deposited at the Guildhall Library (q.v.), includes Lloyd's Captains' Registers 1868 to 1947 listing all holders of masters certificates with full name, place and date of birth and a complete service history. The Information Centre, Lloyd's Register of Shipping, 71 Fenchurch Street, London, EC3M 4BS www.lr.org/about_us/shipping_information/referencelibrary.aspx hold records including: Registers of Ships from 1764 which name the owners and builders of the ships; Registers of Shipyards just prior to 1800 through to 1980 and some Casualty Returns. They do not hold crew or passenger lists or records of naval ships.

The Registrar General holds registers of births and deaths of Merchant Navy personnel 1837 to 1890 and these are found with other records of Civil Registration (q.v.). From 1891 they are held by the Registrar-General for

Shipping and Seamen, Block 2, Government Buildings, St Agnes Road, Gabalfa, Cardiff CF4 4YA.

Requests by dependents of seamen, naval men etc. for assistance were made to Trinity House (founded in 1529 to deal with matters related to safety at sea etc.) in the form of a "petition" from which we can glean interesting family history data. They span the years 1780 to 1854 and are available via FindmyPast (q.v.). See also the published index *Trinity House Petitions: a calendar of the records of the Corporation of Trinity House, London in the library of the SOG* (SOG 1987).

A very large collection of Crew Lists, Agreements and Official Logs 1861-1938 are in the custody of the Memorial University of Newfoundland. Details can be found on The Maritime History Archive website www.mun.ca/mha/about.php, which also lists the whereabouts of other relevant records that are not held by the university.

The Cornish Masters and Mates Project have produced a CD containing some 4,250 names of Cornish-born masters and mates (the Officer class of the Merchant Navy) published as a joint venture between the London Cornish Association (LCA), Cornwall Family History Society (CFHS) and the National Maritime Museum Cornwall (NMMC).

MERCHANT TAYLORS The Merchant Taylors' Company www.merchant-taylors.co.uk is one of the twelve great city livery companies surviving from mediaeval times. It was originally founded by an association of citizens who were tailors and linen armourers but the position of the company gradually changed. By the end of the C17th its connection with the tailoring trade had virtually ceased and it became what it is today, an association of philanthropic and social character, devoting its energies to educational and charitable activities.

The history of the Merchant Taylors' Company is an integral part of the history of the City of London. Their website contains: Downloadable documents that detail the company's history. The history of the company. A chronology of the company's role in church and charity. A chronology of the company's role in education. The history of the hall.

The company's membership index, covering the period from 1530 through to 1928, is now available online. This comprises four huge volumes containing 36,000 names and was compiled in the early 1930s. Name searches online are free and full details are available for a small charge. Alternatively, a CD of the whole index can be purchased outright.

MESNE LORD See also Manorial Records. A middle lord of the manor who himself held under a superior lord.

MESSUAGE A term often found in wills. It meant a house with its outbuildings and yard and sometimes also included the garden.

METHODISTS See also Bible Christians and Wesleyan Methodist Historic Roll. The Movement, an evangelical movement within the Anglican Church [q.v.], was founded by John Wesley in 1729 at Oxford. After Wesley's death in 1791 it broke away from the Anglican Church and split into a number of factions. These included the Methodist New Connexion 1797, the Primitive Methodists 1807, the Bible Christians 1815, the Protestant Methodists 1828 and the United Methodists' Free Churches 1857, amongst others. The various factions eventually came together to form the Methodist Church in 1932.

Most registers of Baptisms and Burials to 1837 were deposited with the Registrar General and are in TNA. There was a Methodist Metropolitan Registry for the registration of baptisms begun in 1818 and surrendered to the Registrar General with other registers in 1840. These can be accessed via www. bmdregisters.co.uk. The Methodist Archives and Research Centre (MARC) was founded in 1961 to house the Connexional records of the Church. It is housed at the John Rylands Library, 150 Deansgate, Manchester, M3 3EH www.library. manchester.ac.uk/deansgate. The John Rylands Library holds runs of denomi-national magazines which include many obituaries of ministers and laymen. Also many collections of private papers of prominent Methodists. They only hold national and district records; circuit and chapel records are kept locally in CROs and similar repositories. There are no genealogical records in the Methodist Archives, no baptismal, marriage or burial records, nor is it possible for any member of the staff to undertake any form of research as the Centre is not financed for this purpose.

The Library does hold official obituaries of Methodist ministers but these are largely concerned with the spiritual life of ministers and not with their temporal affairs. There is little information in the archives on Methodist local preachers and lay persons, the only regularly used source being their index to the obituaries in the major Methodist periodicals.

Each of the 32 Methodist Districts in the country has its own honorary archivist who should be able to direct enquirers to the appropriate repository.

The Wesley Historical Society www.wesleyhistoricalsociety.org.uk concerns itself with all branches of Methodism. See also The Historical Society of the United Methodist Church www.historicalsocietyunitedmethodistchurch.org.

A magazine *The Arminian* was first issued in 1778 and there followed several changes of title. An index covering the years 1778-1839 was published in the *Proceedings of the Wesley Historical Society* Volume 7 1909-10. In later magazines there are many references to members as well as to preachers. Some issues are available online.

The *Local Preachers' Magazine* 1851-1930 contains useful obituary notices and has been indexed.

Minutes of local Methodist Meetings are sometimes found deposited in CROs. These often name individuals, either because they acted in some official capacity or were given financial assistance or for some other reason.

See Leary, William *My Ancestors Were Methodists: how can I find out more about them?* (SOG 1993).

The websites My Methodist History www.MyMethodistHistory.org.uk; My Primitive Methodist Ancestors www.MyPrimitiveMethodists.org.uk and My Wesleyan Methodist Ancestors www.MyWesleyanMethodists.org.uk are all part of the Methodist Heritage www.methodistheritage.org.uk family, sponsored by the Methodist Church. They also administer the site www.mymethodist history.org.uk, which allows the exchange of information related to Methodist history.

MICHAELMAS The Feast of St Michael, 29th September. One of the Quarter Days (q.v.).

MIGRANTS The term is used frequently to describe people moving from one place to another within a country, as opposed to immigrants and emigrants, who move from one country to another. See Camp, A J *My Ancestors Moved in England or Wales: how can I trace where they came from?* (2nd revised ed. SOG 1994).

MILITARY See Army, Navy, Royal Air Force, Royal Marines.

MILITIA From the Anglo-Saxon period, able-bodied men between the ages of 16 and 60 were liable to perform military service for local defence and occasionally further afield. Formal inspections were known as "musters". Militia Muster Rolls from 1522-1640 are in TNA; their research guides *Militia* and *Militia: further research* are available at www.nationalarchives.gov.uk. Later Muster Rolls may be found in Quarter Sessions (q.v.) records deposited in CROs. An enlightening book on the subject is Western, J R *The English Militia in the Eighteenth Century: the story of a political issue 1660-1802* (Routledge and Kegan Paul 1965).

Gibson, Jeremy and Dell, Alan *Tudor and Stuart Muster Rolls* (FFHS 1996) and Gibson, Jeremy and Medlycott, Mervyn *Militia Lists and Musters 1757-1876* (FFHS 2000) give further locations of these documents where extant. The Introductions are most informative. Although not strictly relating to the militia, Alistair Livingstone, Christine Aikman and Betty Hart (ed.) *Muster Roll of Prince Charles Edward Stuart's Army 1745-46* (Aberdeen University Press 1984) contains some 4,800 names culled from almost 50 written sources.

MILLINERS See also Haberdasher. Maker or seller of women's hats.

MILLS ARCHIVE TRUST www.millsarchivetrust.org. This archive specialises in the records of windmills and watermills and is based in Reading. Its website gives further details of its: Archive of original documents, images and artefacts. Library of mill-related books and journals. Research services. Books, publications and other items for sale. Services to family historians. Discussion forum. Newsletter.

The online archive catalogue contains more than one million records from more than fifty collections. There are numerous digital images of documents, whilst the "People Index" contains many photographs and documents. It includes information on millers, millwrights, mill owners, engineers and others with an involvement in milling.

MINING See also Bevin Boys and Industrial Archaeology. Mining history in the UK reflects a diverse collection of industries including coal mining, tin mining, lead mining and quarrying. These distinct industries were very different and were often based in different geographical areas.

The website of the National Association of Mining History Organisations www.namho.org is a good starting point. This was formed in 1979 to act as the national body for mining history in the UK and Ireland. There are now over fifty member organisations, including societies, museums, firms and the like. Links are included to all of the member societies' websites, of which some examples are: Welsh Mines Society. Mining Heritage Trust of Ireland. East Cornwall Mining History Association. Cleveland Ironstone Mining Museum. Northern Mine Research Society.

A website Mining Memorabilia www.mining-memorabilia.co.uk contains links to a large number of mining-related websites. These will be of particular interest to those who want information on coal mining overseas.

A highly recommended website is Ian Winstanley's Mining History UK, which can be found at www.cmhrc.co.uk. This includes sections on mining disasters and the "National Database of Mining Deaths in Great Britain", which commences in 1700.

The National Coal Mining Museum for England at Wakefield www.ncm.org.uk has a museum and library, whilst the website includes a study guide as well as a "virtual" tour of the museum.

A National Archives' research guide of relevance is *Mines and Mining* www.nationalarchives.gov.uk.

Those interested in Welsh coal miners should see www.welshcoalmines. co.uk. For Scottish mining see www.ancestralscotland.com/research-your-roots/working-men-and-women/coalminers/.

The Annual Reports of HM Inspectors of Mines contain information often of help to researchers, such as details of persons killed or injured in a mining accident. These and other records of the coal industry, including those of pre-nationalised mining companies, tend to be held by CROs and local studies libraries. It should be borne in mind that such records might be found in unexpected places. Whilst one would naturally expect to find relevant material in record offices located in counties such as Lancashire, Yorkshire, Derbyshire and Nottinghamshire, the holdings of the Churchill Archives Centre of Cambridge

University www.chu.cam.ac.uk/archives/ are possibly a less-likely source of mining data.

The mining and in particular the coal mining industry spawned a large number of publications in its heyday. These included the: *Directory of Quarries and Pits* (Quarry Managers' Association). *Colliery Year Book*, an annual publication that commenced in 1922. *Mining Journal*, which was published weekly and commenced in 1835. *Colliery Guardian*, a broadsheet newspaper which commenced publication in 1858 and its sister publication the *Colliery Guardian Annual Guide to the Coalfields*, which commenced in 1948.

Publications of this nature can be laborious to use, as they are not indexed and typically contain a lot of technical information that is not really relevant to the family historian. They do however give a good feel for the industries in which our ancestors worked and can be particularly useful when researching an event, such as a mining disaster. Holdings of such publications may be found in the British Library and in larger reference libraries and local studies' centres in the traditional mining areas.

There are many books about mines, miners and mining. See Tonks, David *My Ancestor was a Coalminer* (2nd ed. SOG 2010).

MISSING PERSONS Tracing a relative or erstwhile friend or acquaintance can sometimes prove more difficult than tracing your ancestors. Obvious sources include a mutual contact, internet, telephone directory, letter to a newspaper. Social media sites such as Friends Reunited www.friendsreunited.co.uk and Facebook www.facebook.com might be helpful. For people likely to be in the UK, www.192.com is a good place to start but only limited information is available for free.

The Charity Missing People (formerly The National Missing Persons Helpline) www.missingpeople.org.uk seeks to locate people who have gone missing for whatever reason and which offers support to those left behind. In the event of the missing person being located, a confidential link between the two will be provided.

The Salvation Army Family Tracing Service has branches in several countries. For the UK see www.salvationarmy.org.uk/uki/FamilyTracing.

The Red Cross also run a tracing service see 'What we do' at www.redcross.org.uk. They concentrate on those separated by conflict and disaster.

MISSIONARIES Usually persons sent overseas or into urban areas by a religious community to spread its gospel; they often worked in hospitals or schools. The choice of which Missionary Society a missionary worked for depended on a person's denomination.

The best place to start is the gateway website "Mundus" www.mundus.ac.uk, which provides "a web-based guide to more than four hundred collections of overseas missionary materials held in the United Kingdom. These materials, comprising the archives of British missionary societies, collections of personal papers, printed matter, photographs, other visual materials and artefacts, are held in a large number of libraries, record offices and other institutions."

Some of the largest Missionary Societies were: London Missionary Society (Congregational). Methodist Missionary Society. The Baptists' Missionary Society. United Society for the Propagation of the Gospel (Anglican). The Society for Promoting Christian Knowledge; archives at Holy Trinity Church, Marylebone Road, London NW1. The Church Missionary Society (Anglican).The British and Foreign Bible Society, publisher and distributor of bibles in all languages around the world, deposited its archives in Cambridge University Library, West Road, Cambridge CB3 9DR but they contain very little biographical information.

MODERN RECORDS CENTRE, THE See also Trade Unions. The Modern Records' Centre holds a range of primary sources for modern British social, political and economic history, including records of: Trade unions and related organisations. Trade associations, employers' organisations and related bodies. The motor and related industries, especially through formal agreement with Rover and the British Motor Industry Heritage Trust. Cycling, in the form of the National Cycle Archive. Radical British political movements. Pressure groups and other organisations concerned with social and penal reform, human rights, disarmament, education and health. The organisations whose archives are held at the Modern Records' Centre include the Trades Union Congress, the Confederation of British Industry and its predecessors, the Campaign for Nuclear Disarmament and Amnesty International. The Centre also houses the BP (British Petroleum) Archive. The Centre has also published a number of books and those which are not out of print can be purchased from its website. There is also a series of information leaflets that can be downloaded free of charge from the Centre's website. These are incredibly detailed and should be studied before embarking on any visit to the Centre. The Working Class Movement Library www.wcml.org.uk 51 The Crescent, Salford M5 4WX holds a large collection of records and ephemera for some unions.

MONEY See Coinage and Inflation.

MONUMENTAL BRASSES The website of the Monumental Brass Society www.mbs-brasses.co.uk details the work done by the society on the study, preservation and recording of monumental brasses. It also lists the society's meetings, events and publications and a detailed bibliography for those who want to learn more about the subject.

MONUMENTAL INSCRIPTIONS (MIs) See also War Memorials. These can be very informative and may give dates of birth and death, abodes and relationships. Sometimes those who died overseas, or who were lost at sea (so have no death certificate or burial) will also be commemorated. Older epitaphs are sometimes in Latin. See Parker, John *Reading Latin epitaphs: a handbook for beginners* (new ed. University of Exeter Press 2012). In the 1980s and 1990s, encouraged by the FFHS, many County Family History Societies organised groups of members to record the inscriptions on tombstones in churchyards and in the older parts of cemeteries. These transcripts were then usually deposited in CROs, libraries and in the library of the SOG (q.v.). Increasing numbers are now being made available online. They may include records of stones that have been moved, damaged or become illegible in the ensuing years. Many published collections of inscriptions are listed in the county volumes of Stuart Raymond's series of genealogical bibliographies.

Try www.gravestonephotos.com, a worldwide site of gravestone photographs. With such wide geographical coverage, finding an ancestor will be a matter of luck; it is worth a look nonetheless.

See Burgess, Frederick *English Churchyard Memorials* (SPCK 1979) for chapters on the origins and developments of churchyards and cemeteries; on the types and designs of monuments; the techniques of the masons; a useful glossary of terms associated with memorials and a list of some monumental stone carvers. Kemp, Brian *Church Monuments* (Shire Publications 2010) is a basic introduction to the subject which gives suggestions for further reading.

Memorial inscriptions to people connected with the sea (including ship owners, shipwrights, merchant seamen as well as naval men) are being collected by the National Maritime Museum http://memorials.rmg.co.uk.

An enormous number of monuments dating from C12th to C21st can be seen in cathedrals and churches throughout the country. As well as being part of our historical and cultural heritage, many bear inscriptions of interest and should not be overlooked in the course of research. The Church Monuments Society www.churchmonumentssociety.org encourages the appreciation of church monuments.

A CD *Inventory of Scottish Graveyards* 2nd ed. collates information from over 3,500 cemeteries, burial places, crematoria and individual graves. It is available from The Scottish Association of Family History Societies www.safhs.org.uk.

For an Irish gravestone transcribing project see http://historicgraves.com/.

MORAVIANS The Moravian Church developed as a revival of the "Bohemian Brethren", founded by followers of John Huss in 1457. Their beliefs were spread all over the world by missionaries and churches were set up in this country in the mid C18th.

Their registers were deposited with the Registrar General in 1840. John Wesley was much influenced by their chief belief which was that faith is directly inspired by God. Their established settlements, some of which still survive, hold useful records. These include Mirfield, Fulneck and Pudsey, in Yorkshire; Dukinfield, Cheshire and Fairfield, Lancashire. For details of Moravian church archives see www.moravians.co.uk/index.php/church-house/church-archives.

MORMONS See Church of Jesus Christ of Latter-Day Saints.

MOTOR CARS The museum of the Heritage Motor Centre www.heritage-motor-centre.co.uk at Gaydon in South Warwickshire tells the story of the motor car from some of the very first models to take to British roads, right up to the latest designs. The centre also holds an Archive Collection, which has its origins in the creation of British Leyland Motor Corporation in 1968. Various mergers mean that the archives encompass a total of 97 different companies. The centre's Film & Picture Library contains a wealth of original source material, representing the most comprehensive record of the British motor industry in the world. It consists of over one million original negatives and transparencies and 7,000 film titles dating from the early 1900s.

Licensing records may enable you to trace details of your ancestors' cars. They are listed by Riden, Philip *How to trace the History of your Car* (2nd ed. Merton Priory Press 1998).

MUNIMENTS See also Archives. These are documents which provide evidence of rights and privileges. Family muniments, mainly those of landed families, may still be in private possession but many have been deposited in CROs. For the location of such archives try The Database of Archives of non-Governmental Organisations www.dango.bham.ac.uk; The National Register of Archives and Access to Archives (A2A) (q.v), both available via TNA website www.nationalarchives.gov.uk.

MUSEUMS See also Army Museums, National Army Museum and National Maritime Museum. These provide hours of endless fascination, education, entertainment and background information on a host of subjects. They are to be found in abundance throughout the world, with many being of a specialised nature. Geer, Beverley *Museums and Galleries of Great Britain and Ireland* (Hobson's Guides 1998) provides details of the collections, contents and opening hours of hundreds of British Museums. It is currently out of print but is widely available on the second-hand market. Museums are listed in *The Family and Local History Handbook* (14th ed. Robert Blatchford Publishing 2013).

"National Heritage" http://nationalheritage.org.uk/ is an organisation that supports, encourages and protects museums and galleries in Britain. The journal *Museum News* can be downloaded from their website. It also gives access to the "National Heritage Guide" to current and forthcoming museum and gallery exhibitions.

See the "London Museum Guide" at www.ukguide.org/london/museum.html.

There are a number of regimental museums for those with army ancestors. Many trades and occupations have museums associated with them; some of these are mentioned under the specific trades in this volume.

MUSIC HALL See Theatre.

MUSICIANS There was a London Livery Company of Musicians www. wcom.org.uk. See Crewdson, H A M *A Short History of the Worshipful Company of Musicians* (Knight & Co. 1971). Well-known musicians will be found in Sadie, Stanley ed. *The New Grove Dictionary of Music and Musicians* (29 vols. OUP 2001). See also Dawe, Donovan *Organists of the City of London, 1666-1850* (Donovan Dawe 1983) and Dr Andrew Ashbee's *Biographical Dictionary of English Court Musicians, 1485-1714* (Ashgate 1998).

MUSTERS See Militia.

MY HERITAGE www.myheritage.com. A subscription website allowing family trees to be uploaded and records to be searched. Amongst these are census returns for the UK, USA and Canada, birth, marriage and death records, military records and passenger lists.

N

NAILMAKING This was a thriving industry in the Midlands in the C19th. Bodey, Hugh *Nail making* (Shire Publications 2008) gives an insight into the industry. An Occasional Paper published by the Northfield (Birmingham) Conservation Group entitled *The Nailmakers of Northfield* includes interviews with residents who remember the last of the nailmakers and sketches by a local artist. See also www.sedgleymanor.com/trades/nailmakers2.html.

NAMES See Christian Names and Surnames.

NAPOLEONIC PRISONERS See Prisoners of War.

NATIONAL ARCHIVES, THE (TNA) www.nationalarchives.gov.uk. Throughout this book there are constant references to the amazing collection of national records held by this institution at Ruskin Avenue, Kew, Richmond, Surrey TW9 4DU. The importance of TNA as the premier repository for English and Welsh research can't be underestimated. It also holds records relevant to Scotland, Ireland and former colonies. There are far too many classes of records to list but they include: probate material, records of the armed forces, court records, tithe records, records of taxation and much more. Although it is unlikely to be a place to begin research, all serious family historians with family from the UK, should find their way to the records of TNA at some point.

The website provides access to the "Discovery" Catalogue and to an increasing number of images of original documents that can be downloaded online for a modest fee. The website also includes numerous research guides on many topics and educational pod casts. TNA has an extensive bookshop and online purchases can be made via the website.

TNA does not undertake genealogical research. Readers must either visit the search rooms or employ a record agent. It is vital to check opening times, requirements for reader's tickets and parking arrangements before visiting. Once you have a reader's ticket, it is possible to order documents online in advance, so that they are waiting when you arrive. See Bevan, Amanda *Tracing your Ancestors in the National Archives* 7th ed. TNA 2006).

NATIONAL ARMY MUSEUM See also Army and Army Museums. The National Army Museum is at Royal Hospital Road, Chelsea, London SW3 4HT www.nam.ac.uk. It collects, preserves and exhibits objects and records relating to the regular and auxiliary forces of the British Army. It is the only museum in

Great Britain dealing with the army in general during the five centuries of its existence. It includes the story of the Indian Army to independence in 1947 and of the colonial forces.

The collection includes the papers of such famous soldiers as the 1st Marquess of Anglesey, Lord Raglan and Lord Roberts. Equally important are the hundreds of letters, journals and memoirs of lesser-known men and women of all ranks. The reference library contains over 30,000 books, many of them extremely rare, on British military history. All aspects of army life can be studied from a collection of prints and drawings and photographs. Further information about all the services and publications available, as well as an online collection, can be found on their website, where details of The Society of Friends of the National Army Museum can also be found.

NATIONAL ASSOCIATION OF DECORATIVE AND FINE ARTS SOCIETIES (NADFAS) www.nadfas.org.uk. The Association consists of member societies throughout the country whose aim is to increase enjoyment, knowledge and care of the arts and to stimulate interest in the preservation of our cultural heritage. Events are arranged in different parts of the country in association with museum exhibitions and historic houses and gardens. Study groups are also arranged for those interested in extending their knowledge.

The Voluntary Conservation Corps was started in 1970. Under guidance, they refurbish books in libraries, repair textiles or act as guides for the National Trust. Church recording is another aspect of NADFAS. They photograph and record the history and details of furnishings, memorials, stained glass and the like.

NATIONAL BUILDINGS RECORD See English Heritage.

NATIONAL BURIAL INDEX (NBI) See Burial Indexes.

NATIONAL FARM SURVEY See Farm Survey.

NATIONAL HERITAGE See Museums.

NATIONAL INDEX OF PARISH REGISTERS See Parish Registers.

NATIONAL INSTITUTE OF GENEALOGICAL STUDIES www.genealogical studies.com. They offer a range of family history courses, both online and by correspondence. These cover a range of topics, including research outside the UK.

NATIONAL MARITIME MUSEUM (NMM) See also Monumental Inscriptions. www.rmg.co.uk/national-maritime-museum. Located at Greenwich, the NMM is probably the world's most comprehensive museum of its kind. It has over three million maritime-related artefacts; more than 3,000 oil paintings from the C17th to C20th; some 50,000 prints and drawings; some 300,000 historic photographs; some 750,000 plans of ships built in the UK since the beginning of the C18th; some 3,000 ship models; assorted rare maps and charts, navigational instruments, manuscripts, weapons and uniforms.

Across the whole range of the collection, about 70,000 of these exhibits are now photographed and together with the historic photographs, are the basis of the Maritime Picture Library. Anyone wanting to locate a picture or photograph of an ancestor's ship has a good chance of finding it here.

The Library holds a complete set of *Lloyds' List*, *Lloyds' Register* and the *Mercantile Navy List*. There is a large collection of books and pamphlets on all aspects of shipping in addition to the museum's own publications. The newscutting collection of Frank C. Bowen covering the period from 1880-1940 is of particular importance.

Amongst the manuscript collections, it has Lloyds' Ships' Surveys; applications for masters/mates certificates; agreements and crew lists for specific years and the wreck registers. Many shipping companies have deposited their archives with the museum.

The Marine Society, founded in 1757, indentured some 16,000 boys into the Merchant Navy between 1815 and 1854. It kept detailed records of the boys and their parents or guardians. These Registers of boys placed by private subscription by The Marine Society are at the museum, along with other archives of the Marine Society. Charitable institutions such as The Marine Society and the Maritime Society endeavoured to train poor and orphaned boys. Millington, E C *Seamen in the Making* (J D Potter 1935) gives further details. The Metropolitan Asylums Board established ships for a similar purpose and boys were required to serve two and a half years training. For background of life on board, see Statham, E P *Reformatory and Industrial School Ships* published in *Army Illustrated* 28 January 1899. A copy is available in the museum's library.

The NMM website includes: a history of the museum and of The Royal Observatory at Greenwich; details of its galleries and exhibitions; details of its archive and library collections; information about the museum's Caird Library, which is a comprehensive specialist reference library; details of the Caird Library blog, which carries all of the library's latest news www.rmg.co.uk/library. The website has many research guides, which cover a wide range of topics. They provide information about the Museum's collections and other sources for research into maritime history. The guides are broken up into seventeen categories and each has links to other guides which may be relevant to a researcher. The first four guides (A1, A2, A3 and A4) give comprehensive information about the museum's main collections and records and include specific help for those tracing family history from maritime records. Also on the website is information about the online Royal Museums Greenwich Picture Library, which currently contains some 27,938 online images and details of the Collections blog, which carries the latest news of the museum's collections www.rmg.co.uk/blogs/collections/.

NATIONAL MEMORIAL ARBORETUM The National Memorial Arboretum, Croxall Road, Alrewas, Staffordshire DE13 7AR www.thenma.org.uk commemorates those who have suffered in conflicts or have given their lives in the service of their country. There are memorials for members of many organisations, primarily but not exclusively, regiments or other divisions of the armed forces.

NATIONAL METEOROLOGICAL LIBRARY AND ARCHIVE, THE The library, which contains comprehensive records about the weather of the past, is at Fitzroy Road, Exeter www.metoffice.gov.uk/learning/library. There is an online catalogue.

NATIONAL REGISTER OF ARCHIVES See Archives.

NATIONAL SOCIETY, THE See Education.

NATIONAL TRUST The website of the National Trust www.nationaltrust.org.uk details all of its historic properties and the events that the organisation puts on. The "archives" section of the website considers the family archives of former inhabitants of National Trust properties; documentation which forms an important part of their collections. The Trust's policy is to place family and other archives on permanent deposit with the relevant CRO or other appropriate place, thus allowing for public access.

The Trust has deposited archives of outstanding importance, such as the Bankes papers from Kingston Lacy, now in Dorchester, the Disraeli papers from Hughenden Manor in the Bodleian Library, George Bernard Shaw's papers from Shaw's Corner in Cambridge University Library and the Carlyle papers from Carlyle's House in the National Library of Scotland. The guidebooks for various properties often document the family histories and pedigrees of former occupants.

NATURALISATION See also Aliens, Emigration, Huguenots and Immigration. Naturalisation is the means by which a person of foreign birth obtains citizenship of another, adopted, country. The majority of aliens settling in Britain did not go through the legal formalities of an Act of Naturalisation as it was expensive and only the rich could afford it. It was less expensive to become a denizen by Letters Patent. This gave the status of a British subject but the holder did not have the full rights of a natural-born subject. They were unable to hold public office and whilst they could hold land, they could not inherit it. There are several relevant TNA research guides available at www.nationalarchives.gov.uk. The most useful of these are *Immigrants*; *Naturalisation and British citizenship* and *Naturalised Britons*.

NAVAL & MILITARY PRESS Naval & Military Press www.naval-military-press.com offer specialist books and CD/DVD titles for students of military history. Their publications deal with uniforms, battles, official and regimental histories, medal rolls and casualty lists.

Some of the CD/DVD titles of most relevance to the family historian are *Soldiers Died in the Great War 1914-1919* (q.v.); *Army Roll of Honour 1939-45*; *Official History of The Great War France and Belgium* (data DVD); *Official History of The Great War Other Theatres* (data DVD); *National Archives British Trench Map Atlas: The Western Front 1914-18* (data DVD).

NAVY See Royal Navy and Seaman.

NAVVY See also Railways. This term was applied to a labourer digging canals and later constructing railways.

NEATHERD A cowherd.

NEEDLEMAKER The leading centre for needlemaking was and still is, in the Redditch/Studley area of Worcestershire, some 15 miles south of Birmingham. Needlemaking began in this area in the early C17th, with production peaking at some 70 million needles per week in the late C19th.

A fascinating insight into needle manufacture and the people who made them can be found in the Forge Mill Needle Museum, Riverside, Redditch www.forgemill.org.uk. The museum is housed in an C18th restored water-powered needle scouring (polishing) mill. The museum welcomes enquiries related to the needle industry and families involved. In addition to the museums archives, Redditch Library also has a considerable amount of information. The Needle Museum and Library also have information on the town's other local industries, in particular fishing tackle and Royal Enfield.

The novel by Roy Clews *Young Jethro* (Heinemann 1975), gives a vivid picture of the conditions of the workers in industry at the time when England was at war with Napoleon; the Hollins, John *Needlemaking* (Shire Publications 1981) gives more practical information on the trade.

The Worshipful Company of Needlemakers of the City of London was one of the Livery Companies www.needlemakers.org.uk.

NELSON The Nelson Society www.nelson-society.com has a splendid website detailing lots of historical information about Nelson, listing publications and giving details of the society's journal and events. It collects information on men who served with Horatio Nelson throughout any part of his career; in particular, where they now rest. There were 17,000 sailors of all nationalities in the British Fleet alone at Trafalgar.

Websites giving information about Nelson and the Battle of Trafalgar include: www.ageofnelson.org; British History in-depth from the BBC www.bbc.co.uk;

The Battle of Trafalgar www.nelsonsnavy.co.uk; The Battle of Trafalgar 1805 www.royalnavy.mod.uk; The Minotaur at the battle of Trafalgar www.minotaur.org/trafalgar.htm; the final website has schedules containing many names.

See the Trafalgar Roll on TNA Website www.nationalarchives.gov.uk/trafalgarancestors/. There is a similar list on the HMS Victory website, which also contains other useful background information www.hms-victory.com.

Men at the Battle of Trafalgar - The Ayshford Trafalgar Roll (Ayshford 2010) is a CD that contains information, collected mainly from contemporary documents by Pam and Derek Ayshford, about the Seamen and Marines on board the British ships at the Battle of Trafalgar. The Roll contains the names and details of over 21,000 men who were on the musters of the British ships on 21st October 1805. Details recorded about each man include the ship on which he served, his rank or rating and in most cases his age and place of birth. Where the documents survive other details may include families, former trades, pensions, awards, medals, physical descriptions, pictures, injuries sustained, illnesses and date of death.

NETHERLANDS The Centraal Bureau voor Genealogie or Central Bureau for Genealogy (CBG) is the Dutch information centre for genealogy and family history. It is the starting point for most research into Dutch ancestors or Dutch migrants who settled in other countries in the world. The website of the CBG at www.cbg.nl is in both Dutch and English. The website has the facility to search for surnames in the online catalogue of the CBG. It also contains information about how to start genealogical research in the Netherlands and details the publications of the CBG and the collections that are available for consultation in the CBG reading rooms. It is also easy to "meet" other researchers on the CBG forum, many of whom seem to be knowledgeable and prepared to give guidance and help to fellow genealogists.

NEW POOR LAW See Board of Guardians and Workhouses.

NEW STYLE See Calendar.

NEWGATE PRISON CALENDAR A printed list of prisoners to be tried at Newgate, with manuscript additions. There are 61 such volumes in class HO77 at TNA. They cover the period from 1782 to 1853. After 1822, the results of trials are included.

NEWSPAPERS See also Internet Library of Early Journals, Local History, London Gazette and Obituaries. Newspapers can be an invaluable source of information about people and events in the locality in which your ancestors lived. A research guide available on TNA website www.nationalarchives.gov.uk entitled *Newspapers,* gives links to many online sources of newspapers. The Newsplan Project, in association with the British Newspaper Library, aimed to microfilm old newspapers in order to preserve them. Microfilming halted in 2010, in favour of digitisation. The most important of these is The British Newspaper Archive www.britishnewspaperarchive.co.uk, where millions of pages of national and provincial papers can be searched and downloaded for a fee. This material is also available via FindmyPast (q.v.) www.findmypast.co.uk. See also The Times Digital Archive http://gale.cengage.co.uk/times.aspx/, which is often available free through public library websites and the Burney collection of C17th and C18th newspapers http://gdc.gale.com/products/17th-and-18th-century-burney-collection-newspapers/.

Willing's Press Guide, issued annually and available in large libraries, gives details of current local newspapers. You may be able to find what you need a little nearer home by consulting Gibson, Jeremy *Local Newspapers 1750-1920, England and Wales; Channel Islands; Isle of Man: a select location list* (3rd ed. FHP 2011). It tells you just what papers are available in local libraries, CROs and other repositories.

The National Library of Wales is digitising approximately a million pages of Welsh newspapers and journals. See www.llgc.org.uk/index.php?id=4723.

It is always worth checking in local record offices or libraries to see if local papers have been indexed. Without an index or a date for a specific event, using newspapers can be a very time consuming task. Transcripts and indexes to various regional and local papers are available online. An example is that of the *West Briton*, which covered south-west England http://freepages.genealogy. rootsweb.ancestry.com/~wbritonad/. Overseas newspapers are also becoming more easily available, see uder the individual countries for examples.

NEW ZEALAND See also Army and Parkhurst Boys. The website New Zealand History Online www.nzhistory.net.nz is a good starting point and contains information for family historians. The "Hands on History" section is likely to be the most relevant.

The website for Archives New Zealand is at http://archives.govt.nz/. It includes the "Archway" facility for searching the catalogue. Information about the collections of the National Library of New Zealand can be found at http://natlib.govt.nz/.

The New Zealand Society of Genealogists, PO Box 14036, Panmure, Auckland 1741, New Zealand. www.genealogy.org.nz offers the facilities of many large family history societies, including publications, meetings, a research library and a bi-monthly magazine.

Births, Deaths and Marriages, Historical Records for New Zealand can be accessed at www.dia.govt.nz/Births-Deaths-and-Marriages.
Many historic New Zealand newspapers can be searched and articles downloaded free of charge at http://paperspast.natlib.govt.nz.
See Bromell, Anne *Beginners' Guide to Family History Research in New* Zealand (Whitcoulls 2004).

NEW ZEALAND IMMIGRANTS For emigrants to New Zealand two good starting points are www.nzhistory.net.nz/handsonhistory/genealogy-links and the lists of passengers arriving in Auckland 1838-1889, 1909-1921, which can be searched at www.aucklandcity.govt.nz/dbtw-wpd/passengers/passenger.html.

NISI PRIUS COURTS A court that, in Britain and other English speaking countries, tried an issue of fact before a judge and jury.

NONCONFORMISTS See also Cemeteries, Toleration Act and under the names of various denominations. Non-conformists were those who worshipped outside the established church. Since the Reformation of the 1530s, this could be seen to include Catholics, however the term is usually used to mean the various non-Anglican branches of the Protestant church. Non-conformists have encountered varying degrees of acceptance since the C16th. Prior to the Toleration Act of 1689, it was often thought too risky to keep a register. In general the Quakers were the most conscientious in keeping registers and the Baptists least so. Quaker registrations begin in 1650 and those of Presbyterians from 1662.

For our ancestors, denominational loyalty was often fluid. Chapels too changed their allegiance. Presbyterians often became Independent. One chapel became in succession Presbyterian, Unitarian, Independent and then Baptist. A single nonconformist register might contain entries for several congregations where the minister travelled a circuit and carried the book around with him. It is thus desirable to know which churches were cared for by the same minister and during which years. Early baptisms might be in the register of a minister who preached, virtually as a missionary, in an area before a congregation was organised there and whose church was some distance away.

The Non Parochial Registers Act of 1840 required that all non-conformist registers should be surrendered to the Registrar General. These are now at TNA. Many non-conformist records of baptisms, marriages and burials, covering Methodists, Wesleyans, Baptists, Independents, Protestant Dissenters, Congregationalist, Presbyterians, Unitarians and Quakers (Society of Friends), are now available online on a payment basis at either The Genealogist website www.thegenealogist.co.uk or The Official Non-Conformist and Non-Parochial BMDs website www.bmdregisters.co.uk. The latter is an important gateway to many hundreds of non-conformist registers. Sometimes registers were contained in the same book as minutes of chapel meetings, lists of members, expulsions etc. and these may not have been surrendered. In this way a few have found their way to CROs.

Some nonconformists had their own burial grounds; the most famous of these is Bunhill Fields in London www.cityoflondon.gov.uk/things-to-do/green-spaces/city-gardens/visitor-information/Pages/Bunhill-Fields.aspx, where burials took place between 1713 and 1854. The burial registers have been deposited in TNA. Interment Order Books 1789-1854 are at LMA.

See Steel, D J *The National Index of Parish Registers: volume 2 sources for nonconformist genealogy and family history* (Phillimore 1973).

There is a series of books published by the Royal Commission on the Historical Monuments of England *Nonconformist Chapels and Meeting Houses*. They cover the following counties in volumes: Buckinghamshire; Gloucestershire; Herefordshire, Worcestershire & Warwickshire; Derbyshire; Staffordshire & Shropshire; Northamptonshire & Oxfordshire; Leicestershire, Nottinghamshire & Rutland (Royal Commission on the Historical Monuments of England 1987).

NOTES & QUERIES This journal began in 1849 and is a collection of articles about history, literature and antiquarian matters. It is now published by Oxford University Press http://nq.oxfordjournals.org/. There are also a number of county versions of *Notes and Queries*, many of which can be found online.

NUMERALS See also Roman Numerals. Arabic numerals are those used as standard in the Western World.

NUNCUPATIVE WILL See Wills.

NUNS See Roman Catholics.

NURSE CHILDREN This was a term common in burial registers of the home counties, mainly because many thousands of infants sent out of London to spend the first few years of their life in the country, died in the nurse's parish. Contrary to popular belief, many of these children were not unwanted or illegitimate but were from a wide spectrum of middle-class homes and were often sent to parishes with which their parents had some connection. See Gillian Clark's 'A Study of Nurse Children 1550-1750' *Local Population Studies* 39 (1987) pp. 8-23, digitised at www.localpopulationstudies.co.uk.

NURSING See also Florence Nightingale Museum, Hospitals, Medals and South Africa. The Royal College of Nursing www.rcn.org.uk has a library and archive at its London headquarters at 20 Cavendish Square, London W1G 0RN. This holds a collection of books, journals and periodicals. It includes advice for those researching nurses on its website. The Royal College of Nursing's annual published records of state registered nurses run from 1922-1968. These can be seen at TNA in class DT10.

Burdett's *Official Nursing Directory* (1894-1899) is of interest. There is a copy for 1898 in the Library of the SOG (q.v.). More general reading is Pavey, Agnes *The Story of the Growth of Nursing* (revised ed. Faber & Faber 1959). Baly, Monica *A History of the Queen's Nursing Institute* (Groom Helm 1987). Stocks, Mary *A Hundred Years of District Nursing* (George Allen & Unwin 1960).

Four relevant TNA research guides are: *Royal Air Force: nurses and nursing services*; *British Army: nurses and nursing services*; *Royal Navy: nurses and nursing services* and *Civilian Nurses and Nursing Services*; available at www. nationalarchives.gov.uk.

The records and holdings of London's Florence Nightingale Museum might also be of interest to those with contemporary nursing interests www.florence-nightingale.co.uk.

The Royal College of Nursing's annual published records of state registered nurses run from 1922-1968.

O

OATH OF ALLEGIANCE See also Association Oath Rolls and Protestation Returns. An Act of 1722 made it necessary for persons in England over eighteen years of age to swear an Oath of Allegiance to the Crown at Quarter Sessions (q.v.). This was a result of anti-Catholic feeling following the Jacobite Rebellion. Where these lists survive, they will be found in CROs. Those for Devon have been indexed and are available online at www.foda.org.uk/oaths/intro/introduction1.htm where there is also an introduction to these records.

OBITUARIES See also Newspapers. The website Iannounce www.iannounce.co.uk contains almost five million more recent death and marriage notices, taken from nearly 500 different newspapers and these are updated daily.

OCCUPATIONS See also Shire Publications. A large number of occupations have their own entries in this text. Many occupations are no longer recognisable today. Stuart Raymond's *Trades and Professions: the family historians' guide* (FHP 2011) gives a general overview of occupational sources for family historians. The same author's *Occupational Sources for Genealogists: a bibliography* (2nd ed. FFHS 1996) lists innumerable published sources. Many local sources are listed in the county volumes of his series of genealogical bibliographies, especially *Londoners' Occupations: a genealogical guide* (2nd ed. FFHS 2001). Particularly if you trace your ancestry back before 1733, you may be confronted with the occupation being given in Latin. See Morris, Janet *A Latin Glossary for Family and Local Historians* (FHP 2009), which gives a long list of Latin names. Although you can guess some of them, you might be puzzled if you found your ancestor was an aromatarius (a grocer) or a burriarius (a dairyman). Three volumes of *The Book of Trades or Library of Useful Arts 1811* (4th ed. Wiltshire FHS), edited by Beryl Hurley, describe various trades in the early C19th.

Thompson, E P and Yeo, Eileen (ed.) *The Unknown Mayhew* (Pelican Books 1973) has very detailed descriptions of the work, living conditions and pay of a number of occupations. It covers in great detail silk weavers, needlewomen, tailors, boot and shoe makers, toy makers, merchant seamen, sawyers, joiners, coopers, dressmakers and milliners, hatters and tanners. See also John Burnett's *Useful Toil: autobiographies of working people from the 1820s to the 1920s* (Pelican 1977), which contains the memoirs of Victorian and Edwardian workers in a variety of occupations. Hartley, Dorothy *Made in England* (2nd ed. Century in association with The National Trust 1987) is a fascinating guide to some of the age-old jobs and skills practised in England.

See also Culling, Joyce *An Introduction to Occupations: a preliminary list* (2nd ed. FFHS 1999) and Waters, Colin *A Dictionary of Old Trades, Titles and Occupations* (revised ed, Countryside Books 2002). The Registrar General's *Classification of Occupations* is the basis of classifications used in census. It has been revised and published approximately every decade since the late C19th. See the website of The Office for National Statistics www.ons.gov.uk (formerly the OPCS).

We have given under separate headings some of the important trades in which our ancestors were engaged, with references to books about the London Livery Companies. Although your ancestor may have lived elsewhere, these books could give useful background information about the trade for use in your family history.

The Tools and Trades History Society (TATHS) was founded in 1983 to further the knowledge and understanding of hand tools and the trades and people that used them. It has published numerous interesting articles in its newsletters and it produces publications of use to family historians who are doing an in-depth study of their ancestors' occupations. Further details of this society can be obtained from www.taths.org.uk.

OLD BAILEY See Crime and Criminals.

OLD STYLE See Calendar.

ONE-NAME STUDIES Many people who have unusual surnames are intrigued by them. They tend to widen the scope of their research and record all instances of the name, including those to whom they are not related. It is a temptation to think that all with the same surname must be related but this is seldom the case. Pursuing a one-name study can be quite fascinating. Often this leads to the formation of a One-Name Family History Society. There are a number of long established ones in this country and many thousands in the U.S.A., although the latter often concentrate only on the descendants of one couple.

Anyone conducting world-wide studies of a single name, or thinking of doing so, should consider joining The Guild of One-Name Studies, often referred to as the GOONS, www.one-name.org. It publishes the quarterly *Journal of One-Name Studies*. Other benefits of Guild membership are outlined on their website, which also carries a database of registered names. It is worth checking to see if the surname in which you are interested in has been subjected to extensive study. In April 2012 the Guild of One-Name Studies published *Seven Pillars of Wisdom: the art of one-name studies* as a guide to the running of a one-name study.

ONE-PLACE STUDIES See also Local History. These are local history studies of a single place and are often undertaken by family historians with an interest in a particular ancestral parish. See the Society for One-Place Studies website www.one-place-studies.org. The list of One Place Studies includes some outside the British Isles. Many of those undertaking One-Place studies become the Online Parish Clerk for their chosen place, normally but not necessarily an historic parish. These are not to be confused with the Parish Clerks that form part of the Anglican Parochial Church Councils. The Online Parish Clerk will hold a body of records on the parish they are studying and will answer enquiries from these. See www.onlineparishclerks.org.uk. The south west of England is particularly well served by online parish clerks. As always in these situations, some of those conducting One-Place Studies hold a great deal more information than others.

ONLINE PARISH CLERKS See One-Place Studies.

ORAL EVIDENCE This is a term used by family historians for information handed down in the family by word of mouth. Modern technology enables memories of the past to be preserved exactly as they are related. Recordings of the voices of parents and other relations are a precious addition to family records. The Oral History Society has a website www.oralhistory.org.uk and produces a journal. See Taylor, Lawrence *Oral Evidence and the Family Historian* (FFHS 1984).

ORDNANCE SURVEY See Maps.

ORGANISTS Dawe, Donovan *Organists of the City of London 1660 to 1850* (Dawe 1983) lists the succession of organists for each City of London Church, followed by biographical notes.

ORIENTAL AND INDIA OFFICE COLLECTIONS See Asia, Pacific and Africa Collections.

ORIGINS The Origins website www.origins.net is a pay per view site, with indexes to and digital images of various sources. It has various collections including "British Origins", "Irish Origins", "Scots Origins" and its "National Wills Index". Whilst this site does not hold as many records as some of its competitors, it does have some interesting datasets. For example, "British Origins" includes: London Apprenticeship Abstracts 1442-1850, which comprises over 486,000 names. Militia Attestations Index 1886-1910, which comprises in excess of 110,000 names. Middlesex Baptisms Index 1538-1751, which includes over 300,000 names. The "National Wills Index" includes: Prerogative & Exchequer Courts of York Probate Index 1688-1858, which comprises over 263,800 names. Surrey & South London Will Abstracts 1470-1858, which comprises in excess of 562,700 names.

Many of the indexes are accompanied by images of the original documents themselves, whilst the help pages contain useful summaries of the records, why they came into being and how the researcher should use them.

ORPHANS AND ORPHANAGES See Children's Societies.

OSTLER Sometimes known as a "hostler", an ostler was historically a stableman at an inn. In recent times, a hostler was the name given to a person in charge of locomotives when not in use.

OUT PENSIONERS See Chelsea Royal Hospital.

OVERSEERS OF THE POOR See Poor Law.

OXFORD MOVEMENT, THE A mid C19th intellectual movement within the Anglican Church. Many members were associated with Oxford University. This High Church movement developed into Anglo-Catholicism and aimed to restore ornament and ritual to the Church of England. John Henry Newman and Edward Pusey were key figures in this movement. They were also known as Tractarians, after a series of publications. See Lawrence N Crumb's *The Oxford Movement and Its Leaders: a bibliography of secondary and lesser primary sources* (Scarecrow Press 2009) and Brown, Stuart J and Nockles, Peter B (ed.) *The Oxford Movement, Europe and the Wider World 1830-1930* (Cambridge University Press 2012.)

OXFORD UNIVERSITY Students are listed in Foster, J *Alumni Oxonienses 1500-1886* (8 vols. Parker and co. 1887-1892 reprinted Kraur Reprint 1980). For an online version for the period 1500-1714 see www.british-history.ac.uk. This information is also available via www.ancestry.co.uk.

The archives of Oxford University are held at The Bodleian Library www.bodleian.ox.ac.uk/bodley.

OXFORD UNIVERSITY PRESS (OUP) MUSEUM AND ARCHIVE www.oup.com/uk/archives. Oxford University has been involved with the printing trade since the C15th. The group's archive holds the records of the University's printing and publishing activities from the C17th to date. The archive's website includes: a timeline detailing the development of OUP. "Item of the month", a feature looking at a selected holding in the archive or museum. More detailed information about the archive and its main groups of material. Details of a collection of papers relating to the history of the Oxford English Dictionary (OED), first published between 1884 and 1928. Three short film clips made in 1925 illustrating industrial life and highlighting the Press's work to audiences around the world, which can be viewed online. Information of use to potential visitors to the museum or archive.

The archive also manages the Press Museum in Oxford. This traces the history of Oxford University's involvement in printing and publishing from the C15th to the present day. The museum includes displays on OUP buildings, the C17th Fell Types, the Oxford Almanacs, Alice in Wonderland and The Oxford

English Dictionary. Also on display are a C19th printing press and the latest online publications of OUP. Until recently the OUP owned its own paper mill. This was the Wolvercote Paper Mill, a couple of miles north of Oxford.

OYER AND TERMINER In the Middle Ages, justices might be commissioned by oyer and terminer to hear trials of specific serious crimes, such as treason or murder. The records of these cases are at TNA. Commissions of oyer and terminer were used in Scotland until the C19th.

P

PALAEOGRAPHY Defined as the study of the handwritings and often the manuscripts, of the past. Once you are back to the C17th in your researches, you will certainly need a guide to decipher the handwriting. There are a number of these available, such as Marshall, Hilary *Palaeography for Family and Local Historians* (Phillimore 2010). Iredale, David *Enjoying Archives* (David and Charles 1973, reissued Phillimore 1980), has an excellent chapter on handwriting and reproduces various forms of the letters of the alphabet from the C10th - C18th. Then there is Grieve, H E P *Examples of English Handwriting 1150 to 1750* (Essex Education Committee 1981) and Buck, W S *Examples of Handwriting 1550 to 1650* (SOG 1982). There is a delightful little book entitled *A Secretary Hand ABC Book* by Alf Ison (A Ison 1982). Scottish handwriting is dealt with in the excellent Grant G. Simpson's *Scottish Handwriting 1150-1650: an introduction to the reading of documents* (John Donald Short Run Press 2009). See also www.scottishhandwriting.com.

There is an online palaeography tutorial on TNA website, available at www.nationalarchives.gov.uk/palaeography/.

PALLOT INDEX This index covers more than 98% of marriages in 101 of the 103 ancient parishes of the square mile of the City of London between 1780 and 1837. It also includes many thousands of other marriage entries. There was a baptismal section consisting of twelve million slips, 200,000 of which survived severe damage during the Second World War. Many of the entries are from records which have been destroyed since it was started in 1818. There is a high success rate for those with lost marriages in London.

Initially the property of Messrs Pallot & Co., the original index now belongs to The Institute of Heraldic and Genealogical Studies, 79-82 Northgate, Canterbury, Kent, CT1 1BA England. The index has been transcribed and may be accessed on CD or online from the subscription website Ancestry (q.v.) www.ancestry. co.uk.

PANNAGE This was the right to pasture swine, or the payment for the same right, in woodland.

PAPERMAKERS See also Oxford University Press (OUP) Museum and Archive. The British Association of Paper Historians (BAPH) www.baph.org.uk aims to bring together individuals, companies and institutions with a common interest in: Paper in all its forms and diversity. Papermaking by hand and machine.

Conservation. Paper mill and company histories. Papermakers, their families and communities. Machinery manufacture and development. Watermarks. The association's website gives details about membership, publications and its journal, information about paper and papermaking and links to associated sites. Jean Stirk is compiling a Paper Makers' Index, which is an index of paper-making craftsmen and their families. With a focus on the British Isles, there are currently some 12,000 entries in the index, which are mainly from England. These vary from fragments of information to short biographies. The details have been culled from a variety of sources. Access to the index is through Jean Stirk, who can be contacted via the BAPH website.

PAPIER MACHE See Japanning.

PARISH See also Examinations, Highways, Poor Law (Old), Removal Orders and Settlements. A subdivision of a diocese, having its own church and a clergyman; the area within the responsibility of a parson, to whom tithes and other ecclesiastical dues were paid. In the C16th and C17th, secular administration passed from the manorial courts to the parish, except in matters regarding land transfers. Two important matters of administration which the parish had to contend with were the relief of the poor and the maintenance of the highways. By the end of the C19th, most of these secular matters had become the responsibility of the municipal or county boroughs. See Winchester, Angus *Discovering Parish Boundaries* (Shire Publications 1990). The parish officers: churchwardens, overseers of the poor, constables and highway surveyors (or waywardens) all compiled accounts, which are invaluable sources for family historians. Wiltshire Family History Society www.wiltshirefhs.co.uk have reprinted the 1849 publication *The Handy Book Of Parish Law* and are selling it as an inexpensive A5 booklet.

PARISH CHEST (1) An online retailer, bringing together numerous family history suppliers, whose products can be purchased via www.parishchest.com. It is also possible to purchase memberships to many family history societies through this site.

PARISH CHEST (2) The poor law of 1552 directed the parishioners in every parish to provide a strong chest, having three keys, for holding the alms for the poor. From the early C16th separate legislation required that every parish should have a locking chest to contain the parish registers and all other documents pertaining to the parish. Often one chest was provided, or adapted, to serve both purposes.

In addition to parish registers the contents of the Parish Chest should have included: Churchwardens' Accounts, Charity Accounts, Glebe Terriers, Tithe Records, Vestry Minutes and Agreements, Petty Constables' Accounts, Records of Poor Law Administration, Highway Maintenance, Enclosure, other ecclesiastical and miscellaneous civil records. Any surviving documents are likely to be in CROs or DROs. The standard work on this subject is Tate, W E *The Parish Chest* (3rd ed. Phillimore 2010).

PARISH CLERK The parish clerk normally held this position for life. His duties included the arrangement of baptisms and communions, ringing the church bell and leading the responses at services. He would often have responsibility for completion of the parish register entries.

For further information see Ditchfield, P H *The Parish Clerk* (Methuen & Co. 1907).

PARISH MAGAZINES These date mainly from the C19th and often contain details of christenings, marriages burials and obituaries. Sometimes extracts from early parish registers are reprinted in them. Survival is patchy. The local studies' library might well be able to offer advice on what survives and where.

PARISH MAPS Maps measuring 17" x 13" have been prepared by the Institute of Heraldic and Genealogical Studies (IHGS) (q.v.) www.ihgs.ac.uk. Maps are available for each county of England, Wales and Scotland. The maps show parochial boundaries and dates of commencement of existing registers. Coloured outlines show the jurisdiction of ecclesiastical courts that administered probate and licences. They can be purchased individually but also form part of Humphery-Smith, Cecil R (ed.) *Phillimore Atlas and Index of Parish Registers* (3rd ed. Phillimore 2003). The maps show the ancient parishes that existed before 1832, the ecclesiastical court jurisdictions, the situation of churches and chapels where appropriate and the date of commencement of the surviving registers of the parish. Also included are reproductions of topographical maps from James Bell's *A New and Comprehensive Gazetteer of England and Wales 1834*. In addition, a large index lists the parishes for each county, giving a grid reference enabling the user to find each place quickly. A further feature is a reference to deposited parish registers and parish register copies and their coverage in the variety of local and national genealogical indexes. There is also a listing of nonconformist chapels situated in a particular parish whose records are at TNA. It must be noted that the Index is a consolidated guide to the coverage of these indexes. It will list the earliest and latest dates available but will not state what gaps exist in the series nor will it distinguish between baptismal, marriage and burial registers.

PARISH RECORDS See Parish Chest.

PARISH REGISTERS (PRs) See also Marriage, Parish Maps and Parish Register Transcriptions. Below is a summary of the various stages of development in the keeping of parish registers:

1538 Thomas Cromwell ordered that each parish should keep a register of baptisms, marriages and burials. The entries were to be made after each Sunday service.

1598 Registers were required to be of parchment. All previous entries, that had usually been written on paper, had first to be copied up, particularly those since the accession of Queen Elizabeth. This is the reason so many registers commence in 1558, the previous registers having become unreadable through damp and decay. Up to about 1732 it was common to record the entries in Latin with the Latin forms of Christian names.

1644/5 An Ordinance stated that the date of birth should be given when a child was baptised and dates of death were also to be given (this was not effective).

1653 This was the period of the Commonwealth. The Government took over the custody of registers and appointed civil officers called "Parish Registers" to be responsible for the entries. Unfortunately not many Commonwealth registers have survived.

1667 & 1678 Legislation was passed requiring that all burials should be in a woollen shroud. An affidavit made at each burial that this had been done otherwise a fine was payable. The Act gradually became ignored and was repealed in 1814. Its purpose had been to help the wool trade. Some parishes kept separate Registers of "Burials in Woollen".

1694 A tax of 2/- was levied on each birth, 2/6 for a marriage and 4/- for a burial. Births were to be notified to the incumbent within 5 days and he was to receive a fee of 6d for recording them. This tax was short-lived.

1711 An Act stated that proper register books with ruled lines and numbered pages were to be used (largely ignored).

1754 Hardwicke's Marriage Act, limited to England and Wales, took effect from 25th March. Marriage could be solemnised only in a parish church or public chapel after the publication of banns, or by a licence issued by the bishop of the diocese. Banns books and marriage register books were required to be kept separate from those for baptisms and burials. The marriage had to be performed by a clergyman of the Church of England. Jews and Quakers were exempt and continued to keep their own registers. Minors (under 21) needed the consent of parents or guardians. Some Catholics were married in the Church of England, as well as in their own churches, to ensure legality.

1783 A Stamp Act was passed. This decreed that a duty of 3d had to be paid for every entry of a birth or christening, marriage or burial. The duty was collected by the incumbent who was allowed to retain 10% as a commission. This came into force on 1st October but was repealed 10 years later. It had several interesting consequences. There was a great increase in the number of baptisms in the last few days of September 1783, many of the children being of several years of age and a similar "bulge" after its repeal in 1793. Those in receipt of parish relief were exempt from the tax, no payment being required for any person buried from "any Workhouse or Hospital or at the sole expense of any Charity". The letter "P" appears after numerous entries for the duration of the Act. It is likely that this meant Pauper but the theory has been advanced that it might mean the incumbent had obtained a licence whereby he need not stamp his registers and the P in fact stands for Paid when he did his accounts for the Tax Commissioners.

In more northerly counties of England some parish registers follow the much more detailed format instigated by Bishop Dade. These date from 1777-1812 and may include, for example, date of birth, position in the family, mother's maiden name and parishes of origin of the parents in a baptism entry.

1813 George Rose's Act came into effect requiring that specially printed registers should be used, with separate books for baptisms, marriages and burials. Baptismal entries were to include the names, address and occupation or status (e.g. gentleman) of the parents. Burial entries were to include age and place of residence of the deceased. The form of marriage registers was again changed in 1837. From this date they are duplicates of the civil marriage certificates and can be consulted directly. After 1837, civil records of birth, marriage and death tend to be used in preference to parish registers, although the latter continue to this day.

Most registers have now been deposited in CROs. Many have been indexed by family history societies and others. Many indexes are available online, either via subscription websites such as Ancestry (q.v.) www.ancestry.co.uk and FindmyPast (q.v.) www.findmypast.co.uk or via Family Search (q.v.). Individual parishes may also make indexes available online. Links to these are usually found via GENUKI (q.v.) www.genuki.org.uk. Increasingly, digital images of the original registers are being made available via these means.

For a detailed introduction see Raymond, Stuart *Parish Registers: a history and guide* (FHP 2009).

PARISH REGISTERS OF IRELAND See also Ireland. About two thirds of Irish Parish Registers were destroyed in the Civil War of 1922 but Catholic registers dating from c.1820 had not been deposited and thus survived. Registers can be consulted at the Office of The Registrar General, 8/11 Lombard Street East, Dublin 2.

PARISH REGISTERS OF SCOTLAND See also Scotland. Registers of the Church of Scotland (Presbyterian) commenced in 1558. The original registers are at The National Records of Scotland, Princes Street, Edinburgh www.nas.gov.uk/default.asp. Most Public Libraries throughout Scotland have microfilm copies for their area.

The "English" Church in Scotland is known as the Scottish Episcopal Church. Each local Diocese keeps its own records but those for the Diocese of Aberdeen and Orkney are on microfilm at The Family History Shop, 164 King Street, Aberdeen, AB2 3BD.

Scottish Old Parochial Registers (OPRs) which relate to the Established Church of Scotland (Presbyterian) have more omissions than English Parish Registers but baptismal entries are more detailed, nearly always with the maiden surname of the mother. The Scotland's People website www.scotlandspeople.gov.uk is the key site and enables researchers to download images of OPRs.

PARISH REGISTER TRANSCRIPTS Many have been published by various County Record Societies and in more recent years these have been augmented by publications of FHSs. Copies may well be found in CROs, with FHSs and at the SOG. Some are manuscript, or typescript, copies. Some societies are solely devoted to publishing parish registers e.g. Lancashire Parish Register Society, Staffordshire Parish Register Society and others. They may also hold unpublished transcripts; check with relevant CRO.

It is worth noting that some Record Offices (the Borthwick Institute for one) use "PRT" to mean Bishop's Transcripts.

There is a Parish Register Transcript Society www.prtsoc.org.uk that produces CDs and makes its database available online in exchange for purchased credits.

Phillimore and co. have published marriage registers for about 1500 parishes in many counties. The website www.familyrelatives.com gives a list of which parishes are covered and the transcripts can be search on this site and on a number of others.

There are numerous parish register transcripts on the internet. These can usually be accessed via GENUKI (q.v.) www.genuki.org.uk. Extensive lists of published parish registers are included in the county volumes of Stuart Raymond's series of genealogical bibliographies.

PARKHURST BOYS From 1838, young offenders were sent to Parkhurst Prison, on the Isle of Wight. Many of these boys, aged 12-18, were subsequently sent to Australia and New Zealand, with nearly 1,500 being transported between 1842-1852. For more details see http://members.iinet.net.au/~perthdps/convicts/park.html and Andrew Gill's *A Register of Parkhurst Convicts Apprenticed in WA 1842-1851* self-published in 1992. The Parkhurst Prison registers are in TNA.

PARLIAMENTARY ARCHIVES See also Protestation Returns. The Parliamentary Archives www.parliament.uk/archives was formed following the merger of the House of Lords Record Office and the House of Commons Record Office.

The Parliamentary Archives holds several million historical records relating to Parliament, dating from 1497. These include: Official records of the House of Lords and House of Commons, including Acts, Journals, Deposited Plans and Appeal Cases. Other Parliamentary collections, including the papers of the Lord Great Chamberlain and the History of Parliament Trust. Collections of private political papers and records of political bodies and pressure groups, including Lloyd George, Bonar Law, and Beaverbrook. Records about the Palace of Westminster, including the papers of Charles Barry and A. W. N. Pugin, the drawings of J. Hardman & Co., the Benjamin Stone photographs and the records of various government departments responsible for maintaining the new Palace, as well as many other sources.

See Bond, M F *Guide to the Records of* Parliament (HMSO 1971). A number of guidance booklets can be downloaded from the Parliamentary Archives' website. These include: *Guide to Parliamentary Records. Guide to Personal Political Papers. Sources for Family History at the Parliamentary Archives. Photographic Sources at the Parliamentary Archives. Guide to Digitised Historical Parliamentary Material.* A splendid "virtual tour" is now also available via the same website.

The records of many private matters, such as divorce and naturalisation bills are held in the Parliamentary Archives. There are investigations of peerage claims from 1628. Also many documents dealing with problems of succession to family estates and the Protestation Returns of 1641/2 are held. The catalogue of the Parliamentary Archives can be consulted online at www.portcullis. parliament.uk.

PAROCHIAL CHAPELRY A chapelry within a parish which generally had the right to maintain its own registers. Some parochial chapelries retained the right to marry after 1754. In some cases, duplicate entries were made in the parish register of the mother parish church, in other cases the registers were maintained separately. In either case there should be Bishops' Transcripts (q.v.). Note that not all chapelries were parochial chapelries.

PAROCHIAL REGISTERS AND RECORDS MEASURE 1978 This Act of Parliament came into force on 1 January 1979, with subsequent amendments that came into effect on 1 January 1993. Briefly, this requires parishes to deposit in a DRO all records completed more than one hundred years ago, unless they are still in use. However, if the church opted to keep them in the parish, they had to obtain the consent of the bishop. These registers must be kept in a fire-proof and rust-proof cupboard, observing certain conditions relating to humidity and temperature.

Where registers are retained by the parish, those wishing to see them must be given access "at all reasonable hours". However, no right of access is given to other records in parochial custody. The Measure contains a clause concerning the fees which may be charged for searches to be made in baptism or burial registers. The scale of fees is set out in the Ecclesiastical Fees Order which may be changed from time to time. Marriage registers are not covered by the Measure but in practice fees are required for searches in those registers also. Fees are not charged in DROs. See the Parochial Registers and Records Measure page at www.national archives.gov.uk/information-management/legislation/parochial-registers.htm.

PARSON A parish priest in the Church of England, or any clergyman.

PARTIBILITY A form of inheritance whereby an estate is shared equally between all children, or in some cases all the sons.

PARTNERSHIPS See also Companies. The partnership was governed in former times by principles of case law. In 1890, the Partnership Act was passed to declare and amend the law by statute. Rules determined whether a partnership existed or not and what were its legal effects. Before that time differences between partners over distribution of profit, nature of business, scope and private arrangements as well as the bankruptcy of individual partners led to all sorts of difficulties and litigation. Dissolutions of partnerships in London and abroad were announced in the *London Gazette* (q.v.) www.gazettes-online.co.uk. Partnerships were the usual form of business arrangements before the Companies' Acts and many of these entries probably relate to insolvency.

PASSENGER LISTS See also Emigration. TNA holds lists of passengers arriving in the UK from ports outside Europe and the Mediterranean 1878-1960 and lists of passengers leaving from UK and Irish ports and travelling to places such as America, Canada, India, New Zealand and Australia 1890-1960. There are no comprehensive passenger lists before this date. Images can be downloaded from the subscription websites www.ancestry.co.uk and at Ancestors on Board, now part of the FindmyPast (q.v.) website www.findmypast.co.uk and Genes Reunited www.genesreunited.co.uk.

The work of the Immigrant Ships' Transcribers' Guild might be useful, as they seek to transcribe passengers' lists www.immigrantships.net.

The earliest lists relating to American immigrants are for Philadelphia and date from 1800 but most start in 1820. For details of immigrants see www.castle garden.org and www.ellisisland.org.

PASSPORTS Passports were issued by the Privy Council from at least 1540 to 1683. During the Commonwealth, they were granted to foreign subjects by the two Houses of Parliament. Up to 1794, passports were signed by the King himself and countersigned by the Secretary of State. From 1794, two forms of passport were in existence, the Royal Passport and one issued in the name of the Sovereign but signed by the Secretary of State alone. A record exists of all passports issued between 1794 and 1898. These appear in the 114 volumes of Passport Registers in TNA class FO610. The records show the intended destination of the applicant and are in chronological order. There is an index of names (FO611) covering the periods 1851-1862 and 1874-1898, in eighteen volumes. Other volumes comprise correspondence, the issue of passports by consuls and the passport requirements of foreign countries. A TNA research guide *Passport Records* gives more details www.nationalarchives.gov.uk.

PASTSCAPE See English Heritage.

PATENT OFFICE Although patents were granted by the Crown as early as the C14th, the Statute of Monopolies, which was enacted by Parliament in 1623, laid the foundation for modern patent law. The Patents Law Amendment Act 1852 actually introduced the world's first modern patent law. The same law brought The Patent Office into being on 1 October 1852. This became known as the Intellectual Property Office on 2 April 2007.

In principle, anyone can petition for a patent, so a search of patent literature can be of assistance to the researcher as inventors' names are given in full, usually with their place of residence. The "Business and Intellectual Property Centre" of the British Library www.bl.uk holds a comprehensive collection of British and foreign patents. In addition, some larger reference libraries in other parts of the country have collections of both specifications and abridgements.

In the British Library, there is a name index of patentees covering the period from 1617-1981, with one volume for the period 1617-1852 and then one volume for each year thereafter. The patent number and date the patent was applied for is given and from this information one can discover the full name and address.

A research guide entitled *Inventions: patents and specifications* is available at www.nationalarchives.gov.uk. See also Woodcraft, Bennett *Reference Index to Patents and Inventions* (The Patent Office 1855 reprinted Ulan Press 2012). This lists patent numbers 1 through to 14359, covering the period from 2 March 1617 to 1 October 1852 and refers to any relevant books, journals or law reports in which a particular patent is mentioned.

PATENT ROLLS See Letters Patent.

PATHE See British Pathe.

PATRONYMICS This term is used to denote one of the ways in which surnames evolved, by taking the father's name. For example, Johnson is John's son, which might become Johns, or even by just using the Christian name John. "Mac" before a name, for example MacDonald, also means "son of". "O" before a name, for example O'Connor, means "grandson of". Patronymics are especially common in Wales. Welsh "ap" is a shortened form of Mab meaning "son of". Contractions of this often results in surnames beginning with "B" or "P", for example ap Howell becomes Powell.

PATTENMAKERS They were makers of wooden shoes with high heels of wood or metal, which were designed to raise the feet above the level of mud in the streets. The Worshipful Company of Pattenmakers is a London Livery Company. Its history and details of its treasures can be found on its website at www.pattenmakers.co.uk.

PAUPERS See Poor Law.

PAVIORS A pavior was appointed by a town or village to see to the repair of paving stones etc..

PECULIAR See also Inhibition. This term refers to a parish or group of parishes, not necessarily adjacent or even in the same district or county, which were exempt from the testamentary jurisdiction of the archdeaconry and often the consistory court. Ecclesiastical peculiars were often subject to a dean or dean and chapter, though they might be administered by a locally appointed official. A bishop's peculiar might be administered by the consistory court. A number were royal or archbishop's peculiars, usually locally administered. There were some lay, manorial or collegiate peculiars.

Many Peculiars issued their own marriage licences and granted probate within their jurisdiction. If an area was in a Peculiar, it is necessary to check for separate indexes for these. For example, the Borthwick Institute has some fifty separate Peculiar Probate Indexes for Yorkshire.

PEDIGREE See also Abbreviations, Computer Software and Family Histories. The term "pedigree" usually refers to a formal record of ancestry showing several generations linked together in sequence. Such a record may be in the form of a detailed narrative, often with indents to distinguish the generations, or it may be presented as a chart more familiarly known as a "family tree".

Traditional pedigree charts, often found in published family histories, set out the generations in horizontal lines with the earliest at the top of the page and most recent at the bottom. Parents and their children, in the next generation, are linked by vertical lines. Charts based on this method can become very large but if this is inconvenient, it is possible to split up the pedigree by drawing several smaller charts which may be suitably cross-referenced.

A popular method of presentation is the birth-brief chart or family history record sheet. Generations are set out in columns with the youngest on the left. It is customary to enter one individual in the left hand column, his or her two parents in the next, the four grandparents in the next and so on. The column on the extreme right may provide for sixteen or thirty-two or even more ancestors depending on the physical size of the sheet. Such charts are usually numbered to assist cross referencing.

Other options include the circular chart in which the descendant is placed at the centre and all earlier generations are represented as concentric rings, the earliest ancestors being entered on the outer ring. There are further possibilities based on specially designed pictorial charts, computerised systems or record books.

During the early stages of pedigree compilation, standard formats may be useful but for final presentation one may need a greater measure of flexibility. For instance it is important to be able to accommodate individuals who cohabit or marry several times through death or divorce of spouse(s). Furthermore it may be necessary to be able to show the marriage of close cousins who ordinarily would appear elsewhere on the chart. There is probably no single method of setting out a chart which is universally applicable so it is very much a matter of making a selection on the basis of personal preference. Nowadays most family trees are generated by one or other of the genealogical software programmes and these normally allow for the production of charts in different formats. For hints on how to locate published pedigrees see Family Histories.

See Lynskey, Marie *Family Trees: a manual for their design, layout and display* (Phillimore 1996).

PEDLAR See also Badger. Derived from the word "Ped", a pannier or basket for carrying goods; or the French "pied", one who traveller on foot.

PEERAGE See www.thepeerage.com. G.E. Cokayne has edited the *Complete Peerage* in 14 volumes (reprinted Nabu Press 2011), with a brief biography of every holder of a peerage since records began. This does not however deal with ancestors or children. Collins' *Peerage of England* will give you ancestry and descendants and Volume 9 contains a full index. *Burke's Peerage* and *Debrett's Peerage* are the standard works of reference. The former is the more useful to the genealogist since the pedigrees given are more extensive. Both include extinct and dormant peerages.

Burke's *The History of the Commoners* in 4 volumes appeared in 1836 and deals with titled people; the name was changed for the 2nd edition (1846-1849) and is called *The Landed Gentry of Great Britain and Ireland* (3 volumes). It has an index extending to 311 pages in which there are at least 100,000 names. For Scotland, James Balfour Paul's *The Scots' Peerage* should be consulted. *A Directory of British Peerages* by Francis L. Leeson (SOG 1984), lists British titles of nobility and the surnames of families or individuals who bear, or who have borne, them; it is arranged in one continuous alphabetical run. See Adolph. Anthony *Tracing your Aristocratic Ancestors: a guide for family historians* (Pen and Sword 2013).

PEN & SWORD BOOKS Many of the publications mentioned in this volume have been produced by this Yorkshire firm. Their expanding range of military, family and social history books and DVDs can be browsed on their website at www.pen-and-sword.co.uk. They are also producing a number of guides relating to family history research in particular regions of Britain.

PENSION See also Annuity, Army, Royal Marines and Royal Navy. Pensions were paid to certain state employees. Any surviving records are in TNA. The following TNA research guides can be downloaded from www.nationalarchives.gov.uk: *British Army: soldiers' pensions, 1702-1913. Royal*

Navy: pay and pension records: commissioned officers. Royal Navy: pension records: ratings. Royal Navy: warrant officers' pension records.

PERAMBULATIONS This refers to a custom of walking round the parish boundary. These perambulations are sometimes recorded in parish records and sometimes name those who took part.

In 1861, the Vicar of Lillington in Warwickshire explained to the eighteen parishioners who accompanied him, eight of whom were schoolboys, the purpose of the exercise thus: "The object, for which it is done, is to prevent our neighbours encroaching upon us, and that we may not encroach upon them, and to save us from the expense of strife and ill-feeling, which future disputes might occasion, if the limits of the parish were not ascertained and kept up. Even God himself thought this such an important question, that he pronounced a curse upon anyone who should remove his neighbour's landmark".

PERPETUAL CURATE A clerk or minister in a parish or chapelry where there was no regularly endowed vicarage and where tithes were held in whole or in part by a layman. Also an incumbent of a parochial chapelry with some rights of baptism, burial and the like.

PERSONAL ANCESTRAL FILE (PAF) See Computer Software.

PETTY SESSIONS These were meetings of local justices to deal with minor offences. Records can be found in CROs.

PEW RENTS These were a source of "extra-legal" revenue for the church whereby pews were leased to parishioners in order of social precedence. Seating plans record where our ancestors sat in church and can sometimes be found amongst parish records. For further information, see Tate, W E *The Parish Chest* (Phillimore 2010).

PEWTERER The Worshipful Company of Pewterers is one of the many Livery Companies in the City of London. Its website at www.pewterers.org.uk includes a history of the company, a description of its hall and details of its archives and publications.

PHARMACIST See Apothecaries.

PHAROS TEACHING AND TUTORING http://pharostutors.com/. This firm offers online courses in genealogy and family history, which are delivered by professional genealogists with extensive teaching experience. Their website explains that the researcher will study in their own time but with the assistance of a tutor and interaction with a group of other students. A wide range of courses are available at reasonable prices, with the emphasis very much on UK genealogy.

PHILLIMORE & CO. LTD. See also Parish Register Transcripts. This publisher specialise in books relating to genealogy, local history and allied studies. Their website, which lists their publications, is at www.phillimore.co.uk.

PHILLIMORE ATLAS AND INDEX OF PARISH REGISTERS See Parish maps.

PHOTOGRAPHS AND PHOTOGRAPHERS See also Royal Photographic Society. Many family photograph albums have survived but rarely has the name of the person portrayed been written on the back, though you will usually find a lot of information about the photographer. A very useful addition to your family history is a photographic record of the places with which your family was associated. You should enquire at the appropriate Library or CRO. Many of them do have photographic collections and you can obtain photocopies. The Francis Frith Collection is a remarkable record of Victorian England. Francis Frith was for almost 40 years the most prolific of English photographers and the collection has more than 60,000 of his original glass negatives illustrating over 2,000 towns and villages in Britain. Prints produced from these plates are outstanding for their quality. Images are available to browse or purchase at www.francisfrith.com. There are a number of useful books on this subject. Shrimpton, Jayne *How to get the most from Family Pictures* (SOG 2011); Pols, Robert *Dating Nineteenth Century Photographs* (FFHS 2005); Pols, Robert *Dating Twentieth Century Photographs* (FFHS 2005); Pols, Robert *Dating Old Army Photographs* (FHP 2011); Chapman, Philip J *Basic Approach to Illuminating your Family History with Picture Postcards* (FFHS 2000); Pols, Robert *Family Photographs 1860 - 1945* (PRO 2002); Shrimpton, Jayne *Family Photographs and How to Date Them* (Countryside Books 2008); Storey, Neil *Military Photographs and How to Date Them* (Countryside Books 2009); Oliver, George *Photographs and Local History* (Batsford 1990) whose chapter on interpretation and identification of photographs is of particular value.

A study of fashion also helps to date a photograph. *Wedding Fashions 1860-1980*, 1983 and *Fashion A La Carte 1860-1900*, 1985, both by Avril Lansdell, (Shire Publications), are aids to dating photographs. The photographic process used also helps to date it, as does the photographer's backdrop. For example, balustrades, columns and curtains were popular in the 1880s.

On tracing photographers and their lives see Hannavy, John *The Victorian Professional Photographer* (Shire Publications 1980). The Kodak Company archives have been donated to the British Library and the library of its research department is housed at De Montfort University, Leicestershire. The National Media Museum in Bradford www.nationalmediamuseum.org.uk is also worth a visit. The Royal Photographic Society's Historical Group, www.rps.org/group/historical 38 Sutton Road, Watford, Herts WD1 2QF has lists of photographers who worked in various towns. They produce a quarterly Journal, *The PhotoHistorian* and organise lectures and conferences. See also Pols, Robert *My Ancestor was a Studio Photographer: a guide to sources for family historians* (SOG 2011).

PHYSICIAN See Medical Profession.

PIGOT'S DIRECTORIES See directories.

PINFOLD Also known as a Pound, this was an area in which stray animals were put. They were released on payment of a fine by the owner. The parish officer in charge was known as a Pinder, a Pinfold, a Poundkeeper or a Punder.

PIPE ROLLS These were accounts rendered by the sheriffs to the Exchequer with details of Crown revenues from rents etc. They survive as a continuous series from 1155 to the 1830s, and there are also some for the period 1120-1130. The Rolls are in TNA. See their guide *Early Pipe Rolls 1130-c.1300* at www.nationalarchives.gov.uk. Information from some of these records can be found at www.british-history.ac.uk. Many early pipe rolls have been published by the Pipe Roll Society www.piperollsociety.co.uk.

PLACE NAMES If you discover there is a place corresponding to a surname in which you are interested, do not make the mistake of thinking it was named after one of your ancestors. This was rarely the case. Place names usually date back to a period well before surnames were in use. It is more likely that one of your ancestors originally came from that place. Interpretation of place names should be based on documentary evidence of early spellings. See Gelling, Margaret *Signposts to the Past* (3rd ed. Phillimore 1997).

The Institute for Name Studies http://www.nottingham.ac.uk/ins/index.aspx is the home of research into place names and personal names and is based at the University of Nottingham. The English Place Name Society (EPNS) www.nottingham.ac.uk/ins/placenamesociety/index.aspx is the established national body for the subject; its offices and library are housed in the Institute. For the detailed record and analysis of English place names, from cities to villages, farms and fields, the Survey of English Place Names is the established reference source for historians, linguists and geographers. The EPNS publishes the Survey and other related works, including an annual Journal. County Volumes of the EPNS are important for identifying obscure place names encountered in original sources. See also http://onomastics.co.uk/.

PLANTATION INDENTURES Justices of the Peace were responsible after 1682 for issuing indentures for work on plantations in America or the West Indies.

PLEA ROLLS See Court of Common Pleas.

PLEDGEHOUSE A prison where debtors were kept.

PLUMBER The Worshipful Company of Plumbers is one of the most ancient of the Livery Companies of the City of London. Its Ordinances were granted by the Aldermen of the City of London in 1365. The Company's website at www. plumberscompany.org.uk gives details of its history and explains how to purchase the history that was published by the Company itself in 2000.

PODCAST A podcast is a small audio file that is downloaded onto computer and is listened to either on the host computer, on an MP3 player or Apple "iPod", or following transfer onto a CD, on a CD player.

TNA has an expanding list of pod casts, presentations given by leading historians dealing with many areas of research, which can be downloaded free of charge from media.nationalarchives.gov.uk. Generally, the subjects covered are ones for which TNA has a significant holding of records. A few examples include: *The Navy Board Project*; *Workhouse records for family historians*; *Sources for Army Officers' Commissions*; *Modern Sources for Immigration*; *Army deaths, marriages and births 1761-1913*; *In the name of God, Amen: wills for family history*; *Sources for First World War army ancestry*; *Tracing your Irish ancestors at TNA*.

POLAND The best place to start to research ancestry from Poland is the website "Polish Connections" www.zem.co.uk/polish/history.htm. This contains a multitude of information about Poland and importantly, is written in English. The link takes you into the site's History pages, which includes the section on searching for Polish roots. From there, try "Genealogy in Poland". If more detailed guidance is needed, access the regional links and the link to the "Polish State Archives".

TNA publish a research guide entitled *Polish National and Military Archives: disposal after 1945*, available at www.nationalarchives.gov.uk. The Kresy-Siberia Virtual Museum www.Kresy-Siberia.org is dedicated to researching Polish World War 2 experiences.

POLICE RECORDS See also Constables and Crime and Criminals. The Metropolitan Police Force was formed in 1829. In 1835, the Municipal Corporations Act was passed allowing cities and boroughs to form police forces. The County Police Act was passed in 1839 allowing counties to form forces. In 1856, the County and Borough Police Act was passed compelling all cities and boroughs and counties in England and Wales to have police forces. A comprehensive list of approximate dates of formation of county police forces can be found in John Richardson's *The Local Historian's Encyclopedia* (Historical Publications Ltd. 3rd revised ed. 2003).

Possible sources of information include such publications as the *Police*

Almanac, the *Police Review*, the now defunct *Police Chronicle* and various local police histories.

City of London Police www.cityoflondon.police.uk has a museum. Its website details various books published about the force.The registers of the force exist from 1832 and are in the LMA www.cityoflondon.gov.uk.

Metropolitan Police records are held in TNA, Class MEPO. Their research guide *London Metropolitan and Transport Police* can be downloaded from www.nationalarchives.gov.uk. Much detail about the Metropolitan Police Records of Service can be found on the force's website www.met.police.uk/history/records.htm. The site also contains an official history of the Metropolitan Police, summaries of some famous cases and details of the "The Metropolitan Police Service Historical Archives". This is the place to look for particulars of memorabilia, uniforms, weapons and headgear. The website of the "Friends of the Metropolitan Police Historical Collection" www.friendsof methistory.co.uk has some specific information relating to family history.

Other forces have museums too, which will often contain information about forces that have long-since ceased to exist. For example, Thames Valley Police has a museum at Sulhamstead in the former headquarters of the Berkshire Constabulary. It includes displays on the history of Thames Valley Police and the five police forces that merged to form it, Berkshire, Buckinghamshire, Oxford City, Oxfordshire and Reading Borough. The museum's collections include items from the Great Train Robbery of 1963, uniforms, equipment, medals, photographs, scenes of crime evidence and occurrence and charge books. See www.thamesvalley.police.uk.

The website of the Police History Society www.policehistorysociety.co.uk contains a list of and links to, the websites of all police force museums, as well as much other relevant information. The latter includes a listing of and links to the websites of many police-related historical societies and other bodies.

The Royal Military Police keep their own records and the website of their museum has a very detailed section on "Ancestor Research" www.army museums.org.uk. There do not appear to be any records in TNA for the police of the various railway companies. Some records for the South African Constabulary are however held with Colonial Office papers. Two TNA research guides *Police, Metropolitan (London): records of service* and *Police: transport* www.nationalarchives.gov.uk. It is worth noting that police were at times empowered to issue licences which could yield useful information, for example under the Chimney Sweepers Act of 1875.

For general information on the history of policing in England and Wales see Critchley, T A *A History of Police in England and Wales* (Constable 1978) and Emsley, Clive *The English Police: a political and social history* (Harvester Wheatsheaf 1996). Brewin Books publish a series of County Police histories, including West Mercia, Metropolitan Police, Shropshire and Northamptonshire. For further details, see www.brewinbooks.com. It is also worth keeping an eye open for privately published material relating to police records. For example,

Oxfordshire Black Sheep Publications have brought out a number of books including: *Oxfordshire 1914-1918: special constables, women patrols and July Lists*; *Oxfordshire Constabulary Recruitment Register; Oxford City Police Register; Reading Borough Police Register; Banbury Constables 1775-1925: 150 years on the beat*. An internet search will reveal details of similar titles from other publishers and how to obtain them.

In Scotland, an Act of 1857 established county forces in a similar way to those outlined in the legislation for England and Wales in 1856. Historical records relating to Scottish policing come in various categories. Local authority archives hold some, whilst others are retained by the police forces themselves. In general, a wider variety of records survive for the larger forces, especially the city constabularies. Less survives for some smaller constabularies, particularly those absorbed by larger forces.

A good starting point when researching Scottish police ancestry is the website of the Scottish Archive Network www.scan.org.uk. Its "Knowledge base" contains a great deal of detail. The website of The National Archives of Scotland (NAS) has a research guide *Burgh Records*, which can be downloaded from www.nas.gov.uk. The website of the Glasgow Police Heritage Society and Glasgow Police Museum is another starting point http://gphs1800.tripod.com/.

POLL BOOKS See also Electoral Registers. These are lists of people who voted in Parliamentary elections. During the C18th, the right to vote was restricted to landowners and those who rented property exceeding a particular value. These lists of who voted, which also show for whom they voted, will indicate that an ancestor was in a particular place at a particular time. Some poll books also indicate the trade or profession of the voter.

Poll books are arranged by county. There is a great deal of variation in their arrangement. They might be arranged alphabetically by parish, by hundred, by polling booth or by ward. An excellent aid to using these records is Gibson, Jeremy and Rogers, Colin *Poll Books c1696-1872: a directory to holdings in Great Britain* (4th ed. FHP 2008). Copies of poll books are often found in CROs. In addition, the SOG has a fine collection and has published *Directories and Poll Books in the library of The Society of Genealogists* (6th ed. SOG 1995).

Much other material on poll books has been published. Poll books are being reproduced in facsimile in "Raymond's Original Pollbooks" series. Polls in such places as London, Westminster, Norfolk, Somerset, Suffolk, Yorkshire and Hull feature in the series.

Some poll books have also been published on CD by the Parish Register Transcription Society www.prtsoc.org.uk and by the Anguline Research Archives http://anguline.co.uk. See "Lists of Names: Pollbooks and Electoral Registers" at www.familyhistorypartnership.co.uk, click "Hints and Tips".

POLL TAX This is a tax that may list not just the head of the household but also his family and servants. In the C17th, it was raised in 1660, 1667, 1678, 1689,

1691, 1694 and 1697. Not many of the records survive but those that do are mainly in CROs, though TNA holds some lists of defaulters. Further information is available in *The Hearth Tax, Other Later Stuart Tax Lists and the Association Oath Rolls* by Jeremy Gibson, (2nd ed. FFHS 1996). For details, consult TNA's E179 database (q.v.) www.nationalarchives.gov.uk/e179/.

POOR LAW (NEW) See Guardians, Boards of and Workhouses

POOR LAW (OLD) See also Apprentices, Guardians, Boards of, Settlement and Workhouses. This was administered by the parish after the Act of 1597, which authorised them to levy a rate to be paid by those who could afford to do so. The collection of the rate was the duty of an "Overseer" who also gave relief to those in need, either in money or in kind. Poor Law documents can be a very useful record of people living in the parish since they encompass a wide range of subjects. These include Overseers' Accounts, Settlement Certificates and Examinations, Removal Orders, Apprenticeship Indentures and Churchwardens' Accounts. The duties of Overseers passed to the Boards of Guardians set up in 1834, the Overseers then becoming assessors and collectors. The Rating and Valuation Act of 1925 finally abolished the office of Overseer.

Anne Cole's *An Introduction to Poor Law Documents Before 1834* (FFHS 1994), deals with this subject thoroughly. The author rightly cautions that "It should not be assumed that these records are only of use to researchers with proven pauper ancestors. Those involved with local administration of the Poor Law were certainly not paupers, a very large number of families lived from hand to mouth - an accident could cause the family to become dependent upon poor relief, if only temporarily". Anne Cole's publication cites further reading but see also *Annals of the Poor* by Eve McLaughlin (FFHS 1994). For more detailed coverage see Hawkings, David T *Pauper Ancestors: a guide to the records created by the poor laws in England and Wales* (The History Press 2011) and Burlison, Robert *Tracing Your Pauper Ancestors: a guide for family historians* (Wharncliffe Books 2009).

POPULATION The population of England and Wales in 1801 was about 9 million. Prior to this, there are no reliable statistics to guide us but it is likely that the population was considerably smaller than this. Between 1800 and 1850 the population doubled. As a result of the Industrial Revolution there was a great shift of population from the countryside to the towns. Between 1770 and 1831, Liverpool's population multiplied five times and towns such as Manchester, Birmingham and Bristol saw similar increases.

Prior to the Industrial Revolution, there was much more mobility of population than was originally believed. In pre-industrial England, almost half of the population were servants of one kind or another, if we regard a labourer as a servant. Labourers were hired annually at the hiring fairs and moved to their employer's area.

The Local Population Studies Society (LPSS) publishes a journal *Local Population Studies* (LPS) as well as books on the subject. Its website, www.localpopulationstudies.org.uk, contains information about the Society and its outputs. Its main feature is the archive of back issues of *Local Population Studies*, older issues being available to download free of charge.

The Cambridge Group for the Study of Population and Social Structure have undertaken research and published the results in books and journals such as LPS. A key book is *The Population History of England 1541-1871: a reconstruction* by E A Wrigley and R S Schofield (Cambridge University Press 1989). This is based on an analysis of parish registers. A more recent text is Wrigley, E A and Davies, R S (eds.) *English Population History from Family Reconstitution 1580-1837* (Cambridge University Press 1997).

The Online Historical Population Reports website is at www.histpop.org and covers census reports for Britain and Ireland 1801-1937.

PORTS The website www.portcities.org.uk contains historical information about the maritime heritage of five of England's major ports: Bristol, Hartlepool, London, Liverpool and Southampton.

PORTRAITS TNA has digitised all oil paintings in public ownership, many of which are portraits. This project has been achieved in conjunction with the Public Catalogue Foundation (PCF) and the BBC. See bbc.co.uk/yourpaintings.

The National Portrait Gallery's Heinz Archive and Library was opened in 1993. The archive dates back to 1856 and can assist with research on the Gallery's collection of portraits. There are extensive files of engravings, photographs and reproductions of portraits in collections world-wide, arranged by sitter and artist. The archive also houses most of the Gallery's portrait photograph collection of more than 150,000 original prints and negatives. The library contains some 30,000 books and a number of special collections.

Silhouette portraits were popular in the early C19th. A splendid collection can be seen in the National Portrait Gallery. There is a catalogue of 5,200 named and dated English silhouettes by August Edouart (1789-1861). A huge amount of further information, including details of displays and the catalogue, can be accessed by visiting the National Portrait Gallery's website at www.npg.org.uk. See Ormond, Richard and Rogers, Malcolm (eds.) *Dictionary of British Portraiture* (4 vols. B T Batsford in association with the National Portrait Gallery 1979-1981).

POSTCARDS The first picture postcards in this country were delivered by the Post Office in September 1894 and were immediately popular, with more than two million sent every week. Plain cards had been in circulation for some twenty years previously. Picture postcards are useful as they will show scenes such as a village street and its buildings or an event, such as the opening of a chapel.

Family portraits were also produced as postcards and sent to friends and relatives. The reverse of the cards are also worthy of examination, as there may be family news on them and the addresses could be helpful. *Picture Postcard Monthly* www.postcard.co.uk is published by Reflections of a Bygone Age and contains many advertisements placed by dealers of postcards for sale. Reflections of a Bygone Age have a separate website at www.postcard collecting.co.uk. Both sites carry details of postcard fairs.

Many postcards are held at the Valentine Archive of St Andrew's University Library. This is part of its Photographic Archive. Their website at www.st-andrews.ac.uk/library/specialcollections/photographic/ enables one to browse or seek out subjects or themes. The photographs and postcards themselves can be viewed on-line and saved for future viewing.

Relevant reading includes Godden, Geoffrey A *Collecting Picture Postcards* (Phillimore 1996); Hill, C W *Discovering Picture Postcards* (Shire Publications 1978) and Coysh, A W *Dictionary of Picture Postcards in Britain 1894-1939* (Antique Collectors Club Ltd. 1986).

Old postcards can be obtained from sites such as www.ebay.co.uk, where it is possible to log a search for all items that match a particular place name, so that you are informed if a relevant item is listed. Postcard dealers are also more than happy to receive requests.

POST OFFICE See also Telephone Directories. Some records date back to the C17th and cover every aspect of the Post Office's history and personnel. As well as information on former employees, which begin in 1831, other records document the development of telecommunications and the provision of telegraph, telephone and related services in the United Kingdom and the Commonwealth.

The British Postal Museum & Archive (BPMA), previously known as the Post Office Archives and Records Centre, has a website at http://postalheritage.org.uk/, which contains a great deal of information. This includes a history of the British postal service, details of the Museum and Archives collections and exhibitions, and an opportunity to search their on-line catalogue.

Researchers can also download a *Guide to the Royal Mail Archive*, a number of information sheets addressing particular subjects and a *Family History Research Guide*. For those researching Post Office employees, Staff Nomination and Appointment records and Staff Establishment Books are likely to prove relevant.

See Farrugia, Jean *A Guide to Post Office Archives* (The Post Office 1987) and Smith, Duncan Campbell *Masters of the Post: the authorized history of Royal Mail* (Allen Lane 2012), the first complete history of the Royal Mail up to the present day.

The Post Office Appointment Books 1737-1969, are a collection of 1.5 million records listing the employees of one of the world's largest ever employers. They list the men and women appointed to roles within the service, and detail information on worker appointments, transfers, dismissals, resignations and deaths. They typically include a name, date of appointment, grade or position and location of work, with some showing salaries, references or recommendations. They can be viewed online at www.ancestry.co.uk.

POULTERER A dealer in poultry and game. The Worshipful Company of Poulters www.poulters.org.uk is a London Livery Company that received its first charter in 1504. Its website details its history and its records.

POUND See Pinfold.

PREROGATIVE COURTS OF CANTERBURY AND YORK (PCC & PCY) See also Doctors' Commons and Ecclesiatical Courts. Prerogative Courts of the Archbishops of Canterbury and York had superior jurisdiction over all diocesan courts and had to be used in cases where a will or administration involved property in two or more dioceses. They were sometimes used in preference to a diocesan court as a status symbol. Canterbury took precedence over York.
PCC wills and administrations are held in TNA www.nationalarchives.gov.uk. PCY wills and administrations are held in the Borthwick Institute of Historical Research, which is part of York University www.york.ac.uk.

The majority of PCC wills have been digitised and are available online at www.nationalarchives.gov.uk/records/wills.htm. A variety of other PCC documents are also of interest. See TNA research guide *Wills and Probate: further research*. See also pp 77-80 of Stuart Raymond's *The Wills of our Ancestors: a guide for family and local historians* (Pen and Sword 2012).

PRESBYTERIANS The Presbyterians followed the doctrines of the Reformation leader John Calvin. It was John Knox, who had worked in Geneva with Calvin, who was largely responsible for the spread of Presbyterian ideas in Scotland, where it became the leading church. Churches were also set up in England and Wales.

In 1972, the Presbyterian and Congregational churches in England merged to form the United Reformed Church. This led to a merger of The Presbyterian Historical Society of England with the Congregational Historical Society, with the new name of The United Reformed Church History Society www.urc.org.uk. The society publishes a journal and has a library.

After 1840, English Presbyterian registers were deposited with the Registrar General and with other nonconformist registers, are in TNA.

See Ruston, Alan *My Ancestors were English Presbyterians & Unitarians: how can I find out more about them?* (SOG 2001) and Clifford, David *My Ancestors were Congregationalists* (SOG 1998).

PRESENTMENTS See Churchwardens' Presentments.

PRIESTS See Clergy and Roman Catholics.

PRIMOGENITURE A form of inheritance whereby all is given to the eldest son.

PRINTERS See Papermakers. The Seditious Societies Act of 1799 required printing presses to be licensed by Justices. Records give names and addresses of owners (to 1869) and will be found in Quarter Sessions Records (q.v.). It is important not to confuse Publishing Printers with Textile Printers.

PRISON HULK The body of a dismantled ship used as a floating prison, especially in the early C19th. *The English Prison Hulks* by W Branch Johnson (Phillimore 1970), gives more details.

PRISONERS OF WAR See also Army. A key book on this subject is Paterson, Sarah *Tracing Your Prisoner of War Ancestors: the first world war* (Pen and Sword 2012). With some exceptions, most records in TNA about Prisoners of War before 1914 do not give lists of names or detailed information.

There are several relevant TNA research guides at www.nationalarchives. gov.uk including: *British Prisoners of the Second World War and the Korean War. Prisoners of War in British Hands. Looking for Records of a British Prisoner of War up to the First World War.*

For the French Revolutionary and Napoleonic Wars (1793-1815) there are lists of British Prisoners in France and elsewhere forwarded by the agent for prisoners in Paris. Most prisoners were naval and civilian internees. There are registers of French prisoners in Britain and enemy prisoners on parole but there is no central index for these. In 1813 a register of American prisoners of war in Britain was compiled. French and American prisoners of war were brought into Plymouth in the early 1800s and later transferred to the new prison at Princetown, Dartmoor. The Americans largely built the church of St Michael's, Princetown, which has a stained glass memorial window dedicated to them in 1910. After his release Charles Andrews, an American prisoner, published a book entitled *The Prisoners' Memoirs of Dartmoor Prison* (reprinted General Books 2010). A long list of prisoners who died in this prison 1813-1815 is included, with personal details.

About 8% of the seafaring manpower of the United States, approximately 7,500 Navy and private seamen, were held as prisoners for at least part of the war 1812-14. In addition about 1,000 United States Army or militia personnel were captured and held prisoner. The records relating to those taken prisoner by British Forces during the war are in the TNA and some entries in the relevant General Entry Books for American Prisoners of War are quite detailed.

Some official material relating to Russian prisoners in British hands during the Crimean War (1854-1856) exists at TNA. Records of the Russian Orthodox Church in London give lists of Russian prisoners (in Russian) who received money.

There are registers of Boer War (1899-1902) prisoners arranged by place of confinement (e.g. Natal) and correspondence concerning Dutch, German and French prisoners has survived.

The International Committee of the Red Cross in Geneva www.icrc.org keeps lists of all known prisoners of war and internees of all nationalities in both the World Wars (1914-1918), (1939-1945). These are housed in the International Red Cross Library in Geneva.

3 volumes listing prisoners of war 1939-1945 are available: *Prisoners of War: British army* (Savannah Publications 1990), *Prisoners of War: naval & air forces of Great Britain and the empire* (Savannah Publications 2009) and *Armies and Other Land Forces of The Empire* (Savannah Publications 1990).

During the First World War, deaths of prisoners of war and internees, in military and non-military hospitals in enemy and occupied territory, were notified to the British authorities. These certificates can be consulted at TNA. Also at TNA are lists of British and Commonwealth servicemen who were prisoners of war in Korea (1950-1953).

PRISONS AND PRISONERS See also Crime and Criminals, House of Correction and Parkhurst Boys. Up to the C19th, the main function of a prison was very different from today. They were not principally for punishment or the protection of society since so many offences were punishable by transportation or hanging. The occupants were mainly prisoners awaiting trial or sentence or debtors waiting for their debts to be cleared by whatever means. Very early prisons were located in castles, large houses and fortified gateways. Richardson, John *The Local Historian's Encyclopaedia* (Historical Publications Ltd. 3rd revised ed. 2003) has a list of locations of some, with more specific references to others and only general references to records.

Prison administration was transferred from the counties to the Home Office in 1877. Whilst there should have been a corresponding transfer of archives, some may still remain with the CROs. Records of prisoners in many gaols in the period 1770-1971 are at TNA.

In TNA, there are 207 large volumes classified as Quarterly Prison Returns, dating from September 1824 to March 1876. They contain the names of convicts with their offences, places and dates of conviction and periods of sentence. The returns are from Prison Hulks (q.v.) as well as from ordinary prisons.

Calendars of prisoners awaiting trial exist in connection with the Assizes, and copies may be found in CROs. Relevant TNA research guides, available at www.nationalarchives.gov.uk are *Criminals in the 18th, 19th and 20th centuries* and *Assizes: key to series for English criminal trials 1559-1971*.

The City of London Record Office has an index of people in London debtors' prisons from the mid-1700s. LMA information leaflet 42 *My Ancestor was a Convict*, is a good starting point. It can be downloaded from www.cityoflondon.gov.uk, click on "Things to Do", "Visiting the City", "Archives and City History" and "LMA".

A missing person in a family group in any of the census returns could be explained by the fact that the person was in prison, assuming that no death has been traced, though it is more likely that the person was working away from home. An excellent book is Hawkings, David *Criminal Ancestors: a guide to historical criminal records in England and Wales* (Alan Sutton 1996).

PROBATE, GRANT OF See also Wills. The official proving of a will by the Probate Office. Procedure whereby the executor is formally given the right to administer the estate of the deceased.

PROBATE INVENTORIES See Inventories.

PROCTOR A person employed in civil or ecclesiastical causes, equivalent to a solicitor or attorney at Common Law. Also a University official at Oxford or Cambridge. Sometimes used to refer to a person licensed to collect alms for hospitals.

PROFESSIONAL RESEARCHERS See also AGRA. There are times when it is convenient to employ a qualified researcher to consult records in some distant repository. There are two kinds of researchers, genealogists and record agents. Broadly speaking, the genealogist directs research and interprets the data while the record agent gathers it.

A list of researchers can be found at www.greatauntyalice.com.

PROTESTATION RETURNS In 1641/1642, Parliament organised a national protest against "an arbitrary and tyrannical government", aimed at Charles I. All males of eighteen years of age or over were required to sign a declaration of belief in the Protestant religion, allegiance to the king and support for the rights and privileges of Parliament.

These Protestation Returns are effectively the best male adult census prior to 1841. Most of the Returns are in the Parliamentary Archives (q.v.), arranged within county by hundred. Survival is sporadic, with about a third of the country extant; some counties having good collections, some just a few and some none at all. Further information is contained in *Family History Resources at the Parliamentary Archives*, which can be downloaded from www.parliament.uk. The places for which Returns survive are listed in Gibson, Jeremy and Dell, Alan *Protestation Returns 1641-42 and other Contemporary Listings* (FHP 2009). This book gives details of all published and other transcripts. http://edwardvallance. files.wordpress.com/2011/06/on-lineprotestationreturns.pdf gives links to online transcripts of the returns, although this may now be somewhat out of date.

PROVINCE The diocese over which an archbishop has authority. Before 1858, in England and Wales, this referred to the provinces of Canterbury and York and in Ireland, to the province of Armagh. The prerogative courts of archbishops had superior jurisdiction to all others and Canterbury was superior to York.

PUBLIC RECORD OFFICE Now The National Archives (TNA) (q.v.).

PUBLIC SCHOOLS See Education.

Q

QUAKERS Founded by George Fox, meetings of "The Friends" were held as long ago as the 1650s. The main unit of the Quaker hierarchy was the Monthly Meeting, which was made up of several local or Preparative Meetings. Monthly Meetings were then grouped into Quarterly Meetings, with the London Yearly Meeting overseeing all of these. The names are indicators of how frequently meetings at this level were held.

Before handing over their registers to the Registrar General in 1840, as required by the Royal Commission of 1837, the Quakers indexed all their entries (over 500,000). This digest can now be consulted in the library of the Religious Society of Friends, which is located on London's Euston Road. It has been microfilmed and is available in research libraries as *Friends House Library Digest Registers of Births, Marriages and Burials for England and Wales C17th-1837* (32 microfilm reels World Microfilm Publications 1989).The original records are at TNA; class RG6 is exclusively Quaker records. These can be accessed for a fee via the website www.bmdregisters.co.uk.

The Society of Friends' (Quakers) Registers, Notes and Certificates of Births, Marriages and Burials ranging from 1578-1841 are also available for a fee at www.thegenealogist.co.uk. Generally, Quaker records are more detailed than those of Anglicans at that time and might reveal much more information than expected. Quakers did not believe in the baptism of children but they did record births and continued to perform marriages after 1754, their records often contain the names of almost all those present at the ceremony. Much Quaker material appears in Quarter Sessions (q.v.) because Quakers refused to pay Tithes. Monthly or Quarterly Meetings kept records of fines and persecutions in books of "sufferings", These would be recorded in "The Great Book of Sufferings" at the yearly meeting. There are partial indexes for sufferings up to 1791 at Friends House Library.

The library of the Religious Society of Friends has the largest collection in Britain of photographs and other visual materials and artefacts relating to the wide range of Quaker activities. It has a splendid website at www.quaker.org.uk/library which includes online exhibitions and the library's catalogue. The library has also produced a newsletter since Spring 2008, all editions of which can be can be downloaded from www.quaker.org.uk/library-newsletter. The library's latest news is always announced on its Facebook page at www.facebook.com/libraryofthesocietyoffriends.

The Friends' Historical Society www.quaker.org.uk/friends-historical-society was founded in 1903. It aims to promote the study of Quaker history and holds meetings, publishes research findings and publishes the *Journal of the Friends Historical Society*. The Quaker Family History Society www.qfhs.co.uk produces a journal, holds meetings and has background information about the Quakers and their records on it website.

See Milligan, Edward H and Thomas, Malcolm J, *My Ancestors were Quakers* (2nd ed. SOG 1999).

QUARRYING See Mining.

QUARTER DAYS Days on which quarterly payments are due, tenancies begin and end and the like. In England, they are Lady Day (25 March), Midsummer Day (24 June), Michaelmas (29 September) and Christmas Day (25 December). In Scotland, they are Candlemas (2 February), Whit Sunday (15 May), Lammas (1 August) and Martinmas (11 November).

QUARTER SESSIONS' COURTS Quarter Sessions records are potentially a most useful source for filling in the background in family history research. In addition to the Sessions' role as judicial authority in cases of minor crime (which continued until 1972), they were the administrative body of each county before the establishment of county councils. Their records often extend back to Tudor times.

They offer a "lucky dip" which may mention family members as magistrates, offenders or witnesses, holders of minor administrative office and a host of other occupations.

A great many aspects of local administration were dealt with by the Quarter Sessions, and many such records are of relevance to family historians. The starting point is to ascertain what has been deposited in the local CRO. These are just some of the documents that might survive, many dating from the C18th and C19th: Constabulary Pay Lists and Crime Returns (lists of charges). Lists of Deputy Coroners. Enrolments of deeds and wills and of papists' estates. Gamekeepers' Certificates. Hair Powder Tax Certificates. Woolwinders' Oaths. Declarations of allegiance by Roman Catholics and Protestant dissenters, declarations against transubstantiation and the like. Documents giving the names of pauper lunatics in parishes. Relief of the poor, settlement examinations, removal orders. Apprenticeship records. Calendars of prisoners with sentences. Depositions in criminal cases. Indictment books giving names of offenders, offences and dates of conviction. Insolvent debtors. Lists of prisoners and papers relating to their release. Victuallers' Recognizances. Bastardy Orders. Recognizance Books (q.v.) these were really bonds kept by the Clerk of the Peace which secured the appearance of defendants, prosecutors or witnesses. Failure to appear meant a heavy fine. Lists of properties and occupiers of land in various parishes in the county with lists of amounts assessed. Flax Bounty: to encourage the growing of flax and hemp, provision was made for the distribution of a bounty for growers. Claims had to be sent to the Clerk of the Peace. Freemasons' Lodges, annual returns of members. Returns of persons using weights and measures. Registration of boats, barges and other vessels used on navigable rivers. Court registers of Courts of Petty Session. Coroners' reports.

See Gibson, Jeremy *Quarter Sessions Records for Family Historians: a select list* (5th ed. FHP 2007).

Many records of the Quarter Sessions have been published e.g. Hearing, Terry and Bridges, Sarah (eds.) *Dorset Quarter Sessions Order Book 1625-1638 - A Calendar* (Dorset Record Society 2006) and Blades, Robert (ed.) *Oxford Quarter Sessions Order Book* (Oxford Historical Society 2009). See www. devonquartersessions.wordpress.com for details of the Devon Quarter Sessions Project.

QUEEN ANNE'S BOUNTY See also First Fruits and Tithes. A fund established by Queen Anne in 1704 to receive and use the annates and tenths previously confiscated by Henry VIII, generally used towards supplementing the income of the poorer clergy. The Fund was made responsible by the Tithe Act 1925 for the collection of tithe rent charges. This was abolished by the Tithe Act 1936 and Government Stock received in compensation. In 1948, Queen Anne's Bounty and the Ecclesiastical Commission were formed into the Church Commission for England. A good deal of interesting information is on their website www. churchcommissioners.org. A rare but useful find would be Hodgson, C *An Account of the Augmentation of Small Livings by The Governors of the Bounty of Queen Anne, for the Augmentation of the Maintenance of the Poor Clergy* (Rivington, Hatchard, Parker and Deighton 1826), which listed hundreds of names of benefactors, with the benefices to which they contributed.

QUITCLAIM A formal discharge or release of property. Such documents are often held by CROs. For further information see the research guidance page for quitclaim on www.nottingham.ac.uk/ManuscriptsandSpecialCollections.

QUIT RENT A fixed annual payment made by a manorial tenant to be released, or quit, from services to the Lord of the Manor. Abolished in 1922.

R

RADIO TIMES ARCHIVE See British Broadcasting Association (BBC) Archive Collections.

RAGGED SCHOOLS See Education.

RAILWAYS The records of the railways are scattered, with many in TNA having been assembled by the British Transport Commission on Nationalisation. Equally, some railway records are in CROs or university archives.

Three TNA research guides of relevance can be downloaded from www.nationalarchives.gov.uk: *Railways*; *Railway* Workers and *Railway Workers: further research*. These deal with the records of the companies themselves and with their staff records.

In 1992, British Rail Archives presented 270 volumes of Great Western Railway (GWR) Stockholders Probate Registers 1835-1932 to the SOG. The GWR Shareholders' Index is now available online at the pay per view or subscription website FindmyPast (q.v.) www.findmypast.co.uk.

Key books on this topic are: Hawkings, David *Railway Ancestors: a guide to the staff records of the railway companies of England and Wales 1822-1947* (The History Press 2008); Drummond, Di *Tracing your Railway Ancestors: a guide to family historians* (Pen and Sword 2010) and Richards, Tom *Was Your Grandfather a Railwayman? a directory of railway archive sources for the family historian* (4th ed. FFHS 2002).

The Railway Ancestors Family History Group www.railwayancestors.org.uk offers assistance to those researchers wanting to trace their railway ancestors.

For a fascinating insight into how the railways were originally built, read Coleman, Terry *The Railway Navvies* (Hutchinson 1965, reprinted Pelican 1976).

The Railway and Canal Historical Society has an interesting website at www.rchs.org.uk.

The National Railway Museum Library www.nrm.org.uk has an extensive collection of railway photographs that are predominantly views of locomotives, carriages, wagons and stations, together with general railway scenes of moving trains and railway related subjects such as shipping and road vehicles. Its website contains more details, as well as some online exhibitions. It has a database of railway workers who died during World War One. This includes names of over 20,000 railway workers with rank, military number, rail department, railway occupation, address, information on their families, war memorial and date of death of railway workers. It also includes references to photographs in staff magazines www.nrm.org.uk/RailwayStories/worldwarone. aspx.

RAMBERT DANCE COMPANY http://rambert.org.uk/. This is Britain's national contemporary dance company. It owns one of the most complete dance archives in the UK, which dates back to the foundation of the Company in 1926 and includes a collection of costumes, both current and archival.

RAPE Term used in Sussex for a grouping of several Hundreds (q.v.).

RATE BOOKS These may survive for your area from the mid C18th onwards. They identify the occupants of houses. Where they survive, they are likely to be in CROs.

RECOGNIZANCES These were bonds that ensured that defendants, prosecutors and witnesses required at the Quarter Sessions (q.v.) would appear when needed. They are found in Quarter Session records in CROs.

RECORD OFFICES See also Archives, CROs, Diocesan Record Offices and National Archives, The Record Offices are vital for family historians, as these are the main custodians of the original records that we need to consult. There are different types of Record Office; they may cover a diocese, county or city. Frequently DROs and CROs have now been amalgamated. Some CROs have amalgamated with Local Studies Libraries, e.g. Devon, Surrey and Wiltshire. Most Record Offices make no charge to users but in a few cases a charge is made for Search Room facilities, either per person per day or part of a day or by issue of a season ticket (valid for a certain number of months from date of issue). Each Record Office has different requirements regarding ID and this should be checked prior to visiting, as should opening times. Some Offices require users to book, especially if a film or fiche reader is required. Most Record Offices will allow the use of a lap top and a digital camera, providing the flash is deactivated; some will make a charge for this.

See Archon Directory www.nationalarchives.gov.uk/archon for the location of archives.

RECORD SOCIETIES See also British Record Society. In addition to The British Record Society there are numerous County Record Societies that specialise in printing indexes and transcripts of documents relating to their area. Details of publications may be found on the relevant societies' websites or at the Bibliography of British and Irish History database www.royalhistoricalsociety. org/respubs.php.

RECTOR A clergyman who received all or part of the great tithes, that is one tenth of all crops grown in the parish. The tithe was also levied on farm animals. The rector also sometimes received the smaller or vicarial tithes.

RECUSANTS' ROLLS See also Roman Catholics. A Recusant was one who refused to comply with the rites and ceremonies of the Church of England. It was most commonly used of Roman Catholics but was sometime also applied to Nonconformists and other Protestant dissenters. In Elizabethan times, fines were imposed by the Churchwardens for failure to attend church on Sundays and holy days. In 1581, the offence became indictable and much more stringent fines were imposed by the Sheriffs. The details of such fines were recorded in the Pipe Rolls (q.v.). Failure to pay fines led to seizure of the recusant's goods and much of his land. From 1592, the information was recorded in the rolls on a county by county basis, giving the name of the Recusant, rent, description of land, date of seizure, payments or arrears of payment etc.. These records which cover approximately a century are in TNA classes E376 to E379. Some have been published by the Catholic Record Society.

RED CROSS See Prisoners of War.

REEVE He represented the tenants on a manor in negotiations with the lord of the manor or his steward and arranged such things as the labour which tenants were required to provide for a stated number of days of the year.

REGISTER OFFICE See also Civil Registration and Maps. Often inaccurately referred to as the Registry Office. Certificates of births, marriages and deaths can be purchased from local Register Offices. Before doing so the following points should be borne in mind. The reference numbers of The Registrar General, obtained from sites such as FreeBMD at http://freebmd.rootsweb.com/ are not recognised by local Register Offices, so additional detail may be required in order to obtain a certificate. If there has been an error in the Registrar General's indexes it may be that an elusive entry can be traced locally.

A registration district is an administrative area into which the country was divided for the purpose of registering births, marriages and deaths. Originally these were based on Poor Law Unions. Some registration districts have been amalgamated over the years and it is necessary to ensure that you approach the office that has the appropriate records. The webpage www.ukbmd.org.uk/ genuki/reg/regoff.html provides a full list of registration districts and the addresses of local register offices.

REGISTRATION TAX See also Parish Registers. From 1695 to 1706 a tax was levied on all births, marriages and deaths recorded in the parish registers. Also taxed were bachelors over 25 and childless widowers. The Act required a complete enumeration of the population as it stood in 1695. Virtually none of the tax lists have survived except for the Cities of London and Bristol, a few other boroughs and 16 Wiltshire parishes. Returns for 80 of the 97 ancient parishes within the walls of the City of London and 13 outside have survived and are in the Corporation of London Record Office, with a published index to the City parishes and a card index to the others. The Bristol assessments have been published with an index. In 1783, entries in the registers were again taxed but the act was repealed 10 years later (1794 Act).

REGNAL YEARS This method of dating starts with the date of accession of each sovereign. Thus 3 Henry VII would run from 22 August 1487 to 21 August 1488. A full list of such years appears in Richardson, John *The Local Historian's Encyclopaedia* (3rd revised ed. Historical Publications Ltd. 2003), though you can work it out for yourself having first established the year of accession of each monarch. There are exceptions to this rule (George II being one, because of the change in the calendar). Another useful source is Cheney, C R *Handbook of Dates for Students of English History* (2nd ed. Cambridge University Press 2002). This website may also help http://people.albion.edu/imacinnes/calendar/Regnal_Years.html.

RELATIONSHIPS The meaning of certain terms indicating relationships has changed over the years, see "In-law". The term "cousin" was always rather loosely used and should not be taken too literally.

It is easiest to use a chart to determine a relationship between two people. These often appear in general 'how to' family history books and there are several online, one of the best of these can be found here www.irish-genealogy-toolkit.com/family-history-chart.html. Many family tree software programs have a feature to work out relationships between two individuals.

The chart in this book illustrates the relationship between yourself and a common ancestor. It could be extended indefinitely. Persons with a common grandparent are first cousins. Persons with common great-grandparents are second cousins etc.. It becomes more difficult when the two people whose relationship you are seeking are of different generations.

In order to determine the degree of relationship between person x and any other descendant of a common ancestor:

1. Determine the common ancestor, e.g. gt-grandparent, gt-gt. grandparent.

2. Determine how many generations x is from this ancestor (you are three generations from your great-grandparents).

3. Determine how many generations the other person is from the common ancestor. If he, too, is three generations from the common ancestor, he is x's second cousin. If he is two generations from the common ancestor, he is x's first cousin once removed (x's father's or mother's first cousin). If he is four generations from the common ancestor he is x's second cousin once removed (the child of x's second cousin).

There is an ambiguity in that "first cousin once removed" may be either your father's or mother's first cousin or your first cousin's child. These may be distinguished by "ascending" or "descending".

HOW TO DETERMINE RELATIONSHIPS

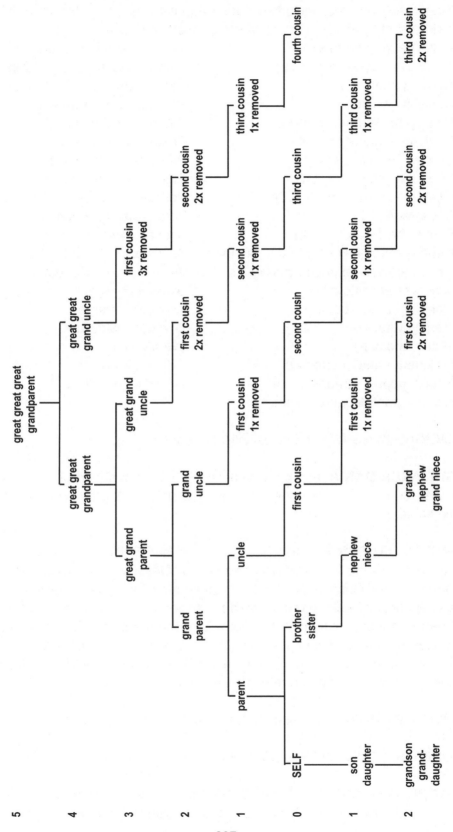

Since early records, including parish registers, were written in Latin the following list of Latin words for relationships may be of use:

Amita - aunt (paternal)
Avuncular - uncle (maternal)
Avus - grandfather
Caelebs - single
Conjugata - married woman
Conjures - married couple
Femina - woman, wife
Filia - daughter
Filiaster - son-in-law, stepson
Filius - son
Frater - brother (or monk)
Gener - son-in-law, or grandson-in-law
Ignoti parentis - of unknown parents
Majores - ancestors
Mariti - married couple
Marita - wife
Mater - mother
Matertera - aunt (maternal)
Nepos, nepus - grandson, nephew
Nepta - granddaughter, niece

Nurus - daughter-in-law
Parens - parent, grandparent
Pater - father
Patruus - uncle (paternal)
Priores - ancestors
Proles - descendant
Propinquities - relation
Relicta - widow
Relictus - widower
Soror - sister (or nun)
Sponsa - wife
Sponsus - husband
Successio - descendants
Uxor - wife
Uxorious - married
Vevodus - widower
Vidua - widow
Viduus - widower
Vir - man, husband

RELIGIOUS CENSUS See Ecclesiastical Census.

REMITTANCE MAN A term used to describe the black sheep of rich families who were sent to the colonies with an annual remittance to stay away and never come home.

REMOVAL ORDERS See also Poor Law (Old) and Settlement. A pauper was considered to be the responsibility of his parish of legal settlement when in need of parish relief. Once a settlement examination had taken place and his settlement determined, an order would be made for him to be "removed" to his last parish of legal settlement. He would be escorted by the Constable (q.v.), being passed from parish to parish and handed over at the boundary.

These documents are often found in the Parish Chest (q.v.) and in Quarter Sessions records (q.v.) at the relevant CRO.

RENUNCIATION When an executor declines to apply for probate.

REQUESTS, COURT OF See Court of Requests.

RETURNS OF OWNERS OF LAND The most useful volumes detailing land ownership are *Returns of Owners of Land*, published from 1873 to 1876 and arranged on a county basis. Most large reference libraries and record offices have a copy of Returns of Owners of Land. The returns for some counties are available in booklet and/or CD form. It can also be searched at http://ukga. org/cgi-bin/DB/search.cgi?action=loadDB&DB=1 or via Ancestry (q.v.) www. ancestry.co.uk.

REUNION See Computer Software.

ROADS See Highways.

ROGUE MONEY Parishes were obliged to contribute to the relief of poor prisoners in the County Gaol. This was collected by the parish constable (q.v.).

ROMAN CATHOLICS See also Recusants' Rolls, Scotland and Strays. Some Roman Catholic Registers date from 1778 when the Roman Catholic Relief Bill was passed but very few were kept before then. Not many were surrendered to the Registrar General in 1840 and those deposited at TNA are almost all from Yorkshire, Durham and Northumberland with only a very few registers from the whole of the rest of the country. Those that were surrendered can be consulted at www.bmdregisters.co.uk. There is a TNA research guide entitled *Catholics*, which can be downloaded from their website www.nationalarchives.gov.uk. After the Reformation, Catholics were most strongly grouped in these counties plus Lancashire and Staffordshire. Some early registers have been published by the Catholic Record Society www.catholicrecordsociety.co.uk but for an analysis of registers see Gandy, Michael *Catholic Missions and Registers 1700-1880* (6 vols. and atlas vol. Michael Gandy 1993). 1. London and the Home Counties. 2. The Midlands and East Anglia. 3. Wales and the West of England. 4. North East England. 5. North West England. 6. Scotland. Two other publications by Michael Gandy are also important *Catholic Family History: a bibliography of good sources* and *Catholic Family History: a bibliography of local sources* both (Michael Gandy 1996). Steel, D J *The National Index of Parish Registers Vol. III: Sources for Roman Catholic and Jewish genealogy and family history* (Phillimore 1974) deals with Roman Catholic entries in Anglican registers. A list of Catholic record Society publications, up to 1958, can also be found in Mullins, E L C *Texts and Calendars* (Royal Historical Society 1958). For later publications see the Bibliography of British and Irish History database www.royalhistoricalsociety. org/respubs.php.

Quarter Sessions Records (q.v.) contain lists of recusants and details of catholic estates. Catholic archives reveal much information about charities, education and the poor. The archives of the Catholic landed gentry may contain details about their tenants. Catholics appear in a great many State and Anglican records and these are thoroughly described in Williams, J Anthony *Recusant History: sources for recusant history (1559 to 1791) in English official archives* (Catholic Record Society 1983).

The Catholic Family History Society www.catholic-history.org.uk/cfhs publishes a journal and other works and holds meetings.

The Catholic National Library is at St Michael's Abbey, Farnborough, Hampshire GU14 7NQ www.farnboroughabbey.org/ccl/index.php. The Catholic Archives Society website is at www.catholicarchivesociety.org. They have produced a large number of publications.

A Catholic Marriage Index of over 30,000 entries covering mainly the period 1837-1880 is held by the Institute of Heraldic and Genealogical Studies (q.v.). It is available on CD from the Parish Register Transcript Society www.prtsoc.org.uk.

In the C18th many prosperous Catholics who died in London were buried at St. Pancras Churchyard. Many refugees from the French Revolution are buried here.

Records of priests and nuns are excellent and often give a great deal of information about their parents and even their brothers and sisters (with C19th Irish nuns this can be the best or only source to determine from whence in Ireland the family had come). Also nuns were prominent in teaching, nursing and social work so their biographies are often very interesting. The Catholic FHS has an index of over 14,000 C19th nuns (estimated at half the total number). All known priests have been listed in Bellenger, Dom Aidan *English and Welsh Priests 1558-1800* (Downside Abbey 1984) and Fitzgerald-Lombard, Dom Charles *English and Welsh Priests 1801-1914* (Downside Abbey 1993). There are detailed biographies of all secular priests 1558-1800, Jesuits, Benedictines, Franciscans, and Carmelites as well as many smaller Orders (see the bibliographies in the books referred to above). An enormous number of biographies will be found in Gillow, J *A Bibliographical Dictionary of the English Catholics* (5 vols. 1887-1902, reprinted Ulan Press 2012). This is also available in a Kindle edition. *Biographies of English Catholics* compiled by Rev. John Kirk, (Burn and Oates 1909), is very strong on the C18th.

ROMAN NUMERALS Those who encounter roman numerals should consult TNA research guide *Roman Numerals*, which can be downloaded from www.nationalarchives.gov.uk.

ROOTSTECH This is a conference that is held annually in the U.S.A. with an emphasis on the use of technology to accelerate the researcher's efforts to find, organize, preserve and share their family's history. Attendees learn skills from hands-on workshops and interactive presentations at the beginner, intermediate and advanced level. Further details from www.rootstech.org. Many of the presentations at RootsTech are recorded and made available online.

ROOTSWEB www.rootsweb.com is part of the Ancestry (q.v.) family. It describes itself as "the oldest genealogical community". It enables individuals or groups to establish mailing lists or message boards to reflect their interests. Many of these are geographically based. Others relate to a particular surname, ethnic group or denomination. Rootsweb is also responsible for the "World Connect" family tree. Users are invited to submit Gedcoms of their own family trees, which can then be searched. Users should be aware that information submitted in this way will vary in accuracy. Rootsweb also hosts a variety of websites and volunteer projects, including FreeBMD (q.v.). In addition, general family history advice can be found within its pages.

ROYAL AIR FORCE See also Medals. The Royal Air Force was formed on 1 April 1918 by the amalgamation of the Royal Flying Corps (previously army) and the Royal Naval Air Service (previously navy). Service records prior to this date will be either army (q.v.) or Royal Navy (q.v.).

For early enlistment in the ranks of the Royal Flying Corps, between May 1912 and August 1914, with Service Numbers 1-1400, consult McInnes, I and Webb, J V *A Contemptible Little Flying Corps* (London Stamp Exchange 1991), which contains potted biographies of the men who served. A Muster Roll listing all NCOs and men who were serving in the Royal Air Force on 1st April 1918 was compiled. It is arranged in service number order, listing date of joining, rank and trade. (It does not give first names, only initials and does not identify the Squadron or unit the airman was serving with.) Officers who served are listed in the *Air Force List*, the date of commission and branch of service can be identified and an officer's career can be traced through these listings. Both the Muster Roll for April 1918 and a complete set of Air Force Lists are available in TNA, which has numerous research guides on the records of the Royal Air Force, the Royal Flying Corps and the Royal Naval Air Service, downloadable from www.nationalarchives.gov.uk.

Army Officers Records of Service (including the R.F.C.) are in class WO339 at TNA. These files are only 60-70% complete. For other records of service contact: Ministry of Defence, Army Records Office CS(R)2b, Bourne Avenue, Hayes, Middlesex UB3 1RF.

Historical information, including details of the Royal Air Force Historical Society is on the Royal Air Force website www.raf.mod.uk/history. Where they survive, service records of the officers and men of the Royal Air Force, Royal Flying Corps and Royal Naval Air Service are in the custody of the Ministry of Defence, not at TNA. A form to request information (for a fee) from service records can be downloaded from www.raf.mod.uk.

The Royal Air Force Museum, London is at Grahame Park Way, London, NW9 5LL www.rafmuseum.org.uk/london. This website also lists a number of useful publications.

Medals (q.v.) awarded to personnel of the predecessors of the RAF, the Royal Flying Corps and the Royal Naval Air Service, for service in the First World War, are recorded on rolls in WO 329 and ADM 171 at TNA respectively. No later rolls are available.

RAF officers' service records 1918-1919; Women's RAF service records 1918-1920; RAF operations record books 1939-1945; Royal Naval Air Service officers' service records 1906-1918 and Second World War Royal Air Force combat reports, official reports filed by pilots or air gunners after they had encountered enemy aircraft on operational flights can all be searched at TNA website www.nationalarchives.gov.uk.

A Biographical Register of all those who served in the Royal Flying Corps, Royal Naval Air Service and Royal Air Force during the First World War is available on CD. This covers both Officers and Other Ranks, aircrew and groundcrew and part of the project involves re-arranging the Royal Air Force Muster Roll of April 1918 into alphabetical name order rather than the compiled service number order. Details of Casualties are also included in the register. Contact David J. Barnes, R.F.C., R.N.A.S., R.A.F. Register, c/o 148 Parkinson Street, Burnley, Lancashire, England, BB11 3LL. His website contains useful background information www.rfc-rnas-raf-register.org.uk/RFCRegister.htm. Mr Barnes has also written *The Military Medal Winners of the RFC, RAF and AFC 1916-1920* (Ray Westlake Books 1993). Three valuable books by Don Kindell are *Royal Navy Roll of Honour - World War 1, By Name: Part 1*, *Royal Navy Roll of Honour - World War 1, by Date and Ship/Unit: Part 2* and *Royal Navy Roll of Honour: between the wars 1918-1939* all (Naval History 2009). See also Jarvis, S & D *Officers who Died in the Service of The Royal Navy, Royal Naval Reserve, Royal Naval Volunteer Reserve, Royal Marines, Royal Naval Air Service and Royal Air Force 1914-1919* (Naval and Military Press 2000).

Aircrew records of those who took part in The Battle of Britain are held in the Operation Record Books of each Squadron, Unit or Station at TNA, Class AIR28. Some squadrons have a long history dating back to the RAF's creation out of the Royal Flying Corps in 1918 but most were formed just before or during World War II.

ROYAL ANTIDILUVIAN ORDER OF BUFFALOES (RAOB) www.raob.org.uk. A fraternal organisation dating back to the early C19th.

ROYAL ARCHIVES These are housed in the Round Tower at Windsor Castle and consist of the personal and official documents of former sovereigns and of other members of the Royal Family up to 1952. The Royal Archives were established in 1911, in order to cope with the large accumulation of royal papers from the reign of Queen Victoria, as well as the official papers of King Edward VII.

The contents of the Royal Archives are particularly useful in relation to persons in the direct employment of the sovereign. They are however the private property of the Queen and are not open to the public. Applications to study papers relating to a specified subject can be made by writing to the Senior Archivist. Further details are available from www.royal.gov.uk.

A National Archives research guides that can be downloaded from www.nationalarchives.gov.uk is *Royal Household and Wardrobe*.

ROYAL BANK OF SCOTLAND (RBS) The RBS Group was founded in 1727 and incorporates over three hundred constituents, the oldest dating back to the 1580s, with surviving banking records from the mid C17th. The RBS Heritage Online website http://heritagearchives.rbs.com details the documents, ledgers, letters, photographs and films held, which relate to the activities of the constituent banks and businesses, their owners, staff and customers over the past three and a half centuries. The website gives: a summary of the available historical records; an alphabetical list or a geographical directory of the banks and businesses covered on the site; a list of supplementary archive collections that were created by people or organisations connected with RBS Group.

Of more general interest, the main RBS website at www.rbs.com/about.html includes links to pages entitled "RBS History in 100 objects", which enables the researcher to explore objects from the bank's heritage collections and "Our banknotes", which enables the researcher to learn about the banknotes issued by RBS since 1727.

ROYAL BRITISH LEGION See National Memorial Arboretum.

ROYAL COMMISSION ON HISTORICAL MANUSCRIPTS Was responsible for publishing details of the location and nature of archives. It became part of TNA in 2003.

ROYAL COMMISSION ON HISTORICAL MONUMENTS OF ENGLAND (RCHME) See English Heritage.

ROYAL DESCENT Descents from members of the Royal Family were at one time greatly prized but they are far from uncommon and today there is much less interest in them. The fluid nature of English society and intermarriage through different social classes over a long period has brought a fine trickle of royal blood to many an ordinary person quite unaware of the fact. By 1911 King Edward III had about a hundred thousand descendants. The number is much greater now. In 1903, the living descendants of Mary, Queen of Scots, numbered 1,440; now it is over 10,000. Beyond Edward III the royal blood flows out in England through Edmund Crouchback the son of Henry III, through Thomas of Brotherton and Edmund of Woodstock the younger sons of Edward I and their sisters Joan and Elizabeth, through Eleanor the daughter of King John, and through illegitimate lines like those from Robert, Earl of Gloucester, the bastard of Henry I. Sir Anthony Wagner has shown in *English Genealogy* (2nd ed. Phillimore 1972), pp.233-240, how descendants of these have acted as gateways to royal ancestry in particular areas of the country. Nineteen settlers in New England before 1650 were descended from Edward I. In Europe it has been calculated that Charlemagne, Emperor of the West, who died in 814, probably has twenty million living descendants.

All the known legitimate descendants of James I were listed in A C Addington's *The Royal House of Stuart* (3 vols. Charles Skilton 1969). There are numerous descents from the illegitimate children of Charles II. Details of the British royal families may be found in *Burke's Guide to the Royal Family* (Burke's Peerage 1973) and most other royal families can be found in *Burke's Royal Families of the World* (2 vols. Burke's Peerage 1977-80). Greater details of some appear in Marlene A. Eilers' *Queen Victoria's Descendants* (2nd ed. Rosvall Royal Books 1998). The most detailed account of the ancestry of the British royal family in all its lines is Gerald Paget's *The Lineage and Ancestry of HRH Prince Charles, Prince of Wales* (2 vols. Skilton 1977). See also Weir, Alison *Britain's Royal Families: the complete genealogy* (Vintage 2008).

ROYAL HISTORICAL SOCIETY, THE This body was founded in 1868 to promote the scholarly study of history www.royalhistoricalsociety.org. it runs conferences, awards prizes for historical books and articles and administers the Bibliography of British and Irish History (BBIH) see Bibligraphies.

ROYAL HOSPITAL CHELSEA See Chelsea Royal Hospital.

ROYAL HUMANE SOCIETY (RHS) The website of the RHS www.royalhumane society.org.uk contains a history of the society and gives details of awards and medal holders. It also notes that the entire archive of the Royal Humane Society, including its original casebooks, minutes and annual reports from 1774 to present date, was formally transferred to the custodianship of the LMA in late 2008. It is now available for research via LMA www.cityoflondon.gov.uk.

First mention of the well known Grace Darling medal is in 1838. By 1989, approximately 127 Gold, 1,328 Silver and 11,143 Bronze Medals had been awarded. The criteria for an award is that it can only be made to a person who "at risk to his own life saves or attempts to save the life of a fellow citizen". The degree of bravery is reflected in the award of medals, testimonials and certificates of commendation. In addition, an "In Memoriam" testimonial is presented to the relatives of those who lose their lives in attempting to rescue others.

ROYAL LIFE SAVING SOCIETY The Royal Life Saving Society was founded in 1891 as the Swimmers' Life Saving Society to combat a rising toll of over 2,000 deaths a year. The society is based in Alcester but its website at www.rlss.org.uk does not indicate that any records of interest to family historians are maintained. Awards are made to volunteer lifesavers in recognition of achievement on attaining certain standards.

Pearsall, Ronald *Lifesaving: the story of the Royal Life Saving Society, the first 100 years* (David & Charles 1991) is indexed and a considerable number of names are listed. Its appendix 2 gives names of Mountbatten Medal Winners (Worldwide) 1951-1988.

ROYAL MARINES See also Medals and Nelson. A key book is Divall, Ken *My Ancestor was a Royal* Marine (SOG 2008). Whilst soldiers had been part of the complement of ships of war from early times the first British military unit raised especially for sea service was the Duke of York and Albany's Maritime Regiment of Foot, 1664. This later became part of the Army establishment and is the direct ancestor of the Buffs. From 1690, extra marine regiments were raised in wartime for sea service; at the end of the war these were disbanded, soldiers discharged and the officers put on half pay. Though these early marine regiments were employed for sea service they were part of the army and were organised like other foot regiments, the exception being that parties serving at sea came under naval discipline and were shown on their ships books (listed separately) for wages and victuals.

In 1749, these marine regiments were disbanded for the last time. In 1755, a new Corps of Marines was formed under Admiralty authority; it was not part of the army. Though it continued to use Army ranks and uniform it had no regimental structure. The fifty companies were divided between three divisions, based at Portsmouth, Plymouth and Chatham. From 1805 to 1869 a fourth division was based at Woolwich. If serving under military command (i.e ashore, as landing parties) the Marines came under military discipline, otherwise they were responsible solely to the Admiralty.

Until the outbreak of war in 1939, the main role of the Royal Marines was to provide detachments in HM ships and ashore. There have always been other calls on their manpower to meet commitments as the situation demanded, such as providing a brigade for the 63rd Royal Naval Division in the 1914-19 war and the nucleus of a Mobile Naval Base Defence Organisation in the 1930s. During the 1939-45 war they continued to man HM ships, but even more personnel were deployed in landing craft and commandos under the auspices of Combined Operations.

Many books have been and continue to be written about the history of the Royal Marines and its units and formations over the years. The official history has been well documented and is contained in four books: *Britain's Sea Soldiers* vols. 1 and 2 by Colonel Cyril Field RMLI (up to 1914) and vol. 3 (1914-19) by General H E Blomberg, KCB (Lyceum Press 1920s). See also *The Royal Marines: history of the Royal Marines 1664-2000* by Richard Brooks (Constable 2002) and Thompson, Julian *By Sea and by Land: the story of the Royal Marines Commandos* (Pen and Sword 2004).

The Royal Marines Historical Society, run in conjunction with the Royal Marines Museum, has published two books of deaths in the two World Wars that contain the names, details, units and burials. These books are *With Full and Grateful Hearts: a register of Royal Marines deaths 1914-1919* and *Bid Them Rest in Peace: a register of Royal Marines deaths 1939-45*, both by J A Good.

All these books and many others, can be found in the library of The Royal Marines Museum, Eastney, Southsea, Hampshire PO4 9PX www.royalmarine smusuem.co.uk, which is well worth a visit. They have published *The Royal Marines: a short bibliography* (1978).

Other troops serving afloat were artillerymen. In 1804 the Admiralty formed companies of marine artillery to man the bombs; in 1859 there was a formal division between the Royal Marine Artillery (stationed at Eastney, Southsea and known as the Blue Marines) and the Royal Marine Light Infantry (known as the Red Marines). The two branches were amalgamated in 1923.

No records of Officers' services for men appointed before 1793 have survived. For officers commissioned after 1793 a search should first be made in the Records of Officers' Services. Only from about 1837 are these records complete. *The Navy List*, published annually, also includes Royal Marine officers. The Corps Historical Records Officer, DRORM, Centurion Building, Grange Road, Gosport, Hants PO13 9XA holds the records of officers and other ranks who joined the Corps after 1918. All other records are held at TNA, which has relevant research guides at www.nationalarchives.gov.uk. Royal Marines' service records 1842-1925 can be search via TNA Discovery catalogue and copies of the records downloaded from the website for a small fee. Those serving between 1842 and 1884 are only included if they were still serving in 1884.

Each division of the Royal Marines kept its own registers of births, marriages and deaths of children and wives borne on the strength. They give the Marine's rank and some information on posting. Registers for Chatham cover 1830-1913; Plymouth 1862-1920; Woolwich (marriage rolls only) 1822- 1869 and for the Royal Marine Artillery 1810-1853 and 1866-1921. No registers survive for Portsmouth Division.

Records survive for Royal Marine wills and administrations and pensions. The Royal Greenwich Hospital catered for the Marines as well as the Navy.

Royal Marines' service records 1842-1925 can be searched and downloaded from TNA website www.nationalarchives.gov.uk.

ROYAL NATIONAL LIFEBOAT INSTITUTION (RNLI) The RNLI was founded in 1824 as the "National Institution for the Preservation of Life from Shipwreck" and early records are sparse. With the introduction of the institution's journal *The Lifeboat* in 1852, records became much better but were still not comprehensive.

People looking for ancestors by name might be lucky if the relative was either a lifeboat officer such as a coxswain or had been awarded some form of RNLI gallantry award. In early days the men who went to sea in the lifeboat were simply local fishermen or gentlemen and their names were not usually recorded. Records may be held by individual Lifeboat Stations or have found their way into CROs.

The website of the RNLI at www.rnli.org.uk gives details of the institution's history and also carries information about the RNLI Heritage Trust, which is based in Poole. The Poole premises house the RNLI library and archive, whilst the webpage also details the half a dozen museums that are maintained by the institution.

Voluntary lifeboat services operate in other countries, including the Netherlands, Sweden, New Zealand and South Africa.

ROYAL NAVAL ASYLUM This was set up in Paddington in 1798 under the title "British Endeavour", for the education and maintenance of orphans and destitute children of sailors and marines. By Acts of Parliament in 1806 and 1807, it came under royal patronage and transferred to new premises, which today house the National Maritime Museum at Greenwich. In 1825, it was amalgamated with the Greenwich Hospital School (q.v.).

Records of the Royal Naval Asylum are in class ADM73 at TNA. These include applications, admission registers, disposal of children, lists of staff and servants. The website "Portcities London" contains further information about and photographs of the Royal Naval Asylum www.portcities.org.uk/London.

ROYAL NAVY See also Greenwich Hospital and Greenwich Hospital Schools, Medals, Royal Naval Asylum and Seamen. Key books on this topic are Fowler, Simon *Tracing your Naval Ancestors: a guide for family historians* (Pen and Sword 2011) and Pappalardo, Bruno *Tracing your Naval Ancestors* (TNA 2003). It is also worth downloading the several relevant TNA research guides from www.nationalarchives.gov.uk.

There are no systematic records listing men serving in the Navy prior to the Restoration (1660). Various classes of C17th records survive at TNA, mostly in class ADM.

The printed *Navy List*s (which began in 1782 as *Steel's Navy List*) are on open shelves in TNA, together with other printed sources. Issues of the *Navy List* are also available via various subscription websites and 120 issues can be searched for a fee at www.navylistresearch.co.uk. From these it is fairly easy to trace the career of a commissioned officer's career in the Royal Navy. O'Byrne, William *Naval Biographical Dictionary* (reprinted Naval & Military Press 2005) gives details of nearly 5000 officers, all those who were serving or had retired by 1845.

Royal Navy officers' service records 1756-1931; Royal Navy ratings' service records 1853-1923; Women's Royal Naval service records 1917-1919 and Royal Naval Division service records 1914-1919 are among the relevant records that can be searched and downloaded for a small fee from TNA website www.national archives.gov.uk.

Chaplains can be traced through succession books though more recent records are still held by the Chaplain of the Fleet. See also Kealy, A G *Chaplains of the Royal Navy 1626-1903* (1903).

The Guildhall Library (q.v.) has records of the issue of certificates by the Barber-Surgeons' company to those intending to serve as surgeons in the Royal

Navy 1705-45. They relate to prospective naval surgeons from the provinces as well as London. After the formation of the new Company of Surgeons in 1745, such certificates were issued by them.

Commissioned Sea Officers of the Royal Navy 1660-1815 published by the National Maritime Museum gives details of careers. Periodicals devoted to military interests can also be a fruitful source of information if you have ancestors in the services. The *United Service Journal and Naval and Military Magazine* was first published in 1829, later becoming *Colburn's United Service Magazine*; it contains notices of births, marriages and deaths, often with detailed obituary notices relating to officers. *The Naval Chronicle* was published monthly from 1799 to end of 1818; an index was compiled by W Jeffery in 1933. Norman Hurst published an index to the births, marriages and deaths in *The Naval Chronicle* in 1989.

The Navy Records Society www.navyrecords.org.uk have a publishing programme. Members have free access to Navy Records Online www.navy recordsonline.co.uk.

There are several other societies which might be able to provide information or background material. Naval Historical Collectors and Research Association www.nhcra-online.org publishes in its quarterly journal *The Review* numerous lists which include medal rolls, casualty lists, ships rolls etc.; many of which come from sources other than TNA.

The Society for Nautical Research www.snr.org.uk Hon Secretary, P D Winterbottom, 6 Ashmeadow Road, Arnside via Carnforth, Lancs LA5 0AE.

The following libraries also contain a wealth of material: The Britannia Royal Naval College Library, Dartmouth, Devon TQ6 OHJ, is open to the public for research.

The Naval History Library is within Plymouth Central Library, Drake Circus, Plymouth PL4 8AL.

The Liverpool Nautical Research Society, Maritime Archives & Library, Merseyside Maritime Museum, Albert Dock, Liverpool L3 4AA http://liverpoolnauticalresearchsociety.org.

Naval Historical Library www.royalnavalmuseum.org HM Naval Base (PP66), Portsmouth, PO1 3NH.

For general background see Phillips, Lt, Cdr. L *The Royal Navy Day by Day* (The History Press 2011) and Rodger, N A M *The Wooden World: anatomy of the Georgian navy* (Fontana 1998).

ROYAL PHOTOGRAPHIC SOCIETY, THE See http://erps.dmu.ac.uk/ for a research database of over 45,000 records from the annual exhibition catalogues of the Photographic Society, London, published between 1870 and 1915.

ROYAL SOCIETY, THE The Royal Society is a fellowship of the world's most eminent scientists and is the oldest scientific academy in continuous existence. It has a recently refurbished library and archive, the former also housing the society's rare book collections. The society's website is at http://royalsociety.org/. In particular, it is worth looking at the society's history, printed works, archives, image library and fellows. The Raymond and Beverly Sackler Archive Resource is a database of biographical information on past fellows of the Royal Society from 1660 onwards. The society also maintains a library and archive blog.

ROYAL WARRANT HOLDERS The website of the Royal Warrant Holders Association www.royalwarrant.org allows all Royal Warrant holders to be searched.

ROYALIST COMPOSITION PAPERS See also Commonwealth, The. During the Civil War and Interregnum the administration of the country was in the hands of Parliamentary Committees. At least two of these committees were involved with so-called Delinquents (q.v.). In many instances a Delinquent, after investigation, was deprived of most of his estate. There were sometimes options to pay a fine based on a valuation of an estate and the extent of an individual's delinquency. Orders and correspondence are at TNA, Classes SP23 and SP28, volumes G61 to 173. Depositions, given under oath by those who were permitted to compound, together with the amount of compositions, at which assessments were made, appear in volumes G174 to 227. Green, Mrs E (ed.) *A Calendar of the Papers of the Committee for Compounding with Delinquents 1643 to 1660* (5 vols. HMSO 1889). There is a TNA research guide *State Papers Domestic 1642-1660* available at www.nationalarchives.co.uk.

RURAL DEAN see Dean.

RURAL LIFE, MUSEUM OF ENGLISH The Museum of English Rural Life at the Institute of Agricultural History of the University of Reading www.reading.ac.uk/merl/ is a national centre for information on agricultural history and rural life. More details of its archives and library and of how to visit the museum, are on its website.

RUSSIA See also Prisoners of War. The Leeds Russian Archive (LRA) was established within Special Collections of the library of Leeds University in 1982 as a joint initiative of the library and the University's Department of Russian and Slavonic Studies. It comprises some 550 collections of manuscripts, photographs and other archival material and also several thousand books and journals, which document Russian history, literature and culture and Anglo-Russian contacts in the C19th and C20th.

Further details can be obtained from the Archive's website at www.leeds.ac.uk/library/spcoll/lra/. Two useful books for those studying the British in Russia by Janet M Hartley are *Guide to Documents and Manuscripts in the United Kingdom Relating to Russia and the Soviet Union* (Mansell 1987) and *The Study of Russian History from British Archival Sources* (Mansell 1986).

S

S & N GENEALOGICAL SUPPLIES An online shop www.genealogysupplies. com specialising in genealogical software and storage solutions but also offering books and CDs. The same firm runs The Genealogist (q.v.).

SACRAMENT CERTIFICATES From 1673 any person holding civil or military office had to produce a certificate signed by a minister, churchwardens and two witnesses that he had received the Sacrament, in other words, that he was a practising member of the Church of England. These certificates, which frequently gave the occupation of the man and of his witnesses, were sent to the Clerk of the Quarter Sessions (q.v.). Some are held in TNA; see their research guide *Oaths of Loyalty to the Crown and Church of* England available at www. nationalarchives.gov.uk Whilst this law was not repealed until 1828, fewer certificates were issued after 1750.

SADDLER The Worshipful Company of Saddlers is one of the very oldest of the City of London Livery companies, with surviving records dating back to the C15th. An account of the Company's history, details of its treasures and charters and information about its archives can be found on the company's website www.saddlersco.co.uk. See Sherwell, J W *A Descriptive and Historical Account of the Guild of Saddlers of the City of London* (3rd ed. 1956).

SAILORS See Royal Navy and Merchant Seamen.

SAINSBURY ARCHIVE, THE The Sainsbury Archive documents the history of one of the nation's oldest retailers from when it was founded in London, in 1869, through to present day. It also provides a unique illustration of the transformation that has occurred in retailing and in shopping and eating habits since the mid C19th.

The Archive is located at the Museum of London in Docklands and is open to the public. Visitors can view displays from the collection and browse a range of digital and paper-based resources from the library and archives, including reference books, image files, films and journals covering the history of Sainsbury's and shopping as well as the history of the docks and the local area. The separate search room is open by appointment for more in-depth research using material from the archive collections.

More details about the archive can be found on the Museum of London Dockland's website at www.museumoflondon.org.uk/sainsburyarchive. That website also contains a link to their Sainsbury's history pages and images from the archive, which are found in the Collections Online website "Story of a Supermarket". A link enables the researcher to browse and search the digital archive of Sainsbury's in-house magazine *JS Journal*, now called *The Journal*, from its first issue in December 1946 up to October 2010.

ST. CATHERINE'S HOUSE See also Civil Registration. This was a former repository of the civil registration indexes. The indexes are still sometimes referred to as the "St Catherine's House Indexes".

SALE OF WIVES See Divorce.

SALTER The Worshipful Company of Salters www.salters.co.uk is ranked ninth of the Twelve Great Livery Companies of the City of London. Its origins lie in the salt trade of medieval London, its first licence having been granted in 1394 and its Charter of Incorporation being obtained in 1559. By the time of the Norman Conquest, the Cheshire towns of Northwich, Nantwich and Middlewich were well established as salt producing towns, as was the Worcestershire town of Droitwich. There is a salt museum in Northwich www.saltmuseum.org.uk.

SALVATION ARMY See Missing Relatives.

SAMPLERS A sampler is an embroidered piece of material displaying stitching skills. Early samplers are believed to be ways of recording new patterns or stitches but from the seventeenth to the early C20th, it was customary for young girls to embroider a sampler. Usually included in the design was their name, a verse or quotation, and the date the work was completed. A few include other family details. See Toller, J *British Samplers, a Concise History* (Phillimore 1980). Also worth reading is *Samplers* by Pamela Clabburn (Shire Publications 1998). Good advice on the treatment and possible repair of these family treasures can be obtained from The Royal School of Needlework www.royal-needlework.org.uk or The Textile Conservation Centre www.textileconservationcentre.co.uk.

SASINES, REGISTERS OF A list of Scottish legal transactions since 1617, although there was a forerunner, known as the Secretary's Register from 1599-1609. There is a General Register, covering the whole country and Particular Registers, which relate to specific areas. Indexes to many Particular Registers have been published and are available from The National Archives of Scotland www.nas.gov.uk/guides/sasines.asp. This webpage includes an introductory guide. Another useful introduction is at "Sasine Abridgements" www.scan.org. uk/knowledgebase/topics/sasine_abbs_topic.htm. More recent transactions can be searched for a fee at Land Registry, Scotland http://landregistryservice.co.uk.

SCHOOLS See Education.

SCILLY, ISLES OF The Isles of Scilly Museum is the main repository of interest to researchers. Details of its holdings are on its website at www.iosmuseum.org. Other sources of information relating to the Isles of Scilly may be found on the mainland at The Royal Cornwall Museum www.royalcornwallmuseum.org.uk, Penzance Library http://db.cornwall.gov.uk and the Cornish Studies Library at Redruth www.cornwall.gov.uk. Contact also Cornwall Family History Society www.cornwallfhs.com and Cornwall Record Office www.cornwall.gov.uk/default.aspx?page=24656.

SCOTLAND See also Civil Registration in Scotland, Parish Registers of Scotland, Emigration, Family Histories and Sasines. A crucial site for those with Scottish ancestors is Scotland's People www.scotlandspeople.gov.uk. It is an online, pay-per-view portal for access to a variety of Scottish records including records of civil registration, census returns, old parish registers and probate material.

National Records of Scotland (NRS) www.nrscotland.gov.uk was formed in 2011 by the amalgamation of The National Archives of Scotland (NAS) www.nas.gov.uk/default.asp and the General Register Office for Scotland (GROS) www.gro-scotland.gov.uk. Their records are available at The National Records of Scotland, Princes Street, Edinburgh. The former GROS records include old parish registers, statutory registers of births, marriages, deaths, still births, adoptions, divorces and census records. The NAS contained a vast collection of material useful to the family historian, including probate material, deeds, records of national government and businesses and court records. Further details of NRS holdings can be found on the GROS and NAS websites.

The National Register of Archives for Scotland (NRAS) www.nas.gov.uk/nras/register.asp was set up in 1946 as a catalogue of collections of private papers in Scotland and to make information about them available. It contains over 4300 descriptions of archives held in private hands, by landed estates, societies and businesses. The NRAS does not actually hold any of these private papers. The Register also includes surveys of similar papers that have been deposited in the archives and libraries of local authorities and universities. In addition, the Scottish Archive Network (SCAN) www.scan.org.uk provides access to the holdings of more than 50 Scottish archives. Many of the NRAS surveys are available on the NRAS Online Public Access Catalogue (OPAC) at the National Records of Scotland, Edinburgh.

The National Library of Scotland www.nls.uk is a major research library with digital sources available and a comprehensive newspaper collection.

Each year from 1855, valuation rolls were returned for the whole country These give details of proprietors, occupiers and tenants as well as values. Those for the years ending in 5, beginning with 1915 and working back to 1855, are being released by Scotland's People www.scotlandspeople.gov.uk.

Another useful website is ScotlandsPlaces www.scotlandsplaces.gov.uk, which enables users to use geographic locations to search national collections from their project partners who are: The Royal Commission on the Ancient and Historical Monuments of Scotland (RCAHMS), The National Records of Scotland (NRS) and The National Library of Scotland (NLS). See also www.ancestral scotland.com, a website designed for visitors to Scotland, with a genealogical bias.

Paton, Christopher *Researching Scottish Family History* (FHP 2010). Clarke, Tristram *Tracing Your Scottish Ancestors: the official guide to research in TNA of Scotland* (6th ed. Birlinn Ltd. 2011) and Bruce Durie's *Scottish Genealogy* (3rd ed. The History Press 2012) are three up to date guides to Scottish research.

The Scottish Genealogy Society www.scotsgenealogy.com 15 Victoria Terrace, Edinburgh EH1 2JL has an extensive library and runs a lecture programme. The Scottish Association of Family History Societies (SAFHS) www.safhs.org.uk is an umbrella organisation for Scottish Family History Societies and similar bodies. The Anglo-Scottish Family History Society www.anglo-scots.mlfhs.org.uk was formed as a branch of the Manchester and Lancashire FHS in 1982 to promote the study of Scottish migrant families and assist with tracing their ancestors back to Scotland.

The Scottish Records Association www.scottishrecordsassociation.org was founded in 1977 and is concerned with the preservation and use of historical records in Scotland. It publishes the journal *Scottish Archives* and organises conferences. The Scottish Records Society published numerous volumes of transcribed documents, some of which are available from the Scottish SOG.

The Association of Scottish Genealogists & Record Agents (ASGRA) www.asgra.co.uk issues a list of members who offer professional Scottish research services. There is also the well established Scots Ancestry Research Society www.scotsancestry.co.uk.

Scottish Catholic Archives www.scottishcatholicarchives.org.uk are at 16 Drummond Place, Edinburgh, EH3 6PL. Scottish Catholic history is well covered by *The Innes Review* www.euppublishing.com/journal/inr published by Edinburgh University Press twice-yearly since 1951. There were substantial pockets of Catholicism in Aberdeen, Banff, Inverness, the Outer Hebrides and Kirkcudbright. In the C19th the growth was mostly in Glasgow, Lanarkshire and Renfrewshire. Johnson, Christie (ed.) *Scottish Catholic Secular Clergy 1879-1089* (John Donald 1992) gives biographical notes for each priest, listed alphabetically within diocese.

The Aberdeen and North East Scotland Family History Society www.anesfhs.org.uk run a shop and study centre at 158-164 King Street, Aberdeen, AB2 3BD.

A CD *Inventory of Scottish Graveyards* (2nd ed. The Scottish Association of Family History Societies) contains information from over 3,500 burial places.

SCOTLAND'S PEOPLE See Scotland.

SCOTTISH EMIGRANTS A useful website is Scots Abroad http://digital.nls.uk/emigration/resources with links to a wide variety of sources including diaries of emigrants. Dr David Dobson www.st-andrews.ac.uk/history/staff/daviddobson.html has written several books about Scottish emigrants including *The Original Scots Colonists of Early America 1612-1783* (Genealogical Publishing Co. Inc., 1988), which lists 7,000 people. The Association of Scottish Family History Societies has published five volumes of Scottish Emigrants into England and Wales and a Digest of library sources of Scottish Genealogy in the Manchester Central Library. The introduction to the former gives a guide to variants of Scottish names. For those with Scottish ancestry who are trying to locate the origins of their migrant ancestor who was born before 1855, this series could be a useful aid. For further details, and to download the Scottish Strays Marriage Index free of charge, at www.anglo-scots.mlfhs.org.uk. The Highlands and Islands Emigration Society helped nearly 5,000 individuals to leave western Scotland for Australia between 1852 and 1857 www.scan.org.uk/researchrtools/emigration.htm.

For Scottish emigrants, consult Whyte, D (ed.) *A Dictionary of Scottish Emigrants* (Magna Carta Book Co. 1973); Whyte, Donald *The Scots Overseas: selected bibliography* (FFHS 1988) and Lawson, James *The Emigrant Scots* (Aberdeen & N.E. Scotland Family History Society).

SCOUT ASSOCIATION, THE The Archive and Heritage Department of The Scout Association is based at London's Gilwell Park. Its website www.scoutsrecords.org gives advice and guidance on researching individuals and groups in scouting and provides information on the preservation and retention of records by scout organizations. The website also contains the archive's catalogue and provides details of and access to the catalogues of those county scout associations that have their own archive services.

SCRIVENER A scrivener was a clerk who specialised in drawing up bonds, wills, charters, legal documents and the like. At a time when many people were illiterate, he offered an important service to the community. The Worshipful Company of Scriveners is a London Livery Company, with surviving records going back to 1565. An account of the Company's history can be downloaded from their website at www.scriveners.org.uk.

SEA DEATHS Christopher and Michael Watts' *Tracing Births, Deaths and Marriages at Sea*, (SOG 2004) is a good starting point. See also Hocking, Charles *Dictionary of Disasters During the Age of Steam (including sailing ships and ships of war lost in action) 1824-1962* (2 vols. Lloyd's Register of Shipping 1969).

TNA holds several classes of record that may be of use including: Registers and wages and effects of deceased seamen, 1852-1881, 1888-1889 (class BT153, indexed in BT154); Monthly lists of deaths of seamen, 1886-1889 (class

BT156); Register of seamen's deaths classified by cause, 1882-1888 (class BT157); Registers deaths of passengers at sea, 1854-1890 (class BT 158, partially indexed in BT158/7 and BT158/8); Registers of deaths of British Nationals at sea, 1875-1888 (class BT159); Registers and indexes of deaths of passengers and seamen at sea, from 1890 (class BT334). See also TNA www.nationalarchives.gov.uk/records/research-guides/shipwrecks.htm guide to ships wrecked or sunk, which contains a bibliography of useful works.

The National Maritime Museum http://www.rmg.co.uk hold Alphabetical Returns of Deaths of Merchant Seamen July 1916–1918 and 1920–1989. That for 1946 also includes a supplement of merchant seamen who died while prisoners of war, 1939–1946. The also have a card index recording deaths of merchant seamen both by enemy action and natural causes. In addition the museum holds Returns of Births and Deaths of Passengers, 1939–1963. These are Transcripts from official log books recording passengers' births and deaths. There are also records of deaths of second world war soldiers on hospital ships and troop ships but the ship's name is needed to use these records.

SEAMEN See Fishermen, Merchant Seamen, Nelson, Royal Navy and Sea Deaths.

SECOND FLEET See Australia, Crime and Criminals, Emigration and Transportation.

SEE Often used as a synonym for diocese, though technically the seat of the bishop or the diocesan centre.

SELF-ACTER MINDER A person who looked after a self-acting "mule" in a spinning machine.

SELON INDEX The South East LONdon index includes census returns for the area, including some that survive from 1811 and 1831, poor law records, some parish registers (chiefly Bermondsey) and miscellaneous items including voters' lists from Camberwell in the 1830s. Enquiries should be addressed to Mr P. R. Shilham, 6 Beckford Close, Wokingham, Berkshire, RG41 1HN.

SEPHARDIC JEWS See also Jewish Ancestry. These Jews are those from the Iberian Peninsula, who reached England in the C16th and C17th.

SERGEANTRY/SERJEANTRY See Manorial Records. A form of English feudal tenure where dues were rendered to the Sovereign, not a mesne lord (q.v.). It was divided into Grand and Petty, the former a special service to the Crown, the latter the renderings of an implement of war to the Sovereign.

SERVANTS See Domestic Servants.

SERVANTS' TAX Between 1777 and 1852, a tax was levied on households employing male servants including gamekeepers and gardeners. Female servants were taxed in 1785, a guinea being payable in each case. The SOG holds a manuscript index to those who paid the Male Servants' Tax in 1780. Further details can be found on their website at www.sog.org.uk.

SERVICEMEN'S WILLS See also Army. Servicemen, including minors on active military service and mariners or seamen at sea, could make nuncupative wills, these being wills orally declared in the presence of witnesses. When on active service, or under orders for this, they could make holograph wills, these being wills in their own handwriting without witnesses. Servicemen of Scottish or Channel Islands domicile could make handwritten wills without witnesses at any time. Servicemen's pay books carried forms for both types of will.

SESSIONS BOOKS Virtually minutes of the proceedings of the Quarter Sessions kept by the Clerks of the Peace. Details of those present, the indictments, verdicts and sentences were included.

SETTLEMENT See also Poor Law and Removal Orders. An Act of 1662 empowered two justices to order newcomers into a parish to leave and to return to the parish from which they had come. This was particularly likely if it seemed they might require help from the Overseers of the Poor. They would undergo an examination to establish which was their parish of settlement i.e. was financially responsible. The precise rules governing to which parish an individual belonged changed over time but broadly, settlement could be gained by birth in a parish, by various rent or rate qualifications, by being apprenticed to a parishioner or by working for a year and a day in the same job in the parish. The resulting documents are of value to the family historian as they are full of personal information. Settlement examinations often give details of parentage, family, occupation and movement from place to place. Anyone from the working class wishing to move from one parish to another had to obtain a settlement certificate saying that his parish of settlement would be responsible if he needed poor relief. The system lapsed early in the C19th. Where these Examinations and Certificates survive, they will be with the poor law records of the parish in the CRO, perhaps amongst the records of the Quarter Sessions (q.v.). Some have been indexed.

SETTLEMENT, DEED OF See Entail.

SEXTON He was appointed by the Vestry, the Incumbent or the Churchwarden. He was sometimes responsible for grave-digging and generally acted as caretaker, cleaner and carried out simple repairs in the church.

SHAKESPEARE See also Theatre. The Shakespeare Centre Library and Archive www.shakespeare.org.uk in Stratford-on-Avon is run by The Shakespeare Birthplace Trust. It is the most important Shakespeare Library in the UK, covering the full range of subjects for the study of Shakespeare. Its collections include: Printed materials and books relating to Shakespeare's times, life and works. A Local History Archive of material relating to Stratford-upon-Avon and South Warwickshire, with records dating back to C12th. There is also a museum. The Archive also holds the records of the Royal Shakespeare Company (RSC), including programmes and photographs from 1879 to the present.

As well as using a reading room, visitors can attend lectures, courses and study days. The repository also maintains a blog at http://findingshakespeare. co.uk. This contains news from the reading room, online exhibitions and an interesting collection of articles. The University of Birmingham Shakespeare Institute holds a wide range of Shakespeare-related collections and is working closely with the Shakespeare Birthplace Trust to develop digital access to both repositories' unique collections. More details can be found on the Institute's website at www.shakespeare.bham.ac.uk.

SHEFFIELD INDUSTRIAL MUSEUMS TRUST (SIMT) SIMT www.simt.co.uk comprises three separate attractions, with aims that include telling the story of Sheffield from its beginning to the present day and telling the ongoing story of how industrial development changes peoples' lives. The three attractions are: Abbeydale Industrial Hamlet; Shepherd Wheel Workshop and Kelham Island Museum.

SHERIFF He was the Crown's representative in the County but there was some overlapping with the duties of Lord-Lieutenant. His duties gradually passed to Justices of the Peace and Coroners; the Lord-Lieutenant became the Crown's Representative.

SHIP MONEY This was a tax first levied by Charles I in 1634 to finance the Navy and protect English ships against pirate attacks and impending threats from the Dutch and the French. Initially, it was imposed on citizens in maritime areas but later on to those in other areas. It became one of the chief issues between King and Parliament and was declared illegal in 1641. Many lists of those paying the tax survive. The documents are at TNA and are listed on the E179 database (q.v.). The Ship Money Returns 1639-1640 for the county of Suffolk have been reproduced on CD by S & N Genealogy Supplies (q.v.) www.genealogysupplies. com.

SHIPWRECKS See Deaths at Sea.

SHIPWRIGHTS Whilst the earliest reference to The Worshipful Company of Shipwrights is in 1387, its livery was granted in 1782. However, it exists "by prescription", which means it is acknowledged to have been in existence before 1199. Today, the Shipwrights' Company prides itself on being the principle maritime Livery Company of London. Further details about its history and treasures can be found on its website at www.shipwrights.co.uk.

See Ridge, C Harold *Records of the Worshipful Company of Shipwrights* (2 vols. Phillimore 1939 & 1946). These volumes include 241 pages of alphabetically arranged names of all known members of the Company, with references to the records in which they are found.

SHIRE PUBLICATIONS Shire Publications www.shirebooks.com produce a wide range of books of interest to the local and family historian. A full catalogue of current titles can be found on their website but it is worth searching second hand outlets for volumes that are not currently in print. Of particular use to family historians is a series of booklets known as "Shire Albums". These provide brief introductions to particular trades and occupations. There is also a "Discovering" series by the same publisher.

SHOEMAKER See also Cordwainer. The nickname of Northampton Town Football Club, the "Cobblers", suggests that the Midlands town has a history steeped in footwear and a visit to Northampton Museum and Art Gallery will confirm that to be the case. Amongst other things, the museum contains a world-famous shoe collection and a display portraying the history of shoemaking. An index to shoemakers is also held. Further details of the museum, its location and its opening times are on its webpage at www.northampton.gov.uk.

SILHOUETTES See Portraits.

SILVERSMITH See Goldsmith.

SIX CLERKS, THE These were the senior clerical officials of the Court of Chancery. In the C17th, each of the Six Clerks began to file cases separately in their respective divisions under their own names, for example Bridges, Collins and Hamilton. The complexities of the system are described in TNA research guide entitled *Chancery Proceedings: equity suits from 1558*, which can be freely downloaded from www.nationalarchives.gov.uk.

SKINNER The Worshipful Company of Skinners was a London Livery Company that obtained its Charter in the C14th. The Company controlled the English fur trade, with furs being part of male attire and much favoured by royalty. The Company's website at www.skinnershall.co.uk gives full details of its history.

SLAUGHTER HOUSES After 1786, owners of slaughter houses had to be licensed by the Justices. Application had to be supported by a certificate from the minister and churchwardens approving the application. The records are with those of the Quarter Sessions (q.v.). They can be useful in tracing butchers.

SMITH A worker in metal. Usually specified as blacksmith (iron), whitesmith (tin), goldsmith or silversmith.

SOCIAL HISTORY BIBLIOGRAPHY It is very important to understand the context for the lives of our ancestors. There are numerous books that can help in this respect. What follows is a small selection.

Davidson, Caroline *A Woman's Work is Never Done: a history of housework in the British Isles 1650-1950* (Chatto and Windus 1986).

Few, Janet *Coffers, Clysters, Comfrey and Coifs: the lives of our seventeenth century ancestors* (FHP 2012).

Fussell, G E *The English Rural Labourer: his home, furniture clothing and food from Tudor to Victorian Times* (Greenwood Press 1976).

Ginn, Peter, Goodman, Ruth and Langlands, Alex *Wartime Farm: rediscovering the skills and spirit of world war II* (Pavilion Books 2012).

Goodman, Ruth, Langlands, Alex and Ginn, Peter *Edwardian Farm* (Pavilion Books 2010).

Goodman, Ruth *Victorian Farm* (Pavilion Books 2009).

Gilbert, Christopher *English Vernacular Furniture 1750-1900* (Yale University Press 1991).

Hartley, Dorothy *Food in England* (Piatkus 1954).

Hutton, Ronald *The Rise and Fall of Merry England: the ritual year 1400-1700* (Oxford University Press 1994).

Mercer, Eric *English Vernacular Houses: a study of traditional farmhouses and cottages* (HMSO 1979).

Styles, John *The Dress of the People: everyday fashion in eighteenth century England* (Yale University Press 2008).

Tannahill, Reay *Food in History* (Penguin 1988).

Vickery, Amanda *Behind Closed Doors: at home in Georgian England* (Yale University Press 2010).

Waugh, Norah *The Cut of Men's Clothes 1600-1830* (Routledge 1987).

Waugh, Norah *The Cut of Women's Clothes 1600-1930* (Faber and Faber 1994).

Worsley, Lucy *If Walls Could Talk: an intimate history of the home* (BBC 2012).

SOCIAL STATUS There was a great preoccupation with social status. One has only to read the novels of Jane Austen to be very conscious of this. The highest social status was accorded to those who were titled, or who were connected with titled people, and those whose wealth lay in the possession of great estates. Those whose wealth came from "trade" were not considered high in the social scale. However, success and fame could be achieved by those born of humble status. Examples include Ben Jonson, Josiah Wedgwood, Richard Arkwright,

Robert Burns and even Jane Austen herself. Cardinal Wolsey is reputed to have been the son of a butcher.

SOCIETY OF FRIENDS See Quakers.

SOCIETY OF GENEALOGISTS (SOG) The Society was founded in 1911 to promote and encourage the study of genealogy. Details of how to join the society can be found on its website www.sog.org.uk. Members and non-members, the latter on payment of a fee, have access to the society's library in London, which is unique in this country and provides incomparable sources for students. There are over 70,000 volumes therein, as well as much manuscript and microform material. Information about the society's library catalogue is available on its website. Some of the other highlights of the society include: A bookshop at its London premises, purchases can also be made on-line. A wide range of books, finding aids and indexes are published, including the useful *My Ancestor was a ..... series. A comprehensive programme of events, including talks and lectures, are held at the society premises throughout the year. In addition, courses for beginners are run on an ad hoc basis. Transcription and indexing projects are undertaken by volunteers. The journal *Genealogists' Magazine* is published quarterly and forwarded to all members.

SOLDIERS DIED IN THE GREAT WAR 1914-1919 In 1921, the War Office published two lists of those who died during the Great War. One volume gave details of nearly 42,000 officer casualties and a further eighty volumes detailed the 662,000 "other ranks" to have been killed in action. These records embrace every regiment and corps of the British Army. They typically include details of the soldiers' regiment, corps and battalion, decorations received, where the individual was born, lived and was enlisted, their rank and number, and how, when and in what location they died. These books are widely available in libraries and are also accessible on line and on CD. They have been digitised by Naval & Military Press Limited and are made available on (a rather expensive) CD as a searchable database containing all 703,000 entries. Further details are at www.naval-military-press.com and www.great-war-casualties.com. It is available online via Ancestry UK (q.v.) www.ancestry.co.uk or FindmyPast (q.v.) www.findmypast.co.uk.

SOLICITOR See Legal Profession.

SOUTH AFRICA See also Emigration. The National Archives and Records Service (NARS) of South Africa's website is at www.national.archives.gov.za. The Pretoria offices of NARS incorporate The National Archives Repository, the Bureau of Heraldry and the National Film, Video and Sound Archives. The website describes where various regional and national records are now held. "The Cape Town Archives Repository, the Free State Archives Repository, the

Pietermaritzburg Archives Repository, the Durban Archives Repository and the Port Elizabeth Archives Repository have devolved their archival and record management functions to the relevant provincial departments. Up until 1994, the Republic of South Africa was divided into four provinces: the Cape Province, Natal, the Transvaal and the Orange Free State. The National Archives has in its custody the records of central government as well as the public records of the former Transvaal Province and its predecessor states. The Free State Archives Repository in Bloemfontein houses the public records of the former Orange Free State and the Orange River Colony. The Cape Town Archives Repository holds public records of the former Cape Province and earlier colonial administrations, while the Pietermaritzburg Archives Repository and the Durban Archives Repository have custody of the records of the former Natal Province and its predecessor states. In addition to the repositories each of the former provinces had what was then known as intermediate depots, or records centres, as they are called today."

The Genealogical Society of South Africa www.genza.org.za has several branches, including an "electronic branch". It publishes a quarterly journal *Familia* and other publications. The society has a large body of research material and arranges meetings. See also the searchable database at www.ancestor. co.za.

A very detailed account of research in South Africa appears in Lombard, R T J *Handbook of Genealogical Research in South Africa* (2nd ed. Institute of Historical Research 1990). See also *South African Genealogies* compiled by Heese, J A ed. and Lombard, R T J (The Human Sciences Research Council). These are a series of volumes based on *Geschlacht-register der oude Kaapsche familien* of 1894 by C C de Villiers, tabling Dutch and Huguenot families who settled in the Cape Colony from 1652 and their descendants to 1810. Another series of volumes that are gradually being published is Spencer, Shelagh O'Byrne *British Settlers in Natal 1824-1857: a biographical register* (University of Natal Press). See http://shelaghspencer.com. *The South African War 1899-1902: service Records of British and colonial women. A Record of the Service in South Africa of Military and Civilian Nurses, Laywomen and Civilians* compiled by Sheila Gray (Shelia Gray 1993) is taken from a wide variety of sources this comprehensive work has over 1,700 names. Currer-Briggs, Noel *Worldwide Family History* (Routledge & Kegan Paul 1982) has a chapter dealing with South African research.

SOUTH PACIFIC ISLANDS See New Zealand.

SPELLING As the study of your ancestors takes you further back in time, you will come up against the problems of spelling variations. Spellings were not consistent, even within the same document, It must be remembered that even in the mid C19th, many people could neither read nor write. They were often uncertain how their surname was spelt. When a baptism, marriage or burial took place, the incumbent or church official would enter the name in the register as it seemed to him it should be spelt. However, the dialect of the informant might mislead him. The same applies to BMD entries made by Registrars after 1837. It is an idea to study the sound of your name and then write down all the possible spellings which would produce the same sound when read. A name such as "Wright" could be found as Rite, Right, Write and many other variants. The more unusual your name is, the more strange variants you may find.

STAMP DUTY See Parish Registers.

STATE PAPERS, DOMESTIC AND FOREIGN These were originally informal reference collections of papers compiled by clerks to successive Secretaries of State. However, in 1610 an official keeper was appointed to register and care for the growing collection. Not every Secretary of State passed over all the papers accumulated during his tenure of office so many remain in private collections although their whereabouts are listed in the catalogue of TNA. State Papers in the official collection are in TNA. When you want to look at the State Papers, the best place to start is the *Calendar of State Papers*. These books list, in date order, the documents that are in the collection and give a summary of each. A number of TNA research guides deal with State Papers available at www.nationalarchives.gov.uk. These cover: *State Papers Domestic: Charles II-Anne, 1660-1714*; *State Papers Domestic: Commonwealth, 1642-1660, State Papers Domestic: Edward VI-Charles I, 1547–1649*; *State Papers Domestic: George I-George III, 1714-1782*; *State Papers Domestic: miscellaneous classes*; *State Papers: foreign*; *State Papers: Ireland, 1509-1782*; *State Papers: letters and papers of Henry VIII*. State Papers Online http://gale.cengage.co.uk/state-papers-online-15091714.aspx makes those from 1509-1714 available to institutional subscribers.

STATIONERS' HALL Copyright (q.v.) presented no problem until the development of printing. The need to sell multiple copies of a single printed work before the final profit was made raised the question. From 1554 until 1924, copyright was normally secured by registration with the Stationers' Company in London. Throughout the period during which registration was necessary to establish copyright, there was widespread disregard of the procedure, partly because of the registration fee but mainly to evade the obligation to provide complimentary copies for copyright libraries. The Worshipful Company of Stationers and Newspaper Makers www.stationers.org is a London Livery Company. The website gives information about the company, its treasures and its archives. See Blagdon, Cyprian *The Stationers' Company: a history 1403 to 1959* (1960).

The Stationers' Company has copyright registers from 1554 to 1842. The entries up to 1709 are in Arber, A (ed.) *A Transcript of the Registers of the Company of Stationers of London 1554-1660* and Eyre, Briscoe (ed.) *A*

Transcript of the Registers of the Worshipful Company of Stationers from 1640 to 1708. For entries from 1710 to 1842, the original registers need to be consulted. The absence of an index makes knowledge of the date of publication essential. Copyright records held at TNA cover the years 1842 to 1924. Since 1911, The Stationers' Company has maintained a voluntary register. The voluntary register and the pre-1842 records are held at the Stationers' Hall. TNA research guide *Copyright Records: Stationers' Hall* gives further details and can be downloaded from TNA website at www.nationalarchives.gov.uk. This research guide includes some useful notes on the various Copyright Acts and gives details of the arrangement of the Registers.

STEP RELATIONSHIP See In-laws.

STEWARD He usually presided over the manorial courts, kept records and dealt with rents and land transfers. The bailiffs (q.v.) were under his supervision. He was accountable to the lord of the manor.

STOCKINNER/STOCKINGER See also FWK. One who worked at a stocking hand loom, a stocking weaver or framework knitter.

STRAW PLAIT See Hatting Industry.

STRAYS See also Deaths Overseas and Migrants. A stray is a recorded event such as a baptism, marriage or burial which takes place outside the area in which the person normally lived. Most family history societies interpret this as "out-of-county", so in the case of a gentleman from Stafford marrying a lady from Warwick at Coventry, only the groom is a stray. Some societies give a narrower interpretation, particularly if they cover a city. Another possible interpretation comes from Yorkshire, where strays are sometimes defined by Riding. The definition of a census stray is often different again, as they are normally considered to be people resident outside their county of birth. Strays appear in all kinds of places and can be of great value in locating lost ancestors. The most frequent types are those found in marriage and census records. Many coastal parishes record numerous stray burials of sailors drowned at sea and washed up on the foreshore and the researcher will also find baptisms, gravestone inscriptions, settlement papers and the like. Many family history societies have a "strays index" for their county or area and details will be found on the relevant society's website. Marriage strays will often be found in the appropriate County Marriage Index, and these are detailed in the book Gibson, Jeremy, Hampson, Elizabeth and Raymond, Stuart *Marriage Indexes for Family Historians* (9th ed. FHP 2008).

SUBSIDIES See also E179 Database. Subsidies were the main means of taxation before the Civil War and during the 1660s. The collection was by instalments, so they are difficult to date precisely. Only the wealthier members of the community were affected, such as gentry, landowners and the more substantial tradesmen. A distinction was made between taxation on goods (moveables) and land. The amounts paid became stereotyped and hence did not relate closely to real wealth, but they are still an indication of status. Lay Subsidies were levied on the laity, as opposed to the clergy.

Names are not given in the C14th and C15th Rolls. The "Great Subsidy" of 1524-27 is probably the most genealogically useful. The last subsidies to be levied were in Charles II's reign. Those records which survive are in TNA and are often in poor repair. Returns are listed on the E179 Database (q.v.) www.nationalarchives.gov.uk/E179. A research guide on TNA website *Taxation Records Before 1689* gives further information and can be downloaded from www.nationalarchives.gov.uk.

The returns for a number of counties have been published. Amongst these are: *The Lay Subsidy Rolls for the County of Sussex 1524-25* (Sussex Record Society 1956) and is now available to view free of charge at www.sussex recordsociety.org. *Subsidy Roll for the County of Buckingham Anno 1524* (Buckinghamshire Record Society 1950) is now available to download free of charge at www.bucksinfo.net/brs. Several subsidy transcripts are available online at www.british-history.ac.uk; individual transcripts are available on other websites.

Fifteenths and tenths were a form of taxation in force from 1134 -1624. The levy was a fifteenth of the amount assessed for rural areas and a tenth for towns and the royal demesne. The records are at TNA class E179. Many of these lists of names for the 1332 assessment have been printed. Some of these appear on British History Online (q.v.) www.british-history.ac.uk. The research guide *Taxation before 1689*, which can be downloaded from www.national archives.gov.uk is relevant. Most records are lists of places and sums payable, rather than names. There are no returns for the counties of Cheshire and Durham, which were exempt as were the very poor.

SUFFRAGETTES The Women's Library, which was previously known as The Fawcett Library, specialises in the history of this movement and the personalities involved. Although part of London Metropolitan University, the Library is available to the public. Details are on its website at www.londonmet.ac.uk.

SUNDAY SCHOOL See Education.

SURGEON See Medical Profession and Royal Navy.

SURNAME INTERESTS' LISTS Sometimes referred to as Directories of Members' Interests, these lists of family historians interested in a particular surname are often created by Family History Societies and relate to a specific area. A typical example of the latter is "OXSIL", the Oxfordshire Surname Interest

List, which can be found at www.oxsil.org.uk. Many such directories of interests are listed at www.genuki.org.uk/indexes.Surnameslists.html.

SURNAMES See also By-names, Deed Poll, One-Name Studies and Spelling. It is doubtful whether knowing the origin of your surname will in any way help you trace your ancestry but it is obviously of interest. Surnames came into general use in the C12th and C13th. There are numerous books on the subject.

Addison, Sir William *Understanding English Surnames* (Batsford 1978).

Barber, H *British Family Names, their Origin and Meaning* (1894 reprinted 1903 and 1968).

Bardsley, C W *Dictionary of English and Welsh Surnames with special American instances* (reprinted Heraldry Today 1981).

Black, George F *The Surnames of Scotland* (New York Public Library 1946).

Guppy, H B *The Homes of Family Names in Great Britain* (reprinted Baltimore 1968).

Hanks, Patrick & Hodges, Flavia *A Dictionary of Surnames* (OUP 1988).

Hey, David *Family Names and Family History* (Hambledon Continuum 2000).

Kennett, Debbie *The Surnames Handbook: a guide to family name research in the 21st Century* (The History Press 2012).

MacGiolla-Dhomnaigh, Padraig *Ulster Surnames* (Dublin 1985).

Mc Kinley, R A *A History of British Surnames* (Longman 1990).

McLysaght, E *The Surnames of Ireland* (6th rev. ed. Irish Academic Press 1985).

Morgan, T J & Morgan, Prys *Welsh Surnames* (Cardiff 1985).

Reaney, P H The *Origin of English Surnames* (new ed. Routledge 1980).

Reaney, P H and Wilson, *A Dictionary of English Surnames* (OUP 2005).

Redmonds, George, King, Turi and Hey, David *Surnames, DNA and Family History* (OUP 2011).

Redmonds, George *Surnames and Genealogy: a new approach* (FFHS 2002).

Rowlands, Sheila & Rowlands, John *The Surnames of Wales: for family historians and others* (Genealogical Publishing 1996).

Titford, John *The Penguin Dictionary of Surnames* (Penguin 2009).

A *Surname Atlas* is available on CD from Archer software (q.v.) www.archer software.co.uk. This provides distribution maps for British surnames, based on the 1881 census.

The key website for surname studies is www.surnamestudies.org.uk (formerly Modern British Surnames), based on the work of the late Philip Dance and maintained by The Guild of One Name Studies. See also The Society for Name Studies in Britain and Ireland www.snsbi.org.uk, http://onomastics.co.uk/ and www.taliesin-arlein.net/names.

For suggestions of variant spellings see www.origins.net/namex/NameX Search.aspx.

SURROGATE Appointed by a bishop to act on his behalf. Often empowered to issue Marriage Licences and to prove wills.

SURTEES SOCIETY This society was founded in 1834 and is named after Robert Surtees, author of the *History of Durham*. The Society was one of the earliest publishing societies, and concentrates on the records of the counties of North-Eastern England. The society's website at www.surteessociety.org.uk details its objectives, lists all volumes published by the society, many of which can still be purchased and also details how to apply for membership.

SURVEYOR OF HIGHWAYS See Highways.

SWEEPS From the earliest times, households possessed fires which over the centuries developed into the sophisticated fireplaces and chimney stacks which we know today. Houses were often enlarged by adding an extension to the back or side, and as most rooms had a fireplace each flue went up to join another, creating a maze which eventually opened to the sky. Irrespective of the number of fireplaces in a household or the type of fuel burnt in them, soot accumulated in these narrow flues. They had to be swept, which was an unpleasant job. One of the most effective means of achieving this was to send a small person up the flue with a scraper and brush. In the majority of cases young boys were used, although it was known for girls to be employed too. Often, these children were foundlings or orphans from the parish workhouse, whose lives were held cheaply. The job of a climbing boy was unpleasant and often fatal. Whilst there would have been exceptions, most sweeps had little regard for their "apprentices". Indeed, the job of a chimney sweep was itself not popular. An Act of 1788, largely brought about by the campaigning of Jonas Hanway, forbade the use of boys under eight for this purpose but it was widely disregarded. In 1803, a society was founded to obtain the abolition of chimney sweeping by climbing boys, whilst in 1817, a Select Committee was set up to examine the whole question. Further Acts were passed in 1834 and 1840 which forbade boys under the ages of ten and twenty-one respectively to sweep chimneys by climbing, but again these Acts were largely disregarded by master sweeps. It took the publication of Charles Kingsley's *The Water Babies* in 1863 to arouse public awareness of the problem. It was finally resolved by Lord Salisbury's Chimney Sweepers Bill of 1875, which provided for the registration of master sweeps with the local police. Some of the licences issued to them may still be found amongst police records.

SWING RIOTS These were agricultural riots in 1830, where a wave of rick-burnings and the destruction of threshing machines in southern and eastern England resulted in nineteen executions and 481 transportations. Threatening letters to farmers were signed "Captain Swing". Although the riots were suppressed by the government, better conditions were eventually won by the labourers. Jill Chambers has undertaken considerable research into these riots, which has enabled her to make contact with a number of descendants of those involved. She has published several books on the subject, under titles such as *Wiltshire Machine Breakers, Volume 1* (Jill Chambers 1993). TNA website at www.nationalarchives.gov.uk contains a research guide dedicated to the Swing Riots. This can be found in the Local History section of the site.

T

TAILORS See Merchant Taylors.

TAXATION See also E179 Database, Game Duty, Hearth Tax, Income Tax, Land Tax, Poll Tax, Queen Anne's Bounty, Rate Books, Registration, Servants, Ship Money, Subsidies, Valuation Office "Field Books" and Window Tax. Not all taxation records are likely to be of value to family historians. A good starting point to establish what records survive and in what location is Jeremy Gibson's *Hearth Tax, Other Later Stuart Tax Lists and the Association Oath Rolls* (2nd ed. FFHS 1996). Two other similar guides of relevance are: *Land and Window Tax Assessments* by Jeremy Gibson, Mervyn Medlycott and Dennis Mills (2nd ed. FFHS 1998) and *The Protestation Returns 1641-42 and other Contemporary Listings* by Jeremy Gibson and Alan Dell (FFHS 1995). The latter includes details of some tax records such as a Poll Tax that was voted in July 1641. Most records of taxation levied before 1690 are listed on TNA's E179 Database (q.v.). There are three interesting research guides about taxation and the men who administered it on TNA website www.nationalarchives.gov.uk: *Hearth Tax, 1662-1689. Customs and Excise Officials* and *Tax Collectors*. Hoyle, Richard *Tudor Taxation Records: a guide for users* (Public Record Office 1994) contains some useful pointers. Numerous other taxes have been levied over the years and a comprehensive list of these national, local and ecclesiastical taxes, with dates, is given in Richardson, John *The Local Historians' Encyclopedia* (3rd rev. ed. Historical Publications Ltd., 2003).

TEACHERS See Education.

TELEPHONE DIRECTORIES See also British Telecom. The earliest telephone directory is dated April 1880 and contains entries for numerous subscribers. Prior to this time, numbers were not published and a caller asked the operator for someone by name and address. An almost complete set of phone books for the whole country is held by British Telecom (BT) at the BT Archives, where they can be viewed in person. These directories have been produced by BT and by its predecessors including Post Office Telecommunications, the National Telephone Company and numerous other private companies. The website of BT Archives www.btplc.com contains an information sheet on British phone books that can be downloaded. It also details the other holdings of BT Archives. BT's historical phone books 1880-1984 are also available online, as they have been scanned by Ancestry (q.v.). The Guildhall Library (q.v.) has an excellent collection of both London and provincial directories.

TENANT IN COMMON A person who has a specific share in a property with others. None of them has exclusive possession of the property since each is entitled to occupy or use the property in common with the others. The interest can be left by will on the occasion of the death of one of the tenants in common. If it is not left by will it will pass under the rules of intestacy. The interest of a tenant in common will not necessarily pass therefore to the other tenants in common unlike in a joint tenancy (q.v.). Business property held by people in partnership must be held as tenants in common and can not be held by them as joint tenants. A joint tenancy can be "severed" and converted into a tenancy in common but not vice versa.

TENANT IN TAIL See Entail.

TERRIERS See Glebe Terriers.

TEXTILES A large collection of archives based around the textile industry are held by the West Yorkshire Archives. These include the records of businesses in the textile industry, as well as trade union records. Further details can be found on the website of the West Yorkshire Archives at www.archives.wyjs.org.uk. That repository has also created a guide to the textiles archives that it holds http://wyorksarchivestreasures.weebly.com/uploads/8/5/9/7/8597192/textiles_to pic_guide.pdf.

TESTAMENT See Wills.

THEATRE See also Shakespeare. The information given below is taken from an article *Family History and the Theatre* by Alan Ruston published in *Hertfordshire People*, No.35 (Winter 1988) the magazine of the Hertfordshire Family & Population History Society. The most useful source of information about actors, actresses, playwrights, producers, theatrical managers etc. is the theatrical press. In these, obituaries are often elaborate. The main theatrical journals are: *The Era* (1838-1939), *Theatrical Journal* (1839-1873: weekly), *L'Entracte* (1873-1906: annually), *Illustrated Sporting and Dramatic News* (1874-1945), *Era Almanac* (1868-1919 annually), *The Theatre* (1877-1897), *The Stage* (1881-date), *Theatre World* (1925-date). *Who's Who in The Theatre* (20th). Of these *The Era* and *Theatrical Journal* are the most important. *The Era* has been digitised and is available at www.britishnewspaperarchive.co.uk or as part of a FindmyPast (q.v.) subscription. *Theatrical Journal* is on microfilm at Westminster City Library www.westminster.gov.uk/services/libraries, which specialises in the theatre. Although these publications concentrate on the London stage they do cover the theatre in the rest of the country, often for quite obscure places. Theatres in virtually every town are mentioned in detail, at one time or another. There is also coverage of the U.S.A. and what were termed the colonies. The main British historical journal *Theatre Notebook* has been published since 1946.

It is fully indexed in separate volumes. Accounts and reviews of plays can be found in *The Times, The Illustrated London News* and local newspapers. The latter are a mine of information for their area especially for pantomimes in December. Pantomimes pre-1870 were very different to those we know today; actors of all types took part in them.

Theatre programmes only came into regular use from the 1800s. Before that all advertisements and lists of players were announced on playbills. Collections of playbills can be found in large Reference Libraries, especially in London. Their location in London is given in Diana Howard's *London Theatres and Music Halls 1850 to 1950* (Library Association 1970). The Guildhall Library's (q.v.) collection goes well beyond London and there are extensive collections in the U.S.A. e.g. at the Harvard Theatre Collection.

Nungezer, Edward *A Dictionary of Actors* (1929) and Baldwin. T W *The Organisation and Personnel of the Shakespeare Company* (Princeton University Press 1927) contain hundreds of names. See also the several volumes of *A Biographical Dictionary of Actors etc 1660-1800* ed. Highfill, Burnim and Langhams (Southern Illinois University Press 1993).

The Theatre Museum is part of the Victoria and Albert Museum www.vam. ac.uk/page/t/theatre-and-performance. There is also the University of Bristol Theatre Collection, Department of Drama: Theatre, Film, Television, Cantocks Close, Bristol BS8 1UP   www.bristol.ac.uk/theatrecollection. The National Theatre archive is based at the National Theatre in London and is the repository for the administrative and technical records of the National Theatre. The collection covers the period from the inception of the company in 1963 to the present day. Material accessible to the public includes programmes, posters, photographs, video and sound recordings of NT productions and platform events, press cuttings, prompt scripts, production drawings, costume, lighting and sound information. The Archive also holds many deposited collections relevant to the National's history including the records of the Shakespeare Memorial National Theatre Trust (1908) and the South Bank Theatre Board. Further details of the archive can be found at www.nationaltheatre.org.uk/ discover-more/archive a website that is intended to be a virtual showcase for the history of the National Theatre and which displays images of the various media held by the Archive. In addition, a catalogue for the research material in the collection is accessible via the website. The Catalogue contains two inter-linked databases, the Archive Catalogue and the NT Performance Database. The NT Performance Database contains details of every play ever staged by the National Theatre. The NT Archive Catalogue contains entries for the items held in the Archive collection.

The British Music Hall Society have a website http://britishmusichall society.com. See Busby, Roy *British Music Hall: illustrated who's who from 1850 to the present day* (Elec. Publishing 1976) and Mander, Raymond and Mitchenson, Jo *British Music Hall* (Gentry Books 1974) are just two of the books available on this particular section of the theatre. See also Shipley, Debra and Peplow, Mary *London Theatres and Concert Halls* (Shire Publications 1987).

THIRD FLEET See Australia, Crime and Criminals, Emigration and Transportation.

THOMAS COOK The website of the travel agent Thomas Cook www.thomascook.com includes a link to a page detailing the company's lengthy history since its formation in 1841. From there, a further link takes us to details of the company's archives, which are situated in Peterborough. The company's archives are said to include: Handbooks, programmes and brochures, 1845-present. Copies of Cook's *Excursionist* newspaper, 1851-1902 and its successor, *The Traveller's Gazette* magazine, 1902-39. Travellers' incidental records (ephemera), 1851-present. Travellers' diaries (originals and copies), 1855-1980. Photographs of premises, staff and travellers, 1860s-1970s. Company business records, 1870s-present. Railway timetables, 1873-present. Travellers' guidebooks, 1874-present. Historical images, a collection of some 500 images. Film material, a series of 45 short films used by the company in the 1950s and 1960s to promote overseas holidays to the new mass market.

THORESBY SOCIETY This society was formed in 1889 and is concerned with the history of Leeds, South Yorkshire and the surrounding neighbourhood. It is named after Ralph Thoresby (1658-1725), Leeds' first historian. Since its foundation, the Society has published books about Leeds, including transcripts of the parish registers. Details of the society's publications, meetings, library, and membership can be seen on its website at www.thoresby.org.uk.

THOROTON SOCIETY This society, named after Robert Thoroton, author of *Antiquities of Nottinghamshire*, specialises in the publishing of historic material relating to that county. Further details of the society, its publications and how to join the society are detailed on its website www.thorotonsociety. org.uk.

TIDE WAITER Tide Waiters and their predecessors, Tidesmen, were customs officers of the C18th whose duties were to board ships coming in on the tide with a view to preventing smuggling and the like. Other officers were known as Land Waiters and King's Waiters. For a more detailed history, see Carson, Edward *Ancient and Rightful Customs* (Faber & Faber 1972).

TIMES DIGITAL ARCHIVE See Newspapers.

TINKERS See Gypsies.

TITHES See also First Fruits, Maps and Queen Anne's Bounty. A tenth part of the main produce of the land and of both stock and labour such as wool, pigs, milk and the like was paid to the local church. Where they have survived, tithe accounts are a useful source of information, particularly as the tithes were paid by quite humble people.

Tithe maps and accompanying schedules, or apportionments, were created in the twenty years or so following the Tithe Commutation Act of 1836. This converted tithe payments into an annual rental. Areas where tithes had already been commuted (converted into an allotment of land or a monetary payment, often following enclosure) did not have a tithe survey. About 75% of the country is covered, with some counties being better served than others. The apportionments detail owners and occupiers of land, together with acreages, land use and values.

Records should be in CROs, with copies at TNA. They are very useful for pinpointing the exact spot where an ancestor lived. Tithes were abolished in 1936. A TNA research guide, *Tithe Records,* can be downloaded from www.national archives.gov.uk. Evans, E J *Tithes, Maps and Apportionments and the 1836 Act* (2nd revised ed. Phillimore 1993) is a good source of further information. See also Beech, Geraldine and Mitchell, Rose *Maps for Family and Local History: records of the tithe, valuation office and National Farm Survey of England and Wales 1836-1943* (2nd ed. National Archives 2004).

TITLE DEEDS See also Bargain and Sale, Entail, Feet of Fines, Ireland, Lease and Release and Scotland. This is a general term for documents relating to the ownership of land and property. They are useful for filling in details of your family history and particularly in tracking down the precise location in which ancestors lived. Occupations are often mentioned on title deeds and the dates shown can also be useful. Many deeds are in collections of Estate Records, which have frequently been deposited in CROs. Deeds often come in bundles, with an abstract enabling you to trace the descent of a property over the centuries.

Relevant publications are Wormleighton, Tim *Title Deeds for Family Historians* (FHP 2012). Alcock, N W *Old Title Deeds* (Phillimore 1986) and Dibben, A A *Title Deeds* (Historical Association 1972) and *An Introduction to Reading Old Title Deeds* by Julian Cornwall (FFHS 1993).

In England, local deeds' registries were established in the early C18th for Yorkshire and Middlesex but this system was not extended to other counties. The registers contain abstracts of deeds including names, addresses and property descriptions and these are now held in the appropriate CRO.

In some locations, abstracts of or indexes to title deeds have been published. An example is Hassall, W O (ed.) *Index of Persons in Oxfordshire Deeds* (Oxfordshire Record Society 1990). It might pay to check what similar material has been published for other counties.

A conveyance was the process of transferring property and also the name of the document relating to it. There are many thousands of conveyances both of crown and private property in TNA. There is no composite index but there are a number of indexes and calendars, usually arranged according to the names of the parties concerned.

These records can be complicated but there are three research guides that can be downloaded from TNA website at www.nationalarchives.gov.uk, which should be of help. They are *Conveyances of Land for Charitable uses in Trust Deeds 1736-1925, Enrolment of Deeds and Registration of Titles to Land* and *Land Conveyances by Feet of Fines 1182-1833*. Conveyances can also be found in CROs.

TOLERATION ACT, THE This Act of 1689 marked a more tolerant attitude towards non-conformists, who could hold their own services providing their meeting houses were licensed in the Quarter Sessions (q.v.) courts.

TOLL See also Turnpikes. The right to levy dues and later described the dues themselves. Tolls were levied at markets and for the upkeep of roads and bridges.

TONTINES See Annuity.

TOPOGRAPHICAL DICTIONARIES These are descriptions of places arranged in alphabetical order. It is important to be able to establish the jurisdiction, civil and ecclesiastical, for each settlement, hamlet, village, town or city, in order to determine the likely whereabouts of archival material.

Samuel Lewis compiled and published a series for England, Wales, Scotland and Ireland during the mid C19th, entitled *Lewis' Topographical Dictionaries.* These listed parishes and the larger administrative units into which they were grouped. This content was updated by F A Youngs to include the 1974 local government reorganisation in his *Guide to the Local Administrative Units of England, Part I: Southern England* (Royal Historical Society 1979). Quite a number of topographies published in the C19th have recently been scanned and reproduced on CD. An example of this is the *Handbook of Essex, Suffolk, Norfolk and Cambridgeshire*, published in 1892 and recently been reproduced on CD by Archive CD Books www.familyhistoryresearch.org. Several other firms have reproduced similar volumes on CD.

TOWNLAND An Irish administrative unit of government. *The General Alphabetical Index to the Townlands and Towns of Ireland* (H.M.S.O. 1901) will help with the location of Townlands.

TOWNSHIP A unit of local government, particularly in northern England.

TOWN WAITER See Tide Waiter.

TRACTARIANS See Oxford Movement, The.

TRADE UNIONS The website Union Ancestors www.unionancestors.co.uk has much background information on unions and their history. See Crail, Mark *Tracing your labour Movement Ancestors: a guide for family historians* (Pen and Sword 2009) and Southall, Humphrey, Gilbert, David and Bryce, Carol *Nineteenth Century Trade Union Records: an introduction and select guide* (Historical Geography Research Group 1994).

Many records relating to trade unions are held at the Modern Records' Centre (q.v.), Warwick University www2.warwick.ac.uk. Bennett, J and Tough, A *Trade Union and Related Records* (University of Warwick 1991) is particularly informative.

TRADES See Occupations and Shire Publications.

TRADING COMPANIES See Companies.

TRAFALGAR, BATTLE OF See Nelson.

TRAINING SHIPS See National Maritime Museum.

TRANSPORTATION See also Australia, Crime and Criminals, Emigration, First Fleet, Second Fleet, Third Fleet and United States of America. This was a very common form of punishment, which often replaced the death sentence. Most were transported to North America the West Indies until the C18th, or to Australia in the C18th and C19th. Arrangements for convicts to be transported were made by the Clerk of the Peace. Records are to be found in those of Quarter Sessions (q.v.) and Assizes (q.v.). Minor offenders were sent to American colonies as "Indentured Servants". An excellent book is Hughes, Robert *The Fatal Shore* by Robert Hughes (Collins 1986).

Records of transportees to Australia 1788-1868 are available on Ancestry (q.v.) www.ancestry.co.uk. Various indexes of transportees have been compiled. These include *The Complete Book of Emigrants in Bondage 1614-1775* and *British Emigrants in Bondage 1614-1788*, which is published on CD. Both of these are by Peter Wilson Coldham and are published by Genealogical Publishing Co Inc. www.genealogical.com. Full details of other indexes can be found in *Specialist Indexes for Family Historians* by Jeremy Gibson and Elizabeth Hampson (2nd ed. FHP 2000).

Relevant to anyone who is trying to trace the subsequent life of a person sentenced to transportation is Reake, Janet *A Convict's Life: a guide to tracing your convict's life* also her *How to Trace your Convict Ancestors: their lives, times & records* (Hale and Iremonger 1987). Further recommended reading is *Bound for Australia* by David Hawkings (Phillimore 1987). This is a guide for family historians wishing to follow the movements and destiny of an ancestor who was transported to Australia. It sets out a systematic sequence by which a convict can be traced from his conviction at court to his life in Australia. It also provides assistance with establishing the convict's place of origin.

The Founders of Australia: a biographical dictionary of the First Fleet by Mollie Gillen with appendices by Yvonne Browning and others (Library of Australian History 1989) is a comprehensive work, researched from primary documents in England and Australia, is an invaluable source of information to those seeking details of the men and women who landed at Sydney Cove on 26 January 1788. Two of the twelve appendices are particularly important: details of those First Fleeters who have previously appeared in error in published works and "The Waysiders", those who were originally on the First Fleet but who never reached Australia. Flynn, Michael *The Second Fleet, Britain's Grim Convict Armada of 1790* (Library of Australian History 1993) is a companion volume to *Founders* and provides similar information, including biographies of the second fleet convicts.

Bateson, Charles *The Convict Ships 1787-1868* (Library of Australian History 1983), tells the story of the convict transportation system, that of the actual conveyance of prisoners to Australia from England and Ireland and of the convict ships, officials and merchants who despatched them.

A G L Shaw's *The Convicts and the Colonies* (Melbourne University Press 1978) is still regarded as a standard reference work on the subject.

The Queensland Convict Transportation Registers Database is at www.slq. qld.gov.au/resources/family-history/info-guides/convicts. Another useful website for those tracing transportees to Australia is www.convictcentral.com. The Descendants of Convicts Group Inc. have a website at http://home.vicnet. net.au/~dcginc/frames.htm#top.

Ask at your CRO if they have any records of convicts awaiting transportation. As an example, the Cheshire Record Office has records which supply names, "make" (e.g. stout), visage (e.g. round), complexion (fair, sallow etc.), eyes, hair, town, character, before whom and when convicted.

TRAVELLERS See Gypsies.

TRINITY HOUSE PETITIONS See Merchant Seamen.

TRONER He was an official in charge of weighing merchandise at the Tron, the scales or weighing machine.

TUITION See Curation.

TURNPIKES In order to finance road maintenance from the late C17th onwards, toll houses were set up at intervals. Travellers would have to pay a toll at each toll house so that, in principle, the roads requiring the most upkeep were appropriately funded. The records of Turnpike Trusts which managed specific sections of roadway often survive in CROs. They include minute books, plans, maps, accounts, local regulations, and even day books of individual toll-house keepers. The records provide evidence relating to those employed by Turnpike Trusts and in a less direct way, highlight the important lines of communication by means of which one's forebears may have migrated.

TYBURN TICKET This was a colloquial name for a certificate granted by the Clerk of the Peace to a person successfully prosecuting a felon. It exempted the person from holding a parish office. It was highly valued and saleable.

U

ULSTER See Ireland.

UNILEVER This company is a worldwide manufacturer of foodstuffs and other products and owns a substantial number of household brands. A brief history of the group can be viewed on their website at www.unilever.com/aboutus/ ourhistory/. The group's archives are based at Port Sunlight, and have a webpage at www.unilever.com/aboutus/ourhistory/unilever archives/. That page details the records that are held that would interest family historians, such as in-house magazines and the records of the former co-partnership scheme. Researchers are invited to visit their searchroom and library by appointment.

UNION See also Workhouses. A grouping of parishes sharing a common workhouse.

UNIONS See Trade Unions.

UNITARIAN This was a religious denomination which developed from Presbyterianism in the C17th. Their churches were run by the congregation. Their registers were deposited with the Registrar General in 1840. For further information, see *My Ancestors were English Presbyterians and Unitarians* by Alan Ruston (2nd revised ed. SOG 2001).

UNITED REFORMED CHURCH HISTORY SOCIETY See also Presbyterians and Congregationalists. The United Reformed Church was formed by the joining together of the Congregationalists and the Presbyterians in 1972. The Historical Society of each denomination joined to form the United Reformed Church History Society. Its website at www.urc.org.uk gives details of its library, journal and how to apply for membership.

UNITED STATES OF AMERICA See also Apprentices, Emigration, Passenger Lists, Prisoners of War and Transportation. A good general research guide is Greenwood, Val D *The Researcher's Guide to American Genealogy* (3rd ed. Genealogical Publishing Co. Inc., 2009. There are a great many Genealogical Societies throughout the U.S.A. and if you know the location of your relative you could contact the appropriate Society for advice.

In America there are no national indexes for births, marriages or deaths, such as we have in the UK. Vital records in America are not inter-state and vital record keeping was not adopted by most states until 1913. Prior to this date there were varying degrees of availability of records. Many vital records can be found on www.ancestry.com.

The US Government has required a census of the population to be taken every ten years since 1790, though until 1850 these recorded only names of the head of the household. Some states have done likewise though they usually appeared five years later than the Federal ones. The state censuses often show more detail of use to the genealogist. There are many census indexes available online at www.ancestry.org up to and including that for 1940. See http:// 1940census.archives.gov/.

The National Archives and Records Service, Constitution Avenue, Washington DC 20408, houses millions of documents that could assist in genealogical research. Their website www.archives.gov/dc-metro/washington gives much useful information. See also Deeben, J P *Genealogy Tool Kit: getting started on your family history at the National Archives* (Foundation for the National Archives 2012). There are Regional Archives in cities such as Boston, New York, Philadelphia, Fort Worth, Denver, Los Angeles, Atlanta, Chicago, Kansas City, Seattle and others. The American equivalent to our British Library is the Library of Congress, (Genealogical Room), Thomas Jefferson Annex, Washington DC 20540. www.loc.gov/index.html. The largest genealogical library in the world is located in that of the Church of Jesus Christ of Latter Day Saints (q.v.) in Salt Lake City https://familysearch.org/locations/ saltlakecity-library.

Federal homestead land records date from the 1860s and may give the location, the man's age, address, date and place of birth, wife's name and size of family. In the case of an immigrant we get details of the country of origin, with port and date of arrival. The latter information may make it easier to find the relevant passenger list.

A TNA research guide *American and West Indian Colonies before 1782* is available at www.nationalarchives.gov.uk.

Coldham, Peter Wilson *American Wills Proved in London 1611-1775* (Genealogical Publishing Co. Inc., 1992) includes will abstracts from the Prerogative Court of Canterbury of testators who include any reference to America. Not just those who lived and died in the New World yet left assets in England but Americans who died in Europe, British mariners who died in the colonies and Englishmen who left bequests to people in America.

For American newspapers see http://chroniclingamerica.loc.gov. The USA First Landowners' Project is at www.historygeo.com. This subscription website maps and names seven million settlers.

UNIVERSITIES See Archives Hub, Cambridge University, Dublin University, Oxford University and University Libraries.

UNIVERSITY LIBRARIES See also Modern Records' Centre, The. The Bodleian Library was named after Sir Thomas Bodley who refounded it in 1602 on the site of an earlier structure. It is first of all the Library of the University of Oxford and one of the six copyright libraries holding a great deal of useful material for researchers. See www.bodleian.ox.ac.uk/bodley for further details and access to the online catalogue.

The University of Glasgow Archive Services also has one of the largest collections of historical business records in Europe. This includes much of the archive of Scottish industries such as banking, retail, distilling and shipbuilding and the archives for the House of Fraser department stores (q.v.). More details can be found at the Archive Services website at www.gla.ac.uk/services/archives.

Online holdings include: The Glasgow Guardian Digital Archive website, which makes available high-resolution scans of every student newspaper produced at the University from 1932-1935 and 1955-2007. The University's "World Changing" website, which celebrates the staff and alumni of the University of Glasgow whose innovations, discoveries or developments in the C20th have changed the world. An "International Archives", which details contributions made by the University of Glasgow and Scottish business to the world. The blog at http://universityofglasgowlibrary.wordpress.com/ details the latest news from the University of Glasgow Archive Services.

Many university libraries are repositories for specific collections; a selection of these are mentioned below. The Special Collections of the Library of the University of Bristol comprise a diverse range of printed books and journals, archival resources and artefacts. The archival collection includes the Brunel Collection, Leicestershire poll books, Penguin Books Limited and the Somerset Miners' Association. Further details can be found at www.bristol.ac.uk, with individual pages giving detailed coverage of the holdings of such collections as "The Penguin Archive".

The Broadlands Archive has been housed at the University of Southampton since 1989, the Broadlands' Archives comprises some 4,500 boxes, which include the papers of the third Viscount Palmerston, successively Foreign Secretary, Home Secretary and Prime Minister, 1830-65; the diaries of the Victorian philanthropist, the seventh Earl of Shaftesbury; and the papers of Earl Mountbatten of Burma and his wife, Edwina, Countess Mountbatten, including extensive documentation for the independence of India and Pakistan; as well as a large group of estate papers, principally for Hampshire and parts of Ireland. See www.broadlandsarchives.com.

Established in 1890, Kay & Co Ltd. of Worcester became one of the largest mail-order companies of the C20th. Offering interest-free cash credit, Kay & Co Ltd. made both fashionable and functional living available to consumers outside the metropolis, selling everything from clothes to carpets, cheerful homewares to live chickens. The archive of Kay & Co Ltd. is held by University Of Worcester Research Collections. Their online research resource www.WorldofKays.org includes information about Kay & Co Ltd. and contains over 1,500 images from the firm's catalogues in digital format. Those interested can also follow and comment on the project at www.facebook.com/CataloguingKays.

The Special Collections of the John Rylands Library of the University of Manchester www.library.manchester.ac.uk include Nonconformist archives (especially of Methodism), archives of recent and contemporary literature and drama, the archives of the University of Manchester and the papers of individual scientists and academics. In addition, the personal papers of distinguished historical figures including Elizabeth Gaskell, John Dalton and John Wesley are held.

V

VACCINATION Vaccination against smallpox became compulsory in 1853. Vaccination certificates were given to parents and local registrars kept registers of vaccinations. In 1867 the responsibility became that of the Poor Law Guardians, rather than the registrars. Vaccination Officers were appointed in 1871, to be responsible for the records. Registrars made returns of births and infant deaths to the Vaccination Officer. These records are very similar to the registers of birth and where extant should be in the CRO. Vaccination Registers listing the children, their ages, parishes and dates of vaccination exist until 1948 but are closed to public inspection for fifty years.

VAGABOND A class of vagrant as defined by the Elizabethan Poor Laws of 1597-1601.

VALUATION OFFICE "FIELD BOOKS" Also known as Lloyd George's Domesday. The Finance Act (1909-1910) required the Inland Revenue to survey all properties in the UK and ascertain their site values. Each unit of property was assigned an hereditament number that was marked for reference purposes on a set of maps in much the same way as Tithe Apportionments and Maps were cross-referenced. To discover the correct number for the house, the researcher needs to look at the Valuation Office Record Maps in TNA class IR121/1-1R135/9. The final record of the survey was written up in standard form and bound in volumes called Field Books, class IR58, which are arranged by hereditament numbers and are also in TNA Miscellaneous records compiled in conjunction with this legislation can sometimes be found in CROs.

The following information on each property is usually included: Names of owner and occupier and whether freehold or leasehold, including any changes between 1910 and 1920 when the act was repealed. Details of term and rental of tenancy. Area of property, date of erection of buildings, number of rooms, their state of repair, liability for rates, insurance and repairs, and the dates of previous sales. The value of the whole property and the market value of the site excluding structures and vegetation. In addition, a sketch plan of the property is sometimes included.

Information was extracted from the Field Books and entered into Forms 37 with a copy sent to the owner. These are to be found in CROs, which may also have duplicates of the Record Maps. TNA has the Domesday Books for the City of London and for Paddington, class IR91.

A research guide, *Valuation Office Survey* is available at www.national

archives.gov.uk. See also Beech, Geraldine and Mitchell, Rose *Maps for Family and Local History: records of the tithe, valuation office and National Farm Survey of England and Wales 1836-1943* (2nd ed. National Archives 2004).

VERDERER He was an officer responsible for the preservation of the King's forest. The post probably dates back to the C11th. The office was held for life. There were four Verderers for each forest, elected by freeholders. The term was also used in the south west for a petty constable.

VESTRY This was the governing body of the parish. There were two main kinds, Select Vestries which were also known as Closed Vestries and Open Vestries. The former were not elected by parishioners but perpetuated by the co-option of new members. The latter were virtually general meetings of all the parishioners. They often proved unsatisfactory and were replaced in some cases by an elected Parish Committee.

VETERINARY SURGEON Details of the Wellcome library of The Royal College of Veterinary Surgeons can be found on the college's website at www. rcvs.org.uk.

VICAR An incumbent (q.v.) in receipt of smaller or vicarial tithes.

VICAR GENERAL A deputy of an archbishop or bishop.

VICTORIA & ALBERT MUSEUM (V&A) The Victorian & Albert Museum is located in the South Kensington area of London and houses a wide range of collections and exhibitions. It also runs courses, conferences and talks and has an online film channel. Full details can be found on the museum's website at www.vam.ac.uk. By way of example, the V&A is home to the "Punch & Judy Archive", which is a treasure-trove of books, scripts, music score covers, drawings, lantern slides and research relating to the Punch & Judy puppet show, a staple of British popular entertainment for nearly four hundred years.

VICTORIA COUNTY HISTORY (VCH) The Victoria History of the Counties of England www.victoriacountyhistory.ac.uk was begun in 1899 and with her approval, named after Queen Victoria. Its aim is to narrate the history of the English counties based on original research and ranging from earliest times to the present.

For each county there is planned a set of volumes, containing both general and topographical volumes therein. Broadly speaking the former consider the pre-history, ecclesiastical and economic history, Domesday Book entries etc., on a county-wide basis, whilst the latter describe in depth each individual city, town and village. Each volume is illustrated and includes maps and plans. Today VCH also produce paperback volumes and web resources. Copies of the volumes may be ordered from any good bookseller and of course, most larger libraries should have at least the volumes for their counties.

Their website gives details of which counties have been covered. The "VCH Explore" section of the website claims to provide "free access to reliable local history materials, produced by academics and volunteers. Photographs, paintings, drawings, maps, text, transcribed documents and audio files are organised thematically and by their geographical location."

VICTORIAN SOCIETY www.victorian-society.org.uk. This was founded in 1958. Its aim is to preserve the best of Victorian and Edwardian architecture and also to study the art and history of the period. It is particularly concerned to protect important C19th and early C20th buildings.

VICTUALLERS' LICENCES See Alehouses.

VIEWFINDER ViewFinder is a browsable library of photographs held by the National Monuments Record, the public archive of English Heritage. They date from the 1850s and are a resource for people interested in England's social, industrial, architectural and archaeological history. For further information and to carry out a search, see the ViewFinder website at http://viewfinder.english-heritage.org.uk.

VISION OF BRITAIN The Vision of Britain Through Time website www.visionofbritain.org.uk provides links to maps, historical travel writings and old photographs. As the site combines listings of administrative units and C19th gazetteers, it provides a comprehensive, searchable index of British place names.

VISITATIONS See also Churchwardens' Presentments and Heralds' Visitations. Ecclesiastical visitations were periodic Inspections by a Bishop or Archdeacon, covering both spiritual and temporal matters. These generated a substantial amount of records including lists of clergy, churchwardens, schoolmasters, charities etc. Bishops' Transcripts (q.v.) were commonly sent in for the visitation. Records are found in DROs. Prior to the visitation, a series of questions would be sent for the incumbent to answer. Some of the responses give useful information about the parish, such as the number of non-conformists or schooling available.

W

WAGES See also Inflation. It is hard to appreciate the changes in the value of money that have taken place in the last four-hundred years. A man leaving £20 in the C17th was not poor. It may help to know the average weekly wages of day labourers which, when converted to decimal currency, were: Early C17th - about 15p. Late C17th - about 20p. Early C18th - about 25p. Early C19th - about 75p. In 1938-9 the average minimum agricultural wage was about £1.75.

For further information, see Munby, Lionel *How Much Is That Worth?* (Phillimore 1989).

WAIFS AND STRAYS' SOCIETY See Children's Societies.

WALES See also Surnames. Research into some Welsh families can be quite straightforward, since the basic sources for England and Wales are the same: civil registration, the census, parish registers and wills may present few problems. The main difficulties lie in the poverty of records in many areas, the relatively late development of surnames (and lack of variety in those names) and in the problems connected with the high proportion of ancestors who were nonconformists by the C19th. Nevertheless, many family historians with only Welsh ancestry find their research satisfying and these problems are not necessarily insuperable.

Key books are *Welsh Family History: a guide to research* (2nd ed. FFHS 1998) and *Second Stages in Researching Welsh Ancestry* (FFHS 1999). These have articles by specialist authors on many aspects of Welsh research and its problems. In particular the books address the need to understand the background to Welsh research, the social and cultural differences (including a different language) and how to cope with them. Another useful book is *Welsh Genealogy* by Bruce Durie (The History Press Ltd. 2012).

There are a number of Welsh Family History Societies. Contact the Association of Welsh Family History Societies (AFHSW) for details. The secretary can be contacted at c/o Adran Casgliadau, National Library of Wales, Aberystwyth SY23 3BU or see their website www.fhswales.org.uk. The AFHSW cannot assist with individual research enquiries but will direct you to the most appropriate county society.

Many Welsh records will be found at the National Library of Wales (NLW), Aberystwyth SY23 3BU www.llgc.org.uk. These include wills, estate records, census microfilms, about fifty per cent of parish registers, bishops transcripts, many nonconformist records, maps, manuscript and printed pedigrees. The

National Library of Wales has digitised Welsh wills and marriage bonds and is in the process of digitising Welsh newspapers and journals. See www.llgc.org.uk/index.php?id=4723.

CROs cover each post-1974 county, with branches in the pre-1974 counties and most hold parish registers, (including, in many cases, films of NLW holdings), parochial records, nonconformist registers and estate records, together with other genealogical sources. Useful and inexpensive leaflets are published describing the holdings of both NLW and CROs (in which there is a measure of overlap) and it is very important to find out what records are available for the area of research and, most important before a long journey, where they are kept. A bonus in Welsh research is that quite ordinary families today can often be connected to noble families in the past, recorded in the large number of Welsh pedigrees in manuscript and printed form. Michael Powell Siddons in *Printed and Manuscript Pedigrees in Welsh Family History* provides the best guide to locating these.

WAPENTAKE Equivalent of a Hundred (q.v.) in some Midland and Northern Counties.

WAR MEMORIALS See also Australia and Commonwealth War Graves Commission. A general term used for the many ways in which those who fought and died during various conflicts are commemorated. The type of memorial varies from a simple tablet to a whole building and can be at national, local or individual level. Schools, places of work and of worship and special groups frequently made a commemoration of their members in some way.

The most usual war memorials are to those who served and died in the two World Wars but there are also those to casualties of the Indian Mutiny, the South African wars and the like. Some memorials are considered works of art in their own right, such as the Sandham Memorial Chapel at Burghclere, which is now in the possession of the National Trust. The details of names on war memorials can vary from a simple list of initials and surname to full details of name, rank, number, regiment and place and date of death.

The National Inventory of War Memorials is a national project administered by the Imperial War Museum (q.v.) to record the location and other details of all war memorials in the United Kingdom, including Channel Islands and the Isle of Man. Further details of the Inventory and a search of the database can be undertaken at www.ukniwm.org.uk.

The website War Memorials Online www.warmemorialsonline.org.uk allows people to upload their own photographs of war memorials and to express concerns about their condition.

The War Memorials trust www.warmemorials.org works to preserve and conserve war memorials.

The website of the Anglo-Boer War Memorials Project at www.casus-belli.co.uk/abwmp/ is of interest and also contains a comprehensive bibliography of relevant books and publications.

WARD (1) Equivalent of a Hundred in parts of Northern England.

WARD (2) A minor, whose estate is in the crown's hands during his minority.

WARRIOR See Royal Navy.

WATCH AND WARD Men were appointed to "police" the area under the supervision of the Constable. "Watch" referred to night duty and "Ward" to daytime duties. Wrong-doers were arrested and placed in the care of the Constable.

WATER-GAVIL A rent paid for fishing in the lord's river.

WATERMEN AND LIGHTERMEN, COMPANY OF Until the mid C18th, boat and London Bridge were the only means by which to cross the Thames. Because of the potential difficulties this posed, the Corporation of London was appointed Conservator of the Thames, its duties including the licensing of boat operators on the river. The Company of Watermen www.watermenshall.org was formed in the latter half of the C16th and they were joined by the Lightermen in 1700. Lightermen unloaded cargo from ships and carried it into port by lighter.

The company's influence on the Thames stretched from Gravesend to Windsor so that its members were often drawn from areas of some considerable distance from the City of London. Since 1857, the western limit of jurisdiction has been Teddington Lock. The company has no livery, possibly because the freedom of the City that the liveried enjoyed would exempt them from impressment into the Navy.

The records of the company are at the Guildhall Library (q.v.) and contain a wealth of information. The trades of waterman and lighterman frequently continued through several generations of a family and so records can often be traced through a long span of years. Those admitted to the freedom of the company did so, until the late C19th, exclusively through apprenticeship so it is best to begin a search for a freeman in those records. The research guide *Records of the Company of Watermen and Lightermen* on the website www.cityoflondon.gov.uk of the Guildhall Library (q.v.) gives detailed information on this company with a listing of the records available.

The Company's website includes a history of the company, and plenty of guidance in a section entitled "Tracing Watermen and Lightermen in your Family History". Some of the Company records have been indexed and this webpage gives details of how to obtain a search.

Legon, James *My Ancestors were Thames Watermen* (SOG 2006), is also very informative. See also the Docklands Ancestors website www.parishregister.com.

WATERMILLS See Mills Archive Trust, The

WAYMAN This can be a surveyor of highways or a shipwright or platelayer who is working on a ship launch framework.

WEALD A term used mainly in Kent, Surrey and Sussex to describe wooded country.

WEAVER The Worshipful Company of Weavers www.weavers.org.uk is the oldest recorded London Livery Company. It is mentioned in the Pipe Roll of 1130 and its earliest Charter, granted to it by King Henry II in 1155, refers to the Guild as being in existence in the time of his grandfather, King Henry I. By this Charter, the Company gained the monopoly of its craft, rights of supervision ensuring a high standard of workmanship, power to punish infractions of its privileges, and full control of its members.

WEDGWOOD MUSEUM The Wedgwood Museum, which opened in 2008 on Stoke-on-Trent, is a treasure trove for those interested in ceramic, social, industrial and art history. Its website at www.wedgwoodmuseum.org.uk details its exhibitions, talks, lectures and workshops, as well as presenting information about its many and varied collections.

WELLCOME INSTITUTE AND LIBRARY See also Medical profession. This is the specialist library and research institute for the history of medicine http://library.wellcome.ac.uk/.

WESLEYAN METHODIST See Methodists.

WESLEYAN METHODIST HISTORIC ROLL The Wesleyan Methodist Historic Roll is a unique set of fifty large leather bound volumes which are located at Westminster Methodist Central Hall in London. The volumes contain the names of over one million people who donated a guinea to the Wesleyan Methodist Twentieth Century Fund (or The Million Guinea Fund) between January 1st 1899 and September 1909 when the fund was finally closed. The majority of the donations were made between 1899 and 1904, although because donations could be made In Memoriam, there are many pages of entries detailing those who had died before that time. Further details of the fund and of the records generated by it can be found at www.methodist-central-hall.org.uk.

Researchers wanting to consult the Historic Roll can visit Westminster Methodist Central Hall by appointment, where an index to the records is available. Microfiche of the entries in the Historic Roll for a former Wesleyan Methodist District, Circuit or Chapel can be purchased. The Eureka Partnership www.eurekapartnership.com have transcribed and indexed the Historic Roll for a number of circuits in Oxfordshire, Berkshire and Buckinghamshire and these are sold in booklet form. The Roll for Devon is available on CD from Devon Family History Society www.devonfhs.org.uk. For more background information see www.thefamilyhistorypartnership.com/hints-tips/the-wesleyan-methodist-historic-roll.php or read Richard Ratcliffe's *Basic Facts About the Wesleyan Methodist Historic Roll* (FFHS 2005).

WEST INDIES See Caribbean Ancestors and Emigration.

WHEELWRIGHT The Worshipful Company of Wheelwrights www.wheelwrights. org is a London Livery Company that received its Charter in the C17th.

WHITESMITH A maker of tin utensils, especially those used in dairying operations.

WHO DO YOU THINK YOU ARE? Is the name of the BBC television flagship series where celebrities are assisted in the tracing of their ancestry www.bbc. co.uk/programmes/b007t575. Other countries have since followed suit with similar series. On the back of the television programmes, is the Who Do You Think You Are? Live family history fair held annually in London; billed as the "biggest family history event in the world" www.whodoyouthinkyouarelive.com. There is also a Who Do You Think You Are? Magazine www.whodoyouthinky ouaremagazine.com.

WIFE SALES See Divorce.

WILLS See also Bank of England, Death Duties, Emigration, Partibility, Premogeniture, Prerogative Courts of Canterbury and York, Probate, Grant of, Servicemen's Wills and United States of America. Wills can often contain a great deal of information to help you to piece together your family history, though it should be borne in mind that the majority of ordinary people did not leave wills. Remember that you will rarely find a will of a married woman prior to the passing of the Married Women's Property Act of 1882. Prior to that all her possessions were legally the property of her husband. Widows and spinsters, however, may have left wills. See Stuart Raymond's *The Wills of our Ancestors* (Pen and Sword 2013) for a detailed guide to wills.

The method of finding wills is very different for those proven before and after 12 January 1858

Wills and Administrations in England and Wales from 1858 are at the Principal Probate Registry, First Avenue House, 42-49 High Holborn, London WC1V 6NP. You may consult the Indexes in person without charge and these are quite informative. They include some facts about the deceased e.g. occupation, address, place of death, sometimes former place of residence, date of death, names of executors or administrators, their address and relationship (if any) to the deceased and the value of the estate. There is one set of volumes for each year. Sometimes the wills and administrations are in one alphabetical sequence but the earlier volumes may be separated, with administrations at the end. The District Probate Registries also have copies of these indexes which can be inspected by the public. Many have been deposited in local Reference Libraries or Record Offices. The indexes for 1861-1966 are available on the subscription/ pay per view website www.ancestry.co.uk. Copies of the wills themselves are available for a reasonable sum (currently £6 each) from First Avenue House www.justice.gov.uk/courts/probate/copies-of-grants-wills. Postal requests should be sent to Postal Searches and Copies Department, Leeds District Probate Registry, York House, York Place, Leeds LS1 2BA. See TNA) research guides *Looking for Records of a Will or Administration after 1858* and *Wills and Probate: further research* and *Wills 1384-1858* for further information www. nationalarchives.gov.uk.

Prior to 1858, however, you do have to do some searching for wills as the whereabouts of the will depends on the court in which it was proved. All the land held by the testator had to be within the jurisdiction of the chosen court. Hence if, for example, land was held in more than one bishopric, the archbishop's court must be used. It was however acceptable to use a court higher up the hierarchy of courts than the property ownership dictated. The Phillimore Atlas and Index of Parish Registers (See Parish Maps) shows which courts had jurisdiction in a particular area. Similar information can be found in Gibson, Jeremy and Churchill, Else *Probate Jurisdictions: where to look for wills* (5th ed. FFHS 2002). The first port of call should be the CRO for the area in which the ancestor lived. See TNA research guides *Looking for Records of a Will or Administration before 1858*; *Wills and Probate: further research* and *Death Duties 1796-1903*. *Wills and Probate Records: a guide for family historians* by Karen Grannum and Nigel Taylor (2nd ed. TNA 2009) will also be useful.

Copies of wills proved at the Prerogative Court of Canterbury can be downloaded from TNA website, www.nationalarchives.gov.uk/records/wills.htm, for £3.50 each. These include wills of people who lived all over the country or even abroad. Non-conformist ancestors are particularly like to have had their wills proved in this court. The Borthwick Institute (q.v.) also holds many wills for those whose property was in the more northerly counties. Many collections of wills are being digitised, including, for example, those from Wiltshire and Wales.

A nuncupative will was one made orally, normally by a testator on his deathbed, written down and sworn to by four witnesses but not signed by the deceased. Holograph wills were in the handwriting of the testator.

Wills may often contain unfamiliar words. Raymond, Stuart *Words from Wills and Other Probate Records 1500-1800: a glossary* (FFHS 2004) may help with this.

WINDMILLS See Mills Archive Trust, The

WINDOW TAX This was a tax, imposed in 1696, which succeeded the Hearth Tax (q.v.). Each household paid a basic two shillings; those with between ten and twenty windows paid a further eight shillings. After 1747, households with between ten and fourteen windows paid six pence per window on top of the old basic two shillings and those with between fifteen and nineteen paid nine pence; those above that paid one shilling per window.

In 1825, all houses with fewer than eight windows were exempted. The tax was abolished in 1851. Scotland was exempted altogether in 1707.

In order to avoid payment of the tax, some owners of property bricked up their windows. Surviving records are rare and will be found in CROs. The book *Land and Window Tax Assessments* by Jeremy Gibson, Mervyn Medlycott and Dennis Mills (FFHS 2nd ed. 1998) lists surviving returns. Ward, W R *The Administration of the Window & Assessed Taxes 1696-1798* (Phillimore 1952) is another useful volume.

WOMEN'S ROYAL VOLUNTARY SERVICE (WRVS) WRVS was founded in 1938 as the "Women's Voluntary Services" to assist in the recruitment of women into the Air Raid Precautions department of the Home Office, ahead of the Second World War. It soon outgrew its original purpose and throughout the C20th provided essential services, from holidays for disadvantaged children to the delivery of meals-on-wheels, for every community in the UK. The charity's focus today is the practical support of older people through volunteering.

The WRVS Archive & Heritage Collection www.wrvs.org.uk/about-us/our-history/wrvs-archive-and-heritage-collection is one of the most important charity archives in the UK and was awarded UK Memory of the World status by UNESCO in 2010. The collection houses approximately two million documents, nearly 15,000 photographs and thousands of unique items of uniform, objects and ephemera. On the website there are details of the society's archive and how to access it. At www.wrvs.org.uk/about-us/our-history/fact-sheets the researcher can download information about the WRVS Roll of Honour, a bibliography of books on WVS and WRVS and a copy of *Ten Years' Work*, published in 1948 by WVS and detailing the work of the service over the previous ten years. A fact sheet on WVS uniform is also available, which looks at the development of the WVS uniform from its inception in 1939 through to 1945. It is compiled using documents and surviving examples of uniform of the time from the Archive and Heritage Collection.

WOODWARD Keeper of wood or forest having charge of the growing timber.

WOOLLEN, BURIALS IN See Parish Registers.

WOOLMEN The Worshipful Company of Woolmen www.woolmen.com is a London Livery Company that can trace its history back to 1180.

WORKHOUSES See also Guardians. Gilbert's Act of 1782 authorised parishes to combine for the purpose of setting up a united workhouse but many parishes continued to act independently in dealing with their poor. This changed in 1834, when the Poor Law Amendment Act compelled parishes to unite into groupings called "Unions", whose responsibility it was to deal with the poor. Institutions to house the poor, known as Union Workhouses, were set up to house the poor. The administration was in the hands of Boards of Guardians (q.v.).

Workhouse records are usually found in CROs and are worth examination if one has "lost" an ancestor as he may have ended his days in such a place. It should be remembered that many workhouses were used as hospitals until well into the C20th. Therefore people who were not necessarily paupers frequently died in the workhouse.

Three leading sources of information on workhouses and their records are *Workhouse* by Simon Fowler (TNA 2007), a comprehensive book looking at workhouses and the records that they generated. The four books in the *Poor Law Union Records* series by Jeremy Gibson, Colin Rogers, and Cliff Webb. (FFHS/FHP 1997-2008) list surviving records. The website "Workhouses" by Peter Higginbotham www.workhouses.org.uk, which provides both background information and details of individual workhouses.

There are also two podcasts (q.v.) of relevance that can be downloaded from the TNA website www.nationalarchives.gov.uk. These are *Living the Poor Life: poverty and the workhouse in the nineteenth century*, which sees Paul Carter explore poverty in C19th England and Wales and *Workhouse records for family historians*, in which Simon Fowler considers conditions in C19th workhouses and suggest ways in which you can research the people who lived therein. TNA research guides are also available; these include *Poverty and the Poor Laws*; *Workhouse Inmates and Staff* and *Workhouses*.

The key archives of the Ministry of Health (MH12) Poor Law Union records of correspondence between local and national poor law authorities 1834-1900 can be accessed via the website of TNA at www.nationalarchives.gov.uk.

WORLDCONNECT See Rootsweb.

WORLD WAR I and WORLD WAR II See also Absent Voters' Lists, Army, Bletchley Park, Home Front, Medals and War Memorials. A wide range of publications exist in connection with the two World Wars. These include books, magazines and websites, as well as sources such as the journals of museums. For example, a huge amount of straightforward information is on the BBC website at www.bbc.co.uk.

A number of books published by TNA deal either wholly or partly with the records of the two World Wars. Naturally, they focus primarily on the records held in that repository rather than elsewhere. *Army Service Records of the First World War* by William Spencer (2001). *Family History in the Wars* by William Spencer (2007). *First World War: the essential guide to sources in the National Archives* by Ian F W Beckett (2002). *First World War Army Service Records: a guide for family historians* by William Spencer (2008). *Home Front 1914-1918: how Britain survived the Great War* by Ian F W Beckett (2006). *Medals: the researchers' guide* by William Spencer (2008). *Tracing Your Naval Ancestors* by Bruno Pappalardo (2003).

The following publications, published by FFHS (q.v.), are available from the FHP (q.v.) www.familyhistorypartnership.co.uk. *The Second World War 1939-1945* by Phil Tomaselli (2006). *World War I Army Ancestry* by Norman Holding and Iain Swinnerton (2004). *Identifying Your World War I Soldier from Badges and Photographs* by Iain Swinnerton (2001).

See also *Tracing your Second World War Ancestors* by Philip Tomaselli (Pen and Sword 2011). *The Great War: a guide to the service records of all the world's fighting men and volunteers* by Christina K Schaefer (Genealogical Publishing Co. 2009). This covers forces from many participating countries.

There are also a significant number of TNA research guides which deal either wholly or partly with the records of the two World Wars. These can be downloaded from www.nationalarchives.gov.uk. Available on the same site is a podcast (q.v.) entitled *Sources for First World War Army Ancestry*. In this, Mark Dunton focuses on the main sources at TNA for documenting First World War army service, covering both the officers and other ranks of the British Army.

The Imperial War Museum have a 'Lives of The First World War' project http://www.1914.org/lives/ described as an "innovative, interactive digital platform, bringing material from museums, libraries, archives and family collections from across the world together in one place for the first time".

WRIGHT A constructor, for example a millwright, wheelwright, cartwright and the like. Hence many surnames end with this word.

WRITING UP It should always be an aim to preserve your family history in some way; whether this be in conventional book form, as an article, website, blog or other means. Some useful books, which ever format you choose, are Beckett, John *Writing Local History* (Manchester University Press 2007). Curthoys, Ann and McGrath, Ann *How to Write History that People Want to Read* (Palgrave Macmillan 2011) and Dymond, David (ed.) *Researching and Writing History: a guide for local historians* (Carnegie Publishing Ltd 2009).

Y

YEOMAN Usually, a man leasing and cultivating, a substantial farm.

YOUNG PEOPLE AND FAMILY HISTORY Several books have been written to encourage younger family historians. Particularly recommended are Anthony Adolph's *Who am I? The Family Tree Explorer* (Quercus 2009). Emma Jolly's *Family History for Kids* (Pymer Quantrill Publishing Ltd. 2007) and Jane Starkie's *Hw 2 *t Ur Fmly Hstry* (FHP 2008). There are a number of "fill in the gaps" family history books for younger children. The FFHS run occasional competitions for young genealogists and Devon Family History Society have an "Acorn Club" www.devonfhs.org.uk/acornclub for those under 18, which has an interest wider than those with Devon Ancestors. *Zap the Grandma Gap* by Janet Hovorka (Family ChartMasters 2013), with its accompanying workbook and website zapthegrandmagap.com is full of ways in which adults can help to inspire the younger generation with a love of family history. Young people might also be interested in the game Family House www.familyhouse.com.

Y